Managing Critical Incidents and Large-Scale Event Security

Managing Critical Incidents and Large-Scale Event Security

Eloy Nuñez
Saint Leo University

Ernest G. Vendrell
Saint Leo University

CRC Press
Taylor & Francis Group
Boca Raton London New York

CRC Press is an imprint of the
Taylor & Francis Group, an **informa** business

CRC Press
Taylor & Francis Group
6000 Broken Sound Parkway NW, Suite 300
Boca Raton, FL 33487-2742

First issued in paperback 2021

Version Date: 20160601

ISBN 13: 978-1-03-224275-0 (pbk)
ISBN 13: 978-1-4987-3150-8 (hbk)

Library of Congress Cataloging-in-Publication Data

Names: Nuñez, Eloy, author. | Vendrell, Ernest G., author.
Title: Managing critical incidents and large-scale event security / Eloy Nuñez and Ernest G. Vendrell.
Description: Boca Raton, FL : CRC Press, [2017] | Includes bibliographical references and index.
Identifiers: LCCN 2016006494 | ISBN 9781498731508 (alk. paper)
Subjects: LCSH: Emergency management. | Special events--Safety measures. | Public safety--Planning.
Classification: LCC HV551.2 .N87 2017 | DDC 658.4/7--dc23
LC record available at http://lccn.loc.gov/2016006494

Visit the Taylor & Francis Web site at
http://www.taylorandfrancis.com

and the CRC Press Web site at
http://www.crcpress.com

First, thank you Lord for your abundant blessings!

This book is dedicated to my wife, Gemma, and my two sons, David and Christopher, for their unending love and patience. It is also dedicated to my parents, Ernest and Oneida, for their steadfast guidance and support throughout the years.

A big thank you to my good friend and colleague, Eloy Nuñez. He is the consummate professional, and was the driving force behind this book. I would also like to express my thanks and gratitude to our friends and colleagues at Saint Leo University. In particular, thanks to Dr. Leonard Territo for his generous guidance and assistance throughout this process. Finally, I would like to thank the various members of our nation's public safety community, as well as the military. Your tireless efforts to keep our country safe, oftentimes under the most difficult of circumstances, are much appreciated!

Ernest G. Vendrell

I dedicate my portion of this book to my wife and love of my life, Maria, without whom I could not have withstood the stress of dealing with hurricanes, riots, bombings, hostage calls, phone calls in the middle of the night, and myriad other critical incidents over the past 40 years. She stood beside me during those times when my knees buckled and I thought I had no more strength to go on.

I also wish to recognize the many police officers and firefighters, the soldiers, Marines, sailors, airmen, and their families, who have dedicated their lives in order to protect us from the wolves and to keep us free.

Last, I thank my good friend, Ernie Vendrell, for without him this book would never have happened.

Eloy Nuñez

Contents

Preface

Over the years, many organizations and communities across the country, and the world for that matter, have had to deal with a variety of high-profile critical incidents as well as large-scale special events. From Super Bowls, political conventions, and incidents of civil unrest, to name a few, these complex events often present a myriad of challenges and potential problems for organizations and communities, as well as their various stakeholders. Unfortunately, far too often, communities are caught off guard and discover that their plans, response personnel, equipment, and infrastructure needs are less than adequate. When this occurs, the results can lead to a number of negative consequences, such as a diminished lack of confidence in government, including the agencies that are sworn to protect the public; the potential impact on life and property; and tarnished reputations. In some cases, the ramifications have been devastating to organizations and communities, resulting in years of work to regain lost trust and rebuild impacted areas.

Fortunately, there are a number of historical and contemporary case studies that clearly illustrate the benefits of effective planning, training, exercises, and testing with applicable stakeholders, thereby ensuring that organizations and communities are prepared to handle large-scale events and critical incidents. In particular, incorporating proven preparedness and response strategies into an overall plan enables organizations and communities to ensure that all participants and stakeholders understand their respective roles and responsibilities, identifies areas of expertise, and maximizes resources while minimizing duplication of efforts and avoiding potential conflicts. However, as is often the case, this requires effective leadership at all levels, an important consideration for those organizations and communities engaged in this important arena.

This book provides the most current and effective resources for managing large-scale special events and critical incidents. The book relies heavily on case studies and after-action reports that examine lessons learned from a multitude of previous events and incidents. In addition, the text identifies and examines best practices and recommended approaches, providing the reader with a variety of checklists and planning tools. Along these lines, we have structured the book as follows:

- *Chapter 1* provides an introduction to critical incident management, presenting the reader with an overview of the scope and potential impact of past events, and why effective preparedness and response strategies are critical for success when dealing with large-scale special events and high-profile critical incidents.

- *Chapter 2* focuses on risk analysis and assessing threats, vulnerabilities, and potential impacts. As is often the case, identifying risk and mitigating its consequences drive the process.
- *Chapters 3 through 5* focus on the importance of operational, tactical, and strategic planning. In particular, the operational, tactical, and strategic levels will be examined in depth in order to provide the reader with a comprehensive approach to planning and responding to large-scale special events and high-profile critical incidents.
- *Chapter 6* examines various training, testing, and exercise strategies. These are important considerations as planning, training, and exercises with applicable stakeholders serve to validate the Emergency Operations Plan.
- *Chapter 7* emphasizes the importance of establishing a culture of innovation and learning. Innovation is critical in today's high-risk and fast-paced global environment, which can often require an organization to quickly adapt to changing conditions. Therefore, being a learning organization is critical.
- *Chapter 8* provides a comprehensive view of large-scale special event planning and critical incident management. This will enable the reader to consider various preparedness and response strategies.

The final components of the book include a Glossary, with resources in the appendices. Our goal is to provide the reader with a valuable resource that can be used to effectively plan for, and respond to, large-scale special events and high-profile critical incidents.

Authors

Eloy Nuñez, PhD, is an associate professor in the Department of Public Safety Administration at Saint Leo University (Florida). He teaches graduate-level leadership in criminal justice and critical incident management, and also conducts Command Schools for various police and sheriff agencies.

Dr. Nuñez has more than 26 years of law enforcement leadership experience. Most notably, as the Lieutenant of the Emergency Operations Unit of the Miami-Dade Police Department—he was one of the principal planners for two Super Bowls (1999 and 2007), the Free Trade Area of the Americas (FTAA) Conference in 2003, and the Presidential Debates of 2004. In addition, Dr. Nuñez has extensive experience in tactical leadership situations, including bombings, hostage incidents, active shooter incidents, and counterterrorism. His long career has also included stints in organized crime investigations, robbery and burglary suppression, and 10 years of uniformed road patrol and field training.

Dr. Nuñez obtained his doctorate degree in global leadership from Lynn University (Boca Raton, Florida) in 2007. His research interests focus on the unintended consequences of corporate social responsibility and how it pertains to antiglobalization protest groups that target specific corporations.

Ernest G. Vendrell, PhD, is a professor and the associate director for the Department of Public Safety Administration at Saint Leo University. He has been teaching at the college level since 1995, primarily in the areas of emergency and disaster management, public administration, and criminal justice. He earned a PhD in public administration and policy, an MS in management, as well as an MS and a BS in criminal justice. Dr. Vendrell was also awarded a Fulbright Scholarship in police studies with the United Kingdom for the 1999/2000 academic year, and was a Visiting Fellow at the University of Leicester, Scarman Centre for the Study of Public Order. Throughout the years, Dr. Vendrell has authored various articles and made contributions to books on the topics of law enforcement, security management, as well as emergency and disaster management. He has also served as a reviewer for various journals.

Dr. Vendrell retired from the Miami-Dade Police Department, serving 27 years in a sworn law enforcement capacity. Throughout his law enforcement career, he worked in a variety of patrol, investigative, administrative, and supervisory assignments. He is a member of various organizations, including ASIS International (where he serves on the Crisis Management and Business Continuity Council), the International Association of Emergency Managers, and the International Association of Emergency Planners. He is a Certified Protection Professional (CPP), a Certified Emergency Manager (CEM), as well as a Certified Law Enforcement Planner (CLEP).

1
Introduction to Critical Incident Management

The Complex Nature of Critical Incidents and Large-Scale Special Events

In recent years, there have been a number of high-profile critical incidents and large-scale special events that have challenged public safety organizations across the country. Complex events such as incidents of widespread civil unrest or venues drawing national and global attention often present a myriad of challenges and potential problems for organizations and communities. Far too often, communities are caught off guard, finding that their response plans and resources are less than adequate. When this occurs, the results can lead to a number of negative consequences, including potential loss of life and property as well as a general lack of confidence in government. As an example, the recent civil unrest in Ferguson, Missouri, had a devastating impact on the local community and law enforcement, and it will take some time to establish requisite levels of trust and rebuild impacted areas.

Clearly, high-profile critical incidents, such as the civil unrest that has recently occurred across the country, serve to illustrate the profound impact that complex events can have on unprepared organizations and the communities that they serve. The initial impact is compounded by the vivid imagery that is continuously broadcast by television and various social and electronic media, which often results in further uncertainty and complexity.

Managing Chaos, Uncertainty, and Complexity

Critical incident management is a complex endeavor. There are many moving parts at many different levels, and at times it can be overwhelming to even the most experienced practitioner. The purpose of this book is to simplify a very complex set of factors so that current practitioners, and students aspiring to be future critical incident managers, can understand and deal with the complexities that are likely to confront them. Indeed, this book follows the same fundamental rules that are endemic to critical incident management. As in the management of critical incidents, this book strives to simplify complexity, to make order out of chaos, and to reduce uncertainty. Figure 1.1 illustrates the fundamental objective of critical incident management, and what this book strives to achieve.

Chaos

All critical incidents are chaotic. It is the job of the critical incident manager to restore order as soon as possible.

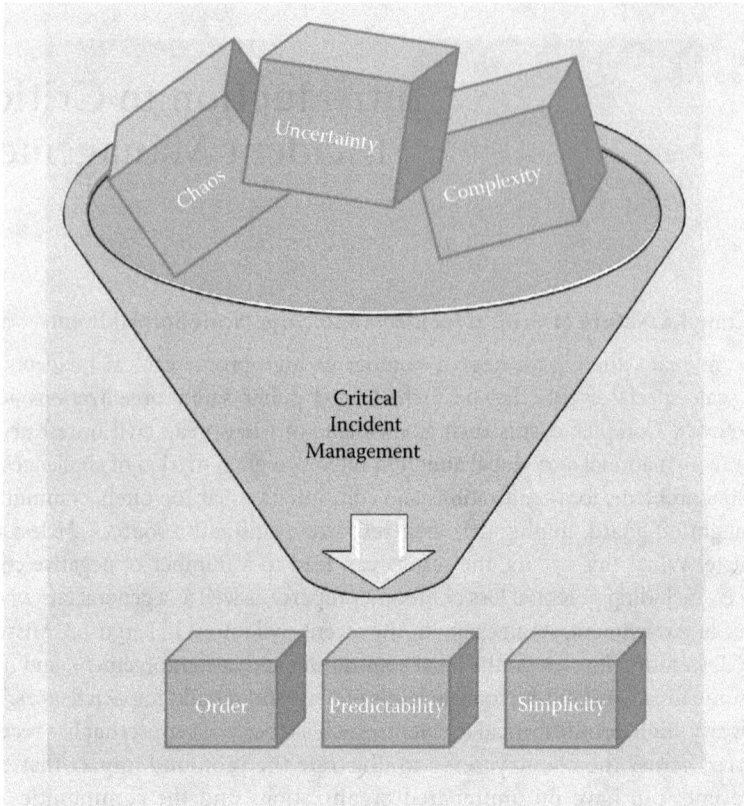

Figure 1.1 The Objective of Critical Incident Management

VIGNETTE 1.1   Stampede at the County Fair

It was one of those crazy Saturday nights for the officers working off duty at the County Fair. It was much busier than the typical night of lost children, people getting sick on rides, and an occasional obnoxious drunk individual having to be escorted out of the fairgrounds. This night, the midways were packed with attendees ... mostly teenagers celebrating the last day of school. Through the late afternoon, and into the early evening, the 25 off-duty officers working the late shift had to deal with several turnstile jumpers who were trying to get into the fair without paying. Reports over the police radio were received about possible gang members ... recognizable by the colors of their clothing ... coming into the fair. Along with the gang members were six undercover Gang Unit detectives keeping an eye on things.

Things started to go bad once the sun went down. First, two Gang Unit detectives arrested a white male juvenile who they believed to be a member of the Latin Kings gang. While effecting the arrest of the white male juvenile, two other female juvenile gang members interfered by coming up from behind and grabbing the detectives' arms. The two females had to be restrained by other uniformed officers who had arrived at the scene, and along with the male gang member were handcuffed and transported to the police office. Subsequent to the arrests, the officers discovered a loaded semiautomatic pistol in one of the females' purses.

Meanwhile, other reports were coming in over the radio about individuals inside the fairgrounds wearing the colors of the Folk Nation and Imperial Gangsters street gangs. There was tension in the air that was felt by all. Sporadic fights were breaking out at different locations in the fairgrounds. There were rumors about individuals who had been observed carrying guns, and that a possible gang fight was brewing. Things were getting so tense that the on-scene commander was discussing with the County Fair manager about closing down the fair early that night. It was only 9:05 PM, and the fair usually closed at 11 PM on weekend nights. An early closing would cost the fair a considerable amount of revenue, but the County Fair manager agreed to the commander's recommendation. By the turnstile count, there were over 20,000 people in attendance that night, and they would have to be herded out of the fairgrounds much earlier than expected. This would not be an easy thing to do.

Before the commander could announce the early closing to the officers via the police radio, three shots rang out around the west side entrance to the fair. As a result, many people panicked and a crowd of several dozen people ran in an easterly direction through the crowd to the midway section of the fair. Several uniformed officers ran in the direction of the gunfire, as did a couple of plainclothes undercover Gang Unit detectives. Some of the fairgoers saw the detectives running with guns at their sides, which further panicked the crowd. The more people panicked, the worse it got, and what was first a crowd of several dozen people morphed into a stampede of several thousand, all along the entire length of the midway. Along the way, several elderly people were knocked out of their wheelchairs, and parents were seen pulling their children into protective cubbyholes between the various exhibits and rides. Just then, two more shots rang out on the east side of the midway, and now some in the crowd that had been stampeding in an easterly direction, turned and ran against the flow in a westerly direction.

The scene was chaotic, and many people were trampled and injured as a result. What had started out as a bad night, was turning really bad. The on-scene commander's job was to get control of the situation and restore order to this chaotic situation. One of the first things he needed to do was gain control of the Gang Unit detectives so that they would not further add to the chaos and panic.

Uncertainty

All critical incidents are uncertain. Amid the chaos in the County Fair stampede vignette, there was also a great deal of uncertainty. The undercover detectives running in the direction of the shots fired only made things worse, as people in the crowd could not discern between the good guys with guns, and the bad guys with guns. Moreover, the uniformed officers responding to the scene of the shots fired may not recognize the undercover detectives, which adds to the uncertainty.

Chaos creates uncertainty, and uncertainty leads to more chaos. It is a cycle that needs to be managed and reversed. It is the job of the critical incident manager to minimize uncertainty at critical incidents. Critical incident managers can minimize uncertainty during the actual incident, but most of the mitigation of uncertainty can be done prior to the incident, and even after the incident occurs. In other words, with proper planning and visioning, critical incident managers can minimize the uncertainty that they are likely to face during spontaneous critical incidents, or at least mitigate its effects. Uncertainty can be reduced considerably with proper planning *before* the incident occurs and by learning from the experience *after* the incident occurs.

Mitigation of the effects created by uncertainty can also be done ahead of time. This will be discussed in greater detail later, but briefly stated, the underlying premise of mitigating the effects of uncertainty has to do with preparing critical incident managers and first responders ahead of time to accept the likelihood that they will face uncertainty and chaos at these incidents. Much like residents of coastal areas weatherproof their homes in anticipation of hurricane season, first responders can "weatherproof" their mind-sets in anticipation of the chaos and uncertainty that are likely to occur during a critical incident.

Vignette 1.2 is an excerpt from the 9/11 Commission Report.[1] This vignette provides a good example of how uncertainty leads to chaos, and how chaos leads to uncertainty. As you read the vignette, consider the uncertainty that the initial "first responders" (the air traffic controllers) were faced with, and the immediate steps that were taken to make sense of the situation.

VIGNETTE 1.2 Excerpt from the 9/11 Commission Report

The FAA (Federal Aviation Administration) Control Centers often receive information and make operational decisions independently of one another. On 9/11, the four hijacked aircraft were monitored mainly by the centers in Boston, New York, Cleveland, and Indianapolis. Each center thus had part of the knowledge of what was going on across the system. What Boston knew was not necessarily known by centers in New York, Cleveland, or Indianapolis or for that matter by the Command Center in Herndon or by FAA headquarters in Washington.

Controllers track airliners such as the four aircraft hijacked on 9/11 primarily by watching the data from a signal emitted by each aircraft's transponder equipment. Those four planes, like all aircraft traveling above 10,000 feet, were required to emit a unique transponder signal while in flight.

On 9/11, the terrorists turned off the transponders on three of the four hijacked aircraft. With its transponder off, it is possible, though more difficult to track an aircraft by its primary radar returns. But unlike transponder data, primary radar returns do not show the aircraft's identity and altitude. Controllers at centers rely so heavily on transponder signals that they usually do not display primary radar returns on their radar scopes. But they can change the configuration of their scopes so they can see primary radar returns. They did this on 9/11 when the transponder signals for three of the aircraft disappeared.

Before 9/11, it was not unheard of for a commercial aircraft to deviate slightly from its course, or for an FAA controller to lose radio contact with a pilot for a short period of time. A controller could also briefly lose a commercial aircraft's transponder signal, although this happened much less frequently. However, the simultaneous loss of radio and transponder signal would be a rare and alarming occurrence, and would normally indicate a catastrophic system failure or an aircraft crash. In all of these instances, the job of the controller was to reach out to the aircraft, the parent company of the aircraft, and other planes in the vicinity in an attempt to reestablish communications and set the aircraft back on course. Alarm bells would not start ringing until these efforts—which could take 5 minutes or more—were tried and failed.

AMERICAN AIRLINES FLIGHT 11

FAA Awareness. Although the Boston Center air traffic controller realized at an early stage that there was something wrong with American 11, he did not immediately interpret the plane's failure to respond as a sign that it had been hijacked. At 8:14 AM, when the flight failed to heed his instruction to climb to 35,000 feet, the controller repeatedly tried to raise the flight. He reached out to the pilot on the emergency frequency. Though there was no response, he kept trying to contact the aircraft.

At 8:21 AM, American 11 turned off its transponder, immediately degrading the information available about the aircraft. The controller told his supervisor that he thought something was seriously wrong with the plane, although neither suspected a hijacking. The supervisor instructed the controller to follow standard procedures for handling a "no radio" aircraft.

The controller checked to see if American Airlines could establish communication with American 11. He became even more concerned as its route changed, moving into another sector's airspace. Controllers immediately began to move aircraft out of its path, and asked other aircraft in the vicinity to look for American 11.

At 8:24:38 AM, the following transmission came from American 11.

American 11: We have some planes. Just stay quiet, and you'll be okay. We are returning to the airport.

The controller only heard something unintelligible; he did not hear the specific words "we have some planes." The next transmission came seconds later.

American 11: Nobody move. Everything will be okay. If you try to make any moves, you'll endanger yourself and the airplane. Just stay quiet.

The controller told us that he then knew it was a hijacking. He alerted his supervisor, who assigned another controller to assist him. He redoubled his efforts to ascertain the flight's altitude. Because the controller didn't understand the initial transmission, the manager of Boston Center instructed his quality assurance specialist to "pull the tape" of the radio transmission, listen to it closely, and report back.

Between 8:25 and 8:32 AM, in accordance with the FAA protocol, Boston Center managers started notifying their chain of command that American11 had been hijacked. At 8:28 AM, Boston Center called the Command Center in Herndon to advise that it believed American 11 had been hijacked and was heading toward New York Center's airspace.

By this time, American 11 had taken a dramatic turn to the south. At 8:32 AM, the Command Center passed word of a possible hijacking to the Operations Center at FAA headquarters. The duty officer replied that security personnel at headquarters had just begun discussing the apparent hijack on a conference call with the New England regional office. FAA headquarters began to follow the hijack protocol but did not contact the NMCC (National Military Command Center) to request a fighter escort.

The Herndon Command Center immediately established a teleconference between Boston, New York, and Cleveland Centers so that Boston Center could help the others understand what was happening.

At 8:34 AM, the Boston Center controller received a third transmission from American 11.

American 11: Nobody move please. We are going back to the airport. Don't try to make any stupid moves.

In the succeeding minutes, controllers were attempting to ascertain the altitude of the southbound flight.[2]

The 9/11 Commission Report from which the above vignette was extracted was released to the public on July 22, 2004. The report was chartered by Congress in 2002 "to prepare a full and complete account of the circumstances surrounding the September 11, 2001 terrorist attacks, including preparedness for and the immediate response to the attacks. The Commission is also mandated to provide recommendations designed to guard against future attacks."[3]

The National Commission on Terrorist Attacks Upon the United States (better known as the 9/11 Commission) was comprised of 10 appointed commissioners and 75 staff members, including investigators, writers, editors, subject-matter experts, lawyers, and clerical staff. The Commission published its findings in a comprehensive 567-page report that was completed nearly 3 years after the

September 11 attacks. The exhaustive review reconstructed the series of events on that fateful day, and methodically put the pieces of a gigantic puzzle together to make sense out of what had occurred. It took nearly 3 years for 85 experts to "make sense" of what had occurred on September 11, and arguably, that sense-making continues to this day, as we get more information of what happened, and what factors led up to that day.

The account as stated in the vignette began at 8:14 on the morning of September 11, with the uncertainty as to why Flight 11 had failed to heed the flight controller's instructions, followed shortly at 8:21, when the aircraft turned off its transponder. Immediately thereafter, the flight controllers began their initial efforts at "sense-making" by examining the empirical evidence available to them, and by creating working hypotheses of what was occurring. The effort to bring clarity to the uncertainty of the situation began almost immediately. Indeed, even with the minimal information available to them, as early as 8:25 AM, the controllers began to notify their chain of command that the aircraft had been hijacked.

Complexity

Most critical incidents tend to be complex. Typically, the larger the incident, the more people are involved in resolving it. Also, the longer an incident lasts, the likelier it will become more complex, as more responders arrive at the scene. The previous vignette highlighted the uncertainty that critical incident managers faced during the September 11 attacks. Vignette 1.3 continues the September 11 account to show how complexity becomes a major factor in critical incidents.

VIGNETTE 1.3   Excerpt from the 9/11 Commission Report

Prior to 9/11, it was understood that an order to shoot down a commercial aircraft would have to be issued by the National Command Authority (a phrase used to describe the president and secretary of defense). Exercise planners also assumed that the aircraft would originate from outside the United States allowing time to identify the target and scramble interceptors. The threat of terrorists hijacking commercial airliners within the United States—and using them as guided missiles—was not recognized by NORAD (North American Aerospace Defense Command) before 9/11.

Notwithstanding the identification of these emerging threats, by 9/11, there were only seven alert sites left in the United States, each with two fighter aircraft on alert. This led some NORAD commanders to worry that NORAD was not postured adequately to protect the United States.

In the United States, NORAD is divided into three sectors. On 9/11, all the hijacked aircraft were in NORAD's Northeast Air Defense Sector (also known as NEADS), which is based in Rome, New York. That morning NEADS could call on two alert sites, each with one pair of ready fighters: Otis Air National Guard Base in Cape Cod, Massachusetts, and Langley Air

Force Base in Hampton, Virginia. Other facilities, not on "alert," would need time to arm the fighters and organize crews.

NEADS reported to the Continental U.S. NORAD Region (CONR) headquarters in Panama City, Florida, which in turn reported to NORAD headquarters, in Colorado Springs, Colorado.

Interagency Collaboration. The FAA and NORAD had developed protocols for working together in the event of a hijacking. As they existed on 9/11, the protocols for the FAA to obtain military assistance from NORAD required multiple levels of notification and approval at the highest levels of government.

FAA guidance to controllers on hijack procedures assumed that the aircraft pilot would notify the controller via radio or by "squawking" a transponder code of "7500"—the universal code for a hijacking in progress. Controllers would notify their supervisors, who in turn would inform management all the way up to FAA headquarters in Washington. Headquarters had a hijack coordinator, who was the director of the FAA Office of Civil Aviation Security or his or her designate.

If a hijack was confirmed, procedures called for the hijack coordinator on duty to contact the Pentagon's NMCC and to ask for a military escort aircraft to follow the flight, report anything unusual, and aid search and rescue in the event of an emergency. The NMCC would then seek approval from the Office of the Secretary of Defense to provide military assistance. If approval was given, the orders would be transmitted down NORAD's chain of command.

The NMCC would keep the FAA hijack coordinator up to date and help the FAA centers coordinate directly with the military. NORAD would receive tracking information for the hijacked aircraft either from joint use radar or from the relevant FAA Air Traffic Control facility. Every attempt would be made to have the hijacked aircraft squawk 7500 to help NORAD track it.

The protocols did not contemplate an intercept. They assumed the fighter escort would be discreet, "vectored to a position 5 miles directly behind the hijacked aircraft," where it could perform its mission to monitor the aircraft's flight path.

In sum, the protocols in place on 9/11 for the FAA and NORAD to respond to a hijacking presumed that:

- The hijacked aircraft would be readily identifiable and would not attempt to disappear.
- There would be time to address the problem through the appropriate FAA and NORAD chains of command.
- The hijacking would take the traditional form: that is, it would not be a suicide hijacking designed to convert the aircraft into a guided missile.

On the morning of 9/11, the existing protocol was unsuited in every respect for what was about to happen.[4]

Mega-scale critical incidents like the September 11 attacks described in Vignettes 1.2 and 1.3 demonstrate how multidimensional and complex these situations are. It is a credit to the men and women who reacted intuitively and reflexively to the many radical and unexpected events that occurred on that day. Indeed, on a day that will always be remembered as the day that everything changed, the mental agility to quickly adapt to a new paradigm makes the actions of these critical incident managers all the more remarkable. The 9/11 Commission Report noted that, "Individual FAA controllers, facility managers and Command Center managers thought outside the box in recommending a nationwide alert, in ground-stopping local traffic, and, ultimately, in deciding to land all aircraft and executing that unprecedented order flawlessly."[5]

The Three-Dimensional Model of Critical Incident Management

We will examine the factors of chaos, uncertainty, and complexity in greater detail throughout this book. In order to understand and manage this very complex topic, we need to do the same thing that critical incident managers in the field do. Fundamentally, this means that we have to simplify a very complex topic into bite-sized portions. To this end, the authors offer a three-dimensional model of critical incident management with the intent of simplifying the complexities associated with critical incidents. Figure 1.2 provides an illustration of the three-dimensional model, on which this book is based. We will deconstruct this model and examine each of the three dimensions separately.

The Incident Command System

The Incident Command System (ICS), which is the structural underpinning for the broader National Incident Management System (NIMS), provides the first

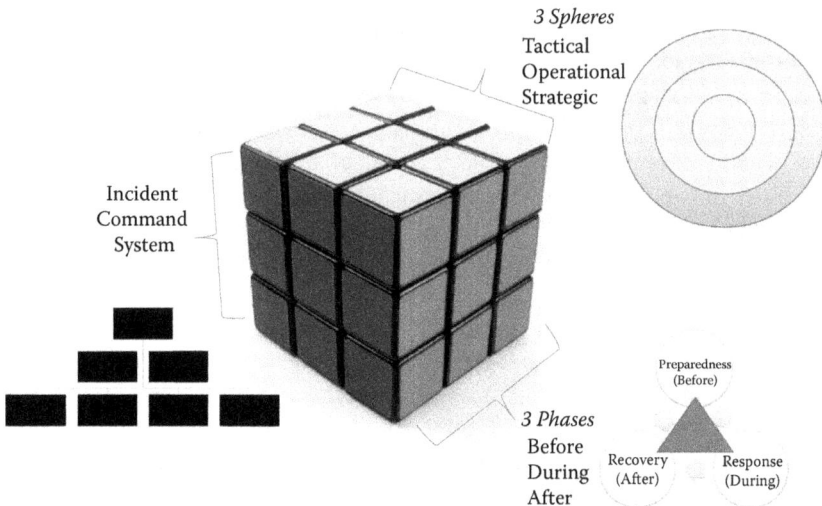

Figure 1.2 Three-Dimensional Model of Critical Incident Management

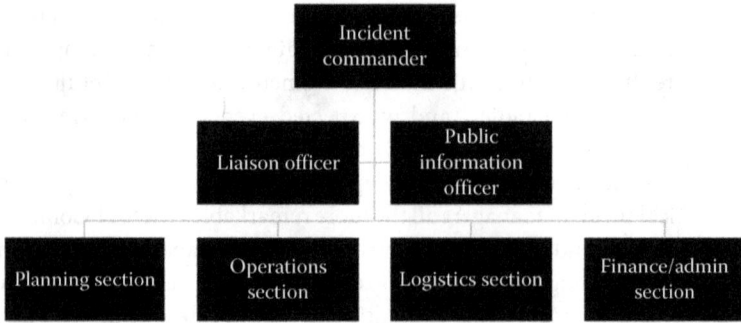

Figure 1.3 Basic Incident Command System Structure

of the three basic tenets of the three-dimensional model used in this book. The ICS organizational structure and related processes have brought much needed uniformity to the field of critical incident management. Figure 1.3 illustrates the most basic ICS organizational structure, which the Federal Emergency Management Agency (FEMA) defines as "The ICS is a widely applicable management system designed to enable effective and efficient incident management by integrating facilities, equipment, personnel, procedures, and communications operating within a common organizational structure."[6]

The great advantage that ICS provides is that it is a fully modular organizational structure, which uses only the elements that are necessary to solve the problem at hand. Detractors of ICS are typically those who erroneously believe that a fully mobilized ICS structure, with all its sections, divisions, strike teams, and task forces must be used for every incident. That erroneous belief is based on a lack of understanding of what the ICS was designed to be in the first place. Indeed, if every element of ICS was to be mobilized for every critical incident, then it would be the cumbersome barrier to nimble decision making that its detractors accuse it of being. But that is not what the ICS was intended to be, and to characterize it as such misses the original intent of the system, and its efficiencies and best practices. Figure 1.3 illustrates the basic elements of an Incident Command System. The boxes in the illustration form the basic building blocks for a modular system that can be small and agile when it needs to be, or very large and complex when it needs to be. ICS is situational by design. That means that the size, scope, and nature of the incident will dictate the size and shape of the ICS for that specific incident. A simple, operations-based ICS may be used for an incident the size and scope of the fairground stampede discussed in Vignette 1.1, or it can be as complex as a full-blown ICS system, with Unified Command components for planning large events such as a Super Bowl, or for very complex mega incidents such as the 9/11 attacks as described in Vignettes 1.2 and 1.3. This book will discuss the ICS's organizational structure and its processes in greater detail, and will provide several examples of specific ICS structures that are used in certain critical incidents.

The Three Spheres of Critical Incident Management

We will examine the organizational structures and processes of ICS in greater detail later because it is such an important part of critical incident management. Yet arguably, reliance on ICS and NIMS alone does not provide the full depth of understanding of what critical incident management is all about. The second dimension of the critical incident management model used in this book is illustrated in Figure 1.4. In this dimension, there are three concentric rings: tactical, operational, and strategic.

Chapters 3 through 5 have been organized along these three concentric rings of the circle. We refer to each of these rings as the three "spheres" of critical incident management. These three spheres comprise the second dimension of critical incident management. Whereas the Incident Command System provides an excellent hierarchical organizational structure that is most effective for managing critical incidents (hierarchical structures work fairly well on noncritical, day-to-day matters, as well), it does not provide a full understanding of the critical incident management universe. The ICS hierarchical structure is flat and one dimensional. Its hierarchical organization chart provides an excellent depiction of the elements (boxes), as well as the lines (the processes) that connect the boxes. These connector lines signify the command process, and clearly define who reports to whom. Clear lines of reporting are integral for any system of command.

What ICS does not do is provide an understanding of the world *outside* its organizational chart. To get a full understanding of the "all-hazards" threat universe that we, as critical incident managers face, it is important to take into account the second dimension of the three-dimensional model. Referring back to the cube illustration in Figure 1.1, the ICS organizational structure is depicted on the vertical axis of the cube. The concentric rings of the tactical, operational, and strategic spheres comprise the horizontal axis of this cube.

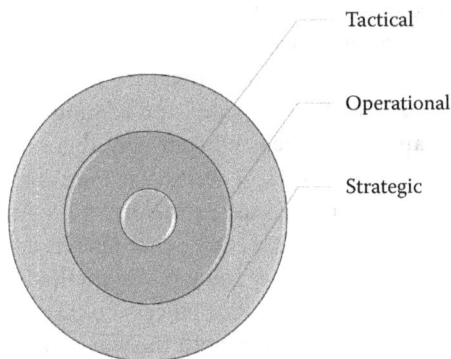

Tactical

Operational

Strategic

Figure 1.4 The Three Spheres of Critical Incident Management

VIGNETTE 1.4 The Genesis of an Idea

Lieutenant Brown was the only police officer in the room. He had been told by his commanding officer to attend a Super Bowl planning meeting that was being held at the County Fire Rescue Department headquarters. He arrived only minutes before the start, and sat in the very last row of the classroom where the meeting was being held. There were five tables with four seats each on the left side of the room, and an equal number on the right side of the room. Every seat was occupied, and there were a few other attendees standing in the back, where pastries and coffee had been laid out on the counter. Judging by the number of seats in the classroom, there were at least 40 fire-rescue men and women in the room ... most wearing short-sleeved white uniform shirts and black pants. Lieutenant Brown was not entirely familiar with the rank insignia designators for the Fire Rescue Department, but as he looked around the room, he saw many with two, three, and even four bugle insignia on their lapels, and figured that these 40 individuals must represent the commanders of various organizational elements within the Department.

Brown recognized the man standing behind the podium at the front as the Chief of the County Fire Rescue Department. The Chief and his upper command staff stood out because they were the only five fire-rescue personnel who were wearing white long-sleeved uniform shirts, black ties, and gold-colored badges and rank insignia on their lapels. Lieutenant Brown surmised that the individuals standing at the front of the classroom were top brass of the Department ... battalion chiefs and assistant chiefs. The Chief shuffled some papers, and looked like he was getting ready to start the meeting. Behind him, there were three large rectangular whiteboards, with one that had five unlabeled boxes of a hierarchical organizational chart that Brown immediately recognized as the basic components of the Incident Command System. Brown had been to several Incident Command System training courses over the past 5 years, and was well versed on the organizational structure of ICS. Indeed, his first exposure to ICS came in the late 1990s, when a County Fire Rescue captain came to the police Training Bureau to teach first-line police supervisors about the newly instituted Incident Command System for the police. The police had been slow to accept the ICS into their incident command procedures, and Brown remembered why there had been so much resistance among his police peers. It seemed at the time that the training had been based on fire-rescue response procedures for fighting fires, and had little to do with the types of incidents that police officers face on a day-to-day basis. Very few officers could relate some of the methodical protocols that firemen used in their jobs. Most police officers could not understand why they would need to wear orange vests with the words *Incident Commander, Operations, Logistics, Liaison,* and so forth. Police work is fundamentally different than fire-rescue work, and most police officers saw these ICS practices as being irrelevant to their profession. Most police officers could not relate to filling out FEMA forms to request more pumper trucks, and what that had to do with their jobs. After all, who has time to fill out a FEMA form, or put on an orange vest, when someone is actively shooting at you? To most police officers, ICS was an impediment to doing their jobs, and many of them resented having fire-rescue personnel teaching them how to handle critical incidents. That was the prevailing view of most police officers in the late 1990s. It had taken several years after the initial training courses before the police department commanders reluctantly accepted fire-rescue's ICS practices as part of their own procedures.

Generally speaking, police officers tend to get impatient with the methodical manner that firemen use to respond to calls. Firefighting tends to rely more on a team-oriented approach, whereas police work is more often done individually, or in teams of no more than two officers. Sometimes, for larger and more complex critical incidents, police officers will organize into larger teams, but for the most part, police work is more of an individual thing. Firemen on the other hand, typically respond to high-hazard calls as a team, in a controlled and methodical manner. They tend to think of police officers as being a bit careless and impatient in the manner that they respond to calls. Firemen jokingly refer to policemen as "canaries." Firemen have come to expect that police officers would act as individuals, rather than as team members, and that they would reflexively rush into high-risk situations, and inevitably find themselves in very bad situations, where firemen would have to come and rescue them. The prevailing saying among firemen was "Why bother bringing chemical agent 'sniffer' equipment to the scene of a hazardous spill, when there's already a policeman on the scene passing out from the toxic gasses?" Policemen and firemen are different in many ways, but one thing they share is a morbid sense of humor.

Lieutenant Brown sat quietly in his seat in the back row of the classroom, as Fire Rescue Chief Frank Fernandez welcomed the attendees to the meeting, and introduced his four command staff personnel, who were standing along the wall at the front of the classroom. The Chief then acknowledged Lieutenant Brown as the only representative from the police department present at the meeting. Chief Fernandez then called up one of his Battalion Chiefs and asked him to give a briefing about what the Fire Rescue Department had done so far with the planning for the upcoming Super Bowl. Brown looked around the room, and although he recognized a few faces, he didn't know anyone's name (other than Chief Fernandez because he recognized him from seeing him on television), and he also didn't know what ranks and positions each person in the room had in the Fire Rescue Department. All he knew was that everyone at this meeting was either in the upper command staff, or at the mid-management level.

As the meeting proceeded past the first 5 minutes, Lieutenant Brown started to realize how far behind the Fire Rescue Department was in the planning phases, in comparison to the Police Department. The Super Bowl was only 3 months away, and the fire-rescue chiefs were just starting to discuss the incident command structure for the coming event. By contrast, the Police Department had started planning for the event 2 years before ... with initial exploratory travels by select supervisory personnel to cities that had held previous Super Bowls. Three months out, and the Police Department had already completed most of its planning and training objectives, yet the Fire Rescue Department was just beginning to think about planning. Lieutenant Brown could not believe how far behind the Fire Rescue Department seemed to be.

The meeting dragged on for 20 minutes, and then past the 30-minute mark, as several fire-rescue commanders took turns on the whiteboard. Each commander would draw boxes, lines, and names inside the boxes of the original ICS diagram that had been on the whiteboard at the beginning of the meeting. The more time elapsed, the more disagreement there was among the meeting participants. One would go up and erase what the previous commander had drawn on the whiteboard, and another would follow and erase that person's diagram. After a while, the discussion started to heat up, and it became clear to Lieutenant Brown that there was a lot of disagreement and tension between some of the commanders of the Fire Rescue Department. It seemed that they were having trouble agreeing to even the most basic aspects of a plan.

At the 40-minute mark of the meeting, Lieutenant Brown sensed that the tension in the room was extremely high. Brown could not believe that with only 3 months to go before the event, this highly respected and nationally acclaimed Fire Rescue Department could not even get out of first gear in its discussion about how the Department's Incident Command System would be structured for this particular event. He found it incredulous that fire rescue was not even aware that the police and the National Football League (NFL) had completed their organization charts months ago, and that the exact names of the commanders of each box had already been assigned. Forty minutes into the meeting, and this group of top commanders had not yet even decided who their incident commander would be, or who would be assigned to the basic positions of operations, logistics, planning, and finance.

A bit frustrated, Brown began doodling on a piece of paper that he had brought to the meeting in order to take notes. Nothing had been decided on, and therefore, the notepad was blank except for a crude diagram of three concentric circles that Brown had drawn on it. Brown thought to himself: "the problem here is that they can't get past the ICS organization structure. They don't seem to realize that there are other agencies and stakeholders involved in the planning process, and that the planning is being done at different levels. They're stuck because they don't seem to realize that they are actually supposed to be making three different plans ... a day-to-day operational level plan ... a tactical plan in case some unexpected incident should break out during the event ... and a broader strategic plan."

Brown had never consciously thought of it in that way before, but by drawing the three-ring diagram on his notepaper, he suddenly realized something that he had already known from before … there are really three levels of planning for large-scale events such as the Super Bowl that they were working on now. Brown hesitated at first, but then raised his hand from the back of the room. He felt a bit uneasy raising his hand since he was the only police officer in a meeting of 40 firemen, but his patience was waning after almost an hour of hearing the fire-rescue commanders argue about the way that the ICS structure was going to look like for the Super Bowl. The Fire Rescue Department director called on him, and Brown stated, "Sir, may I come up front and show you something?"

Chief Fernandez seemed relieved that Brown had interrupted what was becoming a contentious argument, with no resolution in sight. Brown grabbed one of the black erasable markers and on the last piece of whiteboard that remained blank drew the three concentric circles that he had just drawn on his notepaper. Brown pointed to the circles on the whiteboard and said, "Chief, the reason that we're having trouble determining the right incident command structure to use here, is that we're looking at things from one dimension only. There are three things going on here … the operational, the tactical, and the strategic. Each one of these rings requires its own plan, and its own incident command structure."

Suddenly, as if a light switch had been turned on, several of the other fire-rescue commanders chimed in. One of the "two bugle" captains sitting in the front row asked, "Are you saying that we need three separate incident command structures?"

Brown responded, "Well not necessarily … but that may not be a bad idea. I'll have to give it some more thought. However, I think that at a minimum, you need to have a plan that considers these three different spheres. And in your strategic plan, you need to understand that there are many other stakeholders involved in this event, and that you are only one of many key participants." Then suddenly, another idea popped into Brown's head, "… and if you think about it, not only should you be making plans at all three of these levels, you should also be making plans for what happens before, during, and after the incident. Come to think of it, you're actually doing nine different plans … before, during, and after, for each of the three spheres. You can see how complex this event is going to be, and how a flat, one-dimensional ICS structure is not going to give you a full understanding of what is going on, and what needs to be done. That doesn't mean that you need nine different ICS organizational charts. In fact, you should probably only have one organizational chart to keep it simple, but if you look at it from this perspective, you will see how your ICS structure will need to take into account the before, during, and after, for operational, tactical, and strategic spheres."

Brown realized that he was creating new ideas as fast as he could say them out loud. The simple diagram that he had drawn on his notepad only a few minutes prior helped the others in the room understand what they were up against, and it helped him as well. It's not that he didn't already know that there were nine plans instead of one plan. Brown was an experienced planner, and had participated in other Super Bowls, and the planning of other large-scale events as well. It's just that he had never really stopped to think about it like he thought today. The simple diagram helped others see what he himself had never stopped to think about. Brown returned to his seat at the back of the classroom, and suddenly, the fire-rescue commanders began to put together an ICS organizational chart that started to make sense.

From Vignette 1.4, it appears that the stumbling block that the fire-rescue commanders were encountering during their initial planning meeting for the Super Bowl was not because the Incident Command System was a bad thing. The difficulty that they were having was a result of their approach, wherein they started their planning with the solution to the problem in mind, instead of first identifying what the problem was. The construct of the incident command organizational chart that they started with was hindering their ability to frame the problem. The fire-rescue commanders made the fundamental error of trying to fit the problem into the solution, rather than the other way around. The lesson learned from this vignette is that before we start coming up with solutions to problems by making organizational structures, we first need to identify and frame the key issues. In this case, the illustration of the three concentric ringed circle helped the attendees at the meeting visualize a framework to better define the issue, and the task at hand. This simple illustration helped them to think outside of the box that they had created for themselves.

Before, During, and After

The third dimension of critical incident management has to do with time. As stated in Vignette 1.4, Lieutenant Brown came to the realization that in addition to the three spheres of command, the planning also needed to take into account the temporal factor. One of the fundamental errors that the fire-rescue commanders were making in their initial attempt at planning for the Super Bowl was that they did not take into account the things that needed to be done before the incident and after the incident. They were only considering the organizational structures that dealt with the "during" part of the event. To be fair, a fully mobilized ICS structure has a planning component which does much of its work before an incident or event, as well as a demobilization unit, which does most of its work after the incident is over. But even taking into account these two elements in their ICS organizational chart did not give them a full grasp of the temporal dimension that needs to be considered for the planning process.

Temporal factors in the emergency management field are often described as "phases." FEMA uses a four-phase model of emergency management, which is emulated by most emergency management agencies at the state and county levels throughout the United States. The FEMA model is comprised of four phases (mitigation, preparedness, response, and recovery), as illustrated in Figure 1.5.

The FEMA Model of Emergency Management

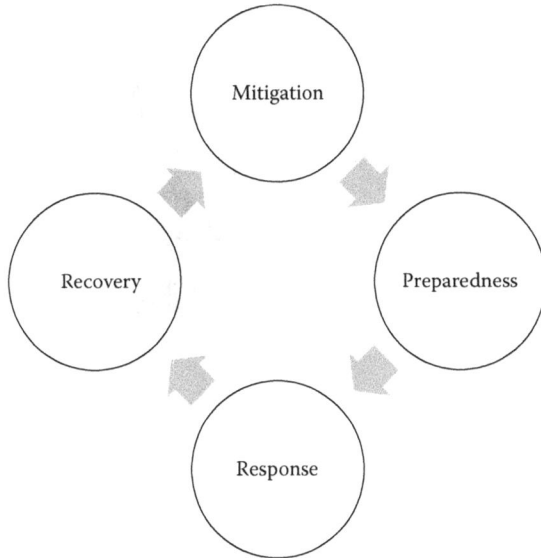

Figure 1.5 FEMA's Four Phases of Emergency Management

Baird[7] examined FEMA's four-phase model and its conceptual origin, as well as other similar various models used by other emergency management agencies. Most of the variations of the FEMA model include the four phases in a circular diagram of interconnected arrows, either spinning clockwise or counter clockwise. Some add the "phases" of *prevention* or *protection,* thus making it a five-part model, instead of reducing it to its most simple manifestation of a three-phase model that the authors utilize. The obvious problem with the FEMA model (and others using four or five phases) is that in a time continuum, there can only be three possibilities: before, during, and after (notwithstanding what some philosophers may argue). The authors argue that anything that is not *before, during,* or *after* cannot be considered a phase per se. As such, for the purposes of this book and for simplicity's sake, we developed a three-phase model, as illustrated in Figure 1.6. This model corresponds with FEMA's phases of preparedness, response, and recovery, but it shows mitigation, not as a temporal phase, but rather as something that is done before, during, and after a critical incident.

In Figure 1.6, mitigation is illustrated as a triangle that is situated in the middle of the three temporal phases, and which touches all three phases. This is because the act of mitigation is not a temporal phase in itself. Indeed, mitigation is something that happens in all the phases. The online Dictionary.com defines mitigation as "the act of making a condition or consequence less severe."[8] Note that a *condition* is something that is preexisting, and a *consequence* is something that happens after an incident. In other words, mitigation is something that happens before and after an action or event.

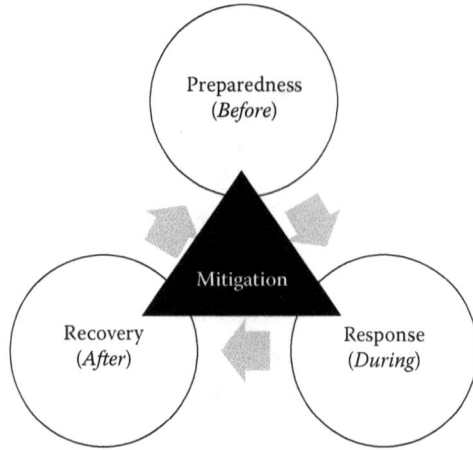

Figure 1.6 The Three-Phase Model of Critical Incident Management

FEMA defines mitigation as follows:

Mitigation is the effort to reduce loss of life and property by lessening the impact of disasters. Mitigation is taking action *now*—before the next disaster—to reduce human and financial consequences later (analyzing risk, reducing risk, insuring against risk). Effective mitigation requires that we *all* understand local risks, address the hard choices and invest in long-term community well being. Without mitigation actions, we jeopardize our safety, financial security, and self-reliance.[9]

In essence, the concept of mitigation has to do with risk reduction. Fundamentally, risk can be reduced in two ways: reducing the likelihood of something bad happening *before* it happens, or reducing the consequences of something bad happening *after* it happens. Chapter 2 is devoted entirely to risk mitigation, and is based on the conceptual model illustrated in Figure 1.6. Clearly, mitigation is not a phase in and of itself. It is something that overarches the other three phases of emergency management. Nevertheless, readers are encouraged to familiarize themselves with the four-phase FEMA model, if for no other reason than FEMA provides grant money to state, county, and tribal governments, and local agencies, and to some nongovernmental organizations (NGOs) as well. For those readers who attempt to navigate the FEMA website, or download grant application documents, we suspect that you may be hard-pressed to discern the difference between a "pre-disaster mitigation" grant and a "pre-disaster preparedness" grant. The funding streams from the federal government will be examined in greater detail in Chapter 5, but it is safe to say that navigating the labyrinth of available grant opportunities would be much easier if one understands the language that FEMA uses. The best advice that can be offered to both novice and experienced emergency managers is to abide by the old saying: "When in Rome, do as the Romans do." In other words, become familiar with FEMA's four-phase model, even if one of those "phases" is not really a phase.

Incidents versus Events

The words "incident" and "event" are often used interchangeably, but for the purposes of this book, they mean two different things. An incident is something that occurs unexpectedly. An event is something that is anticipated and planned for ahead of time. The day, time, and place of the event are known ahead of time. Incidents, on the other hand, occur spontaneously and the place, time, and circumstances cannot be anticipated. Does that mean that incidents cannot be planned for? This is a question that we pose to students at the beginning of our Critical Incident Management for Command Officers courses.

Everyone agrees that special events such as a 5K run, a presidential debate, or a Super Bowl can be planned ahead of time. With these events, we have the luxury of knowing the exact date, time, and place that they will occur, and thus the planning can begin well in advance. The question is whether we can plan for unanticipated incidents. Most would agree that we can plan for hurricanes ahead of time. We may not be able to predict the exact time and location of an approaching hurricane's landfall, but modern weather forecasting models are providing us with better predictions than was the case as recently as 20 years ago. We may be better at predicting the time, place, and force of a hurricane, but we cannot control or cancel it as we could with a concert, a baseball game, or a state fair. This is why hurricanes are considered as incidents and not events.

What about incidents with very little warning such as tornadoes? Can we plan ahead of time for them? Can we plan for an active shooter situation at a local high school? Or a chemical spill at a train derailment, or an anthrax pandemic? None of these incidents can be anticipated with any exactitude. But does that mean that we cannot plan for them? As you read this, and consider each one of these scenarios, it should be evident to you that yes, all these things can be planned for ahead of time. For some incidents such as in hurricanes, there may be considerable warning, as much as 48 hours prior to landfall. For others, there may be very little warning, or no warning at all. The common variable factor that all incidents share is the uncertainty of time and place. The more lead time there is, the more specific the planning can be for that incident. Since the time, place, and circumstances of incidents cannot be predicted ahead of time, critical incident managers have to devise generic plans that are flexible and adaptable to meet a wide variety of situations.

While the *probability* of a hurricane striking a certain place and time cannot be predicted with complete certainty, the *consequences* of the incident can be anticipated by looking at what previous hurricanes did when they reached landfall. It is with these predicted consequences in mind that we base our plans and preparations. It would be foolish not to prepare for future incidents for which similar incidents have occurred in the past, and which have caused great damage and injury. We will discuss in greater depth in Chapter 2 the factors of probability and consequence as they relate to risk analysis.

The distinction between an event and an incident is not whether they can be planned for. It is whether they can be anticipated and controlled. The best way to remember the difference between an event and an incident is to refer to them as *anticipated events* and *unanticipated incidents*. It should also be noted that unanticipated incidents may occur during anticipated events. Indeed, when planning an event, it is a good practice to plan for possible unanticipated incidents that are likely to arise during the event. This practice is called *contingency planning*, and will be discussed in greater depth in various chapters of this book. We now know that we can plan for anticipated events, as well as unanticipated incidents. The only difference is the degree of uncertainty leading up to the event or incident.

Three Types of Incidents

In the realm of *emergency management*, incidents are classified as "types of disasters." We prefer the broader term "incident" because while all disasters are incidents, not all incidents are disasters. The word "disaster" excludes many critical incidents such as hostage situations, unexploded bombs, airplane hijackings, and more. This book is about the broader field of *critical incident management*, not just about the management of disasters. Nevertheless, the two disciplines overlap considerably, and to understand the terminology of one, it is helpful to understand the concepts of the other.

Below et al.[10] identify two generic disaster classifications: natural and technological. They further break down the "natural" category into six disaster groups: biological, geophysical, meteorological, hydrological, climatological, and extraterrestrial. Do not worry. Extraterrestrial merely refers to meteorite or asteroid strike. The typology in this analysis provides an exhaustive list of natural disaster types to include lightning, avalanches, fungal infections, and locusts, grasshoppers, and worms. Notably absent in this typology are man-made disasters.

The U.S. Government website DisasterAssistance.gov lists 15 types of disasters in alphabetical order, including biological threats, chemical threats, droughts, earthquakes, fires, floods, heat, hurricanes, landslides, radiation and nuclear threats, tornadoes, tsunamis, volcanoes, wildfires, and winter storms.[11]

While these lists provide a fairly comprehensive account of the "all-hazards" approach to disaster management, they miss some important types of incidents that critical incident managers are confronted with. Notably missing from these two lists are explosions (both accidental and intentional), active shooter situations, hostage situations, and small unit coordinated military or terrorist attacks.

Similarly, the American Red Cross lists 22 types of emergencies: chemical emergencies, droughts, earthquakes, fires, floods, flu epidemics, food safety, heat waves, highway safety, hurricanes, landslides, pet safety, poisoning, power outage, terrorism, thunderstorms, tornadoes, tsunamis, volcanoes, water safety, wildfires, and winter storms.[12]

All the incident types identified in the three cited classification models are useful for understanding and managing these critical incidents, but for the sake of simplicity, we strive to reduce concepts to their most basic origins. As such, all the types of incidents identified by emergency management organizations can be reduced to three basic categories of incidents:

- Natural
- Man-made accidental (also referred to as "technical")
- Man-made intentional

Not all incidents fit neatly into these categories. For example, in 2011, an earthquake in Japan led to a tsunami that struck parts of the coast, including the Fukushima Daiichi nuclear power plant. This led to a loss of power at the plant, and resulted in a Level-7 nuclear meltdown, and the release of radioactive materials.[13] In essence, one natural disaster led to another natural disaster, which in turn led to a man-made accidental disaster.

Another example where the categories may overlap can be seen with the contention that the process of hydraulic fracturing (commonly referred to as "fracking") may cause earthquakes.[14] If true, this would be an example of a man-made accidental incident leading to a natural disaster.

Order, Predictability, and Simplicity

From the vignettes in this chapter, we get a sense of the magnitude of the challenges that critical incident managers face. To even the most experienced incident commanders, some situations are so chaotic, uncertain, and complex that the mission of returning things to normalcy can be extremely daunting. One such challenge is the planning of a large-scale special event such as a major political convention, or a Super Bowl. These large-scale events typically require at least a year to plan for, and there are hundreds of people involved in the planning process. In the last chapter (Chapter 8), we will synthesize all the lessons learned from Chapters 1 through 7, and apply that knowledge to the planning of a large-scale special event. That chapter includes a list of 27 deliverables that need to be applied in order to achieve a successful plan. Our rationale for choosing a large-scale special event as the capstone project for this book is that planning for such an event entails every possible skill set that a critical incident manager needs in order to be successful.

Before we get to Chapter 8, we start in Chapter 2 by deconstructing and simplifying the concept of risk mitigation, which underlies the entire text. Risk mitigation is what critical incident managers do, and to better understand its principles, we provide some real-life stories that personalize and help us understand risk management in simple terms that we can relate to. Critical incident management can be a daunting challenge, but when we learn that we can apply the same concepts that we use on a daily basis to the most complex situations that we rarely encounter, we can approach these challenges with more confidence.

In Chapters 3 through 5, we will get to the "nuts and bolts" of critical incident management and special event planning at the operational, tactical, and strategic levels, respectively. In each, we will examine the things we need to do to prepare, respond, and recover in a myriad of critical incidents. In Chapter 6, we will explore the many ways that we can teach and learn from each other. We will examine the wide range of training opportunities available to first responders and incident commanders. You will be provided with templates and examples of event scripts that you can use to design your own tabletop or functional level training exercises.

Chapter 7 covers the important topic of creativity, innovation, and institutional change. As the threat landscape changes and new vulnerabilities are exposed, it is imperative that law enforcement, fire rescue, and emergency management agencies adapt to the changes. In Chapter 7, we deconstruct the innovation process and examine the best practices acquired from the successful innovations of organizations across the spectrum. It is our hope that once we get to Chapter 8, you will have a good understanding of the things that you need to know in order to be a successful critical incident manager.

References

1. National Commission on Terrorist Attacks Upon the United States, 2004. *The 9/11 Commission Report.* Online at http://www.9-11commission.gov/ (accessed August 27, 2015).
2. Extracted from the *9/11 Commission Report*, p. 16.
3. National Commission on Terrorist Attacks Upon the United States, 2004. *The 9/11 Commission Report.* Online at http://www.9-11commission.gov/ (accessed August 27, 2015).
4. Ibid., pp. 17–18
5. Ibid., p. 31
6. U.S. Department of Homeland Security, n.d. What is ICS designed to do? p. 3. Online at https://www.fema.gov/pdf/emergency/nims/nimsfaqs.pdf (accessed August 27, 2015).
7. M. E. Baird, 2010. The "phases" of emergency management. Background paper. Intermodal Freight Transportation Institute (ITFI), University of Memphis. Online at http://www.vanderbilt.edu/vector/ research/recoveryphase.pdf (accessed August 27, 2015).
8. Dictionary.com, n.d. Online at http://dictionary.reference.com/browse/mitigation (accessed August 28, 2015).
9. Federal Emergency Management Agency, n.d. What is mitigation? Online at http://www.fema.gov/what-mitigation.
10. R. Below, Wirtz, A., and Guha-Sapir, D. 2009. Disaster category classification and peril terminology for operational purposes. Common accord, Centre for Research on the Epidemiology of Disasters (CRED) and Munich Reinsurance Company (Munich RE). Online at http://cred.be/sites/default/files/DisCatClass_264.pdf (accessed August 28, 2015).
11. DisasterAssistance.gov, 2014. Disaster types. Online at http://www.disasterassistance.gov/disaster-information/disaster-types (accessed August 28, 2015).
12. RedCross.org, n.d. Types of emergencies. disaster preparedness. American Red Cross. Online at http://www.redcross.org/prepare/disaster (accessed August 28, 2015).
13. B. Oskin, 2015. Japan earthquake & tsunami of 2011: Facts and information. *Live Science.* Online at http://www.livescience.com/39110-japan-2011-earthquake-tsunami-facts.html (accessed August 28, 2015).
14. P. J. Kiger, 2015. Could fracking cause an earthquake? *Discovery News*, January 16. Online at http://news.discovery.com/earth/could-fracking-cause-a-major-earthquake-1501161.htm (accessed August 28, 2015).

2
Risk Analysis

Risk Mitigation

Underlying everything that first responders and critical incident managers do is the concept of risk mitigation. We start this chapter with a close look at risk mitigation because risk pervades everything else that follows in the subsequent chapters. Understanding risk and risk mitigation is the bulwark of critical incident management. As stated in Chapter 1, risk mitigation is something that is done before, during, and after an incident. It is the fourth "phase" of the FEMA model that is really not a phase. Risk mitigation is something that all persons and organizations do on a daily basis, even if most of the time we are not consciously aware that we are doing it. The key to understanding risk and risk mitigation starts with seeing it in action in the routines of the day in the life of one person. In this chapter, we will break down the concept of risk into its basic elements so that we can better understand how it affects every aspect of critical incident management—and as we will see in Vignette 2.1—how it affects almost every aspect of our daily lives as well. As you read this story, take note of the number of times that the main character does things to mitigate risk in a day of her life. Consider whether her actions are intended to minimize the *probability* of something adverse happening, or whether her actions are taken to minimize the *effects* of the bad thing if and when it should happen. Finally, as you read this vignette, categorize the mitigation actions into three phases: *preparedness* (the things we do before an incident), *response* (the things we do during an incident), and *recovery* (the things we do after an incident). Understand that the boundaries between the phases are sometimes blurred, and that the things that we do in the recovery phase are likely to overlap into the preparedness phase for the next cycle. For optimal learning effect, it is recommended that you write on a blank piece of paper three separate columns (labeled *before, during,* and *after*), then list each of the risk mitigation actions under the most appropriate column.

VIGNETTE 2.1   A Day in the Life of Officer Annette Williams

As was with every night, Annette Williams tucked her five-year-old son into bed. She leaned over and kissed him on the forehead. "Bobby ... Daddy will read you a story tonight ... I'm running late for work."

Five-year-old Bobby replied, "I love you mom ... be careful tonight."

"I'll see you in the morning little buddy ... sweet dreams ... I love you much. Daddy will be here in a minute." With that, Annette walked out and closed the door behind her, making sure to leave a slight crack so that the hallway light could peek through. She made her way to the master bedroom, where her husband lay on the bed watching TV. "OK Dad … you can take over now." She handed two children's books to him, "He wants *The Gingerbread Man* tonight, but take *Hansel and Gretel* with you in case he asks for a second story."

Fred Williams took the storybooks from Annette and held her in his arms for a minute. "Be careful tonight."

"I will. I'll call you if I'm running late. You may have to get him ready for school if I get a late call."

"No problem, honey. I'll take care of it. I think I can figure things out." With that, Fred Williams … Firefighter Fred Williams … smiled and kissed his wife Annette … Officer Annette Williams one more time.

Annette walked to her closet where her ballistic vest hung. She pulled it over her head and secured the two Velcro straps snuggly across the front. After putting on her police uniform shirt, Officer Williams then strapped on her gun belt that contained an empty holster and compartments for handcuffs, a flashlight, two pouches of 14-round magazine clips, a baton ring, and a small pouch for two latex gloves. She then unlocked a small safe where she kept her loaded weapons and grabbed her semiautomatic service weapon and placed it into the holster. Officer Williams then grabbed an ankle holster with a two-inch, five-shot revolver that she used as an emergency backup weapon. She strapped the holster to the inside of her left ankle and tightened the Velcro straps to make sure it would not slip off during the night. She then pulled the pants leg down so that it would fully cover the secondary weapon. Officer Williams was ready for another night's work.

Officer Williams walked out of the front door of her residence and made sure to lock the top bolt. She knew that her husband would later set the burglar alarm from the inside once she left. Before Williams got into her take-home marked police car which was parked in the front driveway, she made sure to walk around it once and check for any damage, or anything else that someone may have done to it while it was parked unattended. She knew that there had been some vandalism incidents in her neighborhood lately, and there had also been some recent threats to police officers, so she was especially wary. Once she was sure that the vehicle was safe, she got into it and started the engine. Earlier that morning when she returned from the previous night's work, Williams had made sure to back in her police car so that it was facing the street and she wouldn't have to back out of her driveway in the darkness of the evening. That way, if she had received an early emergency call in, Williams' police car would be ready to go and pointed in the right direction.

Officer Williams drove her police car to her assigned patrol area. Since it was a busy Friday night, there would be no roll call scheduled. Since there was no need to drive to the police station, Williams radioed the dispatcher and checked herself into service at 11:01 PM. She was ready for the first call of the night.

It was a fairly typical Friday night, with the typical domestic disturbances, loud music calls, and bar fights. There were over 20 calls holding from the afternoon shift, and Williams and her squad mates quickly handled the backlog, so that by 1 AM there were no more calls holding, and only a few sporadic new calls were being received at the 9-1-1 center.

Williams had not eaten dinner with her family that evening and she decided to grab a quick bite to eat during the brief lull. Being that it was a busy night of the week, she opted to go through the drive-thru of a fast food restaurant and order a hamburger and fries to go. As she approached the drive-thru, Williams made sure that no other cars were in front of her in the line in case she got an emergency call and had to leave in a hurry. She didn't want to put herself in a situation where she would be blocked in by other cars. Williams ordered her food and a minute later picked it up at the takeout window. She drove several blocks until she found a large empty shopping center parking lot where she decided to park and eat her dinner. Williams was an experienced officer, and she remembered several incidents where officers had been ambushed from behind while they were writing reports in their police vehicles. She figured that being in the middle of a large parking area with no other cars around her would give her sufficient time to react to anyone trying to sneak up on her.

Officer Williams quickly gobbled down her hamburger and fries. She had learned to be a fast eater. It's one of the necessary bad habits that police officers pick up. It was a good thing that she finished quickly because she and another one-man unit (Unit 3111) received a call for another loud music complaint from the dispatcher. Williams acknowledged the call and advised on the radio her starting location, so that the other responding unit could get an idea of her distance from the call and the time it would take her to arrive. This was a standard safety practice that most seasoned police officers used. When two one-man units respond to a call from two different starting locations, it's important that they both have an idea of how long until the other unit will arrive on the call. That is because invariably one will arrive at the call before the other. Sometimes it doesn't matter if the two responding officers arrive separately, but more often it is best if both officers arrive at the same time and approach the situation together.

While enroute to the call, Officer Williams observed a male wearing a motorcycle helmet and a long trench coat walking on the sidewalk in the direction of a 24-hour convenience store. This immediately set off alarm bells in Officer Williams' head. There had been several armed robberies of convenience stores in her district by a male wearing a motorcycle helmet and carrying a sawed-off shotgun under his trench coat. This was completely unrelated to the call that she and the other one-man unit were en route to, but in Officer Williams' mind, this was possibly a much more pressing matter. Immediately Officer Williams grabbed her radio mic and raised the dispatcher: "Unit 3115 … request a delay … I think there may be robbery in progress at the 7-11 at 74 and Coral Way. I have a male subject wearing a motorcycle helmet and long trench coat going into the store now. Have Unit 3111 cancel the call he's en route to and respond to my location and go to Tac-4 frequency."

Instead of approaching the front of the 7-11, Officer Williams continued to drive half a block past. She did not know if the subject had seen her, but if he did, she wanted to make it seem like she had not seen him. Williams knew that the subject was already inside the store, and if she approached him now, it could lead to a confrontation. Williams wanted to make sure she had sufficient backup before confronting the subject. She also reasoned that if she confronted the subject too soon, it may force him to possibly take hostages inside the store.

Williams positioned her vehicle in a parking lot across the street behind two dumpsters, where she had a full view of the front of the 7-11, while at the same time staying out of the field of view of anyone inside the store. With her binoculars, she could see the front door of the store, and would be able to tell when the subject came out. Her plan was to take down the subject as he exited the store and walked a sufficient distance so it would be unlikely that he would run back inside. That would be the safest approach. She then raised Unit 3111 on the Tac-4 radio frequency: "Jim, I'm set up half a block east of the 7-11, and I have a partial eyeball on the front entrance of the store. He's in there now, but I don't have a direct view. If you're coming from the west, set up at the corner of 75 and Coral Way in case he runs that way. Don't let him see you pass in front of the store. I want to take him down after he leaves."

Unit 3111 was Officer James Hitchens. He responded on the radio, "Are there any other subjects?"

Williams came back, "That's unknown at this time, but keep your eye out for any possible getaway vehicles."

"I'm arriving at the corner of 75 and Coral Way now, I'll standby here," said Officer Hitchens. "Did you see the black older model SUV parked in the alley behind the Cuban restaurant on the corner?"

"No, I can't see it from where I'm at. What do you have?" asked Williams.

"I can't tell if it's occupied or not, and the head lights are off, but the rear brake lights are on. I think someone may be crouching down inside the vehicle so I don't see them, and is accidentally hitting the brake pedal with their foot."

"OK ... that may be the getaway vehicle ... we'd better get some more units here. I'll go back on the main frequency and see if we can get more backups."

Officer Williams raised the dispatcher and advised of the possible getaway vehicle that Unit 3111 was surveilling, and she asked if there were more units in the area that could assist. Within seconds, two other one-man units arrived in the area. They had been listening to the radio transmissions on Tac-4, and had started heading in the direction of the 7-11. Officer Williams had a solid reputation among her squad members, and everyone knew that when she called for a backup, it was always for a good reason. As the other two units arrived in the general area, Williams observed the subject exiting the front door of the 7-11. On Tac-4 Williams advised: "OK … standby … he's coming out! He's walking fast westbound. Not yet … let him get past the open businesses … we'll take him down close to the vehicle, where the concrete wall is. Watch for crossfire … I'll come up from the east. Jim … approach from the west and take the vehicle. Jeff (Unit 3112), come up behind me from the east … but hold up … not yet … not yet … OK now!"

At that precise moment, the dispatcher raised Officer Williams: "3115, we're now receiving a silent holdup alarm at the 7-11 at Coral Way and 74. Are you OK?" Williams heard the dispatcher, but was not able to immediately answer her because she and Units 3111, 3112, and 3114 were in the midst of taking down an armed robbery subject and a possible accomplice in the getaway vehicle. All four police cars swooped in at precisely the same time, and surrounded the subject who was still walking toward the SUV. At first, it appeared that the subject looked as if he wanted to run, but he had nowhere to go. A row of stores were to his immediate north, and a concrete wall to his west. The four officers surrounded him in a semicircle and his only two other options were to shoot it out, or to surrender. At gunpoint, Williams and two other officers ordered the subject to drop the gun that he appeared to have hidden in his waistband. Cornered, with no place to run, and in no mood to fight, the subject dropped what was later identified as an illegal sawed-off shotgun. Within seconds, the subject was handcuffed and briefly patted down for more weapons.

Meanwhile, Officer Hitchens approached the SUV and saw that it was indeed occupied by another male subject. Hitchens ordered the subject to exit the vehicle, and he too was handcuffed and placed under arrest. Subsequent investigation revealed that the subject in the motorcycle helmet and trench coat had indeed robbed the night attendant at the 7-11. It was also verified that the subject in the SUV was related to the robber, and that he was there as a getaway driver. It was a good job by all involved. Two armed robbers were in custody, and no one got hurt. Robbery detectives later interrogated the two subjects and were able to clear a number of robberies that they had committed over the past few weeks in the district.

Hours later, after completing all the required paperwork, the subjects were transported to jail. Officer Williams made sure to check the backseat of her cruiser to ensure that the subjects had not dropped any weapons or contraband while they were being transported to the jail. This was a routine practice that all officers did after having prisoners riding in the caged backseat of their police cars. Both subjects had been searched carefully prior to be being placed in the backseat cage, but it was a good idea to look under the removable backseat, just in case. Williams looked, but found nothing. It was now almost the end of the shift, and her sergeant wanted to meet her to sign all her reports. Before she met her sergeant on the road, she decided to fill up the tank of her police car at the shop. Williams wanted to make sure that her vehicle was fueled up and ready to go for Saturday night's shift.

Officer Williams had had a good night of patrol. She never did make it to the loud music call that she and Unit 3111 had been dispatched to. But that's OK. Someone else eventually handled the call. Williams' shift ended at 7 AM, and by 7:30 AM, she was already home. As she always does, Williams backed her cruiser up on her driveway ... so that it would be ready to go the next night of work.

Annette came in the front door and was met by her firefighter husband. "Hi sweetie ... how was your night?"

Annette responded, "Pretty good ... got a couple of bad guys robbing a 7-11. Other than that ... another typical Friday night. How about you? Sleep good?"

"Yep ... like a baby." Fred looked over at Annette, and he could tell that she had had a long night. "Uh ... listen honey ... I'll take Bobby to school today. You stay home and get some sleep."

"Aw ... thank you honey ... I appreciate that. I'm really tired today." Annette went to her room and took her sidearm out of the holster and removed the five-inch revolver from her ankle holster. She placed both weapons into the small safe in the closet and locked it shut. She then removed her ballistic vest and hung it up to air out. She would go to bed and fall sleep soon thereafter. Later that afternoon she would pick up her five-year-old son from school, and then start cooking dinner for the family. After that, she would get ready for another night's work that was yet to come before she could rest on her days off, Sunday and Monday.

From this vignette, how many risk mitigation actions did you note? The most obvious ones are when Annette took her guns out of her gun locker, and when she donned her bullet proof vest. The story focuses and chronicles a day in the life of Officer Williams, we tend to focus on the many things that she did to mitigate risk, but there was more to it than just what she did. Consider the risk mitigation actions that the bad guys used prior to committing the armed robbery. One bad guy wore a motorcycle helmet, ostensibly to disguise his identity. That was a risk mitigation strategy. So too was the prepositioning of the getaway vehicle with a driver nearby. What about the dispatcher and the other officers in the vignette? Did they take any actions to mitigate risk? What actions did Annette's husband take to minimize risk? Could the action of taking two different bedtime storybooks to read to his son be considered a risk mitigation strategy? Could this action be an example of contingency planning in case little Bobby did not want to hear the first story?

You can see where this is going. Almost everything that we do on a daily basis has to do with some sort of risk mitigation. Most of the risks are so innocuous that we do not even think about them as being risks. Human beings, and organizations of human beings, as well as other organisms (animals, and arguably plants too), are constantly making risk analyses, and cost–benefit analyses on a minute-by-minute basis. That is how we have adapted and survived as a species. Sometimes we take the right action to mitigate risk, and sometimes we do not. In chronicle of a day in the life of Officer Williams, we note that she made all the right decisions and she survived the night. The risk mitigation strategies used by the two robbers did not work for them this time. This time they lost.

We begin this chapter with a simple story because risk analysis and risk mitigation can be a very complex subject. We want to put it in simple terms that we can all understand and relate to. As we progress through this chapter, we will see how complicated risk analysis can be, but through it all, we ask that you come back to this story to keep the fundamental basis for risk mitigation in perspective.

Risk analysis and mitigation will be at the core of what we do as incident commanders at the operational level (Chapter 3), the tactical level (Chapter 4), and the strategic level (Chapter 5). In Chapter 6 we will look at different types of training, and how the risk factor increases as learning becomes more realistic. For training, the general rule of thumb is that the more realistic and hands on the training is, the longer the knowledge will be retained by the learner. But the trade-off to realistic training is that it increases the likelihood of unintended and adverse outcomes.

Risk also plays a key role in the innovation process. We will examine how risk factors affect innovation in Chapter 7. Finally, as we put all the pieces together by planning for a large-scale special event in Chapter 8, we will again revisit risk analysis and risk mitigation.

How Do We Determine Risk?

Risk mitigation is something that we do to reduce the likelihood of something adverse happening. It is also what we do to minimize its effects if it does happen. Before we take actions to mitigate risk, we need to understand how we assess the factors that determine the risk of something happening. The act of weighing the factors that determine risk is simply called *risk analysis*. The second part of risk mitigation involves a *cost–benefit analysis*. We will deconstruct these two types of analyses in much greater depth later in this chapter, but for now review the risk assessment flowchart provided by FEMA in Figure 2.1.

As was evident in the Officer Williams' story, most of us analyze risk and cost–benefit on an intuitive level, and sometimes even in an unconscious level. In this book, we will learn how to do risk and cost–benefit analyses on a conscious level, taking into account the variables that make up risk. We will deconstruct the factors from the FEMA model to examine each one at a time, and then at the end of the chapter, put them all together for a working model that we can use for managing critical incidents and events, as well as in our daily routines. By the end of this chapter, you should be familiar with methodologies to do qualitative analyses using words to make sense of things, and quantitative analyses using numbers to make sense of things.

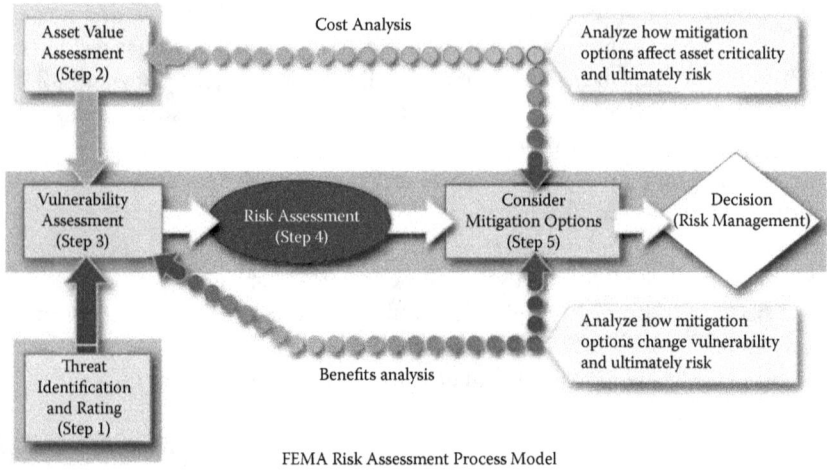

FEMA Risk Assessment Process Model

Figure 2.1 FEMA Risk Analysis Flowchart

EXERCISE 2.1

Before we get into risk analysis at any great depth, we ask that you consider the six scenarios illustrated and described in Figure 2.2, and rank them in the order that you consider them to be from the highest risk to the lowest risk. There is no right or wrong answer to this preliminary risk analysis, and we purposely provided you with very little background information on each of the illustrated scenarios. Once you complete the rank order of these six incidents, we will consider the factors that you used to determine risk.

The impact of a meteor the size of a mountain on Earth would be a devastating incident that could conceivably lead to the extinction of mankind and many other species of animals and plants. Indeed, there is solid empirical evidence to suggest that an underwater crater off Mexico's Yucatán Peninsula was caused by a meteor strike about 65 million years ago, and is believed to have caused the Cretaceous extinction event which led to the mass extinction of dinosaurs.[1]

As devastating as a meteor strike of this magnitude would be, the chances of it happening are very slim. According to the National Aeronautics and Space Administration (NASA), "the impact by an asteroid larger than 1–2 kilometers could degrade the global climate, leading to widespread crop failure and loss of life. Such global environmental catastrophes, which place the entire population of the Earth at risk, are estimated to take place several times per million years on average."[2]

If you chose the meteor scenario as the top ranked risk incident among the six hypothetical scenarios, that means that you think that the consequences of such an incident are so devastating that it should be ranked as the top risk, even though the chances of such an incident occurring in our lifetime is extremely unlikely. In doing so, you are giving the consequence factor greater weight than the likelihood factor.

Figure 2.2 Six Risk Scenarios: (a) Mountain-Sized Meteor Strikes the Earth (From the National Science Foundation http://www.nsf.gov/news/news_summ.jsp?cntn_id=114648.) (b) Radiation Leak Detected at a Nuclear Power Plant (From Flickr—https://www.flickr.com/photos/69383258@N08/6517605543/.) (c) Active Shooter at a High School (Courtesy of the Miami-Dade Police Department. Photographer Unknown.) (d) Car Crashes with Fully Loaded School Bus (From the Missouri State Highway Patrol—http://www.mshp. dps.mo.gov/MSHPWeb/PatrolDivisions/FOB/majorCrashInvestigationUnit/majorCrashInvestigationUnit. html.) (e) Category 5 Hurricane off the Eastern U.S. Coast (From NASA—http://pmm.nasa.gov/node/225.) (f) Passenger Train Derailment in a City (Purchased from Adobe Stock File No.: 89998362 Author: Cylonphoto.)

By contrast, school bus accidents occur relatively frequently. According to the U.S. Department of Transportation, "Since 2003, there have been 1353 people killed in school-transportation-related crashes—an average of 135 fatalities per year."[3] Not quite the mass extinction caused by a large meteor strike, but a concern nonetheless. Are school bus crashes a higher risk than meteor strikes? If you chose school bus crashes as your highest ranked risk situation, it reveals that you place more emphasis on the likelihood that an incident will occur.

Whether you picked the meteor strike scenario, or the school bus crash scenario, or any of the remaining four as your highest risk situation, it should be clear to you now that risk cannot be determined by the likelihood factor alone, or by the consequence factor alone. Asking you to rank order the risk of these six hypothetical scenarios was a bit of a trick question, and was purposely done to show that in order to determine risk, we need to consider both the likelihood (i.e., "probability") and the consequence factors. Figure 2.3 depicts a simple formula to determine risk.

$$\text{Probability} \times \text{Consequence} = \text{RISK}$$

Figure 2.3 Basic Risk Formula

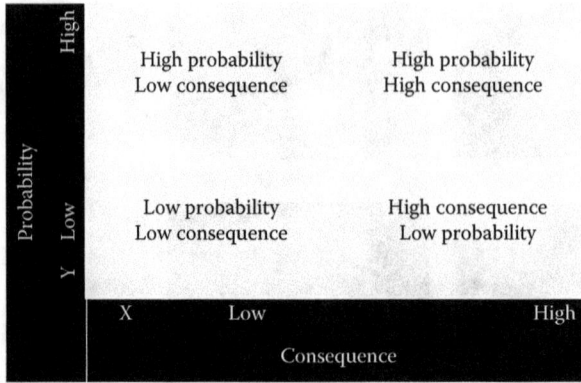

Figure 2.4 Risk Matrix

From Figure 2.3, we see that overall risk is a function of the probability factor and the consequence factor. More simply stated, the left side of the equation (probability) has to do with things that happen *before* the incident. The right side of the equation (consequence) has to do with things that happen *after* the incident. Another way to remember the formula is to think of it as the left side of the equation (probability) being the *cause,* and the right side (consequence) being the *effect.*

Figure 2.4 plots the probability factor on a Y-axis and the consequence factor on the X-axis to show four basic quadrants: high probability–low consequence; low probability–high consequence; low probability–low consequence; and high probability–high consequence. Based on this chart, where would you place the six hypothetical scenarios discussed in Exercise 2.1?

Clearly, the extremely unlikely meteor scenario would be classified as a low probability–high consequence risk because of the devastating effects that it would have. On the opposite quadrant, the school bus scenario would probably be classified as a high probability–low consequence risk. Of course, if it was your own child, or someone you knew personally, you probably would not agree with this classification. What that shows is that at its core, risk analysis is, and always will be, a subjective endeavor. The value that we place on people and things will differ from person to person, and will likely be dictated by our personal values and beliefs.

How Do We Determine the Consequence Factor?

At the root of determining the consequence factor in the risk analysis formula is the attribution of value to the asset being analyzed. Everything has value, and it is the loss of that value that is used to measure the consequence factor. For example, if you are involved in a car crash, and the insurance company determines that your vehicle has been "totaled," they will send you a check for the cost to replace the vehicle (minus a deductible payment on your part). The determination made by the insurance company was based on a cost–benefit analysis that it would cost more to fix the vehicle than to replace it. In order to do that cost–benefit comparison, the insurance company needed to determine two factors: the cost of fixing the car, and the cost of purchasing a new one. Both of these costs can be estimated by taking samples of prices charged by various local repair shops and car dealerships. This example is one of the most common that most of us have dealt with in our day-to-day routines.

It becomes a little more complicated when dealing with insurance companies to recover the losses sustained after a major catastrophe such as a hurricane. Some insurance policies cover the reconstruction of the house or building structure. The better policies also cover the full replacement value of all the contents therein. Regardless of whether it is a simple car accident or a major loss of property as a result of a hurricane, the concept underlying insurance policies is the same. We purchase insurance in order to mitigate the effects (i.e., consequences) of the loss of value to our property. We pay money to a collective pool, and if and when we sustain damage, then part of the money is returned to us to replace and rebuild our losses. Obviously, that pool of money needs to be large enough to be able to pay the victims of catastrophes, both minor and major. To do this, insurance companies calculate and modify as necessary the premiums that they charge to their customers, and most of them take the extra step to obtain "reinsurance" to protect themselves from risk. We won't get bogged down in the intricacies of the insurance trade, but it is important to understand how the industry works because insurance is all about risk mitigation.

If everything has value, how do we go about determining what that value is? In the case of a car, or a house, or the furniture within the house, it is relatively easy to do. For cars, we can walk around the dealership floor and look at the MSRP (manufacturer's suggested retail price) affixed to the vehicle's windshield. If we do our homework ahead of time, we can search online to find out the even lower factory invoice price, and also compare what others have paid for the same type of vehicle in different locations. Either way, whether it is the MSRP or the factory invoice price, it is safe to say that the pricing of the vehicle is ultimately determined by the "invisible hand" of the market. The price of the vehicle is determined by how much the customers are willing to pay for it. Yes, there are supply side factors such as the cost of the parts and labor that affect pricing, but over the long term, it is the demand side of the equation that ultimately sets the price of things.

The price of the car is helpful for determining the vehicle's value, but in itself is not entirely indicative of what the car is worth. That is because cars have moving parts that sustain "wear and tear" and therefore the value of a new car depreciates almost immediately after the purchase. Most things depreciate in value over time. However, some things increase in value over time. For example, over the long run, property values tend to appreciate in value. Likewise, stocks and certain commodities such as gold and silver have historically increased in value over time.

One asset that depreciates in value over time is the life of a human being. For those of you who think that life is priceless, and cannot be quantified or measured, we would ask you to consider the way that life insurance policies and some retirement plans are structured. Actuaries are professionals that gather normative data and use the data to project future trends in an effort to manage risk. Actuaries work for insurance companies, governments, and companies where managing risk is crucial for their survival. Actuaries use a variety of methodologies to determine the value of a person's life. The value of peoples' lives varies considerably depending on a number of factors. According to a *New York Times* article,[4] actuaries working for several government agencies have estimated the average value of a person's life to range from $6 million (U.S. Department of Transportation), to $7.9 million (U.S. Food and Drug Administration), to $9.1 million (U.S. Environmental Protection Agency). These estimates and projections may seem coldhearted, but they play a key role in determining how Congress passes laws and how government policies and procedures are carried out. In the realm of risk management, people are considered assets, no different than machines, buildings, and commodities.

Figure 2.5 shows how the consequence side of the risk formula breaks down into two determinant factors: *intrinsic value* and *symbolic value*. For the most part, the intrinsic value of an asset is easier to quantify and agree upon. For example, the loss of the two World Trade Center (WTC) towers was estimated at between $3 billion and $4.5 billion of intrinsic value.[5] The intrinsic value of an item, or an asset, can be best calculated by how much it originally cost to construct it, or how much it would cost to replace it. The estimate of the original construction costs looks at the past, whereas the estimate of replacement projects into the future. Either method provides a fairly accurate measure of an asset's intrinsic value that most people can agree on.

Most would agree that the terrorists on September 11 chose the WTC towers as much for their symbolic value as for their intrinsic value. Those towers represented the heart of America's financial power. The same could be said for the Pentagon, which by the way had an estimated intrinsic value of $1 billion.[6] The Pentagon symbolizes America's military power. As enormous as the consequences associated with the loss of the intrinsic value to both the Pentagon and

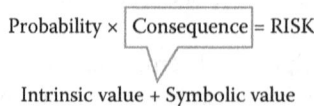

Probability × Consequence = RISK

Intrinsic value + Symbolic value

Figure 2.5 Elements of the Consequence Factor

Critical Infrastructure Asset	Symbolic Value	Intrinsic Value	Level of Consequence
Naval Air Station Jacksonville	3	3	6
Jacksonville Veterans Memorial Arena	2	2	4
Alltel Stadium (Jacksonville Municipal Stadium)	3	3	6
Jacksonville Port Authority (JaxPort)	2	3	5
Jacksonville International Airport	2	3	5
Water Treatment Facility	1	2	3
CSX Corporation Headquarters (Railroad)	2	2	4

Symbolic and Intrinsic Value Scoring Key	Consequence Scoring Key
1 point: Low value	2 points: Low consequence
2 points: Moderate value	3–4 points: Moderate consequence
3 points: High value	5–6 points: High consequence

Figure 2.6 Example Formulation of Symbolic and Intrinsic Values to Determine Level of Consequence

the WTC towers were, the symbolic value is incalculable in terms of dollars. That is not to say that symbolic value cannot be quantified. It can, but not in dollars. Symbolic value is best quantified and measured by assigning numerical values to the assets. Obviously, there is a great deal of subjectivity involved in the attribution of numerical values to an asset in order to signify its symbolic value. What is symbolically important to one person may not be important to another. There are several examples of consequence analyses later in this chapter that take into consideration the intrinsic, as well as the symbolic, values of the assets being assessed. Figure 2.6 provides an example of a basic consequence assessment using a simple three-point scale to assess the intrinsic and symbolic values of certain critical infrastructure assets.

The example in Figure 2.6 uses a basic 3-point scale that corresponds with low, moderate, and high intrinsic and symbolic values. FEMA uses a 10-point scale that gives a wider range of variability in which "10 is considered very high; 8–9 is high; 7 is medium high; 5–6 is medium; 4 is medium low; 2–3 is low; and 1 is very low."[7] Regardless of whether the scale uses a 3-point range, or 5, or 7, or 10, the underlying concept is the same. However, the FEMA model does not differentiate between intrinsic and symbolic values. That model lumps them together into a single score. We recommend that two values be assigned separately because the factors that are considered for determining intrinsic value tend to be money based, whereas the symbolic value is determined by considering more intangible factors. Because of the variation of opinions when it comes to the symbolic values, it is best if the attribution of the scores is done by a large group of raters, rather than a small one. The larger the group of

Critical Infrastructure Asset	Estimated Replacement Cost	Qualitative Value	Quantitative Value
Asset A	$300,000,000	High	3
Asset B	$80,000,000	Moderate	2
Asset C	$7,500,000	Low	1
Asset D	$14,000,000	Moderate	2

Estimated Replacement Cost		Qualitative Value
$0–$10 million	=	Low
<$10 million–$100 million	=	Moderate
<$100 million	=	High

Figure 2.7 Assigning Qualitative and Quantitative Intrinsic Values to Assets

evaluators, the more reliable the rating instrument will be. This mirrors the concept in polling and research where a large sample is likely to be more reliable than a small one.

Figure 2.7 provides an example of how the estimated replacement cost for assets can be used to determine their relative intrinsic values. The lower table provides a range of estimated costs that is used to attribute a qualitative value (low, moderate, and high) for the assets listed on the top table. The range of estimated costs that comprise the three categories can be "guesstimated" by the person or group doing the analysis, or you can hire a statistician to do it for you. The easiest way is to first find out the lowest and highest replacement costs for all the assets being analyzed, and then intuitively guesstimating the ranges for each of the three categories.

While using the estimated replacement cost is a good way to approach the attribution of intrinsic value, it obviously cannot be used for the attribution of the symbolic value. That is not to say that symbolic value should be based only on a "gut feeling" or a wild guess. There are other data available that can be helpful for determining the symbolic value of an asset. For example, we already know that the loss of the twin WTC towers was estimated at between $3 billion and $4.5 billion of intrinsic value, but that amount does not tell the entire story of the loss of value. According to the Institute for the Analysis of Global Security, 83,000 people lost their jobs as a result of the September 11 attack, resulting in a loss of $17 billion in wages.[8] This statistic and others provide a glimpse at the hidden costs associated with the collapse of the twin towers. It is these hidden or intangible costs, that when considered in their totality make up what we think of as being symbolic value.

The task of assigning the symbolic value to assets is admittedly a guess, but we should strive to make "educated guesses" as much as possible. We have at our disposal historical data and past experiences to guide us on this endeavor. The best and most reliable risk analyses are those in which the analysts used hard data to make the best guesses possible.

How Do We Determine the Probability Factor?

Now we turn our attention to the left side of the risk formula, probability (or as some refer to it, "likelihood"). Figure 2.8 illustrates how probability is a function of two factors: threat and vulnerability. You may recall that probability forms the Y-axis on the risk matrix in Figure 2.4.

Determining the likelihood that something will occur in the future is nothing more than a prediction based on the examination of the antecedent factors. In other words, it's a guess. It's a guess about what will happen in the future based on things that have occurred in the past. No one knows for sure what the future holds, but there are predictive models that are very good at predicting future incidents.

Hurricane forecasting is an example of how predictive models have improved over the years. The National Hurricane Center (NHC) uses several forecast models to predict the probabilities of a hurricane making landfall at a certain location. Typically, the NHC and local television weather forecasters use "composite" models that combine the predictions of some or all the models into one. These composite models tend to be more accurate than any single predictive model by themselves. From 1970 to 2015, there has been a steady and significant decrease in the error rate for predicting the track of hurricanes. The improvement in forecast accuracy is probably attributable to better data gathering instrumentation, improved radar and satellite imagery, better and faster computers, and an expanding archive of historical data that is used by the computer models for making forecasts. However, what has not improved significantly is the prediction of a hurricane's intensity.[9] Being able to accurately predict a disaster such as a hurricane gives us a huge advantage in the preparedness phase. However, because these predictions are not infallible, it puts pressure on critical incident managers and government officials to make the right call as to whether to evacuate an area or not. The errors associated with evacuation decisions will be discussed later in this chapter.

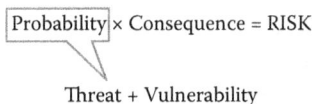

Probability × Consequence = RISK

Threat + Vulnerability

Figure 2.8 Elements That Comprise the Probability Factor

Referring back to the risk formula as illustrated in Figure 2.8, it is the National Hurricane Center's responsibility to identify the threat, and to try to predict when and where that threat will strike. In this case, hurricanes are the threat. The NHC shares the information and its predictions of the threat with state and local governments, and with the public via various media outlets. However, the NHC does not address the vulnerability factor in much depth. They briefly mention some generic warnings about storm surge vulnerability, but they do not access the vulnerability of specific coastal areas. Assessing the vulnerability to hurricanes is generally a state and local emergency management function. For example, the Florida Division of Emergency Management provides storm surge maps to the public via its FloridaDisaster.org website.[10] These storm surge maps are used by the local emergency management agencies to determine the vulnerability of coastal communities, and to formulate evacuation plans.

For someone doing a risk analysis for hurricane strikes in the State of Florida, they would need to rely on information about the *threat* from the National Hurricane Center and about the state's *vulnerability* from the Florida Division of Emergency Management. Only after combining these two factors can a reliable estimate of the probability of an adverse incident be predicted.

Threats, Hazards, and Vulnerability

The words "threat" and "hazard" are often used interchangeably, but they do not mean the same thing. There are subtle differences that need to be defined. Generally speaking, hazards are a type of threat that are passive and are usually preexisting. For example, a pothole on a roadway, a leaking 55 gallon drum, or a weapon left unattended in the presence of a child can all be considered as hazards. The term *hazard* is usually associated with natural or man-made non-intentional threats.

The term *threat* is broader and more inclusive than the word *hazard*. That is because all hazards can be considered threats, but not all threats are hazards. You may recall from Chapter 1, where we identified three types of incidents: natural, man-made intentional, and man-made accidental. In essence, that typology is based on the type of threat that caused the incident. The word *hazard* does not work well for describing man-made intentional threats such as terrorists, active shooters, bombers, mass migrations, and civil disturbances. For this reason, the authors use the broader word *threat* in most contexts, and will use the word *hazard* only to describe preexisting passive threats.

The word *vulnerability* pertains to the state of the asset that is being protected. Vulnerability must be assessed in the context of the threats that are posed to it. For example, when we consider the vulnerability of houses and buildings, and the occupants therein in the context of a hurricane threat, we look at whether those structures have hurricane shutters or shatter-resistant windows. We consider factors such as building codes and to what category level of hurricane winds the structure was built to sustain. We look at tidal surge and flood zone maps to consider whether to recommend an evacuation or a shelter in place. We consider whether there are sufficient food and water stockpiles to last several weeks after the hurricane has passed.

In the context of a man-made accidental incident such as a hazardous material spill from a derailed train, we consider such factors as wind direction and the distance of occupied structures to identify the vulnerability of the affected area. Plume analysis software such as ALOHA is available to critical incident managers who respond to such chemical spill incidents. ALOHA is one tool of a broader system of software applications developed by the U.S. Environmental Protection Agency and the National Oceanic and Atmospheric Administration to assist critical incident managers determine the vulnerable areas that need to be evacuated as a result of the hazardous material spill.[11]

In the context of a man-made intentional threat such as a cyberattack, we assess an organization's security by looking at both the external threats (such as hackers and computer malware) and the internal vulnerabilities and defenses (such as firewalls, antivirus software, and log-in protocols). Regardless of whether the threat is natural, man-made accidental, or man-made intentional, the prediction of probability is based on the interplay between the threat and the vulnerability of a structure or a function. Figure 2.9 provides an example of a *threat assessment* of multiple critical infrastructure assets rated on a simple three-point scale. This particular assessment is focused on man-made intentional threats, namely a terrorist attack. However, with slight modification, it can be adapted for natural threats or man-made accidental threats. For example, instead of: "Generalized, nonspecific information about a threat associated with an attack to the specific

Critical Infrastructure Asset	Threat Score
Interstate I-275 Bridge over Tampa Bay (Howard Frankland Bridge)	1
U.S. Central Command Headquarters	1
Holocaust Museum	3
Raymond James Stadium	2
Port of Tampa	1
Tampa International Airport	2

Threat Scoring Key	
No known threats associated with the specific critical infrastructure asset.	1 point
Generalized, nonspecific information about a threat associated with an attack to the specific critical infrastructure asset. Takes into account the intent and capabilities of terrorist groups that pose the threat.	2 points
Specific information about an imminent threat associated with an attack to the specific critical infrastructure asset. Takes into account the intent and capabilities of terrorist groups that pose the threat.	3 points

Figure 2.9 Threat Assessment for Multiple Critical Infrastructure Assets

Critical Infrastructure Asset	Vulnerability Score
Interstate I-275 Bridge over Tampa Bay (Howard Frankland Bridge)	3
U.S. Central Command Headquarters	1
Holocaust Museum	3
Raymond James Stadium	2
Port of Tampa	2
Tampa International Airport	2
Key: Low vulnerability = 1 Moderate vulnerability = 2 High vulnerability = 3	

Figure 2.10 Vulnerability Assessment for Multiple Critical Infrastructure Assets

critical infrastructure asset," the words "hurricane watch" (a possible hurricane strike within 48 hours). Likewise, the category: "Specific information about an imminent threat associated with an attack to the specific critical infrastructure asset," could be changed to "hurricane warning" (a possible hurricane strike within 36 hours).[12] This shows how this and other similar threat assessments can be adapted for any type of threat.

Figure 2.10 is an example of a *vulnerability assessment* of multiple critical infrastructure assets. As with the threat assessment in Figure 2.9, this one can also be adapted to any type of threat. Some of the factors that are taken into consideration when conducting vulnerability assessments are the following: accessibility to the site via land, sea, or air; visibility and recognizability of the site; physical or natural barriers protecting the site; the level of security; buffer zone protection; credentialing procedures; the presence of on-site hazards; and more.

These are some, but not all, of the factors that can be used to assess the vulnerability of a critical incident asset, or a functional asset.

Figure 2.11 provides a composite view of the probability side of the risk equation (threat + vulnerability), with the consequence side for an overall risk score. Note that this model uses a three-point scale, and the threat and vulnerability are added, instead of multiplied. Figure 2.12 shows the FEMA version of a risk calculation, but in this case, a 10-point scale is used, and instead of adding the threat and vulnerability scores, this model multiplies them. Either way is acceptable, with the first model putting more significance on the consequence factor and the FEMA model putting more weight on the probability side of the equation.

Passive Vulnerability Assessments versus Active Red Team Assessments

A passive vulnerability assessment is one where the assessors observe the existing structures, functions, and daily activities of a critical infrastructure asset.

Asset	Vulnerability +	Threat ×	Consequence =	Risk
Holocaust Museum	High (3)	High (3)	Moderate (2)	12
Shopping Mall	High (3)	Moderate (2)	Moderate (2)	10
U.S. CENTCOM	Low (1)	High (3)	High (3)	12
Super Bowl	Moderate (2)	High (3)	High (3)	15

Figure 2.11 Calculating an Overall Risk Score

Function	Cyberattack	Armed Attack (single gunman)	Vehicle Bomb	CBR Attack
Site	48	80	108	72
Asset value	4	4	4	4
Threat rating	4	4	3	2
Vulnerability rating	3	5	9	9
Structural Systems	24	32	240	16
Asset value	8	8	8	8
Threat rating	3	4	3	2
Vulnerability rating	2	4	8	9

FEMA

Extracted from Table 1–21: Site Infrastructure Systems Pre-Assessment Screening Matrix, pages 1–40

Building Design for Homeland Security   Unit V–9

Figure 2.12 FEMA Critical Infrastructure Risk Table

For example, prior to a large-scale special event such as a presidential debate, or a Super Bowl, teams of experts tour the facilities where the event is to be held to look for potential vulnerabilities. Typically in such cases, the experts on these interagency "mixed teams" include Explosive Ordnance Disposal (EOD) technicians; hazardous material (Hazmat) technicians; Special Weapons and Tactics (SWAT) personnel; dignitary protection personnel; and Department of Energy

RAP teams (Radiological Assistance Program). Other subject-matter experts may be plugged into these interagency mixed teams as needed. These experts look for on-site hazards or other vulnerabilities as they perceive them from their unique perspectives. Some use discipline-specific worksheets or checklists to ensure that they cover all the foreseeable vulnerabilities. Others take a blank sheet of paper and write notes of any potential vulnerability that they observe. Collectively, or individually, the assessors submit their findings to the appropriate intelligence agency that puts it all together and provides a report to the incident commander and all persons who need to know about the potential vulnerabilities of the site. Since the revealing of vulnerabilities to the general public could lead to the information getting into the wrong hands, the release of the information is tightly guarded. At times, policy makers decide that the benefits of releasing the information to the general public may outweigh the risks, but that is usually not the case. Because it usually takes time to correct any problems that the assessor may observe, these passive vulnerability assessments are usually done about a year prior to the scheduled event. That allows sufficient time to make any necessary modifications to the site.

Passive vulnerability assessments do not have to be event based. Many critical infrastructure assets are assessed on a routine basis or when some policy makers get nervous about a similar occurring incident from a different jurisdiction. For example, many government buildings, water and electrical utilities, police stations, schools, airports, seaport facilities, and fuel depots were assessed for vulnerability soon after the September 11 attacks or some other major natural or man-made accidental disaster.

An alternative to passive vulnerability assessments is the use of "red teams" that are used to reveal vulnerabilities that may not be readily apparent from a passive assessment. Red teams are comprised of individuals who take on a simulated adversarial role to infiltrate otherwise well-defended assets. Red teams may be comprised of "undercover" personnel who use subterfuge to gain entry or access to a facility. Or they may play the role of an intruder that attempts to breach the perimeter of a site. Or in the case of cyber security, a red team may be "good guy" computer hackers playing the role of "bad guy" hackers. Red team tests usually involve real people playing the role of bad guys, or adversaries. But sometimes, red team probes can be conducted through computer-generated simulations. We will discuss computer scenario testing and training in more depth in Chapter 6.

The advantage of using active red team probes over the passive vulnerability assessments is that they tend to reveal vulnerabilities that may not be apparent with the latter approach. One reason may be that red team personnel are usually trained ahead of time to "think like a bad guy" and to look for vulnerabilities that the typical "good guy" on a vulnerability assessment team may not pick up on. A second reason is that nobody really knows how people and systems will react until they are actually faced with a challenge. Imagining reality is a good approach, but simulating reality is even better. Red teams will reveal vulnerabilities that would not be revealed otherwise.

VIGNETTE 2.2

For weeks, and even months after the September 11 terrorist attacks, everyone seemed on edge. This was a busy time for police and fire-rescue first responders in general, but it was especially so for bomb squads throughout the entire country. In Miami, Florida, the main areas of concern where most of the calls for service emanated were from Miami International Airport and the Port of Miami.

WSVN, Channel 7, had a reputation for doing investigative stories that would at times embarrass officials by revealing some poor service, incompetence, or corruption in governmental agencies. One such story came about when an investigative reporter and his camera crew breached the security checkpoints at the Port of Miami and were able to videotape the entire escapade. That news exposé was aired for several nights in a row and proved to be quite an embarrassment to the Port of Miami security and county officials. It showed how easy it was for a would-be terrorist to enter and exit the seaport without being challenged by security personnel. If a Channel 7 reporter could do it, why couldn't an al Qaida terrorist do it as well?

Several days after the *Channel 7 News* story had aired, my captain called me into his office. The captain told me that our Division Chief had passed down an order for him to assemble a "red team" to test the security of the Port of Miami in view of the vulnerabilities that the Channel 7 story had revealed. The captain told me that I would lead an undercover team that was comprised of an SRT (Special Response Team) sergeant and four SRT officers to attempt to infiltrate the Port of Miami. The chief wanted us to videotape the whole thing and then report the results to him.

The next day the six of us showed up to work in plainclothes. We all looked like a raggedy bunch … wearing t-shirts, or long-sleeved denim shirts and work cargo pants. Some of the officers brought utility tool belts, hardhats, and lunchboxes to make it look like they were maintenance men or dockworkers. The sergeant and four officers were selected because of their dependability and maturity level. These five had been in SRT for a long time, and several of them were regularly assigned as the unit's counter snipers … telling me that these were the best of the best when it came to self-control and keeping a level head during stressful situations. These were exactly the people I would have chosen if I had been told to choose them myself. I think one of the reasons I was picked to lead this team was because I had previously worked 2 years as the sergeant of a cargo theft investigation squad, and I was familiar with the area.

That morning we drove in three rental vehicles that we had acquired for the day. We headed out to the Port, but we didn't really have a plan of action. Our approach was to stay close together in case something unexpected should happen, and we could each support the others. Our mission was to breach the security at the Port and infiltrate onto the island as far as we could. If we were challenged at any time, we were to simply give up and go away. As it turned out, that never happened. Not once did anyone challenge us.

Our three cars arrived at the first security checkpoint at around 10 in the morning. I was the passenger in the third car, with the sergeant as the driver. Ahead of us were the two other undercover vehicles with two SRT officers in each car. I don't know exactly what the officer in the lead car said to the security guard at the gate, but after half a minute of talking with him, the guard waived him through and he then waived the second and third cars through without asking us for documentation or even an explanation. We obliged and got through the checkpoint without having to even open the window of the car to talk to anyone.

Once we passed the first security checkpoint, we had access to most of the cargo area to the south and east side of Dodge Island (where the Port is located). We turned right into a fenced-in area toward the south side on a road labeled Australia Way, and proceeded east along the seawall unloading area. There we saw these giant robotic cranes unloading cargo containers from ships docked alongside the seawall. Once the cranes lowered the containers onto the ground, some very large forklifts would pick them up and take them to a nearby fenced-in area and stack them on top of each other ... five or six containers high. We took plenty of pictures and video while we were there.

We then proceeded along the southern edge of the island, all the way to the easternmost point where the Port of Miami administrative offices were located. The sergeant and I parked and walked into the main office building. The other four officers waited outside in their two cars. Once inside, the sergeant and I split up and walked in the hallways for about 4 minutes before I was finally asked by one gentleman what I was doing. I thought I was finally caught, but instead of panicking, I simply asked him, "Sir, could you tell me where the restroom is?"

The man pointed in the direction of another hallway and said, "It's right there ... second door to the left."

I responded, "Thank you sir," and then walked into the restroom unescorted and by myself. I never saw that man again, and that would be the only time that day that anyone would ask us what we were doing. The sergeant and I returned to our car in the parking lot, and then we proceeded to tour the Dodge Island for the next 2 hours. We made sure to take lots of photos and videos for the chief.

After leaving the administrative office area, we proceeded westerly and entered a secured area called POMTOC, which I later learned stood for Port of Miami Terminal Operating Company. There, we loitered for a while, and no one asked us what we were doing. We then proceeded westbound along the northernmost roadway, where we encountered another security guard at a checkpoint inside the Port. Once more, all three of our cars were waived through without any of us having to provide an explanation for what we were doing inside the secured area, or where we were headed next. On the north side of the Port is where the cruise ship moorings are located. There, all six of us got out of our cars and walked around freely among dockworkers who were loading supplies into the cruise ships.

Soon thereafter, we decided that we had seen enough, and we returned to our offices at the Special Patrol Bureau (SPB). There, I briefed the captain about what we encountered. I then went into my office and typed up a brief report to the chief. I assumed that from there the chief would share the information with the major of the Police Operations Bureau (POB), which was in charge of policing the Port of Miami.

Several weeks later, I was called into the captain's office once again. The captain told me that the chief wanted me to assemble the red team once more to do a second intrusive vulnerability assessment of the Port. We were told that this time the Port authorities had increased their security by asking the Florida National Guard to augment their security personnel. After the embarrassing *Channel 7 News* story and our subsequent red team incursion, it appeared that the Port administration and POB had finally been prompted to take action.

The next morning, the same undercover red team headed out once more to the Port of Miami. This time, we expected to be stopped and denied entry right away. Along the way, we observed a lot heavier police presence. There was a two-man unit parked on the mainland entrance to the Port on Biscayne Boulevard. I'm not exactly sure what these officers were doing there. They were both sitting in their police car, which had its top red and blue lights activated as if doing a traffic stop, but there was no car there for them to stop. I think they were there just to show their presence. If they were there for the purpose of deterrence, their presence did not deter us. We continued east over the bridge and onto Dodge Island.

There, we saw more police officers standing outside their cars at several intersections. Alongside the officers were several uniformed National Guardsmen holding M-16 rifles. I couldn't get close enough to tell whether the rifles had their magazine clips inserted and whether the weapons were loaded or not. I recalled that for Hurricane Andrew in 1992, the National Guardsmen were issued M-16 rifles, but were not allowed to load their weapons while doing traffic checkpoint duties. I thought that this time their rules of engagement may be different, but I wouldn't be able to get close enough to find out.

We passed several intersections that were manned by police and National Guardsmen. No one made any attempt to stop our three car procession. We then arrived once more at the first security checkpoint, which is about halfway onto the Port. This is the same checkpoint where we were waived through the first time we attempted the incursion. Once more, the security guard waived all three of our cars through. This time, all I needed to do was stop momentarily and open my window and tell the security guard, "I'm with those two cars …" The guard then pushed a button to lift the security gate in front of us to let's through. Once inside that gate, we were able to go all over the same cargo areas that we had breached on our first attempt. After loitering there for about an hour, and taking numerous photographs and video, we decided to head out of the cargo area toward the cruise ship docks. To do so, we had to go through two more security checkpoints. The guards at neither one of the checkpoints questioned us, and they allowed us to proceed out of the secured area unmolested.

Once again, we dismounted from our rental vehicles and we walked all around the cruise ship area. The sergeant and I proceeded to the second floor of the office building where the Police Operations Bureau was stationed. There was no receptionist at the front, and we simply walked in completely unchallenged. Inside the hallways of the police station, we did not see any police officers. The place seemed to be abandoned. It was probably because most of the officers were assigned to traffic duty. The sergeant and I then found the major's office, and opened the unlocked door to go inside. The major was not there. I briefly thought of leaving her a note to tell her that we had been there to visit her, but I changed my mind, and we left without any trace of ever being there. I thought that doing that would have been perceived as being provocative, and that's the last thing that I wanted to do.

As we went down the stairs and were getting ready to get back into our car, an older black gentleman came up to talk to us. He was the janitor assigned to clean the offices, and he had a photo ID attached to his shirt pocket. The man very politely asked who we were, and what we were doing. This was the only person in the two days that our red team had gained access into the Port that had taken the time to ask who we were. At first I lied to him and told him that we were there to fix an electrical problem in the POB office. The janitor seemed skeptical about my story, and again insisted on knowing what we were doing there, and where our photo ID was. At that point, I decided to come clean and I admitted to the gentleman that we were undercover officers doing a red team incursion to test vulnerabilities at the Port. I showed him my real police identification, and I thanked and praised him for his due diligence.

I found it ironic that among all the police officers, security guards, and National Guardsmen that we encountered on our two visits to the Port, only one guy … probably the lowest paid guy, and one whose job it wasn't to challenge us … was the one who did.

After our cover was blown, I decided that it was time to head back to our Special Patrol Bureau office to brief the captain and to prepare my report to the chief. However, this time I made an impromptu decision to raise the on-duty POB lieutenant on the radio and ask to meet him. As a courtesy to him, I wanted to let him know what we had done so he would not be surprised when he heard about it later from his superiors. I thought that if I was in his place, I would appreciate the same being done for me. I also wanted to reassure him that this was not meant to embarrass anyone. I wanted to personally escort him around the Port to show him all the vulnerabilities that we had observed over the past two incursions. I sent the other four SRT officers back to the SPB office, and the sergeant and I stayed behind to meet with the POB lieutenant. I asked the lieutenant to hop in our car, and over the next hour, we toured the entire Port facility, stopping occasionally to talk with the officers on traffic posts to let them know what had occurred. I could tell that the lieutenant was a bit embarrassed at first, but he also seemed appreciative that we had taken the time to personally brief him on the matter, instead of him hearing about it later and getting his butt chewed out.

Soon thereafter, we headed back to our office to discuss what had happened with our captain. I told him that there were two main takeaways that I had learned from the experience. The first takeaway was that I was surprised to find out that it was easier for us to breach the security the second time around. The increased high-profile presence of more police officers and National Guardsmen was not an effective deterrent. I think their presence gave most people a false sense of security, which proved to be counterproductive in that even the officers themselves became too complacent. I think that everyone thought that it was everyone else's job to confront and challenge people trying to enter the Port. That false sense of security may have made people feel good, but it didn't really solve the problem.

The second takeaway from my red team experience was that the only person who challenged us was a nonpolice, or security individual. This tells me that *everyone* should be expected to do their due diligence when it comes to the security of our nation. To me, this was the most important lesson to have learned.

Eloy Nuñez

One example of using red teams to reveal vulnerabilities is with the Domestic Nuclear Detection Office (DNDO) within the Department of Homeland Security. The DNDO is tasked with implementing domestic nuclear detection in the United States, and for coordinating the response to radiological and nuclear threats. The DNDO uses red teams to "independently assesses the operational performance of planned and deployed capabilities, including technologies, procedures, and protocols."[13]

Another example of red team vulnerability assessment was revealed by *ABC News* on a nationwide broadcast of *Good Morning America* on June 1, 2015. According to the report, Department of Homeland Security (DHS) red teams posing as passengers were able to get past Transportation Security Administration (TSA) personnel at security checkpoints with weapons and simulated explosive devices. Out of 70 tests conducted by the DHS red teams, the TSA agents at airport security checkpoints failed to notice the weapons 67 times. That translates to a 95% failure rate, and revealed a major vulnerability in the passenger screening process.[14]

The next day, the headline in an *LA Times* article was, "Red Team agents use disguises, ingenuity to expose TSA vulnerabilities." According to the *LA Times* report, the problems were attributed to two factors: inattentive TSA screeners and poorly designed or malfunctioning equipment.[15]

Clearly, red teams reveal vulnerabilities that passive vulnerability assessments typically miss. However, the obvious trade-off to using red teams is that it is a risky proposition. It is risky to the red teams themselves because they are placed in dangerous positions whenever they try to breach security. No matter the precautions that are taken, risk cannot be eliminated altogether. The second and more important risk is the one that resulted from the *ABC News* report described above. It is clear that the findings of the DHS Red Team were not supposed to be released to the general public, yet somehow it was leaked to ABC, and reported by many other networks that same day and the next. Not only did the general public become aware of the 95% failure rate, it is fairly certain that terrorists around the world became aware of the failure rate as well. The lesson learned from the TSA incident is that the release of information regarding vulnerabilities needs to be tightly controlled in order to avoid the mass release to the public.

Risk Analysis: Threat + Vulnerability × Consequence

Risk analyses can be simple, or they can be complicated. There are a number of risk analysis tools available on the market for a price, or at no cost from the federal government, or some state governments. As critical incident managers, you may be expected at some point to conduct risk analyses, or any of its three components: threat, vulnerability, or consequence assessments as part of your regular duties. These assessments are often formal in nature, and quantitative based. Threat and vulnerability assessments of a formal nature are usually conducted at the tactical and operational levels of command, but the formal consequence assessment component of the risk analyses tends to be done at the strategic level. That is because the attribution of values needed for consequence assessments are usually the domain of policy makers at the highest level of organizations or governments.

On a daily basis, first responders and critical incident managers do all three components of risk analyses all the time. Firefighters conduct threat and vulnerability assessments every time they inspect a building for hazards. They look for flammable material and potential ignition sources. They look to make sure that the building is equipped with fire extinguishers and sprinkler systems. They inquire with the building managers regarding their evacuation plans, and make sure that all doors open properly and that no exits are blocked. Similarly, police officers often do site surveys of private residences and businesses to let the owners know their vulnerabilities to burglars.

Firefighters and police officers do "on the run" consequence assessments as well. These are not the formal consequence assessments that policy makers do at the strategic level. These are the decisions that first responders make every day at an intuitive level. We perceive and weigh the consequences of different courses of action, and then we make decisions instantaneously based on the trade-offs of the costs and the benefits. For example, the fire service uses the term "size-up" to describe a hasty on-scene assessment conducted by the first arriving units: "What's there? What does the situation need? and What have I got?"[16]

The typical "shoot–don't shoot" situations that many police officers face throughout their careers is an example of an informal and impromptu risk and cost–benefit analysis that is usually done in split seconds. As you read this, stop for a moment and consider a "shoot–don't shoot" situation that you have been involved in, or have heard about from someone else's experience. Think of how the threat was analyzed. Was a subject holding a gun, a knife, or some other weapon? Was the subject capable of using the weapon? Did the subject make a sudden move as if to use the weapon?

Think of the vulnerability assessment that was done in the same "shoot–don't shoot" scenario. Were you behind cover, or were you exposed? Were there any other officers or civilians in the line of fire? Now think of the consequence assessment component of your analysis. Is this a deadly force situation? Should a less-lethal weapon be used (such as a baton or a Taser)? Is it appropriate to escalate to the use of deadly force? If I shoot this individual, will I be indicted? If I don't shoot this subject, will he kill me? Embedded in this one or two second risk analysis are components of threat, vulnerability, consequence assessments, and cost–benefit trade-offs. These types of scenarios happen so quickly, and our reactions are very intuitive, so we hardly ever pause to reconstruct them after they occur. But the classic shoot–don't shoot situation is a good example of the type of risk management on the run that all first responders are faced with on a daily basis. Vignette 2.1 also provided a good example of this.

Mitigation Options

The next step after analyzing the risks posed by threats to vulnerable assets and functions is to consider ways to mitigate those risks. The FEMA model shown previously in Figure 2.1 provides a good visual representation of how the "consider mitigation options" step comes immediately after the risk analysis takes place.[17] Risk mitigation, like risk analysis, occurs in all three phases of an incident: before, during, and after. We typically think of risk mitigation as something that we do before, and of course after an incident occurs, but we rarely pay attention to the things we do to mitigate risk in the midst of responding to an incident. Most often, these are tactical "on the run" adjustments of our actions in reaction to any unanticipated new risks that may arise during our response to the incident. But even though not every possible threat and vulnerability can be envisioned ahead of time in response to an unanticipated critical incident, it does not mean that we cannot plan for the eventuality of things going wrong.

In fact, you can almost count on something going wrong. The ability to adjust "on the run" in reaction to unanticipated factors during a critical incident is arguably the most important characteristic of an effective critical incident manager. Risk mitigation actions that occur during the response phase will be discussed in more depth in Chapters 3 and 4, which deal with operational and tactical issues, respectively. In this chapter, we will focus on risk mitigation strategies that are generally taken before and after an incident or event occurs.

FEMA classifies its mitigation strategies into three broad categories: regulatory measures; repair and strengthening of existing structures; and protective and control measures. *Regulatory measures* have to do with the modification of laws, regulations, and building codes to address vulnerabilities that were probably exposed by a vulnerability assessment, or an actual catastrophic incident. For example, in 1992, Hurricane Andrew struck Miami-Dade County and caused over $26 billion in damage.[18] A post-disaster review conducted by a FEMA assessment team (1993) focused on wind-related damage, building structures, and poor workmanship. Those findings led to the strengthening of the Miami-Dade building codes in 1994, followed by similar code changes in Broward County, and later with variations adopted statewide in Florida.[19] Miami-Dade's building codes have been emulated by many coastal communities, and are considered to be among the best in the nation. Indeed, the Insurance Institute for Business and Home Safety (2015) rated the State of Florida codes second only to Virginia among 18 coastal hurricane-prone states.

An example of the *repair and strengthening of existing structures* classification of mitigation strategies is evident in how some federal, state, and local government buildings were outfitted with concrete barriers following the 1995 truck bombing of the Murrah Building in Oklahoma City. The concrete barriers and wider buffer zones help to mitigate the effects of an up-close explosive blast such as the one in Oklahoma City. An example of the *protective and control measures* classification is evident with the imposition of temporary flight restrictions (TFRs) around stadiums during Super Bowl games. These are all examples of risk mitigation actions that were taken as a result of the lessons learned from past disasters.

In regard to man-made intentional incidents such as terrorist attacks, FEMA identifies the following risk mitigation measures: deterrence, detection, denial, and devaluation. FEMA defines deterrence as "The process of making the target inaccessible or difficult to defeat with the weapon or tactic selected. It is usually accomplished at the site perimeter using highly visible electronic security systems, fencing, barriers, lighting, and security personnel and in the building by securing access with locks and electronic monitoring devices."[20]

Deterrence strategy is dependent on the adversary being convinced that the attack is not worth the cost. Thus, deterrence as a prevention or risk mitigation strategy only works in situations involving human-based threats. Obviously, tornadoes, hurricanes, and earthquakes cannot be deterred. Photo 2.1 shows two examples of deterrence strategy. In the animal kingdom, skunks, porcupines,

Neighborhood
Crime Watch

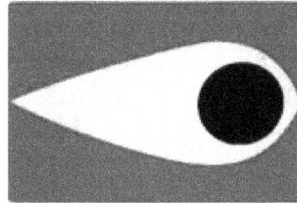

We immediately report
all suspicious activity
to our sheriffs department

Photo 2.1 Two Examples of Deterrence Strategy (Blowfish from Broderbund Clickart, p. 107, Image AAD50468. Neighborhood Crime Watch Sign: http://claycountymn.gov/227/Crime-Watch.)

blowfish, and poisonous caterpillars are just a few examples of deterrence strategy. All these animals rely on a deterrence strategy, either by spraying a noxious chemical agent, or exhibiting sharp quills, or expanding their size to look more menacing, or by showing bright colors to alert a possible predator that they may be poisonous if ingested. Likewise, the Neighborhood Crime Watch sign is supposed to alert would-be criminals that they are likelier to get caught in this particular neighborhood than in others that do not have such signs posted. However, many law enforcement officers will attest that the sign by itself has little if any deterrent effect, unless the neighborhood is actively patrolled by a Crime Watch group, or the police. That is because the adversary (in this case, burglars and robbers) do not take the warning seriously, and they do not perceive any increased risk to themselves. In contrast, a "Beware of Attack Dog" sign posted on a chain-link fence with actual dogs within the fenced-in area is an effective deterrent.

Devaluation strategy is similar to deterrence strategy in that both are dependent on the cost–benefit analysis done by the adversary. While deterrence seeks to psychologically discourage the adversary by making the consequence of their actions too costly, devaluation strategy seeks to devalue the perceived benefits of the actions. The rationale underlying deterrence is: "the cost is too high." The rationale underlying devaluation is: "the benefits are not valuable." Either way, the opponent is doing a cost–benefit analysis and hopefully deciding that the cost to attack the asset is not worth the effort. An example of devaluation strategy is the wealthy person who doesn't wear any jewelry, wears casual clothing, and drives a nondescript car in order to avoid bringing attention to herself. Another example of devaluation strategy is how some major Internet hubs that service metropolitan areas are located in unmarked and nondescript buildings, typically windowless, and gray in color. Set among other downtown buildings, these Internet hubs meld right into the urban topography and are difficult to locate unless one knows the exact address. Typically, there is no roadside parking anywhere around the buildings, and some will take the extra precaution of erecting concrete barriers to keep vehicles from crashing into it from the roadway. That is because even though the average resident of cities such as New York, Miami, Atlanta, Washington, DC, Los Angeles, and San Francisco have no clue of the existence or location of the Internet hubs in their cities, the information is not classified, and indeed is readily available to the general public on the Internet. Anyone who wants to find an Internet hub in their area can look it up online on the TeleGeography Internet Exchange Map website.[21] On that website, the person who wants to find these nondescript critical infrastructure assets can locate their exact address on Google Map, with access to ground-level photographs of the location.

While deterrence and devaluation strategies only work to mitigate man-made intentional threats, the other two, detection and denial, can be applied to natural and man-made accidental threats as well. FEMA defines *detection* as "The process of using intelligence sharing and security services response to monitor and identify the threat before it penetrates the site perimeter or building access points" and *denial* as "The process of minimizing or delaying the degree of site or building infrastructure damage or loss of life or protecting assets by designing or using infrastructure and equipment designed to withstand blast and chemical, biological, or radiological effects."[22] These of course, are stated in the context of counterterrorist risk mitigation, but the concepts can be applied to non-terrorist-related threats. An example of detection in the natural disaster context can be seen as satellite and radar imagery used by National Oceanic and Atmospheric Administration's (NOAA) National Hurricane Center to provide early warning of impending storms. An example of the denial strategy in the context of natural disasters is the construction of buildings that can withstand hurricane force winds, or in the context of man-made accidental disasters—the storing of spent nuclear fuel underwater in storage pools, or in dry casks.

It should be evident by now that the risk mitigation strategies discussed above can be applied under various contexts, and that most of them are emulated from strategies used in the plant and animal kingdoms. Throughout this book, we use examples from the natural world because the comparison helps us to understand the underlying reasons for the various mitigation strategies. As we will see later in Chapter 7, the innovation process is not so much about creating new ideas, but rather about reapplying old ideas in new contexts. Observing and copying animal and plant adaptive strategies provides a wealth of ideas that can be applied in the context of homeland security and critical incident management.

Cost–Benefit Analysis and Trade-Offs

The last step before implementation in FEMA's risk mitigation model involves the analysis of the costs and the benefits associated with any of the mitigation options that are being considered. The underlying assumption is that all actions have a cost associated with them. The costs may not be readily apparent, and may not be easy to quantify, but they are there nonetheless. Cost–benefit analysis is based on this simple premise: when the perceived benefits outweigh the estimated costs, then the decision should be to implement the mitigation action. Conversely, if the estimated costs outweigh the perceived benefits, then the decision should be to not implement the mitigation action. The concept is simple, but the estimates on both sides of the cost–benefit calculation are not. Because of the uncertainty associated with predicting future risk—especially as it pertains to man-made intentional threats—the benefit side of the cost–benefit calculation is very much a guessing game. The cost side of the calculation is also a guessing game to an extent because determining costs can sometimes be like shooting at a moving target. This is because of poor cost estimate practices, or because of the lag time that sometimes occurs between the cost estimates and the actual expenditure for the risk mitigation action. We often hear of cost overruns on government projects. These overruns happen, even when the overruns are calculated into the original cost formulas.

All cost–benefit analyses involve trade-off decisions by policy makers. Generally, the more benefit is desired, the higher the costs will be. The objective of cost–benefit analysis is to determine the *optimal* amount that policy makers are willing to pay for mitigating a perceived risk that they have no way of knowing for sure whether it will happen. Take for example the risk posed by a mountain-sized meteor strike that could lead to the total extinction of our species. The consequences are very high, but the likelihood of that occurring is very small. How much then should our government spend to monitor and detect the extraterrestrial threat posed by asteroids and comets? According to CNN Politics, the amount allocated by the federal government to monitor and detect the threats rose to as high as $20 million a year in 2012.[23] The PBS program NOVA estimates the cost for an asteroid defense system at around $2 billion to build and test from now to the year 2025.[24] Obviously, $2 billion is worth it if indeed the mitigation efforts saved mankind from extinction, but if a large asteroid does not strike the Earth anytime in the near future, such an expenditure would be considered to be reckless waste of money at a time when the funds could be better spent to defend against more likely threats. We chose to use the cost–benefit analysis for a meteor/asteroid mitigation system as an example because of the extreme polarities between its likelihood and consequence factors. However, most risk and cost–benefit decisions are not as clearly separated as this one. In the end—especially with man-made intentional threats—the analyses of risk and cost–benefit are based on the best guesses of intelligent people, taking into consideration the best available information at the time.

In regard to risk analysis and cost–benefit analysis, it is important to note that in the case of man-made intentional threats, our adversaries do the same to us. According to the 9/11 Commission Report, the terrorist organization al Qaida spent approximately $400,000–$500,000 to plan and execute the September 11 attacks.[25] To al Qaida's leadership, that expenditure was well worth the benefits that they derived from it. But as with most decisions, there would be unintended consequences. It is still too early to tell whether al Qaida's cost–benefit analysis achieved its desired outcomes. Only history will tell.

Catastrophic Errors versus Nuisance Errors

We now turn our attention to the examination of catastrophic and nuisance errors as it pertains to critical incident management. It may sound counterintuitive, but the efforts by critical incident managers to reduce risk will invariably lead to errors. This is because the actions taken to reduce catastrophic error are inversely related to the increase in nuisance errors. For example, when a critical incident manager orders the evacuation of a courthouse in response to an anonymous phone call about a bomb being planted inside the building, that incident commander is taking a course of action that minimizes the risk from a catastrophic incident occurring, but is increasing the chances of a nuisance error occurring. In making the decision, the incident commander does not know for sure whether there is a bomb inside the courthouse, and he needs to weigh the possible consequences of ordering an evacuation versus the consequences of not ordering an evacuation. There are four possible outcomes depending on his decision. Figure 2.13 illustrates these four outcomes.

If the incident commander orders an evacuation, and it turns out that there indeed was a bomb inside the courthouse, then he obviously made the correct decision. That outcome is illustrated by the top-right quadrant of Figure 2.13. If the incident commander decides not to order an evacuation, and it turns out that there was no bomb in the courthouse, then he is judged to have made the right decision. That outcome is illustrated on the bottom-left quadrant. If the incident commander does not order an evacuation, and the bomb explodes and kills and injures many people, then it could be said that he made a catastrophic error. That outcome is illustrated on the bottom-right quadrant. If the incident commander orders an evacuation, and it turns out that the bomb threat turned out to be a hoax, then it could be said that he made a nuisance error.

Evacuated	*Evacuated*
Nuisance Error	**Correct Decision**
(False Threat)	(True Threat)
Did Not Evacuate	*Did Not Evacuate*
Correct Decision	**Catastrophic Error**
(False Threat)	(True Threat)

Figure 2.13 Nuisance and Catastrophic Errors

The only way to know for sure whether the decision turns out right is after the consequence occurs, or does not occur. Because the consequences of a bomb exploding are so great, many incident commanders will decide to evacuate the building out of an overabundance of caution. In other words, the incident commander takes a course of action that is commonly referred to as "rather be safe than sorry." That approach is illustrated in Figure 2.14. In this figure, the lower-right quadrant of the catastrophic error is reduced, but the upper-left quadrant of the nuisance error increases.

The problem with the "rather safe than sorry" approach is that evacuations are very disruptive to the daily routines of a business or government entity. Courthouses, schools, and some businesses regularly receive anonymous phone threats that almost always turn out to be hoaxes. The hoax phone calls could be from a defendant who does not want to appear in court that day, or a child who did not study for an exam and hopes that by shutting down the entire school, he won't have to take the test. Evacuations are time consuming, and in the case of private businesses, they adversely affect the company's bottom-line profits. Along with the loss of productivity that ensues from evacuations, there are also increased chances for minor injuries such as sprained ankles. Thieves can also exploit the confusion during evacuations to steal peoples' belongings that are left behind. Evacuations of facilities from such hospitals are even more problematic because of the difficulty involved in moving non-ambulatory patients.

The fundamental decision to evacuate, or not evacuate—to shelter in place, or not shelter in place—will be discussed throughout this book as it applies to different contexts. This is perhaps the most fundamental decision that incident commanders are faced with at the onset of a critical incident. But for now, it is important to understand that errors will occur—both catastrophic and

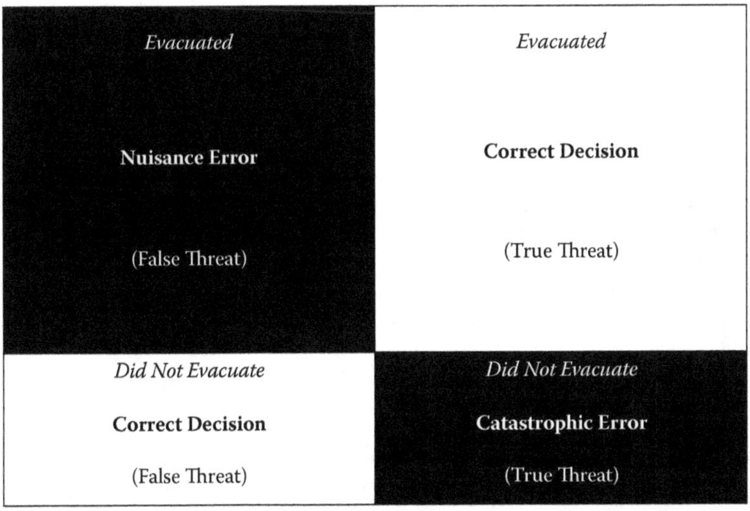

Evacuated **Nuisance Error** (False Threat)	*Evacuated* **Correct Decision** (True Threat)
Did Not Evacuate **Correct Decision** (False Threat)	*Did Not Evacuate* **Catastrophic Error** (True Threat)

Figure 2.14 Catastrophic Error Reduced, Nuisance Errors Increased

nuisance—even when the "correct" decision is made. Being an effective critical incident manager means becoming comfortable with making errors.

References

1. *National Geographic*, 2015. Mass extinctions: What causes animal die-offs? Online at http://science.nationalgeographic.com/science/prehistoric-world/mass-extinction/ (accessed August 30, 2015).
2. National Aeronautic and Space Administration, n.d. The probability of collisions with earth. Online at http://www2.jpl.nasa.gov/sl9/back2.html (accessed August 30, 2015).
3. U.S. Department of Transportation, 2014. Traffic safety facts 2003–2012 data. School-transportation-related crashes. Online at http://www-nrd.nhtsa.dot.gov/Pubs/811890.pdf (accessed August 30, 2015).
4. B. Appelbaum, 2011. As U.S. agencies put more value on a life, businesses fret. *New York Times*, February 16. Online at http://www.nytimes.com/2011/02/17/business/economy/17regulation.html?_r=0 (accessed August 30, 2015).
5. IAGS.org, 2003. How much did the September 11 terrorist attack cost America? Institute for the Analysis of Global Security. Online at http://www.iags.org/costof911.html (accessed August 15, 2015).
6. Ibid.
7. Federal Emergency Management Agency, 2005. FEMA 452—Risk assessment: A how-to guide to mitigate potential terrorist attacks against buildings. Online at http://www.fema.gov/medial-library/assets/documents/4608 (accessed August 30, 2015).
8. IAGS.org, 2003. [Short cite] How much did the September 11 terrorist attack cost America? Institute for the Analysis of Global Security. Online at http://www.iags.org/costof911.html.
9. National Hurricane Center, 2015. National Hurricane Center Forecast Verification. Official error trends, March 25. Online at http://www.nhc.noaa.gov/surge/ (accessed August 30, 2015).
10. FloridaDisaster.org. Online at http://www.floridadisaster.org/index.asp (accessed December 16, 2015).
11. Environmental Protection Agency, 2014. ALOHA software, December 11. Online at http://www2.epa.gov/cameo/aloha-software (accessed August 30, 2015).
12. National Hurricane Center, 2014. NHC glossary of terms, August 1. Online at http://www.nhc.noaa.gov/aboutgloss.shtml (accessed August 30, 2015).
13. Department of Homeland Security, 2015. About the domestic nuclear detection office, May 15. Online at http://www.dhs.gov/about-domestic-nuclear-detection-office (accessed August 30, 2015).
14. J. Fishel et al., 2015. EXCLUSIVE: Undercover DHS tests find security failures at U.S. airports. *ABC News*, June 1. Online at http://abcnews.go.com/ABCNews/exclusive-undercover-dhs-tests-find-widespread-security-failures/story?id=31434881 (accessed August 30, 2015).
15. B. Bennett, 2015. Red team agents use disguises, ingenuity to expose TSA vulnerabilities. *Los Angeles Times*, June 2. Online at http://www.latimes.com/nation/nationnow/la-na-tsa-screeners-20150602-story.html (accessed August 30, 2015).
16. B. Schmidt, 2006. What's in a size-up? *Fire Rescue 1*, January 4. Online at http://www.firerescue1.com/columnists/Billy-Schmidt/articles/14723-Whats-In-a-Size-Up/ (accessed December 16, 2015).
17. Federal Emergency Management Agency, 2005. FEMA 452—Risk assessment: A how-to guide to mitigate potential terrorist attacks against buildings. Online at http://www.fema.gov/medial-library/assets/documents/4608 (accessed August 30, 2015).

18. National Weather Service, 2012. Hurricane Andrew, August 17. Online at http://www.srh.noaa.gov/mfl/?n=andrew (accessed August 30, 2015).

19. C. Morgan, 2012. Impact of Hurricane Andrew: Better homes. *Miami Herald,* June 2. Online at http://www.miamiherald.com/news/special-reports/hurricane-andrew/article1940341.html (accessed August 30, 2015).

20. FEMA, January, 2005. [Short cite, p. 5-5].

21. Internet Exchange Map, 2014. Telegeograpy. Online at http://www.internetexchangemap.com/ (accessed August 30, 2015).

22. FEMA, January, 2005. [Short cite, p. 5-5].

23. T. Cohen, 2013. Money needed to prevent big asteroid strike despite low chance. *CNN Politics,* March 20. Online at http://www.cnn.com/2013/03/19/politics/congress-space-threats/ (accessed August 30, 2015).

24. Veronique Greenwood, 2013. Why can't we prevent an asteroid strike? *NOVA Next, PBS Online by WGBH,* March 26. Online at http://www.pbs.org/wgbh/nova/next/space/asteroid-detection-and-deflection/ (accessed August 30, 2015).

25. National Commission on Terrorist Attacks Upon the United States, 2004. *The 9/11 Commission Report.* Online at http://www.9-11commission.gov/ (accessed August 27, 2015).

3
Planning and Organizing at the Operational Level

This chapter is the first of three that examines critical incident management from the perspective of operational, tactical, and strategic command, respectively. We begin with operational command—the middle ring of the *three spheres of the critical incident management* model—because this sphere provides the best context to understand the basic principles of incident management in action. Figure 3.1 illustrates the position of the operational sphere for which this chapter is devoted.

Operational Command for Spontaneous Incidents

Operational command is at the core of all incident command situations. The operational element is the one that directly addresses the threat. The other major components of incident command (logistics, planning, and finance/administration) exist to support the core operations. In the vast majority of critical incidents, the other three sections are not activated because most incidents are resolved before these components are needed. The strength of the Incident Command System (ICS) is that it is component based, and only those elements that are needed are activated. It is safe to say that every spontaneous incident starts with some sort of operational command, even if it starts with only one first responder arriving at the scene of the incident. That first arriving responder, whether it is a police officer, firefighter, or paramedic, would in essence be the operations section "chief" and incident commander, all rolled into one. In the vast majority of incidents, the ICS does not expand beyond the first arriving responders, as the incident is resolved before a formal ICS is established.

Organizational charts for preplanned events look very different from those that emerge from spontaneous incidents. Preplanned events usually require a full-fledged ICS activation of all the major components because all those components are going to be needed. Figure 3.2 illustrates the organizational chart for a basic ICS in a preplanned event. In this diagram, the operations section has been highlighted so that we can compare it to the development of the operations section of a spontaneous and emerging critical incident.

The organizational chart for a preplanned event has all its components in place at the onset of the event. By contrast, the organizational chart for an unanticipated incident evolves as the incident evolves. Figure 3.3 illustrates how the ICS grows upward, downward, and sideways from the original first-responding units, which form the operations section. ICS is supposed to be a "top to bottom"

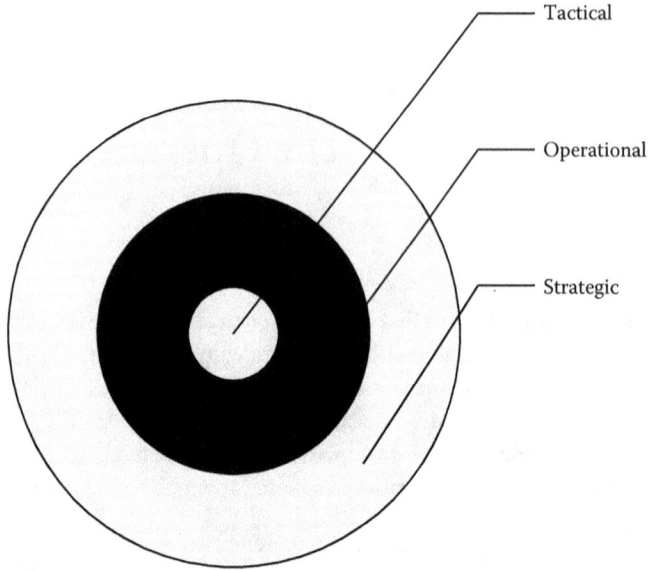

Figure 3.1 Operations Sphere (Developed by Eloy Nuñez and Ernest G. Vendrell.)

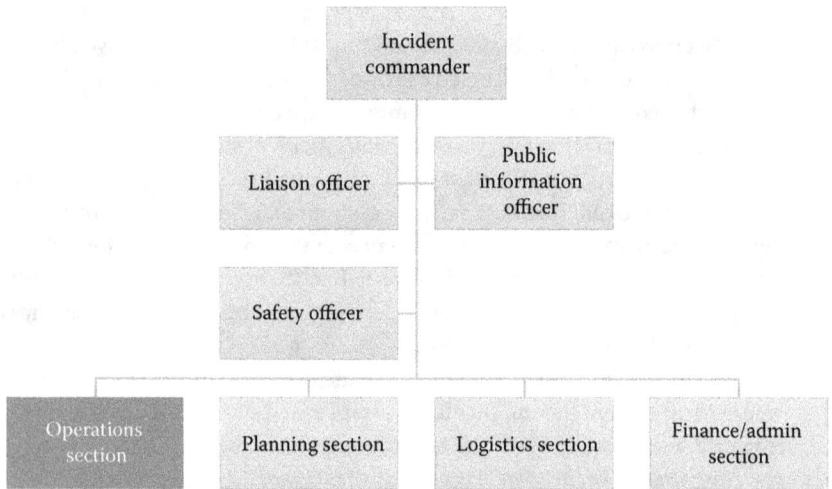

Figure 3.2 Basic ICS Organizational Chart (Adapted from FEMA by Eloy Nuñez.)

hierarchical organization structure, but in the case of a spontaneous incident, the organizational structure builds from the bottom up, down, and then sideways.

Let's consider the case study in Vignette 3.1 so that we can get a better understanding of how an ICS organizational structure evolves during a critical incident. As you read the vignette, consider the approaches taken by police officers at two different incidents. Both incidents start very innocuously, but both

(a)

Early stages

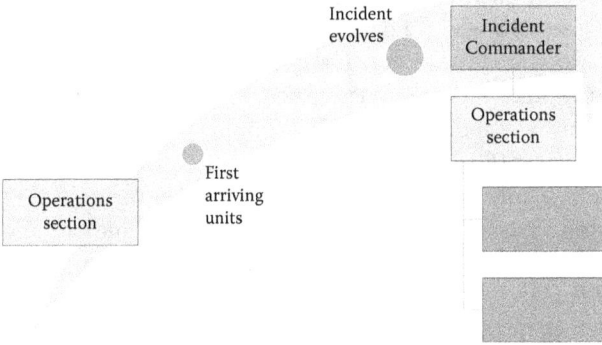

(b)

Later stages

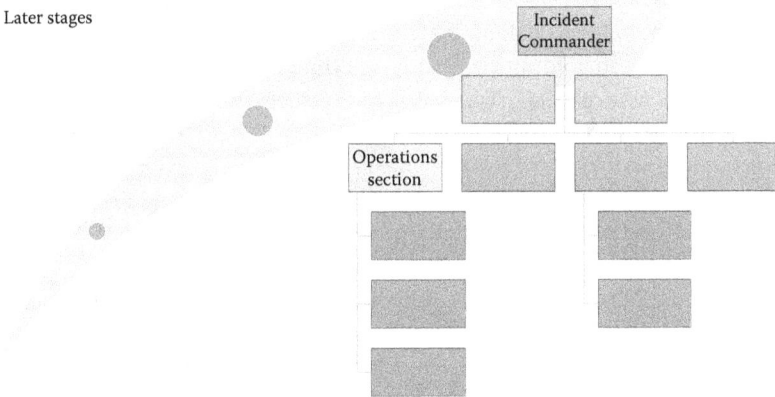

Figure 3.3 (a) Evolution of ICS in a Spontaneous Critical Incident (Developed by Eloy Nuñez and Ernest G. Vendrell.) (b) Evolution of ICS in a Spontaneous Critical Incident

take unexpected turns and become something other than what they started out as. One incident is handled with the regular day-to-day operational resources of the police department, while the other incident grows beyond the capabilities of the regular resources. Consider how and why an incident command structure develops for one, but not for the other.

VIGNETTE 3.1

Field Training Officer Annette Williams and her rookie, Officer Thomas Ford, were riding as a "two-man" unit this evening. Typically, the afternoon shift squad was comprised of eight officers and one supervisory sergeant, but this evening, they were down two officers because one was on vacation, and the other was attending a training course. On a regular night, with a full complement of personnel, Sergeant James Richards liked to put out two, two-man units, and four one-man units. The two-man units are primarily used for responding to calls where a backup officer is required by rule. For such calls, when a two-man unit was not in service, then two one-man units would be dispatched. Since this was a designated field training squad, the two-man units were usually comprised of a field training officer (FTO) and a probationary police officer (PPO) trainee.

This was to be a typically busy Saturday night. As he left the police station at the beginning of the shift, Sergeant Richards checked his car computer and noted that there were ten calls holding, and that all his units were tied up on calls. Fortunately, there were no emergency or priority calls that needed his attention, so he did what he always did on a busy night—he volunteered himself to handle some two-man calls that had been holding for a couple of hours, and which he thought posed minimal risk in responding to them by himself. As a sergeant, Richards had the supervisory discretion to handle certain two-man calls by himself when he saw fit. Calls such as burglar alarms and suspicious vehicles are technically two-man calls, but if the calls have been holding for a while—in this case, over an hour—then the likelihood of a burglar alarm or suspicious vehicle call being an actual burglary in progress are greatly minimized. Sergeant Richards knew that over 95% of burglar alarms turn out to be false, and that the calls were holding for over an hour further lessened the possibility that he would encounter a burglar because no burglar sticks around for more than 5 minutes after an alarm goes off.

Richards cleared some of the suspicious vehicle and burglar alarm calls by himself.

Meanwhile, Officer Williams and her rookie were dispatched as a backup to assist a homicide detective make contact with a possible witness. Officer Williams and Trainee Ford were to respond to a shopping center, where they were to meet up with Detective Maureen Singletary before responding to an apartment complex where the witness was thought to live. Upon arrival at the shopping center parking lot, Williams and her trainee met up with Detective Singletary, and they were briefed on the call. The detective was asking that Williams and Ford come with her to the witness' apartment to provide a "uniform presence" while she sought out and interviewed the witness. Detective Singletary told Williams that she did not expect any trouble from the witness, but that she wanted the uniformed officers with her as a precaution because the witness was allegedly a close friend of the suspect, who was still at large.

Both units left from the parking lot of the shopping center and headed to the apartment complex where the witness was thought to reside. Apartment B-107 was located on the first floor of a 300-unit apartment complex called Oak Tree Villages. Detective Singletary and Officers Williams and Ford parked closer to Building A, so as not to look as if they were heading toward the apartment in the B building. They walked a couple of hundred feet and turned one corner to approach the front door of Apartment B-107. On a hunch, Officer Williams instructed Officer Ford to go around to the back of the apartment in case the witness (a white male, 25 years old) decided to flee out the back. Detective Singletary agreed with this precaution, and waited until Officer Ford was in position in the rear before she and Williams approached the front door of B-107.

As they approached the front door of B-107, Williams and Singletary noticed that the sole window belonging to the apartment was completely covered in brown wrapping paper, and thus they could not see inside. Williams knocked on the door; then stepped back away from it as she always did—on all calls. She knew never to stand in front of a door. There's no way of telling what's behind it—and even though there was no reason to suspect otherwise—this was a precaution that she did all the time, no matter what type of call it was.

After half a minute of no response, Officer Williams knocked on the door again and stepped back. There was no response to the second knock, and moments later she decided to try opening the door. She wasn't sure why she did that, but a gut feeling told her that something wasn't right. The doorknob turned, and the door opened inward to the apartment. Both Williams and Detective Singletary seemed surprised that the door was left unlocked, but intuitively they both decided to proceed. The officer and the detective unholstered their weapons and held them at the low-ready position as they entered through the front door. "Police! Is anyone home?" shouted Williams. There was no response, and the two proceeded to walk inside—Williams in front, and Detective Singletary directly behind her.

Immediately upon entering the living room area, they observed a young white male lying facedown on the tile floor in a pool of blood. The male was motionless and appeared to have a gaping wound in the back of his head. The male was clearly deceased. Next to the deceased male, there was a 9-mm pistol lying on the tile floor. "Stay with him … I'll check the bedroom," Williams told Singletary. Williams then proceeded to check the bedroom, bathroom, and the closets and returned to the living room where Singletary was taking a closer look at the deceased male. "Looks like an exit wound to the back of the head," stated the detective.

Officer Williams responded, "OK … the room is all clear … no one else in the house. Let me call my rookie to the front and get him started to tape off the crime scene."

"OK … but I don't know about this place. Do you smell that?" asked Singletary.

"Yeah … it smells like nail polish remover … acetone … look over there," Williams pointed to the kitchen area. The place was a mess, and among all the dirty pots and pans and unwashed dishes were several glass and plastic containers filled with liquids. There was also a propane tank and various tubes going from one container to another. Some of the containers were labeled as muriatic acid. There was a large bag labeled "Pool Salt" and several plastic milk gallon jugs. There were several 9-volt batteries scattered among the rest of the mess. "This looks like a meth lab," concluded Williams.

"Look over here," called out Singletary as she examined a desk area next to a large screen television. "Is this a meth lab, or is this guy making bombs?" On the desk were several foot-long three-inch PVC pipes with caps on each side. There were also many spent ammunition cartridges of various calibers. On top of the desk were a stack of books, magazines, and loose papers, some of which appeared to contain instructions on how to build pipe bombs. Scattered on the nearby sofa were several publications containing anarchist literature.

"This guy's not going anywhere. We need to back off, in case this place blows up. I'll let the rookie take a quick look at the body for training purposes, but then we're going to back out and secure the front door," said Williams.

Detective Singletary responded, "OK … I'll contact my team and get crime scene over here."

"OK, but before they process the scene, we need to get the Narcotics Unit … or better yet … the bomb squad to take a look at all this stuff, and make it safe. Let's back off … tape off the scene, and wait for bomb squad to clear the apartment," said Williams. "In the meantime, I'll contact my sergeant and let him know that we'll be tied up for a while."

At the same time that this was going on, Sergeant Richards had arrived at a burglar alarm call at a residence that had gone off over an hour ago. He had already responded to and cleared five other alarm calls in the same neighborhood. Richards planned on handling this last one that was holding before heading over to Officer Williams' call that he had heard get dispatched earlier. Sergeant Richards was a charismatic and "hands on" supervisor, who liked to respond to his officers' calls throughout the shift. He especially liked to meet with his FTOs to see how their rookies were doing. As he arrived at the residential burglar alarm call, everything looked OK. The alarm had re-set and was no longer audible. The windows and doors in the front and side looked OK, and it did not appear that there was anyone home at the residence. There was a chain-link fence blocking off the backyard, and Richards could not see if any of the doors and windows around the back had been broken into. To make sure there had not been a break in, Richards decided to go into the fenced-in backyard. As he had done hundreds of times before, Richards intentionally rattled the gate to make sure there weren't any dogs in the backyard. He waited a moment, and after no dogs barked, he opened the gate and proceeded into the backyard, while holding his weapon in the low-ready position … just in case.

It was a good thing he did. Moments after opening the gate to the back-yard, without any warning, a large male rottweiler charged directly at him at full bore. Instantaneously, Richards raised his weapon a couple of inches and pulled the trigger to discharge a single bullet, with the dog's head only two feet away from him. Richards did not have time to aim, or even to point the weapon at the dog. The dog turned 180 degrees and ran back to a small "doggy door" coming out of the side garage. The whole thing happened so fast that Richards couldn't tell if the bullet had hit the dog or not. He hoped not because he was a big dog lover. In fact, as a patrolman, he had served for several years in the K-9 Unit.

Once the rottweiler went back inside, Richards could hear nothing, and he surmised that the owners were not home. There did not appear to be a trail of blood, but that did not mean that the shot missed. He remembered how years ago, the SWAT team had shot a pit bull in the head during a search warrant at a farm, and the dog did not die or even suffer any significant injury from it. That dog must have had a thick skull because Richards remembered how he could see the bullet imbedded under the dog's scalp, with not a trace of blood coming from the injury. In any event, whether the dog had been struck by the round or not was irrelevant. He knew that by discharging his firearm, there would have to be an investigation by internal affairs. Sergeant Richards called his lieutenant on the phone to let him know what had happened. By departmental protocol, the lieutenant would need to respond to the scene and an internal affairs investigator as well. Had the shooting involved a person instead of a dog, then the Homicide Bureau would respond as well. Sergeant Richards was familiar with police shootings, and he knew that he would be stuck at this call for a very long time—probably until the end of this shift, or even beyond.

It was then that Officer Williams called Sergeant Richards to advise him of the details of her call. There were two incidents occurring at the same time, and per protocol, the squad supervisor—in this case, Sergeant Richards—needed to be at Officer Williams' scene. Since Richards was involved in his own firearm discharge incident, he would not be able to respond to Officer Williams' incident. He could not be at two places at the same time. The lieutenant, who is the commander of the afternoon shift for the entire district, also cannot be at both places at the same time. That meant that Officer Williams would be the senior ranking officer on the scene, and the de facto incident commander until such time that someone of higher rank would arrive at the scene and assume command.

Officer Williams was up to the challenge. She was a senior officer who had handled many critical incidents throughout her career. It was now on her to coordinate the responses of various units to the scene. It was clear that the bomb squad needed to respond in order to render safe all the explosive material in the apartment. Fire rescue would need to respond and stand by while the bomb squad worked the apartment. Quite possibly, a Fire Rescue Hazardous Material Unit (Hazmat) would need to respond because of the hazardous materials on the scene. The crime scene unit and the homicide team also needed to respond to investigate the scene and to determine the victim's identity. Because the bomb squad had been requested, that triggered the contact of two federal agencies: the FBI and the ATF. That meant that the Department's Homeland Security Bureau was also notified. Officer Williams would also need uniform units to respond to the scene in order to establish a perimeter around the "hot zone" and to assist in evacuating the entire East Wing of Building B. Because there would be a need to evacuate an entire apartment building, this incident would probably get news media coverage, so Williams also had media relations (PIO) respond. She knew that her scene was going to take quite a while to secure. In fact, it was likely that it would go beyond the end of the shift, and she knew that she needed to start thinking about long-term relief for her officers.

As the evening wore on, a mobile Incident Command Post (ICP) was set up in the parking lot of Building A in the apartment complex. After briefly making an appearance at Sergeant Richards' incident, the afternoon platoon (shift) commander Lieutenant Brian Boyer came to the ICP and formally assumed command of the incident from Officer Williams. Lieutenant Boyer contacted the District major and captain to apprise them of the situation.

The bomb squad sergeant set up his Tactical Operations Command (TOC) closer to Apartment B-107. From there, the bomb squad technicians had ready access to their robots, x-ray machines, and other equipment. There they met with bomb techs from the FBI and ATF. Jointly, they established evacuation and shelter-in-place recommendations based on industry guidelines. The bomb squad sergeant then recommended to Lieutenant Boyer that the area of evacuation be expanded to include all three floors of the entire B-Building and parts of A-Building. Meanwhile, an interagency public information team met with Lieutenant Boyer to draft a brief press release that would be provided to the local television stations for the 11 o'clock news. A media relations area was set up safely outside the hot zone, but within the apartment complex grounds. Television trucks along with their cameramen, reporters, and producers set up their tall antenna booms and began broadcasting live from that location.

Two hours into the incident, an Incident Command Structure (ICS) had been established and was still growing. Lieutenant Boyer was now the incident commander. The operations section was led by Officer Williams. Under Williams were four uniformed officers holding perimeter positions and another two helping with evacuations of the apartment building. In order to meet the manpower needs of the operations section, Lieutenant Boyer moved several officers from other area squads to the scene. The bomb squad and their federal partners formed the Tactical Operations Command directly under the operations section. The bomb squad sergeant would shuttle between the ICP and the nearby TOC to have face-to-face discussions with Lieutenant Boyer and Officer Williams.

Sensing that this incident would continue way beyond the shift that ended at 11 PM, Boyer decided to hold over three of his afternoon shift squads. He also contacted Police Headquarters and requested that the on-call critical incident management unit respond to the scene to provide logistical support in the form of drinking water and electric generators for lighting. Three hours into the incident and the ICS structure had grown to include a logistics section. So far, Boyer did not see the need to activate a planning section or a finance section, but had the incident continued for much longer, these sections would also need to be activated.

Meanwhile, back at the scene of Sergeant Richards' dog shooting incident, only one internal affairs investigator responded. There was no need for anyone else to respond. This particular incident was much smaller in scope and gravity, and thus did not require a formal activation of an ICS structure. Everything that needed to be done at this call was done with the regular resources of the police department.

Postscript—At the scene of the dog shooting incident, the owners of the house, a young family of four, showed up a couple of hours later as the internal affairs investigator and Sergeant Richards were still on the scene. Once inside the residence, the owners were able to check on the rottweiler's well-being, and saw that the dog was OK. Apparently, the single round missed him completely, and the dog had run away from Sergeant Richards because of the sound of the shot. The owners also told Richards that the male rottweiler probably attacked him because it was protecting a female rottweiler and a brood of puppies that were in the garage. Richards was relieved to hear that the dog was not injured; however, he was embarrassed that this incident had occurred in the first place. His intention was to help his squad clear up calls. Instead, he tied himself up on a call for several hours and was not able to be there for his officers when they needed him at the scene of the homicide. Nevertheless, Richards decided to make the best out of a bad situation that could have been worse. He learned what he already knew—dogs bark to warn intruders to stay away, but when a dog is protecting its brood, they may not bark at all. This dog used a silent ambush tactic. This was a lesson that he would learn for the next time he had to enter a backyard.

There are several lessons that can be taken from Vignette 3.1, and also from the illustration in Figure 3.3. First, all spontaneous critical incidents start at the operational level and the ICS structures to deal with them grow upward, downward, and sideways. This is different from preplanned events in which all the necessary components of the ICS are in place before the event starts.

Second, not all incidents require the activation of an incident command organizational structure. All organizations have organizational structures that are designed to deal with the day-to-day business of the organization. Presumably, those structures are organized in a manner that provides the best functionality to the organization. As we saw in Vignette 3.1, one of the incidents was handled on a "routine" basis within the existing operational command of the police department. There was no need to formally activate an ICS structure for that type of incident because it was contained and handled efficiently with the existing units of the organization. In a heuristic sense, it could be argued that every call that a police officer or firefighter responds to begins with the embryo of an operations section. But in police work, the majority of calls for service are resolved without the need to activate a formal ICS structure. In essence, for most calls for service, that "embryo" is never born.

Third, the ICS is meant to be a temporary reshuffling of organizational elements to deal with a temporary problem. Because each ICS activation is specific to the incident that it is intended to resolve, it cannot be left mobilized indefinitely. As soon as the ICS is activated, the incident commander should start thinking of how and when it will be deactivated. For very large and protracted incidents, the demobilization unit under the planning section is the element whose job it is to plan for the phaseout of the ICS activation. More often than not however—especially in police-related incidents—the demobilization planning is done by the incident commander himself.

Fourth, not every incident evolves into a full-fledged ICS structure. As we saw in the vignette, in one incident the ICS did not evolve at all. In the second incident, the ICS evolved from the original operations section and grew upward, downward, and sideways as needed. It grew downward when backup units responded to help secure the scene and evacuate the apartments. It grew upward when the lieutenant responded to the scene and formally assumed the role of incident commander from Officer Williams. It also grew sideways to include a new logistics section and a command staff comprised of a public information officer reporting directly to the incident commander when those functions became necessary. That was as far as the ICS grew for this particular incident. Had the incident commander deemed it necessary, he could have included a liaison officer and a safety officer to his command staff. He could have also activated a planning section and a finance/administrative section if he needed to. This case was a relatively small incident that was probably not going to extend beyond another 8 hours, so the incident commander did not see the need to broaden the scope of his ICS organizational structure. Had it become larger, or extended for a longer time, it is likely that those other support components would have been mobilized.

Why Police Officers Don't Like the Incident Command System

The Incident Command System was invented by firefighters, not by police officers. That basically encapsulates the reasons why police officers have resisted the implementation of the ICS into the law enforcement realm, but the real underlying reasons go beyond petty rivalries between the police and firefighting disciplines. One of the reasons that police officers do not like ICS is because the language of ICS is different from theirs, and oftentimes, words such as *division, section, command staff, unit, task force,* and even the word *officer* have very different meanings. Whenever one word means two different things, or two words mean the exact same thing, there is going to be some confusion. Police officers dislike ICS because they feel like they are being forced to learn a new language that they are expected to use occasionally under certain situations, but not very often.

The second reason that police officers have resisted the implementation of ICS in their departments and agencies is because they view law enforcement work as being very different from firefighting work.

The third reason is that police officers do not like to fill out forms—especially those overly complicated FEMA ICS forms that they perceive as having nothing to do with their jobs. For example, ICS 209, the incident status summary, is comprised of 24 pages of mind-numbing details about almost everything except what is really necessary for solving a typical police incident such as a hostage taking, a bomb evacuation, or an escaped prisoner. Many in law enforcement view FEMA's "one size fits all" approach as being way off the mark.

Lastly, police officers do not like ICS because they feel it is being forced upon them by people who do not understand police work. Are these complaints about ICS valid, or are police officers just resentful that they didn't invent an Incident Command System of their own? Let's now take a closer look at the Incident Command System.

Incident Command System: Does One Size Fit All?

According to FEMA's introduction to the Incident Command System training course (ICS 100), the Incident Command System is designed to be a flexible system that can meet the challenges posed by incidents and events of any kind or any size. Ostensibly, it can be adapted to handle anything in the complexity scale from a Category 5 hurricane to the planning of a Rotary Club fundraising event. It is this flexibility and wide range of use that makes the Incident Command System so intriguing.

Like all good ideas, the Incident Command System was born in response to a catastrophic failure. In Chapter 7 we will examine the innovation process in detail, but it is safe to say in this current chapter that generally speaking, innovation is prompted by failure. That was the case in 1970 when a forest fire in California resulted in the deaths of 16 people and over half a million of acres burned, including 700 structures therein. An after-action review of the incident revealed that there was poor communication and coordination between the different agencies involved in the firefight. That prompted the U.S. Congress to approve funding to the U.S. Forest Service for an incident management system later named as FIRESCOPE (Firefighting Resources of California Organized for Potential Emergencies). A multiagency team comprised of members from the U.S. Forest Service, the California Department of Forestry and Fire Protection; the Governor's Office of Emergency Services, Los Angeles, Ventura; and the Santa Barbara County Fire Departments and the Los Angeles City Fire Department developed the FIRESCOPE concepts that led to the birth of the Incident Command System in 1972.[1]

What was initially designed for a multiagency response to forest fires was expanded as a system to respond to "all hazards" including terrorist attacks, and was eventually adopted at the national level by FEMA in 2004 under the name

National Incident Management System (NIMS).[2] That system is now regarded as the unifying organizing principle throughout the United States for the management of critical incidents and events, and whether we like it or not, it is here to stay. Moreover, as we will examine in greater detail in Chapter 5, the distribution of funding from the U.S. Department of Homeland Security, the Department of Justice, and other federal agencies to the states, counties, and local municipalities is almost always contingent on "NIMS compliance" by the receiving agencies. For that reason alone, many local police chiefs and county sheriffs have put aside their misgivings about the NIMS and ICS.

Regardless of the monetary incentives offered by the federal government for local municipalities and counties to be NIMS compliant, the truth is that the ICS is here to stay. Police chiefs and sheriffs must recognize that the Incident Command System is based on sound organizational principles, and more importantly, it works.

Many police leaders have come to realize that they have already been doing many of the ICS practices for years, but that they have been calling these things by different names. Much of the resistance by police officers to the ICS is partly attributed to a lack of understanding of some of its basic principles and how those principles are applied in real-life situations. The integration of ICS into policing becomes a lot more palatable once we come to the realization that we are not learning many new concepts. The underlying concepts of ICS have been around for ages. What we are learning is a new language—in essence, new words for old concepts.

There are many reasons why local police and fire departments may resist the nationalization of incident management standards as has come about with FEMA's National Incident Management System. Much of the resistance has to do with resentment of the federal government's meddling in the local agencies' operations. While admittedly some aspects of the ICS can be somewhat annoying and dealing with FEMA and the federal government bureaucracy in general can be challenging, we should not throw out the veritable "baby with the bathwater." Earlier we discussed some of the reasons why police chiefs and sheriffs may not like the ICS. In the next section, we will examine the things that make ICS such a valuable tool.

The Four Cornerstones of Critical Incident Management

All structures have a foundation upon which they are built. The same can be said for critical incident management. The foundation upon which the discipline is built is illustrated in Figure 3.4 as the four cornerstones of critical incident management. These "cornerstones" are communication, collaboration, coordination, and command. In this section, we will examine how each of these four cornerstones are related to the core principles of the Incident Command System.

Communications

Communications failure is endemic to the human condition, so it is not surprising that poor communication is cited as a factor in almost every after-action report of incidents or events, no matter the size or complexity. Communications failure played a key role in the response and recovery to Hurricane Katrina in 2005.[3]

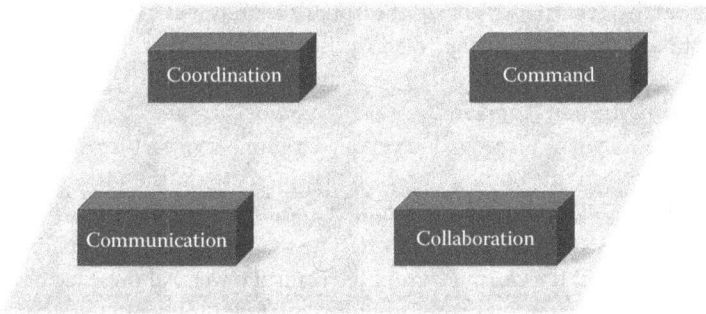

Figure 3.4 Four Cornerstones of Critical Incident Management (Developed by Eloy Nuñez and Ernest G. Vendrell.)

Communications failure played a key role in the police and fire response to the World Trade Center towers on September 11, 2001.[4] Communications difficulties were also prevalent during the first World Trade Center bombing in 1993. An excerpt from the after-action report written by Chief Anthony Fusco of that incident reveals that things were not very much different from 2001 or 2005:

> A major detriment to our ability to strengthen control of the incident was fire department on-scene communications. Communications were a serious problem from the outset. With 156 units and 31 chiefs operating at the height of this incident, try to imagine how difficult it was to gain control of the portable radio operations frequency. Two command channels and one tactical channel were used. In many cases, runners were sent by a sector commander to communicate with the incident commander.[5]

As a result of the lessons learned from the 1993 incident, new radio repeaters were installed near the World Trade Center towers in an attempt to fix the problems that firefighters had experienced then. Despite those technological fixes, the communications problems persisted in the 2001 incident. That is because technology is only one of the factors that affect human communications. Too often, policy makers try to fix communication problems with technology, when indeed, the root cause of the problems have had more to do with language and the ability of the human brain to process information during chaotic and complex situations. FEMA identifies two basic reasons for poor communications: inefficient uses of available communication systems and conflicting codes and terminology.[6] Note that the first has to do with technology, and the second reason has to do with language. Both of these factors are important for determining communication failures, but we will start by examining the language factor first.

VIGNETTE 3.2   Disaster at Tenerife Airport

The deadliest accident in aviation history occurred on March 27, 1977, when the unthinkable happened—two Boeing 747 jumbo jets collided on the runway at the Tenerife Airport in the Canary Islands. All 248 passengers and crew aboard the KLM airliner died in the crash. Another 335 died aboard the Pan Am airplane, or a total of 583 fatalities. Miraculously, there were 61 survivors in the Pan Am plane.

The post-incident investigation revealed a number of factors that contributed to the crash, including poor visibility, pressure on the pilots to adhere to a tight schedule, and the KLM's copilot and flight engineer's unwillingness to challenge their captain's authority despite their obvious reservations about taking off without the clearance from the control tower. All these factors contributed to the disaster, but the communications failure between the KLM crew and the control tower stood above all else as the main contributory factor.

The crash investigators found that the fundamental cause of this accident was due to the KLM captain taking off without clearance from the tower. Notably, in his haste to takeoff after a long delay, the KLM captain did not obey the "stand by for takeoff" instruction from the tower. Moreover, the KLM captain could have aborted his takeoff on time if he had heard or listened to the Pan Am crew reporting that they were still on the runway.

According to the Federal Aviation Administration (FAA) incident review: "In the final minute before the collision, key misunderstandings occur among all the parties involved. And in the end, the KLM pilot initiates takeoff even though Air Traffic Control (ATC) has not issued the proper clearance."

The following are the radio and in-plane conversations of the last minute before the crash, as pieced together by the investigators from the planes' voice recorders.[27]

> 1705:41.5 *KLM copilot speaking to the pilot*: Wait a minute, we don't have an ATC (Air Traffic Control) clearance.
> *KLM pilot responds*: No, I know that. Go ahead, ask.
> 1705:44.6 *KLM copilot to the Control Tower*: Uh, the KLM 4805 is now ready for takeoff and we're waiting for our ATC clearance.
> 1705:53.4 *Control Tower*: KLM 4805 … uh you are cleared to the Papa beacon. Climb to and maintain flight level 90 … right turn after takeoff proceed with heading 040 until intercepting the 325 radial from Las Palmas VOR.
> 1706:09.6 *KLM copilot*: Ah, roger, sir, we're cleared to the Papa beacon flight level 90, right turn out 040 until intercepting the 325, and we're now (at takeoff).
> 1706:11.08 *[Brakes of KLM 4805 are released.]*
> 1706:12.25 *KLM pilot to the copilot*: Let's go … check thrust.
> 1706:14.00 *[Sound of engines starting to accelerate.]*
> 1706:18.19 *Control Tower*: Okay.

At this point, the KLM 747 starts to roll down the runway. Meanwhile, the Pan Am 747 is crossing the same runway, but the low visibility conditions do not allow the KLM crew to see it. According to investigators, they were not sure why the control tower would say "Okay" immediately after the KLM copilot had indicated that the plane was "at takeoff." The investigators hypothesized that the air traffic controller may have believed that KLM crew meant "We're now at takeoff position."

As luck would have it, at this exact moment both the Air Traffic Control tower and the Pan Am plane transmitted on the radio simultaneously, which caused a shrill feedback noise in the KLM cockpit that lasted for almost 4 seconds and made the following communications hard to hear in the KLM cockpit:

> 1706:20.08 *Control Tower*: Stand by for takeoff … I will call you.
> *Pan Am pilot:* No, uh.
> *Pan Am pilot to Control Tower*: And we are still taxiing down the runway, the Clipper 1736.

This radio transmission from the Pan Am 747 should have alerted the crew of the KLM plane that the runway may not have been cleared after all. In fact the flight engineer of the KLM plane questioned his own pilot, even as their plane had already begun rolling down the runway.

> 1706:32.43 *KLM Flight Engineer to his pilot*: Is he not clear, then?
> 1706:34.10 *KLM Pilot responds*: What do you say?
> 1706:34.70 *KLM Flight Engineer to his pilot*: Is he not clear, that Pan American?
> 1706:35.70 *KLM Pilot responds*: Oh, yes. [emphatically]

Moments later, the Pan Am flight crew saw the KLM coming straight at them out of the fog. The Pan Am captain said, "There he is … look at him! [expletives deleted] is coming!" and his copilot yells, "Get off! Get off! Get off!" The Pan Am pilot accelerates the engines but not in sufficient time to avoid the collision. At 1706:47.44, the collision occurred.

As we read in the KLM–Pan Am case study, communications failures are rarely attributed to a single cause. The communication breakdown in this case study was due to a combination of unfortunate factors. The coincidence of two separate transmissions at the exact same time led to a shrill sound on the radio that made it difficult for the KLM crew to hear the control tower at the most critical time possible. There was not much that could have been done to avoid that chance occurrence from happening. However, the part of the communication breakdown that was attributed to the use of unclear language could have—and should have been avoided. In fact, the lessons learned from that tragic incident led to recommendations for future radio communications procedures in civil aviation. Those same recommendations can be applied to other high-risk disciplines.

Because poor communication is so prevalent during critical incidents, perhaps the best thing that ICS contributes to the discipline is its practice of using *common terminology* and *clear text communication*. Common terminology refers to the use of standardized words in order to avoid confusion among the people who are communicating. Each word has a very clear and specific meaning. No word means two different things, and no two words mean the same thing. At least that is the intent of common terminology. ICS seeks to standardize and universalize the terminology used in the emergency management discipline in order to avoid miscommunications. ICS is not the first system that has attempted to universalize language. Esperanto is an artificial language that was created in the late nineteenth century as a way of breaking down barriers between people and help everyone see each other as neighbors.[7]

Another example of *common terminology* is evident in the universal use of the English language for civil aviation internationally. The International Civil Aviation Organization (ICAO), under the charter of the United Nations, has instituted over 10,000 international Standards and Recommended Practices since its inception in 1944. As such, the 191 participating member states and global aviation organizations use these recommended practices to formulate their respective national civil aviation regulations.[8] One notable practice was adopted in their *Resolution A38/8 Proficiency in the English language used for radiotelephony communications*, which formally codified the use of English for all communications between flight crews and air traffic controllers. The use of common terminology in the civil aviation field is one of the best practices that have been instituted to minimize the chances of a communication breakdown such as the one that contributed to the KLM-Pan Am disaster at Tenerife.

Like the ICAO, the Department of Homeland Security (DHS) (and FEMA under it) seeks to standardize language throughout the United States in order to avoid communication failures at critical incidents. Unlike the artificial Esperanto language, DHS does not intend to create an entirely new language. The National Incident Management System and its ICS component is only meant to standardize certain words, not to rewrite an entire language. In essence, ICS provides a "glossary" of terms, not an entire dictionary. Nor does DHS intend to force the local agencies to integrate the terminology into their day-to-day activities. The words *section*, *division*, *unit*, and *task force*, which have certain specific meanings for ICS terminology, may not mean the same thing for the local agencies. That is OK. When a local agency is deemed to be "NIMS compliant" by the federal government, it only means that the agency understands and knows how to speak "ICS language." It does not mean that they must radically change the names of their existing organizational structures and functions. It only means that during a multi-jurisdictional critical incident, they must understand and be able to speak in the common accepted language of the ICS.

Clear text (or "plain language") is when codes and discipline-specific jargon are avoided. Some police and fire departments use Q-codes radio terminology, while others use 10-code jargon on their radio transmissions. In addition, most agencies have their own code systems for different types of calls. Therefore, a great deal of confusion and miscommunication can be avoided when firefighters and police officers from different agencies are working together at a critical incident. The use of plain language is something that many tactical teams have been doing for years. Tactical units such as bomb squads, SWAT teams, and Hazmat teams tend to prefer the use of plain language in their point-to-point radio transmissions as a way of avoiding confusing communications. Under the ICS best practices, the use of plain language is something that all responders would adopt—not just tactical units.

Collaboration

The second cornerstone of critical incident management is *collaboration*. Throughout the evolution of humankind, we have become more specialized in the things we do. The more complex our economies and technologies become, the more we rely on specialists to accomplish tasks that most of us do not have time to focus on. In complex economies, no one can be an expert at everything.

In the realms of law enforcement, firefighting, and homeland security, we have taken upon ourselves the responsibility of protecting our citizens from an "all-hazards" threat environment, not because we wanted to, but because our enemies have given us no choice. We are responsible for defending our homeland from attacks by adversaries that may use a wide array of weapons to kill us. We are also responsible for protecting our homeland from natural disasters, as well as man-made technological accidents. The range of possibilities of things that can harm us seems endless, and nobody can be expected to be an expert at defending us from every possible threat imaginable. We now have bomb squads to render safe explosives, Hazmat teams to clean up chemical agent spills, Department of Energy radiological experts to deal with nuclear and radiological threats, and biological experts at the Centers for Disease Control (CDC) to deal with pandemics and biological terror attacks. We have SWAT teams to deal with hostage takers and active shooters, and we have Mobile Field Forces (MFFs) to deal with riots and civil disturbances. We have weather experts to predict the path of storms and seismologists to provide early warnings for earthquakes and tsunamis. There are many more areas of specialization in the homeland security field that were not listed here. The point is that in today's very complex environment, we rely heavily on highly trained specialists to solve problems caused by a set of specific threats.

Sometimes, the threat can come from a single source—for example an earthquake or an airplane hijacking. In the case of an earthquake, a fire-rescue urban search and rescue team (USAR) would be an example of a highly specialized team that is specifically designed for the task of finding and rescuing victims that have been pinned down under collapsed buildings. In the case of an airplane hijacking, we rely on specialized assault teams that have been trained to breach airplane fuselages to make dynamic entries and neutralize the hijackers. These are examples of single-purpose specialized teams that are created to solve a specific problem. In ICS language, these single-purpose specialists are called *strike teams*. FEMA defines strike teams as "A set number of resources of the same kind and type with common communications operating under the direct supervision of a Strike Team Leader."[9]

Photo 3.1 A Mixed Team Collaborates to Solve a Problem: A Mixed JHRT (Joint Hazard Response Team) Comprised of the Miami-Dade PD Bomb Squad, Miami-Dade Fire Rescue, Miami PD Bomb Squad, ATF, FBI, and the Florida National Guard 44th Civil Support Team Meet to Problem-Solve a Multi-Threat Scenario during the Preparations for the 2007 Super Bowl in Miami-Dade County, Florida (Courtesy of the Miami-Dade Police Department.)

Dealing with a situation that presents multiple threats requires teams of experts from different disciplines. These mixed teams work together to solve crises where more than one threat exists. For example, the 1999 Columbine incident was much more than an active shooter threat. In addition to the semi-automatic rifles, pistols, and shotguns used by the two subjects, it was later determined that there were also more than 90 incendiary and explosive devices that either exploded or were rendered safe by bomb technicians. Over a thousand law enforcement personnel and 172 fire and Emergency Medical Services (EMS) personnel from 15 different law enforcement and fire rescue/EMS agencies were needed to resolve this mass casualty, multi-threat incident.[10]

Given the complexity of a mass casualty incident such as in Columbine, the cooperation of many people from many disciplines and agencies becomes paramount. The typical first responders such as uniformed patrolmen, firefighters, and paramedics are "jacks-of-all-trades" in their particular fields. These first responders are trained and equipped to handle a broad spectrum of situations, and are typically the first to arrive at the scene of a critical incident. They are not, however, trained or equipped to handle highly specialized tasks such as making tactical entry of a building to find and neutralize an active shooter, or to render-safe explosive devices, or to investigate a crime scene, or to issue press releases to the media. These specialized tasks, along with perimeter security, staging area and command post security, and triage (among many others) require a great deal of cooperation between the different agencies and different disciplines involved. Without the cornerstone concept of collaboration, the Columbine massacre would have lasted longer, and probably would have resulted in more deaths and serious injuries.

Coordination

Coordination is the process by which the many collaborating elements work together to set and execute their often divergent priorities. Coordination is not the same thing as collaboration, although these two constructs go hand-in-hand. Coordination has to do with the management of time so that the actions of multiple elements occur either simultaneously or consecutively as desired to solve a problem. For example, in an active shooter incident such as the Columbine massacre, there are usually different players involved with different priorities. The critical incident managers on the scene need to figure out whether the rescue of injured persons inside the school needs to be done first, or whether the SWAT teams need to neutralize the gunmen first, or whether the bomb squads need to render safe all explosives first. In some incidents, on-scene hazards may further complicate matters. Decisions have to be made regarding the timing and sequencing of actions. The planning of those sequences and the execution of those plans either on a concurrent or consecutive basis is what is referred to as coordination.

One example of coordination is how military units execute movements in a certain sequence and direction as planned by commanders. Another example of coordination is how project managers plan and execute the sequencing of milestones toward the end goal of building a skyscraper in a crowded downtown area.

At the core of coordination is the factor of time. As such, the tools of coordination have to do with things that keep the tempo or record the time so that the movements between elements can be executed in unison or consecutively depending on the desired result. Instruments of coordination include but are not limited to the following: clocks, metronomes, timelines, project benchmarks, drums, whistles, horns, radios, cell phones, hand signals, marching cadence, and the rapping of shields by mobile field force riot control officers. All these things are used to coordinate the movements of groups of people.

Communication is obviously important for coordination, but does not necessarily need to be language based. For example, throughout history military commanders have used sounds from horns, whistles, and drums to coordinate the movements of their units. Other means of coordinating movement include the use of signal flags, signal lamps, and even smoke signals. Nowadays, cell phones and text messaging have become a preferred means of coordinating action among political movements, peaceful protest groups, and even terrorist organizations.

Command

The fourth cornerstone of critical incident management is *command*. During critical incidents, communication, collaboration, and coordination among groups can occur without a clearly identified leader, but not very effectively, and not for very long. In chaotic situations, people look for leaders ... or at least symbols of leadership to coalesce around. Amid the chaos of some spontaneously

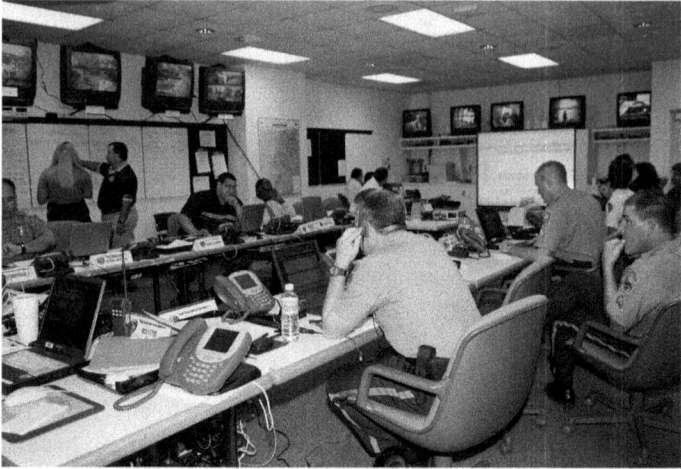

Photo 3.2 Command Post Coordination: A Command Post Makes Use of Telephones, Television, Police Radios, and Whiteboards to Coordinate the Actions of Personnel during the 2003 FTAA Conference Event (Courtesy of the Miami-Dade Police Department.)

occurring incidents, it is likely that some people will take on leadership roles, while others will follow. Many examples abound of regular citizens being thrust unexpectedly into leadership roles during a crisis. It is difficult to predict who will emerge as a leader at the scene of a bombing, or an active shooter, or a train derailment. Sometimes, the person who you would least expect to rise to the occasion is the one who does—and conversely, sometimes the persons who we expect to take on the leadership role do not. The formation of leadership roles at the onset of critical incidents often happens organically. That is to say that the leadership at the early stages of critical incidents is often of an informal nature, whereas it is likely that leadership behaviors will emerge from some of the people at the beginning of a critical incident that is not the same thing as an established *command*.

The concept of *command* is defined as the formalization of the leadership function. That formalization could come in the form of rank insignia, or a uniform, or any other recognizable symbol that clearly delineates the authority of the persons in those leadership roles. Command is also formalized by organizational charts such as those in the Incident Command System. In ancient warfare, kings and generals were clearly identified by coat of arms, flags, and regalia, which provided the visual symbolism as the organizing principle that soldiers rallied around. ICS provides the structure and symbolism that clearly defines leadership during a critical incident. Key to the success of any incident resolution is that every participant be aware of their role and position in relation to everyone else. A formal organizational chart makes it clear to everyone as to who reports to whom, and it provides the "big picture" of what everyone's purpose is. As such, a clearly defined organizational structure is imperative for an effective response to critical incidents.

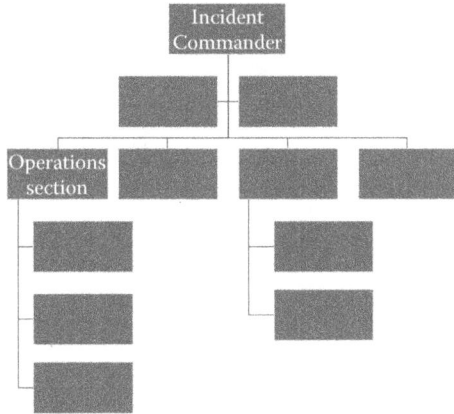

Photo 3.3 Incident Commander (Photo by Robert Rose—August 28, 2011. Courtesy of FEMA, Westminster, Vermont, August 29, 2011—Incident Commander and Westminster Fire Chief, Cole Streeter, observes damage caused by flash flooding following Tropical Storm Irene in the state of Vermont. FEMA provides funds to help homeowners recover from a disaster. Location: Westminster, Vermont.)

The Stages of a Critical Incident Response

Earlier, we identified the three phases of critical incident management: preparedness, response, and recovery—or more simply put—things we do before, during, and after an incident. In this section, we will focus on the response phase and further break down the things we do during an incident into five identifiable stages: initial onset, first response, the dust settles, incident resolution, and post-incident review.

Stage 1: Initial onset. Every incident has a beginning. For some incidents such as bomb explosions, shootings, train derailments, and tornadoes, the initial onset is very clear. For others that develop more slowly such as hurricanes, the onset is not as clear. Does a hurricane begin when it attains hurricane status (74-mile-per-hour winds), or does it begin when a hurricane watch or warning is declared, or when the gale force winds are first recorded on land, or when the eye makes landfall? In truth, it really doesn't matter. It starts when you say it starts. The initial onset stage, like all the other stages, is meant to be a conceptual construct to help us better understand things. Real life has very few clear-cut boundaries, especially those between temporal phases or stages. By definition, Stage 1 begins when an orderly state becomes chaotic. The initial onset is when things are most chaotic and uncertain. At this stage, the situation is likely to be unmanageable. Unless the incident occurs during a preplanned event, the incident manager will likely not be on the scene during this phase, therefore there will likely be an absence of command at this point.

We like to use the metaphor of an explosion to describe the five stages of incident response because the visualization of an outward explosion provides the best

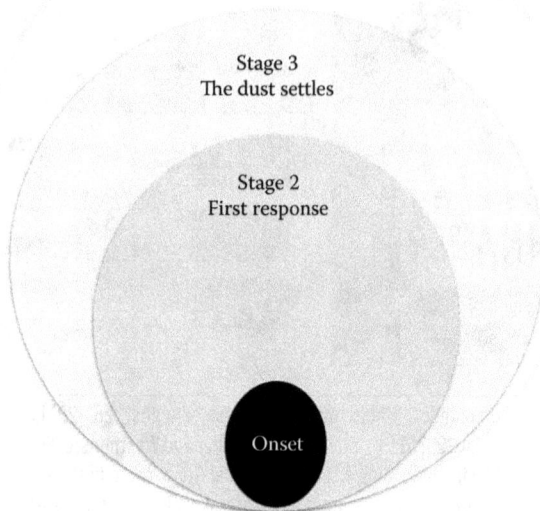

Figure 3.5 Stages of a Critical Incident (Developed by Eloy Nuñez and Ernest G. Vendrell.)

description of what these five stages entail. Figure 3.5 illustrates the initial onset stage as if it was the point of detonation of a bomb. Explosions expand quickly, and continue moving outwardly until something stops them. Conceptually, this illustration can be applied to any critical incident.

Stage 2: First response. Stage 2 starts when people begin the initial attempts to restore order to a chaotic situation. This may include the efforts of first responders or untrained civilians on the scene. At this stage chaos and uncertainty remain high, and complexity grows as more responders arrive on the scene. The prime objective for first responders and critical incident managers in this stage is containment: in other words—to keep the threat from getting bigger or worse. This stage ends when the threat is contained, and the incident is no longer getting bigger.

Stage 3: The dust settles. This stage begins when the threat is effectively contained, but not yet neutralized. That means that the threat is not likely to get outside the containment area, but that it could still cause harm within the contained area. We call this the "dust settles" stage because although the danger still exists, at least things are not getting any worse. Things finally begin to settle down. The incident manager's objective in this stage changes from containment of the threat to actively neutralizing the threat. This is the stage where the incident manager begins to restore order and certainty. Typically, most of the time devoted to the resolution of an incident occurs during this stage. An extreme example of a very prolonged Stage 3 was evidenced in the Branch Davidian Standoff in Waco, Texas from February 28 to April 19, 1993, which took 51 days to bring the incident to an end.[11]

Stage 4: Incident resolution. This stage begins when the threat is effectively neutralized; however, the incident is not over because there is still a lot of work to be done. One example of things that occur in Stage 4 is when the tactical teams do a secondary search after the hostage taker has been placed into custody or shot dead. The known threat has been neutralized, but as an extra precaution, the tactical teams will conduct a secondary search before releasing the scene in case a previously unknown threat is still there.

Another example of the types of actions that occur in this stage is that of crime scene technicians processing the scene after the threat has been neutralized. Clearly, after the threat has been dealt with, there are still a lot of things that need to be done. Stage 4 does not conclude until the entire scene is cleaned up and returned to the previous state of normalcy.

Stage 5: Post-incident review. This is the stage where post-incident reviews and after-action reports are conducted. This stage is actually part of the recovery phase of the things that we do after an incident. We mention it here as the fifth stage of the response phase because in real life there are often overlaps where Step 4 actions and Step 5 actions are done concurrently. For example, after the resolution of a hostage call in which the hostage taker was shot and killed by the tactical team, the team will have an on-scene debriefing (also referred to as "hot washes") immediately afterward while the memory of the incident is still fresh. Meanwhile, homicide investigators and crime scene technicians have just begun their part of the incident resolution. In essence, the SWAT team is in Stage 5, but the homicide investigators and crime scene techs are still in Stage 4. The post-incident review process may take hours, days, weeks, months, and even years, depending on the scope and complexity of the incident.

The Fundamental Principles for Planning Events

There are things we know that we know. There are known unknowns. That is to say, there are things that we now know we don't know. But there are also unknown unknowns. There are things we don't know we don't know.[12]

—Former Secretary of Defense, Donald Rumsfeld

The study of spontaneously occurring incidents provides us with a context to better understand the response phase of critical incident management. Similarly, the examination of preplanned events provides us with a context where we can better understand the things we do before, and after an incident, or event. That is not to say that we cannot plan for spontaneous incidents. As discussed in Chapter 1, we can plan and prepare for unanticipated incidents, but planning for an event where the time and place is known ahead of time is different from the planning for an unanticipated incident where the time and place are not known. The principles of operational planning for events and incidents are similar, except that

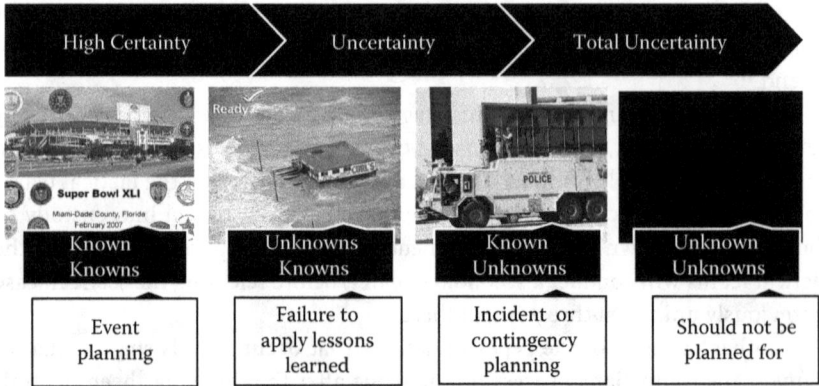

Figure 3.6 Uncertainty Scale (Credits: Known Knowns: Photograph by Eloy Nuñez; Unknown Knowns: [Photograph by Jana Baldwin—December 15, 2015—FEMA Collection https://www.fema.gov/media-library/assets/images; Known Unknowns: Photograph by Lynn Scrimshaw, Courtesy of the Miami-Dade Police Department.)

planning for events focuses on the "known knowns," while planning for unanticipated spontaneous incidents focuses on the "known unknowns."[13]

Figure 3.6 illustrates how uncertainty affects the way we plan for events and incidents. For special events, we are dealing in the realm of the "known knowns." We know the time, date, and location of the event, so therefore we can use timelines and maps to help us plan the event. Having this knowledge ahead of time gives the planners a huge advantage. It allows the planners to take steps to mitigate likely threats and to address the most obvious vulnerabilities. Planners of special events can take steps to control access in and out of the area of operations, therefore minimizing risk. Special event planners have the advantage of being able to preselect the locations of their command posts, staging areas, logistics, First Amendment zones, joint information centers, triage areas, decontamination areas, and more. In essence, planners of special events have the advantage by being able to minimize their own uncertainty, while increasing their adversaries' uncertainty.

That is not to say that special event planners will have absolute certainty, or that they can control every possible circumstance. That is why every special event plan must take into account the "known unknowns" and plan for foreseeable incidents that *may* occur during the event. Planning for the known unknowns is called contingency planning. No one can predict the future with absolute certainty, but it is reasonable to expect that things that have happened in the past could happen again in the future. It is reasonable and prudent for planners to account for certain unanticipated incidents to happen during anticipated events. For example, an event planner may not have specific intelligence of an attack being planned by terrorists, but given the generalized threats against the entire Western civilization from al Qaida and the Islamic State organizations, it would behoove the planners to account for the possibility of such an attack, and to make certain sensible precautions such as buffer zone setbacks, canine explosive sweeps, and having strict credentialing procedures and access control for the event.

Does that mean that special event planners need to account for every possible threat? The answer to that of course, is no. While it is reasonable to plan for the "known unknowns," it is not reasonable, or cost effective to plan for the "unknown unknowns." For example, would it be smart to plan for the possibility of protestors showing up for a presidential debate, even if no intelligence exists of a specific protest being planned for the event? Most would agree that this is an example of a known unknown, and should be planned for as a contingency. On the other hand, would it be reasonable for the organizers of a Rotary fundraising event to plan for protests when there has never been a protest at such an event, nor is there any information indicating that a protest is likely? Most would agree that it would be unreasonable to account for such an unlikely unknown unknown.

The fourth level of certainty *not* mentioned by Former Defense Secretary Donald Rumsfeld is that of the "unknown knowns." The philosopher Slavoj Žižek refers to "unknown knowns" as practices that we pretend not to know about.[14] In other words, these are things that we should be aware of, but that we choose to willfully ignore, or to carelessly disregard. In the realm of critical incident management, an example of *unknown knowns* would be how some planners ignore or fail to acknowledge the existence of after-action reports that identify the errors made by previous planners, and the lessons learned from those errors, as well as the best practices established from previous successes. The phenomenon of unknown knowns is a failure to apply the lessons learned from others who have already experienced similar situations. This, unfortunately, is a more common occurrence than it should be. So often, after-action reports are written and then filed away, or put on a shelf, never to be read by anyone. Sometimes, the failure to apply the lessons learned from others has to do with the lack of due diligence on the part of the event planner. Other times, it is due to the hubris of the planner, and not wanting to learn from others. More often than not, it is just plain lack of awareness by the event planner that others may have already experienced what the event planner is now facing. Either way, this inability or unwillingness of learning from the past errors and successes of others puts us in the position of making the same mistakes over and over. It also leaves the planners and executors of special events with many missed opportunities. The topic of institutional learning and the passing of lessons learned and best practices will be covered in greater depth in Chapter 7.

Murphy's Law and Contingency Planning

It is reasonable to expect that in every preplanned special event, there is a likelihood that unanticipated problems will occur. Sometimes there are unanticipated benefits as well. We will discuss the concept of unanticipated benefits later in Chapter 7, which deals with the innovation process, but for now we will focus on the things that go bad.

The acceptance of things going bad during an event or incident has become part of our common folklore. We commonly refer to the phenomenon of *Murphy's Law* in which "If anything can go wrong, it will." The acceptance of Murphy's Law is a tacit admission of our inability to foresee every possible outcome and to control every possible factor. Most of us have participated in or observed a well-planned event that did not turn out as well as expected due to unanticipated circumstances occurring. The notion of things turning bad unexpectedly goes back a long way. The Scottish poet Robert Burns wrote in his 1785 poem *To a Mouse*:

> But Mousie, thou art no thy-lane,
> In proving foresight may be vain:
> The best laid schemes o' Mice an' Men
> > Gang aft agley (go astray)
> An' lea'e us nought but grief an' pain,
> > For promis'd joy!

This poem is all about humility. The comparison of men to mice in the line: "the best laid schemes (or plans) of mice and men" going astray reminds us that we are not that much different from the smallest of animals. This is a reminder of how insignificant our species can be in relation to the power of nature. Plans that go astray can happen to the lowest creatures (mice), and to men as well. The line: "In proving foresight may be vain," shows that even when the mouse (or the man) can see things coming ahead of time, they still may not be able to avoid a catastrophe. Understanding this notion—that even with ample warning and good planning things can still turn out bad—is one of the most important principles of event or incident planning.

Contingency planning is the term used to describe the planning that we do ahead of time to minimize the probability of something adverse occurring—and if it does occur, to mitigate the effects from it. Contingency planning is what we do in anticipation of Murphy's Law. For even in preplanned events, where we can control the factors of time and place, there are likely to be unanticipated incidents occurring within the event that we need to account for. Contingency plans should be a subset of the overall event plan. In essence, the event plan is about controlling the "known knowns," while contingency planning is about reacting to the unanticipated "known unknowns." In simple terms, contingency planning is about having the flexibility to make mid-course corrections to adapt to unanticipated threats. Examples of contingency planning include, but are not limited to, the design of redundant systems in aircraft, continuation of operations plans (COOP) for organizations, and the staffing of extra personnel to act as a rapid response unit during a civil disturbance.

Let's now refer back to Figure 3.6, where on the far right of the continuum, the uncertainty is complete. This is the realm of the "unknown unknowns." It is difficult, if not impossible to plan for the things we do not know about, or cannot even think about. This is different from the "failure of imagination" that was reported by the 9/11 Commission.[15] The use of hijacked aircraft as man-guided explosive devices against the World Trade Center (WTC) towers could have and should have been foreseen. After all, explosive-laden vehicles had been used by terrorists for years, including the 1993 truck bomb attack against the very same WTC target. Likewise, aircraft had been hijacked before. It is certainly not a leap of faith to have envisioned the possibility of an attack such as those on September 11. The use of hijacked aircraft to crash into buildings is an example of a "known unknown" that should have been planned for on a contingency basis. The authorities may not have known ahead of time of the specific attack, but they should have known of the possibility of such an attack. As noted in Figure 3.6, these types of "known unknown" attacks can and should be planned for. An example of a contingency plan to deal with the generalized threat from hijacked aircraft is the temporary flight restrictions (TFRs) that are imposed during certain large-scale special events such as Super Bowls or presidential debates. This is a prudent step that the event planners should take, even if there is no specific knowledge of an imminent attack.

By contrast, planning for the "unknown unknown" is virtually impossible. That is because the planners have no way of knowing what they do not know, and therefore cannot begin to think of ways to mitigate the threat. It is impossible to try to imagine every threat or delivery mechanism for the threat. Some people can dream up outlandish scenarios, which sometimes come true in real life. When that happens, some critics (with the benefit of hindsight) will claim that the incident was foreseeable, and that steps should have been taken to prevent the incident from occurring. Such criticism is unfair and unwarranted. If something has never happened before, there would be no point of reference for the planners to start from. Moreover, it would make very little economic sense for planners to spend money and resources on something that has never happened before, and that there is no indication will ever happen. Contingency planning is appropriate for the "known unknowns" but not for the "unknown unknowns."

Nine Steps of Pre-Event Operations Planning

Chapter 8 will take a close look at a 31-item list of things to do for the planning of a large-scale special event. This comprehensive list encompasses the planning that takes place at the tactical, operational, and strategic spheres of command. Not all events are the same, but the core principles of planning can be applied to many types of events, ranging from small town Fourth of July parades to very large events such as multinational economic forums, presidential debates, or Super Bowls. For now in Chapter 3, we will focus on a few basic steps that critical incident managers should take for the planning of special events at the operational level.

The nine steps of operational pre-event planning for special events are the following:

Step 1: Conduct a Threat Assessment
Step 2: Meet with Event Organizers and Stakeholders

Step 3: Conduct a Site Survey (Vulnerability Assessment)
Step 4: Develop a Site Plan
Step 5: Develop a Crowd Control Plan
Step 6: Determine Necessary Resources
Step 7: Develop an Organizational Chart
Step 8: Assign Specific Personnel
Step 9: Conduct Training and Rehearsals

Step 1: Conduct a Threat Assessment

We discussed earlier in Chapter 2 how threats can be natural, man-made accidental, or man-made intentional. Threat assessments that are conducted in the planning stages of a special event should take into account all three of these basic types of threats, no matter whether the event is small or large. In very large and complex events such as political conventions, threat assessments are usually conducted by intelligence analysts working in a fusion center, or on a Joint Terrorism Task Force (JTTF). Threat assessments for smaller events tend to be conducted by the incident commander or his/her appointed staff.

Obviously, the weather plays a role in most special event planning, especially those that take place outdoors. For communities located on the east coast, or in proximity to the Gulf of Mexico, hurricanes during season must always be accounted for in the planning. For example, planners of the 2012 Republican National Convention in Tampa, Florida, had to adjust their plans in order to react to the possibility of Hurricane Isaac making landfall around the time and place of the convention week. Even though the hurricane did not make a direct impact on the Tampa Bay area, it came close enough to affect the weather, and for planners to change the itinerary so that the convention had to briefly convene on the Monday as planned, but the activities originally planned for Tuesday had to be postponed.[16] While Hurricane Isaac forced planners to make mid-course adjustments, it also provided an unforeseen and unintended benefit in that it kept many nonlocal protestors away, and thus helped the Tampa Police Department manage the civil unrest that often accompanies these major political conventions.

Accounting for natural and man-made accidental threats is much easier than accounting for man-made intentional threats. Rarely do event planners get information about an imminent and specific terrorist attack targeting their event. When this does happen, the event planners and policy makers may consider cancelling the event, or taking preemptive action to arrest the plotters. More common is the generalized threat of terrorism during an event where a large crowd of people gather. As we saw with the 2013 Boston Marathon bombings, large crowds and the presence of live television broadcasts make such events very attractive for terrorists who want to get the "biggest bang for the buck" for their actions. The large crowds make it easier for them to kill more people with less effort on their part. More significantly, the presence of live broadcast media provides the terrorists with the "free" dissemination of the imagery associated with the terror attack. Today, any event that brings large numbers of people to a specific place and time is a tempting target for terrorists. Small town parades and festivals are not immune from the threat of terrorism. Lesser security makes these "soft target" events more enticing to persons considering a terror attack. Terrorists and criminals make their own risk calculations, much in the same way that we do. While a brazen attack on New York City's Time Square during the New Year's Eve celebration would be a huge win for terrorists, they also know that they face the challenges of increased security, and thus the likelihood of success would be less than it would be for a soft target such as a Fourth of July celebration at a park in Topeka, Kansas. Just like we have to calculate trade-offs, so do the bad guys.

Unless we have specific knowledge of an imminent attack, planning for the possibility of terrorism during a special event is an example of Rumsfeld's "known unknowns." Nowadays, it is prudent to consider and plan for these types of attack at all large gatherings. The U.S. Department of Homeland Security now issues advisory alerts to the affected law enforcement agencies, or sometimes directly to the public via email or social media whenever there are credible or specific, and impending terrorist threats against the United States. The National Terrorism Advisory System (NTAS) issues "Elevated Threat Alerts" to warn the public of credible terrorist threats. An even higher advisory level is the "Imminent Threat Alert" which warns the public in instances where there exists a "credible, specific, and impending terrorist threat against the United States."[16]

The NTAS took the place of the ill-conceived color-coded Homeland Security Advisory System that had been established shortly after the September 11 attacks of 2001. That system was comprised of five color-coded levels of risk, ranging from "low risk" green, to "guarded risk" in blue, to "elevated risk" in yellow, to "high risk" in orange, and "severe risk" in red. This system caused more harm than good because the risk levels were poorly defined and thus resulted in confusion and the expensive deployment of resources when no threats actually existed. Very few people, including law enforcement agencies, knew exactly what they were supposed to do in the face of such ambiguous threats. The biggest weakness of this color-coded system was when the perceived risk subsided. For policy makers, it made political sense to raise the risk level whenever there was a credible threat. However, the problem they faced was when it was time to lower the risk level. No policy maker or politician wants to be the one who lowers the risk level from red to yellow, and then an actual attack occurs shortly thereafter. The accusations of incompetence would be pervasive if such an incident were to occur immediately after the risk level was lowered. In other words, it was a lot easier to raise the risk level than it was to lower it. That was the inherent weakness of the color-code threat advisory system. By contrast, the new system has a "sunset provision" whereby the threat advisory is issued for a specific time period and then automatically expires. This relieves the policy makers of having to lower the threat levels and risking public ridicule should an attack occur immediately after the announcement to lower the level is made. This sunset provision is perhaps the best aspect of the new warning system. The Department of Homeland Security's NTAS provides a Daily Open Source Infrastructure Report to the general public.

There are four major sections of the report, which cover *production industries* (energy; chemical; nuclear reactors, materials and waste; critical manufacturing; defense industrial base; and dams); *sustenance and health* (food and agriculture; water and wastewater systems; healthcare and public health); *service industries* (financial services; transportation systems; information technology; communications; and commercial facilities); and *federal and state* (government facilities and emergency services). You can receive this report via email on a daily basis by requesting it online on the DHS website http://www.dhs.gov/ntas-public-guide.

Terrorism is not the only man-made threat that could cause harm during a special event. There are other disruptive individuals and organizations that need to be accounted for. Special events which have large gatherings of people, and which are broadcast live on television and on the Internet, tend to attract protestors. There are countless organizations that regularly attend such gatherings in order to make a political or social point and have their message conveyed by the media who are covering the event. It is a relatively inexpensive way of getting one's message disseminated widely to the public.

There are too many protest organizations to name in this book. Some are environmental and animal rights groups. Others represent "fair trade" and antiglobalization agendas. These groups are as varied as are the social and economic grievances that they protest against. Some of the organizations are large such as the Teamsters Union with 1.4 million members,[17] or the AFL-CIO with 12.5 million members.[18] Other self-proclaimed protest organizations have only a handful of members.

Organizations span the entire political spectrum, with far-right and far-left groups, and everything in between. The political affiliation of these organizations is not relevant to the event planner. What matters most is the groups' past behavior. Past behavior is a good indicator of future behavior. Successful event planners use market segmenting strategies similar to the practices used by businesses to identify their customer base. Businesses realize that not all customers are the same. Similarly, special event planners must realize that not all protestors are the same. Some protest groups are nonviolent and compliant. Others are nonviolent, but not compliant. Others have demonstrated a history of being violent. For the sake of simplicity, we like to use a color code to categorize these three common types of behaviors. Figure 3.7 illustrates the "market segmentation" approach using colors to identify the predominant behaviors of certain protest groups. The color red is used to signify groups that predominantly rely on violent tactics. Most notable among the red groups are the various organizations that claim to be anarchists. Members of these groups come to events with the specific intent of destroying property and causing injury to others. These individuals tend to be armed with knives, slingshot, Molotov cocktails, or will acquire weapons of opportunity such as rocks, bottles, large dumpsters, and telephone poles as ramming devices. Members of red groups can be easily identified because they often wear gas masks, body padding and other protective equipment in anticipation of a clash with police. Red groups come ready for a fight and create many challenges for law enforcement agencies.

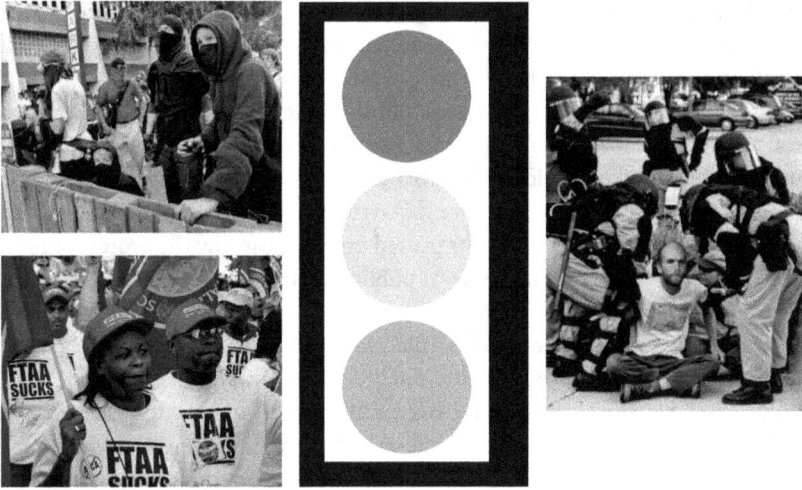

Figure 3.7 Green Yellow and Red Behaviors (Courtesy of the Miami-Dade Police Department. Photographs by Lynn Scrimshaw.)

The color yellow is used to categorize the market segment of protestors that use peaceful but noncompliant tactics. While yellow groups do not pose the threat that violent red groups do, their noncompliance tactics pose a different set of unique problems to law enforcement officials. A prime example of yellow groups is evidenced with the Occupy Wall Street movement that started from a simple blog post in July of 2011 and quickly spread throughout the United States and around the world.[19]

Although there were some instances of violence, for the most part the main tactic of the Occupy Wall Street Movement was simply to occupy space on public and private land. Protestors camped out on the streets and parks in many cities. When the police were called to remove the protestors, the protestors used techniques of noncompliance such as sitting on the ground while clasping each other's arms to form a chain of nonviolent resistance. This tactic causes problems for the police because they are forced to disentangle the protestors one at a time, often resorting to nonlethal pain compliance techniques in order to handcuff and arrest them. This can be exhausting work for the officers who have to separate, handcuff, and then pick up the dead weight of each noncompliant protestor who refuses to walk to the awaiting paddy wagon. Police officers have to remain mindful that any overt use of force such as pain compliance techniques or pepper spray will likely result in loud complaints from the protestors being arrested. It is also likely that the incident will be videotaped by the many onlookers at the scene with cell phone cameras.

To make things even more difficult for the police, some protestors will chain themselves to fences or to each other with locks or handcuffs. Others use the "sleeping dragon" technique, whereby protestors chain themselves together and cover the chains with PVC pipes to make it more difficult for the police to separate them. Police have adapted to these techniques by implementing specially trained and equipped CUT teams that use power saws to defeat the obstructions, while safely separating the protestors. While these CUT teams have improved the arresting officers' efficiency and reduced the likelihood of injuries to the protestors, they still take considerable effort and time to get it done. Yellow protest groups put a heavy burden on police departments. Moreover, the imagery from the hundreds of videos of the arrests posted online is used by the protest organizers to gain sympathy from the general public and to recruit more individuals to their organizations. An organization named the *Ruckus Society,* which was established in 1995 out of Oakland, California, claims to work closely with 43 partner organizations, including *Greenpeace, Earth First*, and the *War Resisters League*. The Ruckus Society claims to have over 100 trainers and volunteers who provide training and action support to like-minded organizations and individuals. According to their website, the Ruckus Society promotes and teaches the "implementation of strategic nonviolent direct action against unjust institutions and policies."[20] In addition to the training camps where these protestors are taught the techniques of passive resistance, the organization also publishes a number of informational manuals, including a 14-page Scouting Manual for Activists, which is available for download on their website.

The third category of protestors in our market segmentation typology is identified by the color green. Green protestors are neither violent nor do they use the passive resistance techniques that the yellow groups use. These groups attend parades and rallies and often carry signs and placards. They may be vocal and loud, but they are peaceful and compliant with the law, and they disperse when given lawful dispersal orders by the police. The color green is used to identify these peaceful protestors, but it has nothing to do with the common use of the word "green" to describe environmental issues. In this typology, the color green simply corresponds to the green light of a typical traffic signal in relation to the amber and red lights. In this context, green means "go" and serves as a reminder to police officers that these peaceful protestors have the legal right to protest, and that their right should not be impeded by police action.

The color-coded typology that corresponds with the colors of a traffic signal provides a simple and easy to remember market segmentation analysis of the protest groups that are likely to come to mass gatherings of people during special events. This typology helps us to understand that the protestors are not a monolithic bloc. It would be a mistake for police to treat all protestors the same. Some of their actions are legal, and some are not. The typology helps us to better understand the challenges posed by protest groups at mass gatherings and how to react accordingly. The practice of the police using a specific approach to react to the specific tactics used by protestors is called *situation-driven tactical approach*, and is based on the concepts in contingency and situational theories of leadership as espoused by Fiedler,[21] Hersey and Blanchard,[22] and others. The situation-driven tactical approach is akin to picking the right tool out of a toolbox in order to fix a problem. It would be foolish to select an adjustable crescent wrench from the toolbox in order to pound a nail. Likewise, it would be foolish for the police commander who is faced with a certain type of protestor to choose the wrong approach to deal with those protestors. For example, sending regular uniformed police officers with no helmets, padding, or shielding to counter the actions of a violent red group would imperil the officers and would probably not work. This would be a severe underreaction that could make things worse instead of better. On the other hand, sending in a mobile field force of heavily armed and protected riot officers to disperse a peaceful rally would be a gross overreaction, and could lead to an unwanted escalation of the situation. The effective management of protestors requires the right tool and tactics at the right time. That is easier said than done because it is possible that members of different groups mix together in a large crowd, making the distinction of the different market segments more difficult. Moreover, event planners need to account for the possibility that peaceful protests can quickly morph into violent ones when the different groups mix with each other. Red groups like to mix into larger green groups for their own protection, and also as a force maximizer by appearing to be bigger than they really are. It is because of this that escalation from nonviolent behavior to violent behavior of the combined groups becomes more likely. The challenge to police commanders comes in recognizing the various groups, and understanding their intentions. There are several ways that police commanders can do this, but one that is often neglected is to meet with the leaders of the groups ahead of time, whenever possible. The next section covers this important step.

Step 2: Meet with Event Organizers and Stakeholders

Meeting with the organizers of an event is one of the first things that an incident commander and his staff should do. For example, when local agencies prepare for a Super Bowl about a year and a half before the event, it is a standard practice for the agency's leaders and assigned incident commander to meet with representatives of the National Football League (NFL) security, as well as the Host Committee representatives. This initial meeting is crucial for the "feeling out" process whereby the participants get to know each other and to exchange contact information. This is an important first step that helps everyone understand each other's roles and capabilities. A large-scale event such as a Super Bowl is a massive undertaking that involves hundreds of people in the planning process. Among those hundreds of planners, there is typically a core group of four to six individuals who play a key role in the planning process. The early meeting and establishment of clear objectives among those core individuals is integral to the success of the event.

The initial meeting of the core planners and stakeholders should not be the end of the interactive process that goes all the way through the event, and should continue after the event is over. For smaller events such as Fourth of July fireworks or holiday parades, the meetings may be brief and involve only a few stakeholders. For larger events such as a Super Bowl or a major political convention, the meetings are conducted often and involve multiple subcommittees to address the various complex issues associated with large events. For example, there may be subcommittees that plan for the mass evacuations, decontamination, and treatment of victims in the event of a mass casualty incident. Another subcommittee may arise for the discussion of total flight restrictions over the venue. Yet another subcommittee may be formed to plan for response to CBRNE (chemical, biological, radiological, nuclear, and explosive) attacks. Another may be formed to deal with protests, civil disturbances, and mass arrest situations. The number and type of committees that are formed will depend on the size and complexity of the event. For a small town Fourth of July fireworks festival, the initial planning meeting may just involve the town manager and a police sergeant or lieutenant representing the local police department. There is no need to overcomplicate things. The more people involved in the planning process, the more chance there will be miscommunications between those involved. The basic rule of thumb is, if the event is small—keep it simple. If the event is very large and complex, then the number of planners will need to expand out of necessity. For very large events, no one person can be expected to do all the planning by themselves.

One important reason for meeting with the various stakeholders is to listen to each other's expectations. That means listening to what others' expectations are of you, and also letting them know what your expectations of them are. The more this is done ahead of time, the less the chances are of misunderstandings happening later. In other words, the purpose of the meetings with the stakeholders prior to the event is to minimize uncertainty. Most incident commanders will meet with event planners and partner organizations. However, the concept should extend to adversarial stakeholders as well. One example of this was when Tampa Police Department Assistant Chief John Bennett and his staff met with media attorneys and attended three ACLU forums prior to the 2012 Republican National Convention in Tampa, Florida. Chief Bennett's progressive approach for meeting with potential adversaries ahead of the event was credited by many for minimizing the number of violent confrontations between the police and protestors that had been experienced at prior political conventions in New York City and St. Paul, Minnesota.[23]

The Miami-Dade Police Department (MDPD) conceived the idea of the Special Event Response Teams (SERTs) in 1993 in anticipation of the political demonstrations by opposing groups for the Summit of the Americas the following year. Prior to this event, there had been several skirmishes between pro-Castro and anti-Castro protestors that had made the news. One highly publicized melee at Miami International Airport was recorded by television stations and brought considerable criticism to MDPD for failing to take the necessary steps to separate the two opposing groups. These skirmishes usually involved just a few individuals, and did not rise to the level where mobile field force riot police were needed to quell them. On the other hand, the regular patrol officers at the airport were not trained or equipped to deal with these types of skirmishes. As a result, the SERT concept was born as an intermediate step between regular patrol and a full blown mobile field force deployment. With SERT teams, the officers would be dressed in regular patrol uniforms, rather than in riot gear. However, they would receive special training on conflict resolution between two opposing groups of protestors. One of the important tenets of SERT was that the leaders would meet with the protest organizers prior to the event in order to discuss the expectations of all parties involved. Whenever there are two or more groups of protestors at the same event which are expected to be diametrically opposed, then the planners need to take steps to ensure that the opposing groups are kept apart from each other. In order to do that, it was important that special sections be delineated with bicycle style "French" barricades, with a buffer zone separating the two groups. The meetings between the SERT commanders and the opposing groups' leaders in advance of the event proved to be critical for establishing these clear parameters and expectations. It is important to note the SERT commander (or any other incident commander) should meet with the opposing groups separately, at different times. It is not a good idea to meet the leaders of the two groups at the same time because invariably there will be a conflict during the meeting. The SERT commander should meet them separately, and must ensure that he or she is perceived as an impartial intermediary. It would be counterproductive if one side perceives that the police are playing favorites.

There is one last thing about the pre-event meetings with stakeholders. Obviously, not every adversary is willing to meet with the police, nor should the police meet with all groups. Terrorist organizations would not want to meet with the police, nor would the police want to meet with them (other than to arrest them). Typically, police commanders would meet with green and yellow types of protestors, and not with the red types. Pre-event meetings with adversarial stakeholders are solely for the exchange of expectations between the groups. They are not meant to be a friendly exchange of pleasantries. Let's not forget that the intent is to explore mutual interests, and to clearly delineate each other's expectations in order to minimize surprises during the actual event. At no time should the police commander allow him/herself to lose any advantage that they may hold. This includes the tight control of any information that if inadvertently leaked by the police commander would give one of the groups a competitive advantage over the other, or over the police. In conclusion, these meetings are not supposed to be friendly. The exchanges between parties should be cordial and businesslike. At all times, the police commander needs to maintain authority and control over the meeting.

Step 3: Conduct a Site Survey (Vulnerability Assessment)

A site survey can be something as simple as a quick walk-thru of the event venue by the incident commander and his team prior to the event, or can be as complex as a comprehensive vulnerability assessment conducted by subject-matter experts. Obviously, the bigger and more complex the event, the more involved the site survey should be. The site survey not only reveals possible vulnerabilities of the event venue, but it also sets the stage for the development of the site plan in Step 4. The following passage was taken from the Ruckus Society's *Scouting Manual for Activists* for pointers on what the site survey should be from the perspective of the protestors.[24]

> A scout should provide information that will allow her (or the coordinator, if different) to evaluate site access, security, the kind of image the action will provide (especially relevant if visual messaging is important), safety concerns, and probability of success. Thinking about weather, lighting, finding useful symbols or signage, and understanding traffic and security patterns are all concerns that are critical for action planning. Experienced scouts and action coordinators can look at the site and visualize the action unfolding.

The site surveys for police and fire-rescue commanders are no different than the site surveys that the adversaries do. They may see things from the opposite perspective, but experienced commanders who conduct site surveys can also visualize the action unfolding. The *Scouting Manual for Activists* explains how online services such as *Google Maps*, *Google Earth*, and *Microsoft Bing Maps 3D* are useful tools that are available to the general public. Getting an aerial perspective of the site prior to visiting it can be very useful. The measuring tool in Google Earth is especially useful for planners. The "street view" feature of these online programs is also a useful tool for getting a ground-level perspective of the site prior to visiting it. Nevertheless, physically visiting the site allows the commanders to gain a perspective that would otherwise not be available through the street view feature. The use of maps and satellite photography are useful, but they are no substitute for physically walking the site and using all the senses to get a feeling for what is likely to occur.

Step 4: Develop a Site Plan

The satellite photography from Google Maps and Google Earth can be used to provide the underlying layer of the basic site plan for the event. Simple and commonly used programs such as Microsoft Word and Microsoft PowerPoint provide shapes (rectangles, circles, solid, and dotted lines) that can be overlaid on the background aerial photographs to create a workable site plan. Figure 3.8 is an example of how PowerPoint shapes were used to overlay the Google Maps satellite imagery of Dolphin Stadium for the 2007 Super Bowl in Miami, Florida.

Many municipalities and counties now have GIS (Geographic Information System) capabilities which provide multiple layers of information to be displayed on a single map. This information can be very useful for identifying critical infrastructure assets on, or near the site of the event.

One of the first things that needs to be done at this step is to clearly define the *area of operation* for the event. The area of operation should serve as the focal point for the planning and organization of the entire event. The area of operation may be small, such as the venue for a county fair, or it may be large, such as an entire downtown area for a major urban area like New York City. For the 2003 WTO (World Trade Organization) Conference in Cancun, Mexico, much

Figure 3.8 Google Map with PowerPoint Overlays (Photograph by Eloy Nuñez.)

of the mainland city of Cancun and the entire barrier island were designated by Mexican authorities as the area of operation. The area of operation may contain fenced-in secured exclusionary areas, or could simply be open to the public with no barriers at all, depending on the type of event.

Other important features that should be included in the site plan are buffer zone designations, locations of command posts and staging areas, traffic control posts, perimeter posts, parade routes, evacuation routes, and "First Amendment zones" where protestors are encouraged to converge. When dignitaries are part of the event, then we need to consider motorcade routes, points of entry, and emergency evacuation routes. Another important consideration in the design of the site plan that goes hand-in-hand with buffer zone protection are traffic checkpoints to control the ingress and egress of delivery vehicles. Of course, this only pertains to large-scale events that last a while and that require deliveries of goods and the entry of authorized personnel. In those situations, great care should be taken so that non-authorized vehicles cannot drive into the secured area at a high rate of speed. In 1983 in Beirut, Lebanon, 241 U.S. Marines and service personnel were killed by a terrorist truck bomb laden with approximately 2000 pounds of explosives. The terrorist drove the truck at a high rate of speed straight into the four-story building where the Marines were stationed and blew himself up.[25]

Ever since this horrific tragedy, many event planners have taken extra precautions to prevent similar incidents from occurring. An effective practice used to address the threat of an explosive-laden vehicle approaching unabated at a high rate of speed is to create a *chicane* or *serpentine* configuration for all approach roadways. Figure 3.9 illustrates the serpentine configuration with three concrete or water-filled barricades along the roadway to force all incoming vehicles to slow down as they drive around the curves. A counter sniper at the top right of the diagram ensures that any vehicle that ignores the order to stop from the security personnel positioned at the gate will be squarely in the sniper's field of fire. Other less-lethal measures can be taken, such as remotely deployed "stop sticks" to puncture the tires of any wayward vehicle in order to slow its approach. The

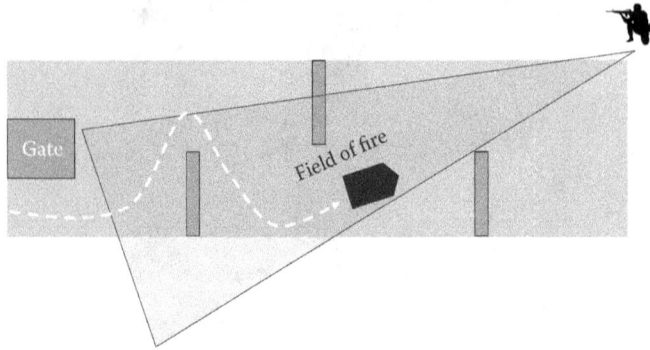

Figure 3.9 "Chicane" or Serpentine Configuration with Concrete Barriers (Developed by Eloy Nuñez and Ernest G. Vendrell.)

cone-shaped area labeled "field of fire" is also referred to as the "sacrificial area" because that is the location that the site planners have designated as the best (least harm) location for the truck bomb to detonate in the event that the terrorist decides to prematurely detonate the explosives. It is possible, and even likely that the security personnel positioned at the gate, and even the counter sniper, may sustain life-threatening injuries if this should happen, but in the realm of critical incident management, sometimes the best decision is the one with the "least worst" outcome. It is better that the explosive-laden vehicle detonates in the sacrificial area than if it explodes close to where more people have congregated.

Landing zones for helicopters and emergency medical treatment areas can also be part of the site plan. Broader aerial photographs and maps can be used to designate total flight restriction zones with concentric circles at 15 and 30 miles (or any other distance) from the center of the defined area of operations, as illustrated in Figure 3.10.

Figure 3.10 Temporary Flight Restriction (TFRs), Miami-Dade Super Bowl, 2007 (Photograph by Eloy Nuñez.)

Step 5: Develop a Crowd Control Plan

Central to all special event planning is the question of how to deal with large numbers of people congregating at the same place and time. In the site plan from Step 4, we briefly discussed some of the aspects of crowd control, such as the designation of "First Amendment" protest zones. In Step 5, we will consider in greater detail the factors involved for developing an effective crowd control plan.

Control of crowds of people starts with the determination of who is allowed access to the site, and who is not. There are two basic categories of access: *free access* and *restricted access*. There are variations of each of these categories, and many events combine more than one type. In this section, we will examine the different variations of free access and restricted access. Free access means that any person can move freely within the site. Because people can come and go as they please, there is no need for fencing, or perimeter barriers. An example of a free access event is a Veterans Day parade on Main Street in a small town or a Fourth of July fireworks show at a county park.

A variation of the free access category is the *engineered enticement approach*, whereby the event planners modify the site layout in ways that entice people to converge in a desired area, while dissuading them from converging in an undesired area. The First Amendment zones mentioned earlier are an example of an engineered enticement approach. This is where planners identify and set aside an area where they hope to persuade protestors to converge. Planners do this by engineering the site plan in ways that appeal to the protestors' lower- and higher-end needs. For example, an event planner can appeal to the protestors' basic needs by setting aside an area that has sufficient shade or shelter from the rain. Having restroom facilities and providing drinking water are also good ways to entice people to a certain location. For the 2003 WTO Conference, the Mexican authorities allowed many of the protestors from out of town to camp for free at a city park and at a baseball stadium near the location of where they wanted the protestors to protest. Some may criticize the Mexicans for collaborating with the adversaries by allowing the out-of-town protestors to squat for an entire week at these two public locations, but in effect, it was a very smart thing to do. By setting aside these areas, and making them a comfortable place to camp out, the authorities kept the protestors 5 miles away from the center of the restricted area on the barrier island of Cancun. Moreover, both of the campsites were located within visual range of a police station building. This allowed the authorities to survive and monitor the movement of the protestors from the comfort of their air-conditioned police building.

The flip side to enticing protestors to a desired location by providing them comfort is the practice of dissuading people from going to places that you want to keep them out of by making the area very uncomfortable. Extreme heat or extreme cold weather can help dissuade people from congregating in a certain place. These two factors work best when the contrast between the two is made clear to the people that you intend to entice.

In addition to appealing to people's lower-end needs, higher-end enticements can also be helpful. For example, it is a good idea to consider the underlying motives of the protestors and why they intend to attend the event in the first place. More than likely, protestors want to be in the thick of things, and they want to be seen and heard. If they perceive that they are too far from the main event, they will try to move closer. Event planners can modify the site plan to give the illusion to the protestors that they are nearer to the center of activity than they really are. Much of this has to do with the understanding of imagery and symbolism. For the most part, people like to turn and face the symbolic object that they are protesting. Ideally, the site plan can be engineered in a way that provides people with an easily recognized symbol, preferably on high ground so that it can be seen from a distance. Planners can create the illusion by signifying that the event is being held in one easily recognized place, while it is actually being held in another less descript location nearby. Another thing that site planners can do to entice people to go to a certain place is to entice the television media to the desired location. Protestors want to be seen and heard, and more importantly, they want their message to be disseminated widely. The best way to do this is to be on television.

Enticing people to voluntarily converge at a certain place is similar to the concept of "if you build it, they will come," from the movie *Field of Dreams*. The trick is not only to build it, but to build it in the right place. If planners designate the First Amendment zone too close to the center of the event, then the risk to the persons inside the restricted area increases. If the First Amendment zone is too far from the center of the event, then two adverse things can happen. First, the protestors backed by groups such as the ACLU (American Civil Liberties Union) may seek an emergency injunction in court to allow them closer access. This is an eventuality that planners should try to avoid because once the courts get involved, it becomes difficult to regain control of the situation. The second thing that can happen if the First Amendment zone is designated too far from the center of the action is that the protestors simply ignore it. The trick for site planners is to hit the "Goldilocks" zone, where the designated area is not too far and not too close. Again, we recommend that site planners meet early with stakeholders (as stated in Step 2), and get a feel for what they want and expect. To a limited extent, site planners can use subterfuge and illusion to make it seem that the protestors are closer than they think; however, we caution planners to be careful in taking this approach. If during the initial meetings, the protestors feel that they are being "jerked around" (for the lack of a better word), then they will likely lose faith in the planners' authenticity, and quite possibly, the communications between the parties will break down. If that happens, then planners will have very little influence on the actions of the protestors for the remainder of the event.

One last thing about First Amendment zones. The term "First Amendment zone" is a misnomer and can be interpreted in the wrong way. The term suggests that people in the zone have First Amendment rights, while those outside do not. Obviously, that is not the case. By definition, the entire United States of America is a First Amendment zone. Event planners have the authority to restrict access to certain areas in order to ensure the public safety. However, at no time do the planners have the authority to restrict free speech. Unfortunately, "First Amendment zone" has been accepted widely as the term to describe the patch of land that is designated for protestors to muster at, but it does not truly describe what that patch of land is for. A better term for that piece of land would be "designated protest area."

Next, we will examine the *restricted access* category. There are two basic types of restricted access: *ticketed access* and *credentialed access*. Ticketed access simply means that a person has to provide a ticket to gain entry into the site of the event. Because there is no control as to who purchases, or obtains the tickets, there is no way of knowing ahead of time the identity of the persons attempting to gain entry. A ticket is basically a conditional agreement by which the attendee is granted access to the event as long as he or she consents to certain reasonable precautions imposed by the event organizers. For example, the tickets of major sporting events and concerts have fine print on the back that outlines the conditions imposed by the event organizer. One of those conditions may be that the attendee agrees to a limited search of his or her belongings. This may include a visual search at the point of entry of all bags and purses. Or it may require the attendees to leave all bags of a certain size behind. Some point of entry searches may involve airport-style security scans such as x-rays, or walk-thru or handheld magnetometer scans used to detect metallic devices.

The advantage of ticketed access is that it funnels the flow of incoming attendees to a limited number of entry points that can be used to screen the persons and their belongings. This provides a better control of access to the site, and therefore minimizes the risk. There are several disadvantages. The most obvious disadvantage is cost. In order to limit access to a few entry points, the entire perimeter of the site must be fenced or delineated by natural or man-made barriers. There are many types of fences and barriers. Typically, the more elaborate the fence system is, the more expensive it will be. Fencing can be anything from a simple chain-link fence, or a chain-link fence with barbed wire or concertina wire on top. Electrified fences add an additional layer of prevention and deterrence, but at a higher cost, and at a higher risk of unintended consequences.

History has shown us that there is no fence or barrier that cannot be breached by a determined adversary. No matter how formidable a fence or barrier may seem, it can be breached by an intruder going over, under, around, or directly through it. Photo 3.4 is an example of the typical fencing used to delineate and keep out unwanted people from the secured area of a large-scale special event. This photograph was taken in Cancun, Mexico, for the 2003 WTO Ministerial Conference. This eight-foot fence is comprised of segments that are linked together for easy setup and breakdown by the organizers. There is barbed wire on top of the fence to make it more difficult for an intruder to climb over it. The outer side has a flat base that is designed to make it more difficult for an intruder to topple the fence because the intruders would have to push against the weight of their own bodies as they stand on the base. Photo 3.5 shows the same style fencing, but reinforced

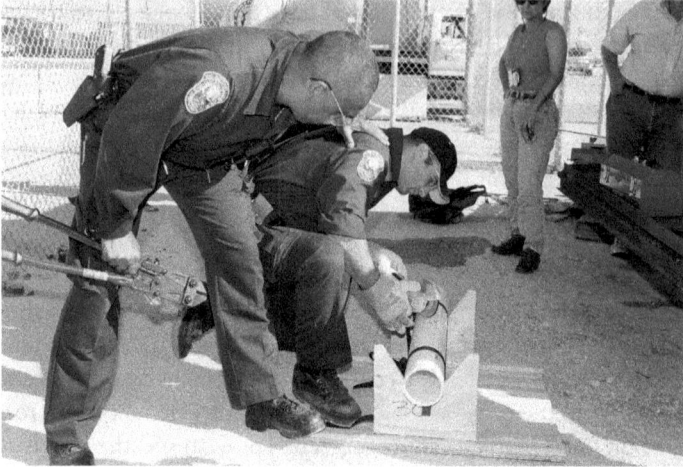

Photo 3.4 CUT Teams in Training (Courtesy of the Miami-Dade Police Department. Photograph by Lynn Scrimshaw.)

Photo 3.5 Barricade Fencing, WTO Ministerial Conference, Cancun, Mexico, 2003 (Photograph by Eloy Nuñez.)

with an extra layer of bicycle style "French" barricades arranged in a triangular manner to add extra stability to the fence line. This reinforced fence line was erected by the Mexican authorities at the critical northern entry point onto the Cancun barrier island where the WTO was being held. On the other side of the fence were an estimated 10,000 protestors staged on the mainland at Cancun City, who intended to breach the fence. Photo 3.6 shows how just a few protestors

Photo 3.6 Barricade Fencing, at Mainland Cancun City, Mexico, WTO Ministerial Conference, 2003 (Photograph by Eloy Nuñez.)

were able to breach the fence on the second day of the conference. Shortly after this photograph was taken, the entire fence collapsed on top of the police officers holding the front line. Amid the tangled mess of metal and barbed wire, many officers sustained injuries and had to be carted away to hospitals. Despite the entire fence line collapsing, the police were able to hold the line that day.

That the 10,000 protestors chose not to trespass further into the barrier island where the conference was being held probably had more to do with the distance (over 5 miles) that they would have had to walk to get to the center of the venue. A heavy police and military presence may also have been a deterrent factor. Nevertheless, the Mexican authorities were able to reconstruct the fence line the next day, about 100 yards east of the original line. This time, they doubled the width of the fence, making it seemingly impenetrable. Photo 3.7 shows the construction of that second reinforced fence line. It is not shown here, but by the fourth day of the conference, that second line was also breached with grapple hooks, ropes, and a 20-foot-long sawed-off wooden telephone pole that the protestors used as a ram. The lesson learned from this incident is that no fence or barrier will hold out intruders by itself. In order to be effective, fencing needs to be actively defended by security personnel. In this particular case, the Mexican authorities took a very passive approach and allowed the protestors to climb on the fence and attach hooks and ropes to it. Without an assertive intervention by the police, the fence was breached rapidly and easily.

The next higher level of restricted access control is called *credentialed access control*. Credentialed access control has all the benefits associated with ticketed access control, but has the added advantage of allowing the event coordinators

Photo 3.7 Barricade Fencing Breach at the Mainland in Cancun City, Mexico, WTO Ministerial Conference, 2003 (Photograph by Eloy Nuñez.)

Photo 3.8 Second Barricade Fence Line, at the Mainland in Cancun City, Mexico, WTO Ministerial Conference, 2003 (Photograph by Eloy Nuñez.)

to limit entry to specific persons whose identities are known ahead of time. Credentialed access allows the event coordinators to prescreen all persons coming into the secured area. This allows the authorities sufficient time to weed out any undesirable person who may pose a threat to the event. Doing the screening ahead of time also cuts down on backups at the point of entry and thus minimizes the errors that may occur when security guards feel rushed to get people through the line. It also creates more accountability in that the names of the attendees are accounted for, and those using a photo credential can be identified and challenged once inside the secure area. Some credentials also have computer bar codes that allow the individual to open certain doors and gates to gain further access. These bar coded credentials can be remotely disabled by security personnel from a central control room if necessary. Of course, more sensitive critical infrastructure sites such as nuclear power plants can have even more sophisticated mechanisms such as hand scans for fingerprint recognition or retina scans of the eye. While photo credentials can be forged, retina and fingerprint scans cannot. Like the ticketed access discussed prior, the main disadvantage of credentialed access is its cost. The more precise and accurate the identification process for credentialing is, the more costly it will be. Many events are a combination of the ticketed access and the credentialed access. For example, for most sporting events, the general public gains entry by showing a ticket at the gate, while the employees, security personnel, media, and delivery personnel are usually credentialed in some form or another.

Step 6: Determine Necessary Resources

This step requires an estimate of what resources are needed to accomplish the mission. The resources include manpower and equipment. There are no "hard and fast" rules on the best way to determine how many personnel are needed to accomplish the mission or what type of equipment and supplies will be needed. The best way to do this is to rely on one's own experience, other peoples' expertise, and to review the after-action reports from previous similar events for guidance. One common error that event planners make is to underestimate the number of personnel that is needed. They fail to account for relief personnel to take the place of frontline officers on a regular rotation schedule, or they fail to account for the personnel that may be needed to react to unanticipated circumstances. This author recalls an incident which occurred during the Y2K deployment in anticipation of civil unrest on New Year's Eve in the year 1999. One young public service aide (PSA) was left alone on a traffic control post on a busy intersection in Miami Beach for over 8 hours without anyone relieving him. His supervisor had forgotten him, and had failed to properly account for a relief schedule. The poor fellow was left on his own with no water to drink and no restroom breaks. He was new to the job, and too timid to ask for help. The situation was eventually resolved when this author ran into this individual and heard his story and called his supervisor to let him know what had transpired. That supervisor failed his most fundamental duty, which is to take care of his subordinates.

A good way to start the estimate is to account for every task that needs to be accomplished, and how many personnel are needed to accomplish the task. For example, let's say that we are planning for a simple Saint Patrick's Day parade down Main Street in a small town in mid-America. The parade is 1 mile long, and there are three intersections along the way where barricades need to be deployed in order to redirect the regular traffic flow. From past experience, we know that it takes two officers at each of those intersections, for a total of six officers. In addition, we need to ensure that the spectators who line the entire parade route are kept on the sidewalk out of harm's way. This year we are paying special attention to this matter because we heard the news from a small nearby town about a little boy that was run over and killed by one of the pickup trucks pulling a parade float. Apparently, the boy wandered onto the street during the parade and the driver did not see him. In order to keep the parade route safe, the planners have strung yellow caution tape along the entire route and have taken the extra precaution of staffing the route with an officer on each side of the street every 300 feet. In order to accomplish this task, the planners calculated that they will need 34 personnel. The entire event only lasts 4 hours, but the planners should account for extra personnel to relieve the officers on fixed posts. To account for the 40 officers already committed to fixed posts, the planners should consider staffing extra personnel to account for the relief of these officers. Relief can be on an "as needed" basis, or it can be planned for on a rotational relief schedule. Figure 3.11 shows a simple formula on an Excel spreadsheet that gradually increases the "relief factor" as time on post elapses. The longer the anticipated time of the event or incident, the higher the relief factor is. The assumption is that people will get increasingly fatigued over a prolonged period of time. Any event or incident that lasts over 12 hours would probably require a shift change to relieve on-post personnel. For example, according to the calculation in Figure 3.11, planners of the small town Saint Patrick's Day parade would need to staff a total of 46 officers. This number accounts for the 40 personnel assigned to fixed posts, plus another six to act as "floaters" for relief purposes. This calculation was derived by multiplying 40 officers times a 1.15 *relief factor* because the event was not expected to last any longer than 4 hours. If it was expected to last for 6 hours, then the chart would recommend a total of 48 officers, with eight assigned to relief duties ($40 \times 1.2 = 48$). This relief factor formula is only provided as a general guideline. There may be different rules in your particular agency that you may need to account for in formulating your own relief calculations.

Figuring out how many personnel are needed to staff the fixed posts and relief schedule for a special event is only the start. Some events such as Super Bowls or major political conventions can last an entire week, and must be staffed on a 24-hour basis. The objective of planners is to assign personnel to shifts that

	<2 hours	4 hours	6 hours	8 hours	10 hours	12 hours +
Relief factor	1.1	1.15	1.2	1.25	1.3	1.4
Personnel on fixed posts	40	40	40	40	40	40
Total personnel	44	46	48	50	52	56

Figure 3.11 Formula for Calculating Necessary Reserve Personnel (Developed by Eloy Nuñez and Ernest G. Vendrell.)

will achieve the optimal results. Since most of the activity occurs in the daytime, it would make sense to assign the majority of personnel to daytime shifts. Figure 3.12 illustrates the 24-hour assignment schedule that the Miami-Dade Police Department used for crowd control during the 2003 FTAA (Free Trade Area of the Americas) Conference. The figure shows how the 1181 personnel were assigned to crowd control duties. This figure only accounts for MDPD personnel, and not for the Mobile Field Forces of the Miami PD, or the other participating agencies. It also does not account for specialized units such as the bomb squad, Special Reaction Team (SRT), aviation unit, canine unit, and marine patrol. Intelligence and past incidents of a similar nature indicated that the peak hours for civil disturbance would be between 1 PM and 5 PM. Thus, the schedule was formulated so that the maximum number of officers (1053) would be deployed during those peak hours. The hours between 1 AM and 6 AM were expected to be the least busy, and thus only 128 personnel were assigned crowd control duties during those off-peak times. As the week progressed, there were minor adjustments in reaction to the protestors' actions, but for the most part, the schedule remained the same. This is an example of a 24-hour staffing schedule for optimal effect.

Step 6 is not just about manpower resources. In this step, we also need to consider what types of equipment and supplies are going to be needed to successfully complete the event. The adage, "An army marches on its stomach," is attributed to Napoleon Bonaparte to show his understanding of how important it is for his soldiers to be well fed in order to fight battles. The same holds true for police and fire fighter first responders. But even more important than food are drinking water and restroom facilities. It is imperative that the logistics section provides ample supplies of drinking water, and a place where personnel can go to the restroom.

Other details such as the procurement of special weapons, ammunition, tools, or protective equipment also need to be considered in this step. Most often, the equipment is already on hand or can be borrowed on short notice from a partner agency. However, under certain unusual circumstances, the mass procurement of new equipment may be warranted. For example, the Miami-Dade Police purchased or leased over $900,000 worth of specialized equipment in preparation for the FTAA Conference in 2003. These purchases included Pepperball munitions, fire extinguishers, new flame-retardant clothing and body padding for the frontline Mobile Field Forces, CUT team tools, six water cannon trucks, and much more. One of the untold success stories behind the planning for the FTAA Conference was the manner in which the Miami-Dade County government rose to the occasion and expedited these purchases so that the frontline officers would be well equipped and protected. Anyone who has ever experienced the bureaucratic delays of the procurement process in a very large government organization will appreciate how expeditiously the purchases were made. Most of the purchase orders were processed and the products delivered within two months of the initial requests. For a county government that was known to take six to eight months to approve a routine purchase order, the relative lightning speed of the

Timeline →	# Pers. →	AM							PM												AM					
		6	7	8	9	10	11	12	1	2	3	4	5	6	7	8	9	10	11	12	1	2	3	4	5	6
Task Force 1 (6 AM–6 PM)	228	228	228	228	228	228	228	228	228	228	228	228	228													
Task Force 2 (1 PM–1 AM)	128								128	128	128	128	128	128	128	128	128	128	128	128						
Task Force 3 (7 AM–7 PM)	208		208	208	208	208	208	208	208	208	208	208	208	208												
Task Force 4 (1 PM–1 AM)	124								124	124	124	124	124	124	124	124	124	124	124	124						
Task Force 5 (9 AM–9 PM)	208				208	208	208	208	208	208	208	208	208	208	208	208										
Task Force 6 (9 PM–9 AM)	128	128	128	128													128	128	128	128	128	128	128	128	128	128
MIA MFF (9 AM–9 PM)	64				64	64	64	64	64	64	64	64	64	64	64	64										
Bike Platoon (10 AM–10 PM)	33					33	33	33	33	33	33	33	33	33	33	33	33									
SERT (10 AM–10 PM)	60					60	60	60	60	60	60	60	60	60	60	60	60									
Total (on any given hour):	1181	356	564	564	708	801	801	801	1053	1053	1053	1053	1053	825	617	617	473	380	380	380	128	128	128	128	128	128

Figure 3.12 24-Hour Distribution of Crowd Control Personnel for the FTAA Conference, Miami, Florida, 2003 (Developed by Eloy Nuñez and Ernest G. Vendrell.)

FTAA purchases were astounding. Much of the credit for this goes to the county manager at the time, who had the vision and wisdom to listen to the frontline police supervisors about the threats to the community posed by the thousands of protestors that were expected to be in town during the conference. Credit also goes to the dozens of anonymous civilian procurement specialists who worked hard to get the job done.

Step 7: Develop an Organizational Chart

Organizational charts are important because it provides everyone with a clear understanding of who reports to whom. The confusion that sometimes occurs during critical incidents and special events can often be attributed to the lack of knowledge about the organizational structure. This is especially true when the organizational structure was newly created for the incident or event at hand. People may be working with new and unfamiliar persons, and having an organizational chart to display to all can go a long way to minimize the confusion.

One easy way to create organizational charts is with Microsoft PowerPoint. As with most Microsoft products, the organizational chart feature of PowerPoint is very intuitive and can be learned quickly by novices. Another excellent software program that can be used to formulate organizational charts is called *eSponder*. This program does much more than create organizational charts. It is a fully integrated incident management tool that incident managers can use to capture data, track personnel, create schedules, fill out ICS forms, create maps and site plans, directly contact participants, and much more.[26]

Step 8: Assign Specific Personnel

There is not a lot to this step, other than the underlying principle of choosing personnel for key positions wisely. It is likely that special event planners will have to use whatever resources are available to them at the time. In most cases, planners have no choice but to use the personnel that are made available to them. This is especially true for specialized tactical units such as SWAT, bomb squads, canine, aviation, and marine units. Frontline personnel for traffic and checkpoint posts, as well as Mobile Field Forces, usually come from regular patrol, or may be on temporary loan from another police department. In this case, the event planners have very little choice in who they use for the event. Nevertheless, there are some critical positions that the event planner/incident commander needs to make sure to staff with people that they can count on. This is especially critical for leadership positions. There are too many types of incidents and events to cover all the possible critical positions that planners should strive to staff with the best possible person; however, we will name a few of the most critical positions.

Undoubtedly, the position of *incident commander* is the most critical of all. Ideally, this person has considerable experience, and has served either as an incident commander or second in command at previous events and incidents. The ideal incident commander is one who has previous experience and a functional understanding of command, operations, logistics, planning, and finance.

Past experience in media relations, safety, and liaison with other agencies is also a plus. The ideal incident commander does not have to be an expert at all these functions, but should have a good working understanding of what each of them does, and how they interact with each other.

The second most critical position that needs to be staffed with a dependable and knowledgeable person is the incident commander's *executive officer*, or second in command. This is usually an experienced "go-to person" who works behind the scenes to get things done, and can readily fill in as the incident commander if necessary. Not every event or incident is so large that an executive officer position is required, but when it is, this person needs to be handpicked for the role. This person is probably the most critical for the success of the event—at times, even more so than the incident commander.

Obviously, the four sections of incident command (operations, logistics, planning, and admin/finance) are also key positions that should warrant special consideration to choosing the best possible person to head them. The same holds true for the three *command staff* positions (liaison, safety, and media relations). Another key position that is not listed as one of the main ICS positions is legal advisor. For large and potentially controversial events such as political conventions where out-of-town protestors are expected, it is almost certain that the police departments and local governments will be sued. Many protest groups hire attorneys prior to the events, and suing the authorities is an integral part of their overall political strategy. In these situations, it is almost inevitable that the authorities will be sued, even if nothing happens. That is why a competent legal advisor reporting directly to the incident commander is so important.

Step 9: Conduct Training and Rehearsals

The last step of operational planning is to conduct training and rehearsals when possible. For smaller events, training may not be necessary, and the rehearsal may take the form of a last minute walkthrough of the event site with the assigned personnel. This last minute walkthrough is important so that all personnel become familiar with each other and what their roles are.

For large and complex events, there will probably be a need for different types of training prior to the event. For example, the 2003 FTAA Conference required all the following training to be done prior to the event:

- Task force and mobile field force commanders' training
- General mobile field force training
- CUT team training
- Chemical agent and Grenadier training
- Water cannon training
- Less-lethal munitions training
- Bicycle response team training
- SERT (Special Event Response Team) training

- Dignitary protection training

In addition to all these training courses, the Miami-Dade Police conducted a realistic 8-hour tabletop exercise with all the task force captains and Mobile Field Force lieutenants several weeks before the event. As it turned out, this tabletop exercise almost mirrored the events that were to unfold weeks later during the actual FTAA event. The tabletop was so realistic and on the mark that when the actual riots began, the commanders reacted as if they had already experienced them. That is because they had experienced them in the simulated tabletop exercise. The exercise also revealed a legal question that had not been considered prior.

Lastly, several live rehearsal exercises were held at nighttime in Downtown Miami to avoid disruption of businesses during daytime hours. Every task force and MFF participated in these live rehearsals. Special Response Team personnel in civilian clothes played the role of the adversary protestors. These rehearsals were so realistic that by the time that the real disturbances occurred, the frontline officers felt like they had experienced them before. The pounding that these officers took from the SRT role players during the live rehearsals was more severe than anything that the real protestors did to them during the actual riot. One of the main reasons why the line officers maintained their discipline throughout the week of the FTAA protests was in large part due to these realistic training exercises and rehearsals. Another unintended and unexpected benefit derived from the nighttime rehearsals downtown was that several dozen early arriving protestors who were staying in nearby hotels actually got to witness firsthand how disciplined the frontline field forces were. Some credit this display as having had a deterrent effect on some of the protestors during the actual event. This view was corroborated by several anecdotal accounts from protestors who were interviewed after the FTAA was over.

This concludes Chapter 3. In Chapter 4, we will examine the issues faced by critical incident managers from a tactical command perspective and delve deeper into some of the issues briefly examined in Chapter 3. Much of what incident managers do at the operational and strategic levels is dictated by tactical concerns. A good example of this was how the Miami-Dade County government responded to the concerns of tactical supervisors who pointed out the need for new and better munitions and protective equipment for its frontline officers in anticipation of the civil unrest associated with the FTAA Conference. In this case, tactics dictated operational deployments and strategic expenditures for the purchase of the necessary equipment. As we will see in upcoming chapters, the operational, tactical, and strategic spheres are distinct entities, but these three spheres are constantly interacting with each other.

References

1. FIRESCOPE, 2003. Some highlights of the evolution of the incident command system as developed by FIRESCOPE, March 26. Online at http://www.firescope.org/firescope-history/Some%20Highlights%20of%20the%20Evolution%20of%20the%20ICS.pdf (accessed September 10, 2015).

2. Federal Emergency Management Agency, 2004. NIMS and the incident command system. Federal Emergency Management Agency, November 23. Online at http://www. fema.gov/txt/nims/nims_ics_position_paper.txt (accessed September 10, 2015).

3. U.S. House of Representatives, 2006. A failure of initiative. Final Report of the Select Bipartisan Committee to Investigate the Preparation for and Response to Hurricane Katrina, February 15. Online at http://www.nola.com/katrina/pdf/main report.pdf (accessed September 10, 2015).

4. National Commission on Terrorist Attacks Upon the United States, 2004. *The 9/11 Commission Report*. Online at http://www.9-11commission.gov/ (accessed September 10, 2015).

5. Department of Homeland Security, 1993. U.S. Fire Administration/Technical Report Series. The World Trade Center Bombing: Report and Analysis, New York City, New York USFA-TR-076/February 1993. Online at http://www.usfa.fema.gov/ downloads/pdf/publications/tr-076.pdf (accessed September 10, 2015).

6. Federal Emergency Management Agency, n.d. ICS 100 course overview. Online at http://emilms.fema.gov/IS100b/ICS0101summary.htm (accessed September 10, 2015).

7. Lernu, 2002. About Esperanto. Lernu! Online at http://en.lernu.net/enkonduko/ pri_esperanto/ideo.php (accessed September 10, 2015).

8. International Civil Aviation Organization, 2013. Language proficiency requirements (LPR). Online at http://www.icao.int/safety/lpr/Pages/Language-Proficiency-Requirements.aspx (accessed September 10, 2015).

9. Federal Emergency Management Agency, n.d. ICS 100—Lesson 3: ICS organization: Part II. Online at http://www.usda.gov/documents/ICS100Lesson03.pdf (accessed September 10, 2015).

10. Department of Homeland Security, 1999. Wanton violence at Columbine High School Littleton, Colorado. Online at http://www.usfa.fema.gov/downloads/pdf/ publications/tr-128.pdf (accessed September 10, 2015).

11. E.S.G. Dennis Jr., 1993. Evaluation of the handling of the Branch Davidian stand-off in Waco, Texas—February 28 to April 19, 1993. [Redacted Version] U.S. Department of Justice, October 8. Online at http://www.justice.gov/publications/ waco/evaluation-handling-branch-davidian-stand-waco-texas-february-28-april-19-1993 (accessed September 11, 2015).

12. D. Rumsfeld, 2002. Press Conference. NATO Speeches. NATO Headquarters, Brussels, Belgium, June 6. Online at http://www.nato.int/docu/speech/2002/s020606g .htm (accessed September 11, 2015).

13. Rumsfeld, Press Conference, 2002.

14. S. Žižek, 2006. Philosophy, the "unknown knowns" and the public use of reason. *(English) Topoi* 25(1-2), 137–142. Online at http://www.egs.edu/faculty/slavoj-zizek/articles/philosophy-the-unknown-knowns-and-the-public-use-of-reason/ (accessed September 11, 2015).

15. National Commission on Terrorist Attacks Upon the United States, 2004.

16. A. Sosnowski, 2012. Republican National Convention delayed by Isaac, August 25. Accuweather.com. Online at http://www.accuweather.com/en/weather-news/isaac-may-impact-2012-republic/70534 (accessed September 15, 2015).

17. Teamster.org, 2015. Fast facts, about the teamsters. Online at http://teamster.org/ content/fast-facts (accessed September 15, 2015).

18. AFL-CIO.org. AFL-CIO Unions. Online at http://www.aflcio.org/About/AFL-CIO-Unions (accessed September 11, 2015).

19. National Public Radio, 2011. Occupy Wall Street: From a blog post to a movement, October 20. Online at http://www.npr.org/2011/10/20/141530025/occupy-wall-street-from-a-blog-post-to-a-movement (accessed September 15, 2015).

20. The Ruckus Society, n.d. Who we are. Online at http://ruckus.org/section.php?id=71 (accessed September 15, 2015).
21. F. E. Fiedler, 1964. A theory of leadership effectiveness. In L. Berkowitz, ed. *Advances in Experimental Social Psychology* (Vol. 1). New York: Academic Press.
22. P. Hersey and K. H. Blanchard, 1969. An introduction to situational leadership. *Training and Development Journal*, 23, 26–34.
23. L. Chapa, n.d. No journalists were arrested at a national convention for the first time in 20 years. Reporters Committee for Freedom of the Press. Online at http://www.rcfp.org/browse-media-law-resources/news-media-law/news-media-and-law-fall-2012/no-journalists-were-arrested- (accessed September 11, 2015).
24. M. Leonard, J. Downey, and B.W., n.d. Scouting manual for activists. The Ruckus Society. Online at http://ruckus.org/downloads/Ruckus%20Scouting%20Manual.pdf (accessed September 11, 2015).
25. CNN Library, 2014. Beirut marine barracks bombing fast facts. *CNN News*, November 2. Online at http://www.cnn.com/2013/06/13/world/meast/beirut-marine-barracks-bombing-fast-facts/ (accessed September 11, 2015).
26. NC4. E-sponder. Online at http://www.nc4worldwide.com/Pages/esponder.aspx (accessed December 16, 2015).

4

Planning and Organizing for Tactical Response

The strategic bombing campaign against Nazi Germany during World War II played a pivotal role in the eventual victory by the allies. The relentless bombing campaign consisted of nighttime raids by the British Royal Air Force, and daytime bombing raids by the U.S. Army Air Corps against strategic targets such as German U-boat and aircraft factories, as well as other manufacturing and critical infrastructure targets. Although the American bombers sustained heavy losses at the beginning of the campaign, they persevered and caused considerable damage to the German industrial production of war materiel and the supplies needed to sustain the war effort.

The famously rugged B-17 "Flying Fortress" bombers used by the U.S. Army Air Corps were comprised of 10 crew members. The pilot sitting in the left seat of the cockpit was the commander of the aircraft. Sitting next to him in the right seat was the copilot, who was the crew's executive officer and second in command. One of the next two most important crew members was the navigator, whose job was to plot a course to get the aircrew to the bombing target, and then get them back to their base in England. The other very important crew member was the bombardier, whose job was to make sure that the bombs were dropped on the intended target. The aircraft's engineer, radio operator, and four gunners comprised the rest of the 10 man crew. All the positions were important, and all the crew members had to be familiar with each other's roles in case they needed to fill in during an emergency. However, the position that was at the core of what bombers do—bomb enemy targets—was the exclusive role of the crew's bombardier. From a technical perspective, the jobs of the navigator and the bombardier were the most challenging of all.

One of the technical advances of the times which greatly improved the accuracy of the bombing runs, and thus the effectiveness of the bombers, was the *Norden Bombsight*. The Norden Bombsight contained an early analog computer that was used to calculate the many variables such as altitude, bomb ballistic characteristics, wind velocity, and the aircraft's airspeed, all of which affect the bombs' flight to the target. The bombsight also contained a linkage to the aircraft's automatic pilot, which allowed the bombardier to make slight corrections to the plane's flight path in order to bring it to the best position possible in order to accurately drop the bombs on the target.

According to the *Duties and Responsibilities of the Bombardier* section of the *B-17 Pilot Training Manual—1943*: "When the bombardier takes over the airplane for the run on the target, he is in absolute command. He will tell you what he wants done, and until he tells you 'Bombs away,' his word is law."[1] The Manual goes on to say that in order for the bombardier to do his job correctly, the pilot needs to ensure that he gets the aircraft in the general area, or otherwise, the mission will fail. That is the type of teamwork that is needed in order to successfully deliver the bombs to the intended target. The pilot flies the plane to and from the target, but for a few minutes while the bombardier makes slight adjustments using his Norden Bombsight, the plane is actually being controlled by the bombardier. The pilot regains control as soon as the bombs are released from the bomb bay, and the "bombs away" signal is given. They can now return back to their base in England.

Command or Control?

We begin this chapter with a brief vignette about the teamwork and the exchange of responsibilities among B-17 crew members during America's strategic bombing campaign of Nazi Germany during World War II. This vignette provides a good basis for understanding the relationship between operational command and tactical command. In this case, the pilot plays the role of operational commander, and the bombardier is the *de facto* tactical commander for the mission. Not mentioned in the vignette is the strategic command level, which in this context would be the general staff back in England making the overall strategic targeting decisions. We will examine the strategic command level further in Chapter 5, but we briefly mention it here so that you can see how the three levels of command relate to each other. Figure 4.1 illustrates the position of the tactical sphere of command as it relates to the other two spheres, which is our focus in this chapter.

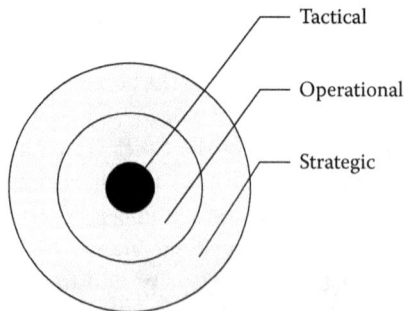

Figure 4.1 Tactical Sphere

Tactical command is the one that occurs closest to the threat. It is "up close and personal" to the adversary. By contrast, strategic command is usually located at a great distance from the theater of operations. Tactical command is all about the "little picture" and strategic command is about the "big picture." In the B-17 example, the pilot has operational command of his aircraft and over his entire crew. The operational command of the pilot over the aircraft and crew was maintained, even in those times where the copilot outranked the pilot. For example, there were missions where the pilot was a first lieutenant by rank, but during the mission, that first lieutenant had command authority of the copilot, who was a captain by rank. That captain may outrank the lieutenant under normal circumstances, but during that specific mission, the pilot is considered the commander, and the copilot is second in command.

The same thing holds true for fire rescue and police during critical incidents. A chief or a major may arrive at the scene of a critical incident, but unless he or she decides to assume command of the incident, that individual must subordinate his or her rank under the incident commander already on the scene. For example, during a hostage situation in which a lieutenant is the incident commander, he or she would have command authority over any captain, major, or chief who arrived at the scene afterward. Of course, at any time, a higher ranked officer may assume command of any incident if he or she deems it necessary. Most do not. That is because they realize that the incident commander who has been on the scene is likely to have a better understanding of the situation than they have, since they are late arrivals. Unless the incident commander is completely overwhelmed by the situation, there is no reason why he or she should be relieved of command by a higher ranked individual.

In the B-17 scenario, the pilot temporarily delegates tactical *control* of the aircraft to the bombardier so that the bombardier can use his Norden Bombsight to make slight adjustments to the aircraft's flight pattern. The reason that the pilot temporarily relinquishes control to the bombardier is because the bombardier is uniquely trained to operate the technology, and thus, he is best suited to do the task correctly and to successfully complete the mission. Operational commanders temporarily delegate control to the tactical level when the mission tasks become very complex, and the skills needed to accomplish the mission become very specialized. In the tactical sphere, commanders are specialists in their field. In the operational sphere, commanders are considered generalists.

The operational commander—in this case, the pilot—delegates the task to the "tactical commander," the bombardier. That does not mean that the pilot relinquishes the responsibilities of his operational command. In that sense, the quote from the *Pilot Training Manual—1943* is incorrect in its use of the word "command." That quote was "When the bombardier takes over the airplane for the run on the target, he is in absolute command." Perhaps a better way of saying it would have been: "When the bombardier takes over the airplane for the run on the target, he is in absolute *control*."[2]

That may seem like a nuanced play on semantics, but it isn't. The words *command* and *control* are similar, but they are not the same. For our purposes, the term *control* will be used in a narrow context. It has little to do with rank or authority. As we saw in the B-17 example, control is temporary and task specific. By contrast, *command* is a broader term and is usually related to rank and authority (although not always). It is more than temporary, and it is more formalized than *control*.

We used the B-17 scenario as an example because it is similar to the relationship between the incident commander (i.e., the operations command) and the tactical commander on the scene of a building collapse, a hazardous material spill, a bomb call, a hostage taking, or an active shooter situation. These are all very complex situations that require a certain degree of expertise, along with very specialized equipment. That is why fire and police departments have specialized units such as Urban Search and Rescue (USAR), Hazmat, bomb squads, and Special Weapons and Tactics (SWAT) teams. The regular firefighter or uniformed patrolman is simply not trained or equipped to handle these highly complex and specialized situations. This is why the incident commanders at the scenes of these types of threats will cede a considerable amount of control to the tactical commanders on the scene. The tactical commander may be the leader of a USAR or Hazmat unit, or the sergeant of a bomb squad, or a lieutenant of a SWAT team, or any other specialized tactical team.

It is a smart thing for an incident commander to temporarily cede control of the "hot zone" or "kill zone" (depending on the type of incident) to the tactical commander. After all, the tactical commander presumably has an up-close perspective of the situation, and is thus assumed to have better situational awareness than the incident commander. The tactical commander is presumably better trained, better equipped, and more experienced at resolving the particular situation than the incident commander is. For all these reasons, it behooves the incident commander to listen and pay close attention to any advice that the tactical commander gives. That does not mean that the incident commander should ever relinquish his or her command of the overall incident to the tactical commander. One thing is to temporarily give someone else control of certain parts of the situation, another is to completely abdicate the responsibility of command for the overall incident. Unfortunately, that is a common error that occurs during critical incidents. Some incident commanders—especially those with little experience—will back off and assume that when the tactical commander arrives on the scene, they give command of the entire incident to the tactical commander. That is not the way it is supposed to be. The incident commanders that abdicate their command responsibility do it either because they feel intimidated and insecure, or they simply do not know how the interplay between incident command and tactical command is supposed to be. If you recall the B-17 vignette, you will understand what the role and responsibilities of the overall incident commander is. That command role should never be relinquished, unless and until the commander is relieved by someone of higher rank, or by the incoming incident

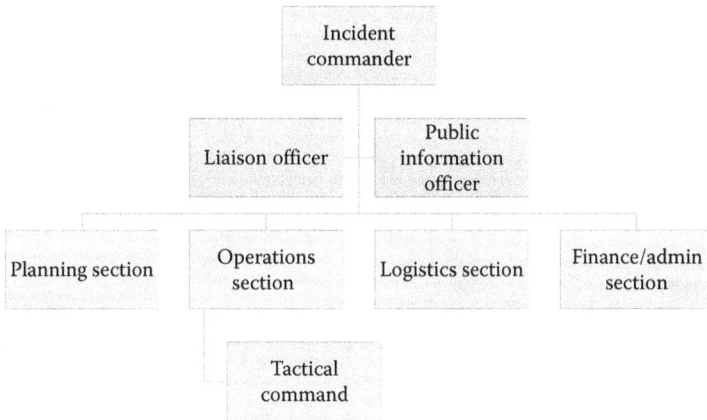

Figure 4.2 Tactical Command in Relation to Operational Command

commander from a new shift. Figure 4.2 illustrates the relative position of the tactical commander to the operational commander in a typical incident command organizational structure.

Specialists and Generalists

No one is an expert at everything. In today's complex all-hazards threat environment, we rely heavily on experts from various fields to solve problems. Some problems are so complex that teams of experts from different fields need to be assembled in order to fix them. We will discuss the composition and use of interdisciplinary mixed teams later in this chapter. But first, let's look at the different specialists that are needed in today's all-hazards environment.

For the purposes of this book, we will define the term *tactical team* as any group of individuals specifically assembled to perform a specialized task. These individuals are presumed to be specialists at their specific discipline and may be assembled either as ad hoc teams to resolve an issue occurring one time or as permanent teams to address a recurring or ever-present threat. There are varying degrees of specialized subject-matter expertise among these tactical teams, but at a minimum, they all share the commonality that its members have received some sort of specialized training that nonmembers have not. With this definition, a hastily assembled team of regular patrol officers that respond to an active shooter incident at a school does not meet the criteria of a tactical team. However, an ad hoc team of patrol or school resource officers that have previously trained in the *diamond formation* in response to an active shooter incident at a school would fit the definition of a tactical team. There is some gray area as to whether a hastily assembled team meets the definition of tactical team, but the two key elements that distinguish tactical teams from hastily assembled teams are specialized training and accessibility to specialized equipment. It is the specialized

Table 4.1 Matrix for Tactical Teams Response Capabilities

	Bomb Squad (EOD)	SWAT	K-9	Aviation	Hostage Neg. Team	USAR	Hazmat	Mobile Field Force	Nat. Guard Civil Support Team	Dept. of Energy RAP Team	CDC
Chemical	•						•		•		•
Biological	•								•		•
Radiological	•								•	•	
Nuclear	•								•	•	
Explosive	•		•								
Active shooter		•	•		•						
Suicide bomber	•	•			•						
Hazardous material	•						•				
Hostage taking	•	•	•	•	•						
Barricaded subject	•	•	•	•	•						
Collapsed building			•			•					
Civil disturbances		•						•			
Escaped prisoner/manhunt		•	•	•				•			

training and specialized equipment that define and set apart tactical teams from non-tactical teams.

There are many types of tactical teams, with varying degrees of expertise and requisite training. Table 4.1 shows some of the more commonly known tactical teams, and how their capabilities relate to the different types of threats encountered in the "all-hazards" threat environment. This table is by no means exhaustive, either in the listing of tactical teams or in the types of threats that the tactical teams respond to. Moreover, some of the types of threats may be very similar, as is the case with chemical agent warfare and hazardous material spills. The table is intended as a generic representation of what these specialized tactical teams are capable of doing. The table does not show the variation of expertise and capabilities of the various types of units. For example, there is a considerable variation of response capability for civilian and military bomb squads in the United States. The Department of Homeland Security/FEMA classifies bomb squads throughout the United States as Type I, II, and III, depending on their capability to perform in various environments, including CBRNE (chemical, biological, radiological, nuclear, and explosive) situations. The lowest level of capability is described by the Department of Homeland Security as follows:

> Type III—A full-time or part-time bomb squad, capable of handling a small incident. Teams shall consist of a minimum of 2 bomb technicians. Team(s) must have basic IED render-safe capabilities. Teams should be capable of working in a CBRN environment absent of vapors and liquids.[3]

The highest capability level for bomb squads in the United States is categorized as Type I, and described in the following manner:

> Type I—A dedicated full-time bomb squad, capable of handling a complex incident. A complex incident may include multiple or simultaneous life-threatening or time-sensitive Improvised Explosive Device Disposal (IEDD) incidents, involving sophisticated improvised energetic materials, electronic/remote firing systems, and tactical explosive breaching support.

Teams shall consist of a minimum of 10 bomb technicians and 2 supervisors. Team(s) must have render safe capabilities up to and including large vehicle borne IEDs (capable of containing up to 60,000 lbs. of explosive material) and CBRN dispersal devices. Team(s) shall be capable of working in a CBRN environment and support tactical team operations.[4]

As noted by the DHS/FEMA typology, not all bomb squads have the same response capabilities. In many rural counties throughout the country, a Type III bomb squad is all that is needed most of the time. If the need arises for a higher level of response, mechanisms exist via standard mutual aid agreements and Memorandums of Understanding (MOUs) between agencies. These agreements are crafted so that specialized units with a higher typology rating can legally respond outside their normal jurisdiction. Type I bomb squads are typically those from large urban areas. These bomb squads are trained and equipped to handle a wide array of CBRNE situations, including large vehicle bombs, and in some limited cases, the capability to render safe nuclear devices. Nowadays, many bomb squads have entered into the realm of explosive breaching in support of SWAT teams during hostage and barricaded subject situations, in addition to their traditional render safe mission.

The typology of capabilities provides a quick reference guide of every team's response capabilities, so that all jurisdictions can determine ahead of time who they need to turn to for assistance during situations where the local resources are incapable or overwhelmed by the nature of the circumstances that they are confronted with. The DHS/FEMA capability typology includes not only bomb squads but also law enforcement aviation (helicopters and fixed wing), a mobile field force (for crowd control), public safety dive teams (for underwater rescue and recovery), and SWAT (Special Weapons and Tactics teams). Not all jurisdictions are large enough or have a sufficient economic base to afford the training and equipment for Type I levels for all these specialized tactical teams, and therefore must make mutual aid agreements with adjoining counties or with state or federal agencies to ensure that all eventualities are covered. Clearly, knowing what capabilities one's own agency has, or does not have, is a starting point for the proper SWOT (strengths, weaknesses, opportunities, and threats) analysis leading up to drafting an emergency response plan. Second to that is the knowledge of what everyone else's capabilities are. The worst time to find out that your tactical teams are not properly equipped, trained, or otherwise not capable is during a critical incident. These are issues that need to be discussed and resolved ahead of time.

While this chapter focuses on tactical teams, and the tactical response to critical incidents, the intended audience is not the tactical commander. This chapter, indeed, this book is targeted at the critical incident manager. The critical incident manager, much like the captain/pilot in the B-17 vignette is a generalist, not a specialist. Like the pilot of the B-17, the critical incident manager needs to know how to "fly the plane" in order to complete the mission. Just like the B-17 pilot, the critical incident manager needs to have a good understanding of all the moving parts of his/her "aircraft" in order to succeed in the mission. But just like the B-17 pilot, the critical incident manager does not need to know every technical detail of every specialized tactical unit under his/her command. It is helpful for the B-17 pilot to have a general knowledge of navigation techniques, and must be familiar with each of the machine gun positions on the airplane, and what they can and cannot do. It is very important for the B-17 commander to also know how the *Norden bombsight* works because that is the instrument that is most important to the successful culmination of the core mission, which in that case is the delivery of the bombs to their intended target. It is not, however, important that the commander of the aircraft becomes proficient in the use of the bombsight. All he needs to know is how it works, and what it can and cannot do.

It would be an unrealistic expectation, indeed counterproductive, for the incident manager to be all-knowing, of all things, all the time. It makes no economic or operational sense for the incident commander to be an expert at everything, but it does make sense for him/her to be somewhat knowledgeable of all the various disciplines involved in the planning and response to critical incidents. The old saying, "jack of all trades, master of none" comes to mind when describing the role of the incident commander. Often, but not always, incident commanders are promoted to their positions after having previously served in a unit or units that were highly specialized. It is not unusual for the critical incident manager to have had some previous experience in such specialized fields as hazardous material spills cleanup, or bomb disposal, or hostage negotiation, or some other tactical unit. The knowledge acquired in that particular discipline will be helpful to the new incident commander, but by itself is not sufficient to be successful. The most effective critical incident managers are those who consciously make a decision to learn a little bit about every moving part on their "aircraft." While the manager cannot be expected to be a master of all trades, he or she must learn enough from each discipline to make the best decisions for the goodwill and safety of all concerned. Indeed, being a generalist is in itself a specialty that requires considerable knowledge and skill. This chapter, and indeed, this entire book is intended for the generalist critical incident managers or those who aspire to be managers in the future.

Mixed Teams

In Chapter 3, we briefly mentioned single-purpose *strike teams* that in ICS parlance are defined as "A specified combination of the same kind and type of resources with common communications and a leader."[5] An example of a single-purpose strike team is illustrated in Figure 4.3, which shows the composition of a multiagency Hazardous Devices Team comprised of bomb technicians from Miami-Dade Police Department (MDPD), the Federal Bureau of Investigations (FBI), and the U.S. Bureau of Alcohol Tobacco and Firearms (ATF) during the 2007 Super Bowl, in Miami, Florida. Large-scale special events such as Super Bowls attract a lot of attention due to their high visibility and symbolic value.

```
          ┌──────────────────────┐
          │   MDPD Bomb Tech     │
          │    Lead Worker       │
          └──────────┬───────────┘
                     │
     ┌───────────────┴───────────────┐
┌────┴─────────────┐      ┌──────────┴──────────────────┐
│      FBI         │      │          ATF                │
│ Special Agent SABT│      │   Special Agent EEO         │
│   (Bomb Tech)    │      │(Explosives Enforcement Officer)│
└──────────────────┘      └─────────────────────────────┘
```

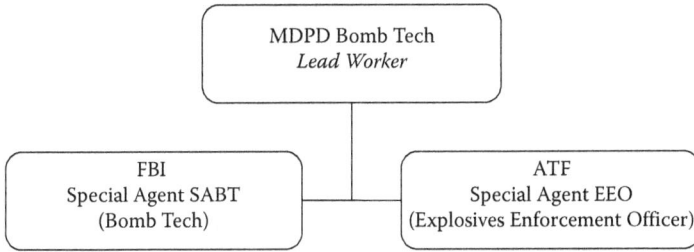

Figure 4.3 Typical Hazardous Devices Team Composition

For this reason, federal agencies provide considerable manpower and equipment assistance to the local authorities in order to prevent, or mitigate a terrorist attack during the event. The purpose of the Hazardous Devices Strike Teams was to respond to, and render safe any reported improvised explosive devices (IEDs) during the week of the Super Bowl events.

There were eight teams, each comprised of any combination of an MDPD bomb tech, an FBI bomb tech, and an ATF explosives enforcement officer. Also participating in these Hazardous Devices Teams were bomb techs from Miami Police Department, Broward County Sheriff's Office, and Palm Beach County Sheriff's Office. The reason for staffing these teams with personnel from different agencies was twofold. First, it creates a "mini" Unified Command at the tactical level. In doing so, the benefits of a Unified Command are replicated from the top to the bottom to include a Unified Command at the strategic (incident command), operational (operations section), and tactical spheres. This organizational configuration is done primarily to improve communications between the various agencies, at all levels of command. The second benefit of pairing the bomb techs from the various agencies is more of an unintended by-product. Although all of these bomb techs have attended similar training throughout their careers, there is a considerable amount of learning from one other that occurs in the short time span leading up to, and during the week of the event. When people from different agencies get together to work for a common cause, good things generally occur. We will discuss this unintended benefit more in Chapter 7, where we will closely examine the innovation process.

Figure 4.4 illustrates the assignments for each of the eight Hazardous Devices Teams during the 2007 Super Bowl. In order to ensure quicker response, and also to disperse the resources in order to protect them from incapacitation resulting from a catastrophic attack, the eight teams were assigned to various locations, inside and outside the stadium grounds. Two of the teams were responsible for regular county-wide response to IED calls. Two other teams were assigned to the *Vehicle and Cargo Inspection System* (VACIS)[6] with the capability to render safe any large vehicle bombs discovered at the incoming cargo and delivery checkpoint.

The second type of mixed teams is what ICS calls *task forces*. FEMA defines task force as "A combination of single resources assembled for a particular tactical

```
                        ┌─────────────────────┐
                        │   EOD Operations    │
                        └─────────────────────┘
```

HDT Team 1 *Stadium inner perimeter*	HDT Team 2 *Stadium inner perimeter*
HDT Team 3 *Outside perimeter—West*	HDT Team 4 *Outside perimeter—East*
HDT Team 5 *County-wide response*	HDT Team 6 *County-wide response*
HDT Team 7 *(VACIS/ARTS)*	HDT Team 8 *(VACIS/ARTS)*

EOD–Explosives Ordnance Disposal
HDT–Hazardous Devices Team
SABT–Special Agent Bomb Tech (FBI)
EEO–Explosives Enforcement Officers (ATF)

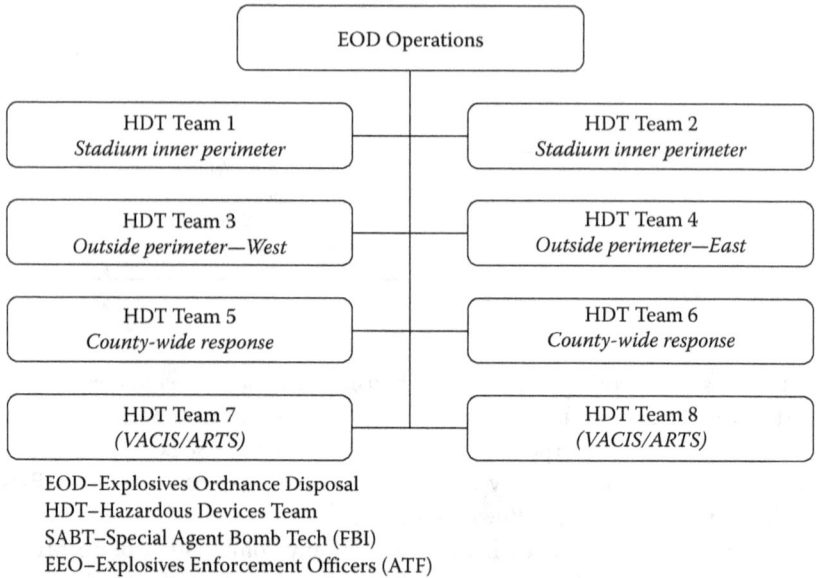

Figure 4.4 Super Bowl EOD Operations

need with common communications and a leader."[7] Task forces are different from strike teams in that they are comprised of interdisciplinary elements. For example, many SWAT teams now have their own paramedics assigned to their entry team "stacks." Sometimes, these paramedics are from a different agency or department, and they are usually cross-trained in both special weapons and

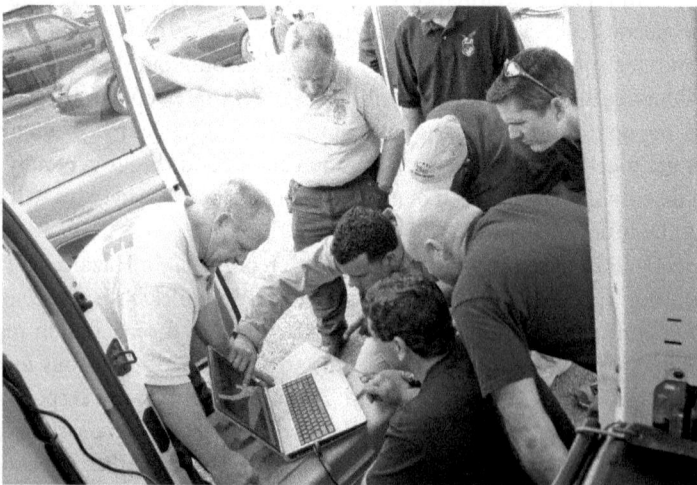

Photo 4.1 Multiagency Hazardous Devices Team in Training (Courtesy of the Miami-Dade Police Department. Photographer Unknown.)

Photo 4.2 A Member of the Florida National Guard 44th Civil Support Team and Her JHRT Team in a Rehearsal Prior to the 2007 Super Bowl (Courtesy of the Miami-Dade Police Department. Photographer Unknown.)

tactics, as well as emergency medical response. Another example of a task force type of mixed team is evidenced in the 2007 Super Bowl, in which multiagency and interdisciplinary *Joint Hazardous Assessment Response Teams* (JHRT or JHAT as some referred to it) were employed. Figure 4.5 illustrates the composition of this mixed team.

The purpose of the JHRT teams was to respond to any suspected CBRNE type of call to *assess* the threat and report back to the Bomb Management Center at

JHRT Team Composition

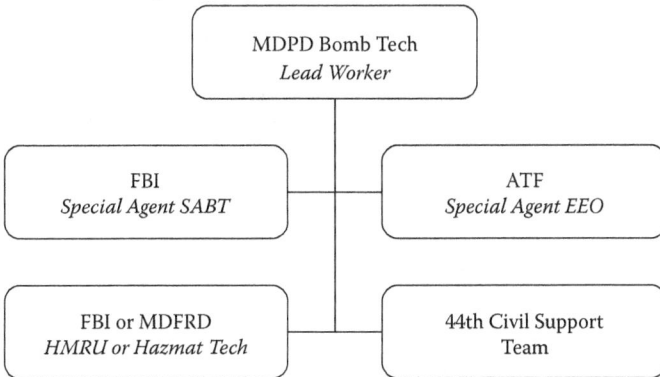

Note: A Canine Team and a Department of Energy RAP team (not seen on this chart) are assigned to support each JHRT.

Figure 4.5 Joint Hazard Assessment Response Team (JHRT)

the Incident Command Post. This mixed team is different from the Hazardous Device Team which is comprised of several different disciplines including bomb technicians, Hazmat technicians, K-9 handlers, Department of Energy RAPs (Radiological Assistance Program), and National Guard Civil Support Team (CST) CBRN technicians. The concept behind the JHRT mixed teams is to have the combined expertise of multiple disciplines to assess an unknown threat. The idea for the JHRT evolved from the earlier Hazardous Agent Assessment Teams (HAAT) and the Hazardous Devices Assessment Teams (HDAT) that were used in the 2003 Free Trade Area of the Americas Conference in 2003, and then for the 2004 Presidential Debates at the University of Miami, in Coral Gables, Florida. The problem with those two teams was that one was for assessing explosives, and the other was for assessing CBRN threats. Since it is not always clear at first what the nature of the threat is, both teams would be dispatched to the same call, but there was some miscommunication between the two teams, and there was a dual reporting structure in which each team reported their assessments via separate chains of command. This organizational structure led to confusion and duplication of effort during the rehearsals prior to the Presidential Debate. For these reasons, we decided afterward to merge the HAAT and HDAT teams into a single element, which comprised experts from various disciplines, and which reported their findings and recommendations through a unified chain of command as illustrated in Figure 4.6.

Like the Hazardous Devices Teams (HDT), the JHRTs were dispersed throughout the stadium grounds for quick response and to ensure continuation of operations in the event of a catastrophic incident. The mission of the JHRT teams was to respond to any suspected CBRNE incidents and to collectively

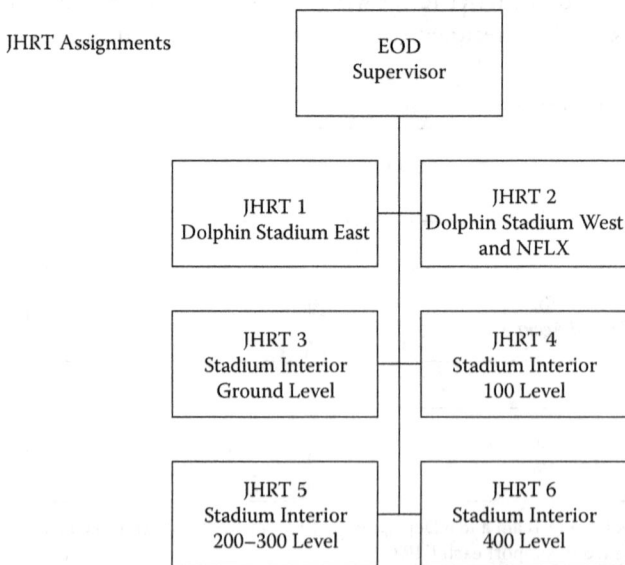

Figure 4.6 JHRT Assignments for the 2007 Super Bowl

Table 4.2 Capabilities and Areas of Expertise of JHRT Team Members

Team Member	Capabilities/Areas of Expertise
MDPD Bomb Squad Bomb Tech	Render safe of suspected explosive devices. Has some basic understanding of CBRNE issues and possesses basic diagnostic tools for radiological and some chemical threats.
FBI SABT (Special Agent Bomb Tech)	Render safe of suspected explosive devices. Also is a handler of an explosives detection canine. Has some basic understanding of CBRNE issues.
ATF EEOs (Explosives Enforcement Officer)	Render safe of suspected explosives devices. Also has some basic understanding of CBRNE issues. Expertise with the large vehicle bomb system.
FBI Hazardous Materials Response Unit (HMRU) or MDFRD Hazmat Tech	Expertise with hazardous materials and CBRNE. Possesses equipment for radiological and chemical diagnostics.
Florida National Guard 44th Civil Support Team	Expertise with diagnosis of all CBRNE threats. Does not have a render safe capability for explosives.
MDPD Canine Unit	Canine handlers with explosives detection dogs. Have no render safe or diagnostic capabilities for CBRNE.
Department of Energy Radiological Assistance Program (RAP)	Expertise in radiological detection and diagnostics.

assess the situation and report back to the Bomb Management Center. Depending on the scope of the situation, the responding JHRT teams could act as a "mini" Unified Command at the tactical level. In addition to identifying and assessing the threat, the JHRT teams would be expected to identify the hot zones, establish perimeters, recommend evacuation or shelter-in-place actions, coordinate safe response routes for Hazardous Devices Teams and/or Hazmat teams, and recommend forward staging area sites for other responding units. The JHRT teams also had the delegated authority to render safe certain threats if they deemed it necessary under exigent circumstances. Table 4.2 shows the capabilities and areas of expertise of the various JHRT team members.

The Fundamentals of Tactical Response to Critical Incidents

As stated before, this book is not intended as a primer for tactical commanders. There are simply too many types of incidents, and too much knowledge and expertise from the myriad disciplines to put in a bottle and share it within a single book, much less in one chapter of that book. Nevertheless, there are some fundamental concepts and practices that critical incident managers from all the disparate disciplines need to fully understand. As a critical incident manager, you do not need to know the details about the weapons and tactics of SWAT teams, or the properties of chlorine gas, because you will depend on the expert advice of your tactical team leaders. But you do need to know the basics of perimeter control and personal protective equipment (PPE) because it falls upon you to ensure that the personnel under your command are safe. So for a brief moment, we will delve into the basic concepts that every critical incident manager needs to know in order to be successful and to protect the officers and firefighters that work for them.

Perimeters

The guiding principle in medicine "above all, do no harm," is applicable in critical incident management as well. The most fundamental application of that principle is to first contain the threat. No matter the type of critical incident, the use of perimeters is essential for keeping threats contained so that they can be managed. Whether it is the sudden shift of wind that turns a forest fire toward the command post or the hostage taker who has gone mobile with his hostages, the threat increases dramatically when it escapes the perimeter that was intended to keep it contained. Fundamentally, there are two types of perimeters. The purpose of the *inner perimeter* is to keep the threat in so it does not escape. The purpose of the *outer perimeter* is to keep undesired outside influences from coming in and making the situation worse. Containment of a critical incident works best when these two types of perimeters are employed in unison. Figure 4.7 illustrates the basic concept with concentric circles, but we all know that perimeters come in all shapes and sizes. In urban areas especially, perimeters tend to take on the contours of existing streets and avenues, and thus are usually square or rectangular in shape. The concentric circle representation of perimeters in this section was selected only because it portrays the concept of perimeters in a way that is easy to understand, but we acknowledge that in life things rarely conform to perfect circles or other polygon shapes.

Figure 4.7 also shows a third layer of perimeter, which in this case is referred to as the traffic control perimeter. This third perimeter is sometimes used in large

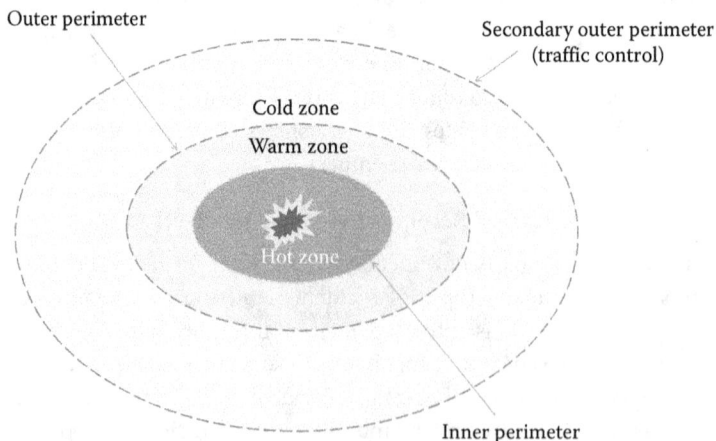

Figure 4.7 Perimeters and Zones

incidents such as manhunts for armed and dangerous escaped prisoners, along with traffic checkpoints at strategic points of ingress and egress. The purpose of this third perimeter can be either to keep things in, or keep them out. Defined by those perimeters are the hot, warm, and cold zones. The term *hot zone* is used primarily by firefighters, whereas police officers typically refer to it as the *kill zone*. For the purposes of this book, we will refer to the area within the inner perimeter as the *hot zone,* since that is the term most used by emergency managers and the National Incident Management System. Everything outside the outer perimeter is referred to as the *cold zone.* The ground between the inner and outer perimeter is the *warm zone.* These zone designations are more than graduations of danger intensity. They provide clearly defined areas where command posts, staging areas, treatment areas, and decontamination corridors can, and cannot be located. These zones have clearly defined purposes as to who can enter and exit, and who cannot. Table 4.3 provides definitions for each of these zone designations and perimeters.

Perimeters can be on the ground, in the sea, or in the air. An example of a perimeter in the air is the *temporary flight restriction* (TFR) at certain special events such as Super Bowls, presidential debates, or any other National Special Security Event (NSSE) as designated by the Department of Homeland Security. TFRs are commonly referred to as "no fly zones" and typically are designated in concentric circles around stadiums or NSSE event venues at intervals of 10 miles for the inner ring, and 30 miles for the outer ring. Usually, there are military

Table 4.3 Perimeter and Zone Designation Definitions

Term	Definition
Hot zone	Area of a critical incident where there exists the possibility of imminent death or serious bodily injury. The nature of a hot zone varies according to the threat and may be defined in terms of line-of-sight threats posed by gunfire, or by a radioactive or chemical "plume" in the case of a CBRNE incident.
Warm zone	Area of a critical incident that is in between the hot zone and the cold zone. This area is often used as a location for a forward staging area or a Tactical Operations Command (TOC). The warm zone is considered to be "safe" from the threat contained in the hot zone.
Cold zone	Area of a critical incident that falls outside the hot and warm zone. This area is also considered to be safe from the threat inside the hot zone. This area is often used to establish Incident Command Posts, staging areas, bases, and helispots. Media and other liaison functions are usually located in the cold zone.
Inner perimeter	Line of demarcation that separates the hot zone and the warm zone. The main purpose of the inner perimeter is containment of the threat. In other words, "to keep the threat in."
Outer perimeter	Line of demarcation that separates the warm zone and the cold zone. The main purpose of the outer perimeter is control of the scene. In other words, "to keep the outside world out."
Traffic control perimeter	Line of demarcation that separates the cold zone from the rest of the world. The main purpose of the traffic perimeter is also control of the scene. Like the outer perimeter, the traffic perimeter is designed to "keep the outside world out." The traffic perimeter helps by controlling the ingress and egress of emergency units to the area. This extra layer of control may or may not be deployed depending on circumstances.
Decon corridor or point of insertion	A controlled area located in the warm zone that acts as a pathway between the hot zone and the cold zone. In a Hazmat or CBRNE incident, this location is used to decontaminate the entry teams. In a SWAT situation, the point of insertion is identified as the location in which a SWAT or rescue team goes in or out of the hot zone.
Treatment area	Location used for the collection and treatment of victims prior to transport to a hospital. The treatment area is typically set up in the cold zone.

aircraft that enforce the 30-mile TFR mark with direct radio warnings to any trespassing aircraft, followed by visual aircraft-to-aircraft contact. Wayward aircraft that continue to trespass into the 10-mile TFR, face the distinct possibility of being shot down after several warnings.

Yet another type of "perimeter" that we do not give much thought to is the conceptual perimeter that strives to control information from being released prematurely, thereby increasing the risk to first responders and other citizens in the area. For example, news media helicopters now have very powerful telescopic cameras that are gyroscope steadied, and can shoot a live feed of ongoing tactical situations. This can be problematic for tactical teams that rely on surprise when they make their move to enter the building where armed subjects are holding hostages. If the hostage takers see the SWAT teams moving in, the element of surprise will be compromised, and thereby increasing the risk to the entry team. This has been an ongoing and unresolved issue for many years, and there is no legal mechanism that prevents news media from broadcasting live action shots during hostage or barricaded subject situations. However, much can be done ahead of time by the media relations or public information officers (PIO) of police departments to impart an informal understanding with local media regarding each other's expectations. More often than not, when a good relationship exists between the police department's PIO and the local television stations, there is a better chance that the TV stations will agree to postpone live broadcasts of critical situations. Nobody, not even the most aggressive media outlets, want to have the burden of having a police officer shot as a result of an irresponsible broadcast. For that reason alone, most television outlets will cooperate with all reasonable requests made by incident or tactical commanders. Again, the key is to have good relations with the media ahead of time. A professionally managed PIO section is essential for this to happen.

The management of media relations could be a chapter in itself, but we will not spend much more time on the topic. The key to effective information control is a professionally managed Public Information Office. It is no accident that the PIO position is considered to be a direct-report command staff position in the Incident Command System hierarchy (see Figure 4.8). The timely release of information is one of the most important aspects of effective critical incident management. In very large events or incidents involving Unified Command structures, the PIO function will likely focus around a Joint Information Center (JIC) whereby representatives of the PIOs of all the major participating agencies will meet in order to plan out and release information to the public in unison, and with "one voice." One of the worst things that can happen during critical incidents is that officers on the scene speak out of turn and give premature or misleading information to the media, and that information is leaked out to the public. That is how false rumors get started, and the problems of the original incident get compounded. When that happens, it is because the invisible "perimeter" that controls the release of information has been breached.

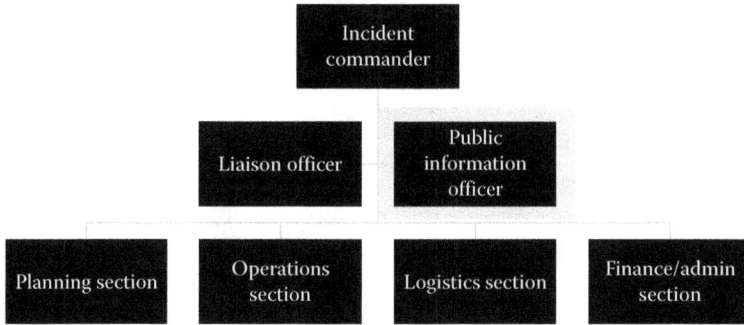

Figure 4.8 The Public Information Officer in the Incident Command System Hierarchy

Personal Protective Equipment

As important as the containment of the threat within the established perimeters is the protection of the police and firefighters whose job it is to enter the hot zone to quell the threat. That is *the* most important job of the critical incident manager. For that reason, we will devote this section as a brief overview of personal protective equipment (PPE) that these officers and firefighters will depend on to survive in the hot or warm zones. This is not meant to be a comprehensive overview of all PPE issues faced by tactical and operational commanders. The purpose of this section is to provide the critical incident manager a general overview of the different types of PPE, and when and where each level is appropriate for use.

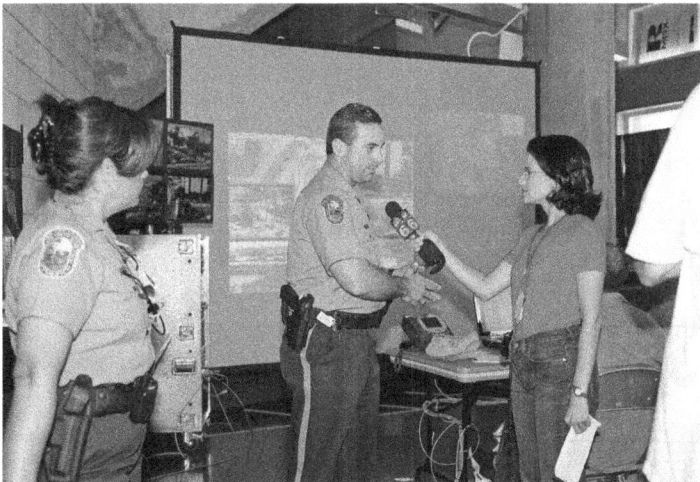

Photo 4.3 Television Interview at the Tactical Command Post, Downtown Miami, Florida, during the FTAA Conference, 2003 (Courtesy of the Miami-Dade Police Department. Photograph by Lynn Scrimshaw.)

PPE can include ballistic-resistant vests for regular patrol officers, bomb suits for bomb technicians, and heavy ballistic vests and ballistic helmets for SWAT personnel in the police realm. In the fire department, PPE can include fire-resistant wear, helmets, gloves, and self-contained breathing apparatus (SCBA), among other things. For the purposes of this section, we will briefly examine the standardized categorization of PPE as it relates to protection from CBRNE and hazardous materials. There are four main levels of PPE, ranging from Level A, providing the highest protection, to Level D, providing the least protection. The levels of PPE are set by the Occupational Safety & Health Administration (OSHA), under the U.S. Department of Labor.

Level A PPE Level A PPE is a positive air pressure, totally encapsulated chemical protective suit with a self-contained breathing apparatus (SCBA). According to OSHA guidelines, Level A protection should be used when the greatest level of skin, respiratory, and eye protection is required. Specifically, Level A protective wear should be used when:

1. The hazardous substance has been identified and requires the highest level of protection for skin, eyes, and the respiratory system based on either the measured (or potential for) high concentration of atmospheric vapors, gases, or particulates; or the site operations and work functions involve a high potential for splash, immersion, or exposure to unexpected vapors, gases, or particulates of materials that are harmful to skin or capable of being absorbed through the skin
2. Substances with a high degree of hazard to the skin are known or suspected to be present, and skin contact is possible
3. Operations must be conducted in confined, poorly ventilated areas, and the absence of conditions requiring Level A has not yet been determined[8]

Level A protection is used by trained personnel to enter the hot zones of some CBRNE hazards. Firefighters and police officers who do Level A protection should be Hazmat trained and certified. Because of the cumbersome properties of the Level A suit and butyl gloves, it is not practical for SWAT usage, although many SWAT teams have trained with Level A PPE. The same holds true for bomb techs. Type I bomb squads are certified for Level A PPE; however, the wearing of Level A suits precludes the wearing of the regular bomb suits that provide limited fragmentation protection. Depending on the variables of the situation, bomb techs must choose either Level A protection, or fragmentation protection from the bomb suit, but not both.

Level B PPE Level B PPE is described by OSHA as, "the highest level of respiratory protection is necessary but a lesser level of skin protection is needed." Level B protection is also based on self-contained breathing apparatus (SCBA), but is much less cumbersome than the totally encapsulated positive air pressure Level A suit. Unlike Level A, the Level B suit does have practical application by SWAT

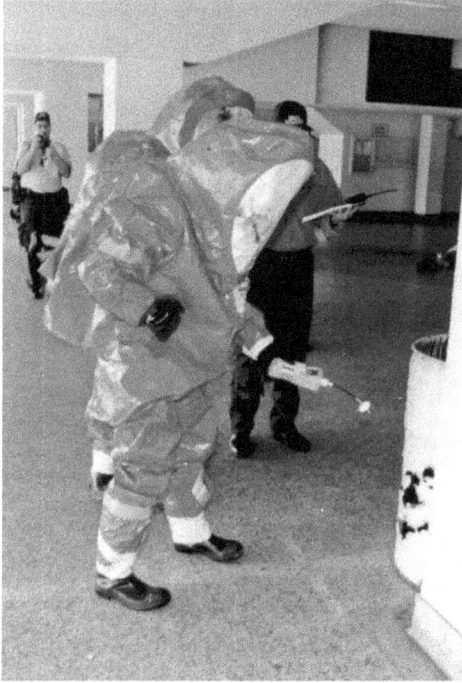

Photo 4.4 Level A PPE (Courtesy of the Miami-Dade Police Department. Photographer Unknown.)

and bomb squad officers. The smaller gloves used in Level B allow for the SWAT officers to insert their trigger fingers inside the trigger guard of their weapons, which is almost impossible with the larger gloves used with Level A PPE. The head gear and respirator of Level B make it difficult for the SWAT personnel to aim their weapons at their targets, but it is not as restrictive as the Level A head-gear. Similarly, Level B PPE has a better application for bomb squad personnel in that it can be worn underneath the standard bomb suits. However, the trade-off for better protection against CBRNE hazards of Level B PPE is that it encumbers movement, and the weight and heat retention of the garb severely limits the time that the officers can remain downrange in the hot zone. Downrange time is also limited by the amount of air supply in the SCBA tanks.

According to OSHA, Level B protection should be used when

1. The type and atmospheric concentration of substances have been identified and require a high level of respiratory protection, but less skin protection
2. The atmosphere contains less than 19.5% oxygen
3. The presence of incompletely identified vapors or gases is indicated by a direct-reading organic vapor detection instrument, but vapors and gases are not suspected of containing high levels of chemicals harmful to skin or capable of being absorbed through the skin[9]

Photo 4.5 City of Miami SWAT Team in Level B PPE (Courtesy of the Miami-Dade Police Department. Photographer Unknown.)

Level C PPE   Level C PPE differs from Levels A and B in that it does not rely on self-contained breathing apparatus (SCBA). For Level C to be appropriate, the oxygen level in the immediate atmosphere must be sufficient to sustain the user's respiration. Level C respirators can be augmented with a *Powered Air Purifying Respirator* (PAPR) to make breathing easier for the user.

According to OSHA, Level C protection should be used when

1. The atmospheric contaminants, liquid splashes, or other direct contact will not adversely affect or be absorbed through any exposed skin
2. The types of air contaminants have been identified, concentrations measured, and an air-purifying respirator is available that can remove the contaminants
3. All criteria for the use of air-purifying respirators are met[10]

Level D PPE   Level D PPE is defined by OSHA as, "A work uniform affording minimal protection: used for nuisance contamination only."

Level D protection should be used when

1. The atmosphere contains no known hazard
2. Work functions preclude splashes, immersion, or the potential for unexpected inhalation of or contact with hazardous levels of any chemicals[11]

Decontamination Procedures

Let's return now to the guiding principle of "above all, do no harm." In critical incident management, one of the best ways to "do no harm" is to make sure that

Photo 4.6 Hialeah Police Department SWAT Team in Level C PPE (Courtesy of the Miami-Dade Police Department. Photographer Unknown.)

the hazards within the contained hot zone are not inadvertently dispersed outside the contained area by personnel returning from the contained area. Those personnel who may be contaminated with chemical, biological, or radiological hazards may include the Hazmat or CBRNE technicians sent in to resolve the threat; or victims who are being rescued or are trying to leave the hot zone on their own accord.

Photo 4.7 Miami-Dade Police Mobile Field Force Officers in Level D PPE (Courtesy of the Miami-Dade Police Department. Photograph by Lynn Scrimshaw.)

Decontamination procedures may be as simple as washing one's hands after accidentally coming into contact with bodily fluids at the scene of an injured person or crime scene; or as complex as the decontamination of a major radiological catastrophe such as the Fukushima Daiichi nuclear power plant breach.[12] Perhaps the most elaborate decontamination efforts ever were the protocols used by NASA upon the return of the Apollo 11 capsule and crew from the first landing on the moon in 1969. The extraordinary efforts to isolate and decontaminate the crew and all the materials returning from the moon were done as a precaution to avoid the unlikely but worst-case scenario whereby an unknown "alien" biological threat would be spread throughout the Earth, thereby potentially causing a pandemic among humans or other species on the planet. Immediately upon splashing down in the Pacific Ocean, the crew of Apollo 11 donned respirator aided biological isolation garments (BIG suits) similar to today's personal protective equipment garb, but unlike modern PPE, the BIG suits were designed to keep any biological hazards in, rather than out. The three astronauts and their command module capsule were wiped down with a sodium-hypochlorite solution prior to bringing them aboard the aircraft carrier U.S.S. Hornet. Once onboard the Hornet, the three astronauts were transferred to a fully encapsulated *Mobile Quarantine Facility* (MQF), where they stayed until the ship reached Houston, Texas. In Houston, the entire MQF, with the astronauts inside, were moved to an especially designed quarantine facility called the Lunar Receiving Laboratory (LRL) at the Johnson Space Center, where they were held in quarantine for 21 days. The LRL was an 83,000 square foot facility that was designed to house the astronauts and all support staff who had come into contact with them, including crew surgeons, recovery engineers, medical laboratory technicians, cooks, and stewards. The LRL also kept the command module capsule and even the helicopter used to transport the crew and capsule to the Hornet. These extraordinary efforts were taken by NASA because they were dealing with the unknown as to what possible biological hazards may have existed on the moon.[13]

The National Fire Protection Association (NFPA) classifies six levels of decontamination as A—light hazards; B—medium hazards; C—extreme hazards; D—dry contamination for water-reactive substances; E—etiologic agents and certain dry pesticides; and R—radiological materials.[14] This classification system is important for the technicians who deal with the decontamination of hazardous materials, but for the purpose of the critical incident manager generalist, a simple three-level categorization is better suited. These three types of decontamination are listed in the order of small to large: tactical, technical, and mass decon.

Tactical decon is defined as the decontamination equipment that one person can carry, and is used for hasty cleanups of light or medium hazards when no other option for decontamination exists. Tactical decon kits typically include some sort of alcohol-based foam or liquid cleanser, and other materials that can wash off or blow off contaminants from the person's clothing or body. These kits are often provided to police and fire-rescue first responders as part of Level C protective gear, and are intended for emergency decontamination of oneself, or some other person in proximity. Tactical decon is intended to hastily mitigate the effects of an accidental exposure to certain hazardous materials. It is not meant as a way of decontaminating hazardous material technicians and their equipment as they exit a contained hot zone.

The controlled protocol used to decontaminate Hazmat techs and their equipment as they exit a contained hot zone is called *technical decon*. This is the procedure that we typically think of when we think of decontamination, whereby technicians in either Level A or Level B protective gear are washed off by other technicians (usually wearing Level C PPE) as they exit the hot zone through a carefully controlled *decon corridor*. The decon corridor is the designated pathway that technicians use to enter and exit the hot zone. This corridor is located in the warm zone, and acts as a vestibule to contain the spread of the hazard from the hot zone to the cold zone. Typically, the decon corridor contains shallow plastic "kiddie" pools to contain the washed off hazardous materials so that it does not run off and seep into the ground. The contaminated water runoff is later placed in containers and disposed in a manner that renders it safe.

Unlike the hasty use of tactical decon, technical decon is done in a very controlled and methodical manner. Great care is taken to contain the hazardous materials from getting outside of the containment area. Typically, the persons who are being decontaminated move through different stations along the decon corridor, where in the end, they doff (remove) their personal protective equipment and then return to the safety of the cold zone for a likely debriefing session. One of the challenges confronted by technical decon, is the decontamination of expensive and sensitive equipment such as firearms and tactical robots that should not be exposed to the water/bleach solution that is typically used to wash off personnel.

The third type of decontamination is called *mass decon*. Like tactical decon, mass decon is also used "hastily" to mitigate the spread of contaminated elements from the hot zone to the cold zone. Mass decon is used to decontaminate large numbers of people who are evacuating or fleeing from a CBRNE incident in a place with large concentrations of people such as a crowded subway station or a preplanned event like a Super Bowl. Mass decon is basically a series of firefighting ladder trucks set up with hoses attached to booms extended high over a designated mass decon corridor. The hoses on the extended booms act as a high volume, low pressure water shower to rinse off large numbers of people who may have been contaminated by some hazardous material. After being decontaminated by these giant showers, the victims are triaged by first responders, and isolated if necessary in a designated refuge/observation area.[15]

For Super Bowl XLI, in 2007, we had four mass decon corridors established for the day of the game. Two parallel corridors were set up to funnel the evacuees westbound toward the NFL Experience area, and two other parallel corridors were to funnel the evacuees eastbound toward a parking area outside the designated exclusionary zone around the stadium. These four corridors were intended to provide a quick, but orderly mass decontamination of up to 90,000 people, including fans, players, coaches, media personnel, stadium staff, and halftime performers. That was the plan, at least. How that plan would actually turn out during a real CBRNE incident at a fully loaded stadium is another matter. It would be impractical to simulate an actual evacuation and decontamination of 90,000 people who would presumably be in a state of psychological distress, if not panic. However, there are a number of science-based computer simulation programs that ostensibly can mirror real conditions, and which can be used for planning the evacuation and mass decon aspect of large-scale special events. These computer programs combine the properties of particle movements in physics with psycho-social aspects of crowd dynamics to predict the direction and rate of movement of large numbers of people under certain conditions. These crowd simulation computer programs provide a valuable tool for planners of large-scale special events.[16]

Tactical Response to Non-CBRN Incidents

Whether it is an attack by Islamic State terrorists, a disgruntled ex-employee, or a student with mental illness issues, incidents involving the use of high velocity assault weapons and explosives seem to be an almost daily occurrence around the world. Regardless of political affiliation or ideology, persons who seek to gain attention by causing great harm are using these basic weapons to kill a lot of people, and then count on television media to instantaneously broadcast the incident worldwide. The more people are killed, and the more spectacular the explosions are, the more likely the media will cover the incident. That is why terrorists of all types—ideologically based organizations or individual narcissists—will tend to choose the means that are most readily available to them, which will give them the highest rate of *return on investment*. For both the terrorist and the narcissist, the *return* is the public attention that they seek, and the *investment* is usually either their own death or incarceration. Both the terrorist and the narcissist are more than willing to make that trade-off.

Today, explosives can be easily manufactured using improvised material legally available to average consumers. Instructions on how to improvise an explosive device are easily found on the Internet. Assault rifles and handguns are readily available. While attacks with chemical, biological, radiological, and nuclear weapons may be deadly, the manufacture and dissemination of these weapons take a considerable level of expertise. An attack with assault weapons and/or explosives is loud, and the effects are immediately apparent. By contrast, the effects of CBRN weapons may not be as immediately visible. In the case of a biological agent release, the effects may not be evident for days. The promise of spectacular imagery, coupled with ease of access to the weapons, makes the combination firearm/explosives attack a much more likely scenario than the CBRN type of scenario. Police departments know this and are prepared.

While Hazmat teams and bomb squads take the tactical lead for CBRN situations, the active shooter or military-style assault situation is the realm of the SWAT teams. Bomb squads also provide support in these situations, when the subjects use improvised explosive devices, and some bomb squads can also provide support with explosive breaching capabilities. In calls involving hostages, or barricades subjects, negotiator teams also play an important role. In all SWAT calls, fire-rescue units respond to standby to treat injuries. At the center of all tactical responses is the SWAT commander—usually a police lieutenant or captain. Because situations involving armed subjects can happen anywhere, at any time, the *Tactical Operations Command* (TOC) is a mobile command post that is usually set up in close proximity to the hot zone, but never inside the hot zone. The TOC is the place where the SWAT commander sets up his command post. In some situations, the TOC may be nothing more than the immediate area around the commander's vehicle. However, more often than not, the TOC is centered on a specially designed command post vehicle that most county and large city jurisdictions have. These command post vehicles come in different shapes and sizes, but they bring with them many tools and conveniences that make the job of managing a tactical situation much easier. Typically, these command post vehicles are equipped with white boards and markers to draw diagrams of where the subject are; a canopy for shade; laptop computers; bottled water; and extra tools of the trade such as pole cams, extra ammunition, and chemical agents.

The TOC serves as both a tactical command post and a reporting and staging area for SWAT and bomb squad personnel as they arrive. If a negotiating team is needed, they typically will set up their own area close to the TOC, but not right on top of it. The lead negotiator must keep in face-to-face contact with the SWAT commander throughout the entire incident. The TOC can be a busy and crowded place, so it is important that security is established around it, so that other non-tactical police personnel do not hang around and add to the chaos. SWAT teams often use stanchions to mark an area around the TOC so that nonessential personnel stay out of it.

Because the TOC is both a command post and a staging area, it has to be fairly close to the hot zone. Sometimes, the TOC is inadvertently set up too close, and needlessly puts the SWAT team commander and his staff at risk. A good practice is to place the TOC one block up and one block to the side of the building where the subjects are thought to be. Doing so usually puts it out of the line of fire from the threat. A good rule of thumb to remember is: if you can see the subject, then he can see you. Establishing the TOC at least two city blocks away from the identified hot zone puts it close enough so that the SWAT team personnel do not have to go too far to enter the area where the subjects are presumed to be, yet not too close.

Typically, fire rescue is staged at a safe location from which they can respond within a minute or two in the event of injuries. Bomb squad, canine, and aviation units may respond to the scene as needed, depending on the type of call. Another important component of active shooter/bomber calls is the public information officer (PIO). Typically, PIO sets up a media staging area where television satellite trucks park and set up their extended boom antennas. This media staging area must be well in the cold zone, at a safe distance from the hot zone.

Next, we will discuss the relationship between the TOC and the Incident Command Post (ICP). Often, these two command elements are colocated, but they are not the same thing, and ideally, they should not be located at the same place. The TOC is where the tactical commander (in this case, the SWAT commander) centers his/her command. That tactical commander must focus his/her full attention on the threat in the hot zone. The tactical commander should not be distracted by the goings on outside the tactical sphere. The broader mission of the critical incident must be the realm of the overall Incident Commander, and that mission must be centered at the ICP, not at the TOC. These are two different command posts doing two different missions by two different commanders. There is nothing wrong with having these two command posts fairly close to each other—preferably, walking distance—so that the incident commander and the SWAT commander can meet face-to-face and plan out their strategy. The job of the incident commander requires that he or she have a broad view of the entire situation. He or she must deal with issues related to perimeter control and information control. Depending on the situation, the incident commander may have to designate mustering locations for the families of victims to meet at. It is the incident commander's job to decide whether to evacuate or shelter in place the areas affected by the threat. If the incident is large, or growing uncontrollably outside the defined hot zone, the incident commander needs to redefine the hot zone and area of operation. Clearly, the incident commander has his or her hands full during active shooter/military attack situations. In order to do all these things effectively, incident commanders must keep a broad perspective throughout the incident, and cannot afford to focus on the threat inside the hot zone. That is the tactical (SWAT) commander's job.

Although the incident commander runs the entire incident, he or she must rely heavily on the SWAT commander's advice and recommendations. However, at no time should the incident commander abdicate his/her command to the SWAT commander. That is a common error that occurs with many inexperienced incident commanders. These incident commanders are under the incorrect belief that once the SWAT commander arrives on the scene, the SWAT team takes over. That is not the way it is supposed to be. It is vitally important that the incident commander and SWAT commander confer often (hopefully, face-to-face), and that they work collaboratively to resolve the incident. The incident commander would be wise to listen to the SWAT commander's requests, but in the end, the incident commander has full responsibility over the outcome of the incident. The relationship between an incident commander and a SWAT commander is no different than the relationship between a B-17 pilot and the plane's bombardier.

We will conclude this chapter with a brief mention of suicide bomber scenarios. The suicide bomber adds yet another compounding factor to the police response to active shooter/military attack scenarios. Police SWAT teams have been successfully dealing with barricaded subject and hostage calls for years. The Columbine mass casualty incident in 1999 combined the active shooter factor with over 30 improvised explosive devices.[17] The pairing of active shooters and explosive devices is as deadly as the pairing of barbed wire and machine guns in

World War I. Active shooters need to be dealt with quickly in order to minimize their carnage. However, the presence of secondary explosive devices left inside the buildings and vehicles considerably slows down the tactical response. Add to that milieu the suicide bomber factor, and now we have a real difficult challenge on our hands. On November 13, 2015, in Paris, France, we saw the carnage that a squad-sized group of Islamic State terrorists were able to inflict on innocent bystanders with a combination of assault rifles and suicide explosive vests.[18] The addition of explosive vests to the mix of deadly factors further complicates the task of neutralizing the threat. Police officers that have been trained their entire careers to aim at the center mass when they shoot now have to consider that their shot at center mass may inadvertently set off the explosive vest, thereby putting themselves and others around them in further risk. SWAT officers are trained to shoot at an armed subject's head under certain circumstances, but the regular patrol officer rarely encounters this situation, and is usually not trained on how to deal with it. We expect that attacks such as the one in Paris will happen more frequently in the United States.

Because the suicide bomber threat is expected to grow in the United States, we strongly recommend that readers of this book consider attending the excellent training for first responders, which is provided under the auspices of the U.S. Department of Homeland Security at New Mexico Tech's Energetic Materials Research and Testing Center.[19] Some of the courses that are currently being offered to first responders include the following:

- Incident response to terrorist bombings
- Prevention of and response to suicide bombing incidents
- Understanding and planning for school bomb incidents
- Initial law enforcement response to suicide bombing attacks
- Medical preparedness and response for bombing incidents

The next chapter examines the strategic sphere of critical incident management. We have gone from the examination of operational command in Chapter 3, and then zeroed in on the smaller sphere of tactical command in this chapter. In Chapter 5, we will expand our examination into the realm of broad strategic command. To use the B-17 analogy, Chapter 3 was about the pilot/commander of the aircraft. Chapter 4 was about the bombardier, and Chapter 5 will be about the Allied commander of strategic Air Force command.

References

1. E. C. Miller. B-17 Crewmen duties and responsibilities. *Hell's Angels, 303rd Bomb Group (H)*. Online at http://www.303rdbg.com/crew-duties.html (accessed December 2, 2015).
2. Ibid.
3. FEMA. Law Enforcement Resources. Resource: Bomb squad/explosives teams. National Mutual Aid & Resource Management Initiative. Online at http://www.oema.us/files/Law_Enforcement_Resource_Typing.doc (accessed December 2, 2015).

4. Ibid.

5. FEMA, 2008. ICS Glossary. Online at https://training.fema.gov/emiweb/is/icsre-source/assets/icsglossary.pdf (accessed November 28, 2015).

6. PNG Logistics, 2013. Online at http://pnglc.com/what-is-a-vacis-exam/ (accessed November 28, 2015).

7. FEMA, 2008. ICS Glossary.

8. U.S. Department of Labor, 1994. Occupational Safety and Health Standards. General description and discussion of the levels of protection and protective gear. Online at https://www.osha.gov/pls/oshaweb/owadisp.show_document?p_table=STANDARDS&p_id=9767 (accessed November 29, 2015).

9. Ibid.

10. Ibid.

11. Ibid.

12. B. Oskin, 2015. Japan Earthquake & Tsunami of 2011: Facts and information. *Live Science*. Online at http:// www.livescience.com/39110-japan-2011-earthquake-tsu-nami-facts.html (accessed August 28, 2015).

13. A. Tarantola, 2012. How NASA Prevents a Space Plague Outbreak. *GIZMODO*, September 25. Online at http://gizmodo.com/5945743/how-nasa-prevents-a-space-plague-outbreak#_ga=1.199365678.1879235282.1449061060 (accessed December 2, 2015).

14. National Fire Protection Association, 1997. Guidelines for decontamination of fire fighters and their equipment. *NFPA Supplement 10*, 5. Online at http://www.disas-ter-info.net/lideres/english/jamaica/bibliography/ChemicalAccidents/NFPA_Sup10_GuidelinesforDecontaminationofFire%20FightersandTheirEquipment.pdf (accessed December 2, 2015).

15. W. Lake, S., P. Schulze, and R. Gouglelet, 2013. *Guidelines for Mass Casualty Decontamination during a Hazmat/Weapon of Mass Destruction Incident: Volumes I and II.* Edgewood Chemical Biological Center. U.S. Army Research, Development and Engineering Command. ECBC-SP-036. Online at http://www.nfpa.org/~/media/Files/Research/Resource%20links/First%20responders/Decontamination/ecbc_Guide_MassCasualtyDecontam_0813.pdf (accessed December 2, 2015).

16. M. C. Lin and D. Manocha, 2010. *Simulation Technologies for Evacuation Planning and Disaster Response.* Institute for Homeland Security Solutions. Online at http://sites.duke.edu/ihss/files/2011/12/IHSS_Research-Brief_Lin.pdf (accessed December 2, 2015).

17. Department of Homeland Security, 1999. Wanton violence at Columbine High School, Littleton, Colorado. Online at http://www.usfa.fema.gov/downloads/pdf/publications/tr-128.pdf (accessed September 10, 2015).

18. *BBC News*, 2015. Paris attacks: What happened on the night, November 16. Online at http://www.bbc.com/news/world-europe-34818994 (accessed December 2, 2015).

19. Energetic Materials Research and Testing Center, 2010. *Course Offerings.* New Mexico Tech. Online at http://www.emrtc.nmt.edu/training/ (accessed December 2, 2015).

5
Strategic Planning—A Systems Approach

Strategy without tactics is the slowest route to victory. Tactics without strategy is the noise before defeat.

Sun Tzu

Strategy or Tactics?

We start this chapter with the examination of *strategy* and *tactics*, and how they relate to each other. These concepts are intertwined like two conjoined twins attached at the head. For the sake of discussion and analysis, we can separate the two concepts, but as a matter of practicality, *strategy* and *tactics* should always go hand-in-hand. As the Sun Tzu quote suggests, leaders who concern themselves with tactical matters and ignore the broader strategic concerns are sure to fail in whatever endeavor they undertake. This is true in war, in business, and in critical incident management. The old saying, "can't see the forest for the trees," comes to mind when considering how some leaders regard tactics as being more important than strategy. Leaders who place an emphasis on tactics over strategy are likely to get lost in those forests.

Most would agree that plans conceived without a clear strategic direction are likely to fail. Strategy, not tactics, should ultimately drive a leader's actions. On the other hand, leaders who devise strategic plans without taking into account tactical considerations are living in a fantasy world, and they too are likely to fail. For a strategy to be viable, it must be driven by the realities on the ground. It is a mistake for a leader to not acknowledge the tactical realities that he or she is confronted with. Strategic planning that does not take into account tactical considerations is an exercise in futility. Nowadays, it has become vogue for companies and organizations to conduct a strategic planning process that involves multiple steps. Typically, the process starts with the formulation of a "vision statement," followed by the setting of strategic priorities (or goals), and then with the enumeration of specific objectives to reach those goals. There is nothing wrong with doing this type of strategic planning. In fact, the authors highly recommend that organizations do this. However, this chapter is not about the strategic planning process that many organizations use as a standard roadmap for their actions. There are plenty of management books and journal articles on how to do strategic planning. That is not what this book is about. This book—and this chapter in particular—examines the interplay between the tactical, operational, and strategic spheres of critical incident management. It is not the intent of the authors to get into a "chicken and

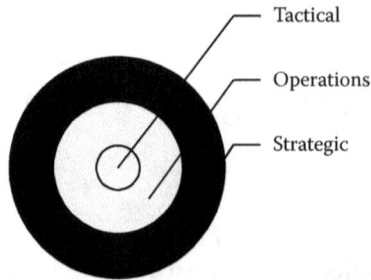

Figure 5.1 Strategic Sphere

egg" discussion as to what came first, and what is more important. Suffice it to say that strategy and tactics go hand-in-hand. Figure 5.1 illustrates how the broad strategic sphere relates to the tactical and operational spheres.

You may recall Vignette 4.1 in Chapter 4 regarding the American B-17 bombing missions over Germany during World War II. In that story, the pilot was the commander of the aircraft, while the bombardier was the specialist who was delegated temporary control of the airplane during a short bomb run. Using the typology illustrated in Figure 5.1, the bombardier is equivalent to the commander of the tactical sphere, while the pilot is the equivalent of the commander of the operational sphere. In this World War II analogy, the equivalent of the strategic level commander would be General Dwight Eisenhower, the Supreme Commander of the Allied Forces in Europe. It was General Eisenhower and his command staff's responsibility to devise the overall strategy of the Allies to defeat Nazi Germany. One of the tenets of Eisenhower's strategy involved a strategic bombing of critical infrastructure assets in German-controlled areas in order to weaken the enemy's manufacturing capabilities and supply lines. General Eisenhower did not fly the B-17s, nor did he control the *Norden Bombsight* during a bombing run. His job was to weigh the risks, and to consider the costs and benefits of the overall strategy. In other words, as the Supreme Commander of the Allied Forces in Europe, it was Eisenhower's job to see the "big picture," and to devise battle plans as guided by the broad strategic direction. That broad strategic direction was not conceived in a vacuum. It took into account the tactical realities on the ground. Strategies such as invading North Africa first, the strategic bombing campaign in German-held territory, and keeping the North Atlantic shipping lanes open with antisubmarine warfare were dictated as much by the tactical realities on the ground, as with the strategic intent of the Allies. Eisenhower's broad strategic intent was to inflict pain on the enemy until they surrendered unconditionally. Nowadays, that broad strategic intent would be referred to as a "vision statement." Back then, everyone understood this, and there was no need to write down a fancy vision statement. In World War II, nothing short of total victory would have been acceptable.

In keeping with the organizing principles of this book, this chapter will examine real-life case studies, and consider simple and practical solutions to problems faced by today's critical incident managers and policy makers. In this chapter, we will examine some of the things that went wrong in incidents such as the civil disturbances in Ferguson, Missouri, and Baltimore, Maryland. We will look at critical incident management from the broad *systems* perspective and we will consider some practices that managers and policy makers may consider implementing in order to "weatherproof" their communities against disruptive civil disturbances or other unanticipated critical incidents. Before we proceed, we first need to briefly examine what is meant by the term *systems approach*. A systems approach helps us to look at the "big picture" as it relates to the strategic sphere of critical incident management.

A Systems Approach to Strategic Planning

Before we can discuss what a systems approach to strategic planning is, we need to define the term "system." A *system* is defined as "A group of interacting, inter-related, or interdependent elements forming a complex whole."[1] Systems have a defined boundary. Anything outside that boundary is considered to be part of a larger *meta system*. Systems are comprised of *elements* and *processes*. Elements are the parts that comprise the total system. In a sense, a system is more than just the sum of its parts. The word *process* is used to describe the interactions between those elements within the system, as well as with other systems. Figure 5.2 illustrates the elements of a system as boxes in a typical organization chart. The solid and dotted lines represent the processes between the elements. Examples of processes include, but are not limited, to communication (information flow), funding (resource flow), coordination, integration, and command.

Simply stated, the boxes in Figure 5.2 represent the *elements* of a system. Elements are things that we can see, hear, and touch. An element can represent an organization, a division or department, a place, an object, or even an individual person. Processes are the lines that connect the elements. Another word for *process* is *relationship*. For example, the hierarchical structure depicted in the Incident Command System organizational chart illustrates a chain of command relationships between the boxes. Other processes between elements are depicted in diagrams to show relationships such as information flow. Figure 5.3 depicts the flow of information in the Central Intelligence Agency's (CIA) Intelligence Cycle.[2]

Figure 5.4 illustrates side by side the two processes by which the U.S. Department of Homeland Security (DHS) money trickles down to the local level

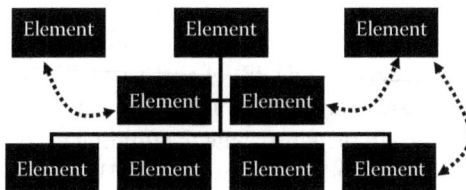

Figure 5.2 Elements and Processes

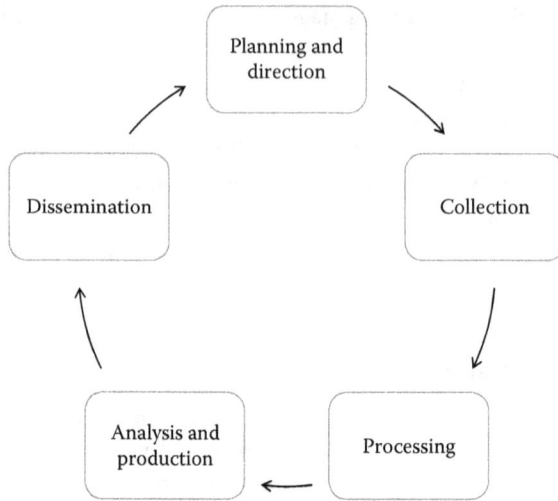

Figure 5.3 The Intelligence Cycle (From the U.S. Central Intelligence Agency.)

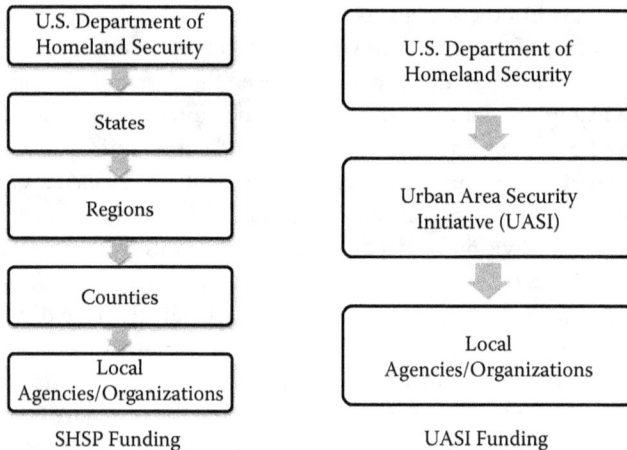

Figure 5.4 Two DHS Funding Streams

police and fire-rescue agencies. The funding stream on the left depicts the flow of money in the State Homeland Security Program (SHSP) and Law Enforcement Terrorism Prevention Program (LETPP) of past years. These two programs are funded by the DHS as block grants to the states. In turn, the states distribute the funding to regions, which in turn distribute the funding to counties, and eventually to local agencies. The second process by which DHS allocates funding to local agencies is through its Urban Area Security Initiative (UASI). This money focuses on high-density metropolitan areas that are deemed to be high-risk targets for terrorism. For example, New York City, Washington, DC, Miami, Atlanta, Boston, San Francisco (Bay Area), Los Angeles, Houston, and other large urban areas that have had a history of terrorist attacks are the prime recipients of UASI funding.

Table 5.1 denotes the funding of the states and territories of the United States under the SHSP program for Fiscal Year 2014.[3] Table 5.2 denotes the distribution

Table 5.1 FY 2014 SHSP Allocations

FY 2014 SHSP Allocations

State/Territory	FY 2014 Allocation	State/Territory	FY 2014 Allocation
Alabama	$3,733,000	Montana	$3,733,000
Alaska	$3,733,000	Nebraska	$3,733,000
American Samoa	$854,000	Nevada	$3,733,000
Arizona	$4,568,000	New Hampshire	$3,733,000
Arkansas	$3,733,000	New Jersey	$8,354,000
California	$60,035,000	New Mexico	$3,733,000
Colorado	$3,979,000	New York	$76,742,000
Connecticut	$3,978,000	North Carolina	$5,489,000
Delaware	$3,733,000	North Dakota	$3,733,000
District of Columbia	$4,119,000	Northern Mariana	$854,000
Florida	$11,010,000	Ohio	$7,698,000
Georgia	$6,807,000	Oklahoma	$3,733,000
Guam	$854,000	Oregon	$3,837,000
Hawaii	$3,733,000	Pennsylvania	$10,026,000
Idaho	$3,733,000	Puerto Rico	$3,733,000
Illinois	$16,357,000	Rhode Island	$3,733,000
Indiana	$3,978,000	South Carolina	$3,733,000
Iowa	$3,733,000	South Dakota	$3,733,000
Kansas	$3,733,000	Tennessee	$3,978,000
Kentucky	$3,978,000	Texas	$21,448,000
Louisiana	$3,978,000	U.S. Virgin Islands	$854,000
Maine	$3,733,000	Utah	$3,733,000
Maryland	$6,125,000	Vermont	$3,733,000
Massachusetts	$5,622,000	Virginia	$7,414,000
Michigan	$6,658,000	Washington	$6,493,000
Minnesota	$3,978,000	West Virginia	$3,733,000
Mississippi	$3,733,000	Wisconsin	$3,978,000
Missouri	$3,978,000	Wyoming	$3,733,000
Total			$401,346,000

Source: Department of Homeland Security Funding Opportunity Announcement, FY 2014. Homeland Security grant program. Online at http://www.fema.gov/media-library-data/1395161200285-5b07ed0456056217175fbdee28d2b06e/FY_2014_HSGP_FOA_Final.pdf (accessed July 30, 2008).

Table 5.2 FY 2014 UASI Allocations

FY 2014 UASI Allocations

State/Territory	Funded Urban Area	FY 2014 UASI Allocation
Arizona	Phoenix Area	$5,500,000
California	Anaheim/Santa Ana Area	$5,500,000
	Bay Area	$27,400,000
	Los Angeles/Long Beach Area	$67,500,000
	Riverside Area	$1,000,000
	Sacramento Area	$1,000,000
	San Diego Area	$16,874,000
Colorado	Denver Area	$3,000,000
District of Columbia	National Capital Region	$53,000,000
Florida	Miami/Fort Lauderdale Area	$5,500,000
	Orlando Area	$1,000,000
	Tampa Area	$3,000,000
Georgia	Atlanta Area	$5,500,000
Hawai	Honolulu Area	$1,000,000
Illinois	Chicago Area	$69,500,000
Indiana	Indianapolis Area	$1,000,000
Louisiana	New Orleans Area	$3,000,000
Maryland	Baltimore Area	$5,500,000
Massachusetts	Boston Area	$18,000,000
Michigan	Detroit Area	$5,500,000
Minnesota	Twin Cities Area	$5,500,000
Missouri	Kansas City Area	$1,000,000
	St. Louis Area	$3,000,000
Nevada	Las Vegas Area	$1,000,000
New Jersey	Jersey City/Newark Area	$21,800,000
New York	New York City Area	$178,926,000
North Carolina	Charlotte Area	$3,000,000
Ohio	Cincinnati Area	$1,000,000
	Cleveland Area	$1,000,000
	Columbus Area	$1,000,000
Oregon	Portland Area	$1,000,000
Pennsylvania	Philadelphia Area	$18,500,000
	Pittsburgh Area	$3,000,000
Texas	Dallas/Fort Worth/Arlington Area	$15,500,000
	Houston Area	$24,000,000
	San Antonio Area	$1,000,000
Utah	Salt Lake City Area	$1,000,000
Virginia	Hampton Roads Area	$1,000,000
Washington	Seattle Area	$5,500,000
Total		$587,000,000

Source: Department of Homeland Security Funding Opportunity Announcement, FY 2014. Homeland Security grant program. Online at http://www.fema.gov/media-library-data/1395161200285-5b07ed0456056217175fbdee28d2b06e/FY_2014_HSGP_FOA_Final.pdf (accessed July 30, 2008).

of UASI funding to select high-density/high-risk urban areas for the same fiscal year. The underlying reason for the two separate funding streams goes back as far as the dilemma faced by the framers of the U.S. Constitution in 1787. It was then that a fundamental disagreement about representation emerged. The smaller states (population wise) wanted an equal number of representatives to Congress. The larger states thought that they should be represented in Congress in proportion to the population in their states. The Great Compromise of 1787 resulted in the inception of a bicameral legislature in which one house (the Senate) was created to appease the smaller states, while the other (the House of Representatives) was created to appease the larger states. That there are two different funding streams—one for the low-population states, and the other for high-population states—comes as no surprise. Nevertheless, according to DHS, law enforcement agencies can receive allocation from SHSP, UASI, or both. In the end, the money reaches the local agencies, regardless of the path that it takes to get there. These two separate funding streams are examples of a process that links the federal elements with the state and local elements of the homeland security system.

Systems, Subsystems, and Meta Systems

Systems are often comprised of smaller *subsystems*. For example, the human body is a system that is comprised of several subsystems such as the skeletal, muscular, circulatory, digestive, nervous, respiratory, reproductive, urinary, and lymphatic systems. These subsystems have clearly distinct functions, but they interact with each other to keep us alive. Another example of a system is the solar system. The elements of the solar system are the sun, the planets, their moons, asteroids, and comets. Each of these elements can also be considered to be subsystems. For example, the Earth has its own magnetic field, atmosphere, and is also comprised of various ecosystems that can be considered to be subsystems or systems in their own right. In fact, every plant or animal on Earth can be considered as being a distinct system of its own. Systems can be as large as galaxies, or as small as atoms. As it pertains to the discipline of critical incident management, the primary systems that we will be dealing with are the emergency management system, the criminal justice system, the homeland security system, the economic system, and the federated system of government. The term *meta system* refers to a larger system of systems. For example, in astronomy, galaxies are meta systems that are comprised of billions of solar systems. Figure 5.5 illustrates a system and its subsystems within, as well as other systems outside its boundary in the meta system. The "U" in the middle stands for *unit of analysis*. The unit of analysis is the central element that we will use for our systems analysis.

> If you know your enemy and you know yourself you need not fear the results of a hundred battles. If you know yourself but not the enemy for every victory gained you will also suffer a defeat. If you know neither the enemy nor yourself you will succumb in every battle.
>
> **Sun Tzu**

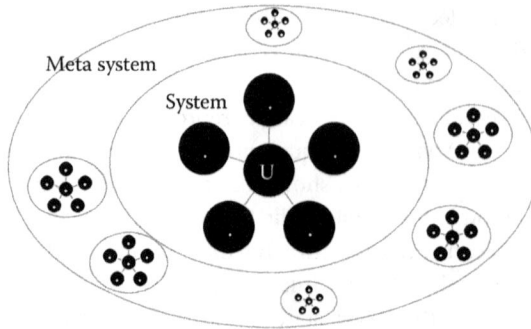

Figure 5.5 Unit of Analysis in Relation to the System and Its Meta System

A *systems approach* to strategic planning is well suited for addressing the complexities of modern day homeland security and emergency management spheres. Failure to consider the many moving parts of a complex system will likely lead to poor results. As Sun Tzu points out, it is important to know oneself, but it is essential that we know our adversaries as well. The systems approach provides planners with an understanding of where their organization stands in relation to other organizations, both friendly and adversarial. We recommend a holistic approach to systems analysis that starts with a stakeholder analysis, and is followed by a SWOT (strengths, weaknesses, opportunities, and threats) analysis. The SWOT analysis is followed by risk analysis and then a cost–benefit analysis. This holistic approach is illustrated in Figure 5.6.

Stakeholder Analysis

The first step is to gain an understanding of our organization's operating environment. To do so, we start by identifying stakeholders associated with the central *unit of analysis*. Stakeholders can be any group or individual that has a vested interest or effect in the outcome of an issue or event. Stakeholders may either be adversarial, cooperative, or situational. Freeman and Reed define the term *stakeholder* as, "groups to whom the corporation is responsible in addition to stockholders: those groups who have a stake in the actions of the corporation."[4] This definition focuses on corporations as the unit of analysis, but the term *stakeholder* can be applied to all types of organizations, not just corporations. Okes and Westcott describe the term stakeholder as, "individuals, groups, or organizations who will be directly or indirectly affected by an organization carrying out its mission."[5] According to Okes and Westcott, "all stakeholders have particular issues, priorities, and concerns, and it is important that an organization understand each of the stakeholder groups and the issues most important to them."[6]

Stakeholder analysis does not need to be very complicated. One commonly used approach is to make a list of all organizations or individuals that have an effect or are affected by the actions of the organization at the center of the analysis (i.e., the unit of analysis). Those organizations and individuals that are listed

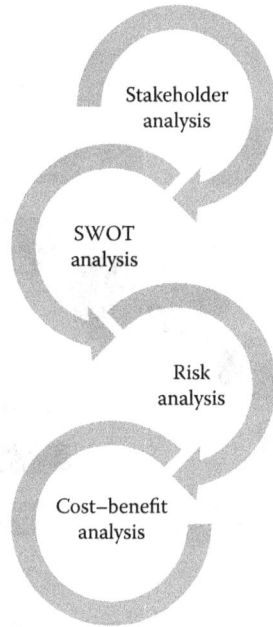

Figure 5.6 Holistic Systems Approach

are then examined closer to determine whether they are friendly or adversarial to the unit of analysis. The analysis of the listed stakeholders would also take into account their common issues of concern, and whether there are possible points of agreement, or possible points that may lead to conflict. A good practice for doing a stakeholder analysis is to conduct a SWOT analysis from the perspective of each of the stakeholders. In other words, a SWOT analysis from the outside in. More on SWOT analysis will follow in the next section.

Another useful way to start a stakeholder analysis is to draw a stakeholder map in which all the stakeholders are illustrated—preferably on one page—in a way that best portrays the relationships between the stakeholders and the unit of analysis. Figure 5.7 illustrates an example of a simple stakeholder map, whereby the central unit of analysis is a local law enforcement agency. In this stakeholder map, the diagram that portrays the stakeholder system is divided into four quadrants: public, private business, local government, and federal government. For this particular stakeholder map, each of these quadrants would be considered systems of the overall system that is being portrayed.

If the stakeholder map in Figure 5.7 looks to be overly simplistic, it is because it was meant to be that way. The whole point of a stakeholder map is to oversimplify our perspective of the system so that we can better understand it. That is why we recommend that the stakeholder map be drawn on one page. The one page serves a role similar to an executive summary of a report. It puts it all together in an organized and simple to understand picture. Later, the analysis can get more detailed,

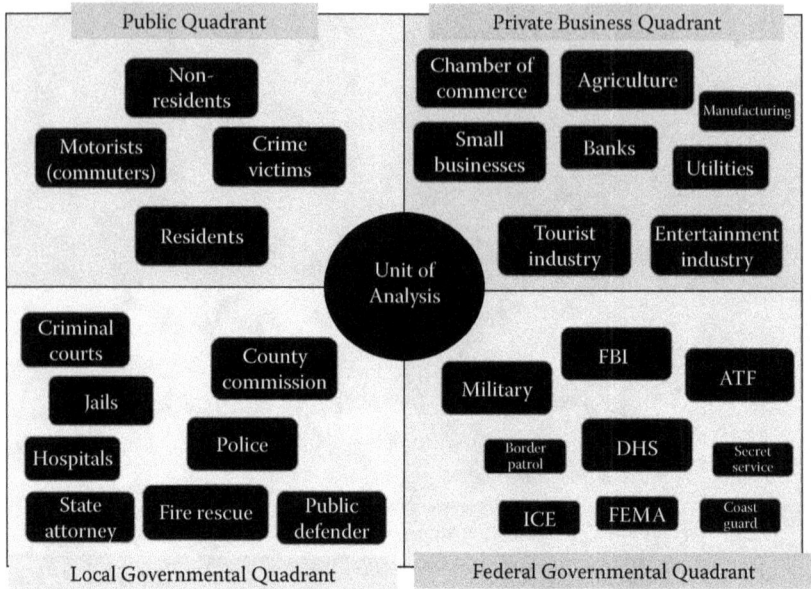

Figure 5.7 Stakeholder Map with Four Quadrants

and more pages can be added as needed. The purpose of stakeholder maps is to provide the analysts with "the big picture." The microanalysis of the relationships between the elements is done afterward, mostly in the form of a SWOT analysis.

VIGNETTE 5.1   Gaining the Competitive Advantage

The Kansas City Chiefs of the National Football League list 27 coaches on their coaching staff. Included among those 27 are the *Head Coach; Assistant Head Coach; Spread Game Analyst/Special Projects Coach; Statistical Analysis Coordinator; Offensive Coordinator; Quarterbacks Coach; Assistant Quarterbacks Coach; Running Backs Coach; Tight Ends Coach; Offensive Line Coach; Assistant Offensive Line Coach; Defensive Coordinator; Defensive Line Coach; Assistant Defensive Line Coach; Linebackers Coach; Assistant Linebackers Coach; Defensive Back Coach; Assistant Secondary Coach; Special Teams Coordinator; Assistant Special Teams Coach; Quality Control and Director of Video Operations; Assistant Director of Video Operations;* two *Video Assistant Coaches;* a *Strength and Conditioning Coach;* and two *Assistant Strength and Conditioning Coaches.*[7] Each of these positions has a specific and specialized role in the overall operations of the team. Not only does this practice say a lot about the age of specialization that we're in right now, but it also shows the lengths that professional football teams go to in order to gain a competitive advantage over other teams. In the United States, professional football is a serious matter. Coaches who lose more than they win don't last very long.

One would expect this type of specialization and attention to detail in the highly competitive profit-based stakeholder environment such as the NFL and its 32 teams. Not far behind are the college football teams of the NCAA (National Collegiate Athletic Association). For example, the University of Alabama lists 13 coaches in its football program, but it also makes use of another 24 individuals in roles as *Football Analysts* and *Graduate Assistants*.[8] Each of these specialized positions has a very specific role in the operations of a football team. For example, it is the responsibility of the offensive coordinator to devise a game plan and a set of offensive play calls to be used for various situations during a game. Likewise, the defensive coordinator is responsible for devising the defensive game plan to counter the opponent's offensive game plan. The defensive game plan includes a number of coverages and blitz packages to put pressure on the opponent's quarterback. Most teams have a general offensive and defensive scheme that they use throughout the season. All teams scout their opponents and look for tendencies that the other team may rely on. After all, if certain play calls are successful during games, they are likely to be repeated. Plays that don't work out very well are often discarded. Thus, every team develops tendencies—in other words, they get into habitual ruts. This can be a good thing, and a bad thing. Success in football often has to do with key players being in the right place, at the right time. If the opponents can chart the tendencies of your team, then they are more likely to be in the right place, at the right time to counter your plays, and therefore achieve a competitive advantage.

As a coach of a football team, knowing your opponents' tendencies will give you the advantage in key one-on-one matchups. Sometimes, winning or losing a game can hinge on just one or two plays where an individual player is in a "mismatch" with the opponent, thereby giving that player the temporary advantage. Both professional and college football teams employ assistant coaches, whose jobs are to scout the opponents' tendencies.

Coaches who scout other teams are looking for the threats that their opponents present. In other words, these scouts consider the opponent's strengths, and they view those strengths as threats to their own teams. For example, Seattle Seahawks quarterback Russell Wilson is known as a dual threat quarterback who can throw the ball, or run with equal proficiency. Coaches and scouts know that Wilson becomes especially effective when he is flushed out of the pocket and starts to run. Most defenses counter this dual threat by putting steady and equal pressure in the form of controlled blitzes and by dropping back extra men on coverage. On the other hand, less mobile quarterbacks, like Peyton Manning (formerly with the Denver Broncos), are less likely to break out of the pocket and run the ball. Therefore, teams tend to blitz extra men through the "A-gap" hole between the center and the guards in order to make quarterbacks like Manning less comfortable. Without getting too technical, it is clear that different types of players, with different skill sets, pose different types of challenges for their opponents. That is why the coaches/scouts look at their opponents' threats, but they also look at their opponents' weaknesses. Most teams have weaknesses that their opponents find and seek to exploit. This becomes especially evident as the football season drags on, and many of the key players become injured, and are either forced to play with handicaps, or replaced by less-talented backups.

There is another set of coaches that do nothing else other than scout their own teams. These coaches are responsible for looking at their teams as if they were their opponents' scouts. Their job is to look for their own team's strengths and weaknesses. More importantly, these coaches look for tendencies that their own play callers develop, so that they don't become predictable to their opponents. Typically, the head coach, and the two main coordinators (offensive and defensive) will devise a game plan for the next opponent based on how well their teams do. It makes perfect sense to repeat doing what has been successful in the past. In the business world, this is a strategy called "relying on *core competencies*." Relying on one's core competencies makes sense because the things that have worked in the past are likely to work in the future.

It's generally a good idea to repeat the things that you're good at, while at the same time trying to improve the things that you're not very good at. For example, the Georgia Tech University football team uses a triple option offensive scheme that is very simple, but it creates all kinds of problems for their opponents. That is because very few teams nowadays employ that type of offensive scheme, and it is very difficult for opponents to practice and prepare against it. That's because no other teams use that scheme, and opponents don't get to see it very often. Secondly, the opponents find it difficult to compose a "scout team" that is equally adept as the Georgia Tech offense. That mismatch of personnel and scheme gives the Georgia Tech team a huge competitive advantage on the field. The disadvantage that Georgia Tech has is a strategic one. Because most college football players aspire to eventually play for the NFL and make a lot of money, they tend to choose university teams that employ offensive schemes that are similar to those used by NFL teams. Georgia Tech's triple option scheme is rarely used by the NFL. That's because the NFL teams don't want to expose their multimillion dollar quarterbacks to the risk of injury from the constant pounding that triple option quarterbacks take. While Georgia Tech's triple option offensive scheme may provide it with a competitive advantage on the football field, it also saddles the team with a huge strategic disadvantage in that the top high school prospects usually choose other university teams that run a "pro scheme" for their offense.

Like in any business, in football there are internal strengths and weaknesses, and external threats and opportunities. Like in any other business, the head coach of a football team must understand the advantages and disadvantages of every move they make, and like in any other business, they learn to make trade-offs in order to maximize their chances of winning.

SWOT (Strengths, Weaknesses, Opportunities, and Threats) Analysis

Vignette 5.1 provides an example of how football teams conduct SWOT analyses of their own internal strengths and weaknesses, as well as their external opportunities and threats as posed primarily by their opponents' strengths and weaknesses. The analysis of opportunities and threats is not just in relation to their opponents, but must also take into consideration other factors in their environments. For example, teams from the Pacific West Coast that travel to play teams in the Atlantic East Coast tend to be at a temporary competitive disadvantage due to the lasting effects of jet lag. For this reason, some traveling teams will go to the cities where they will be playing a couple of days earlier so that their "body clocks" and circadian rhythms can adjust accordingly. The same holds true for teams from the East that travel out West. Certain teams, such as the Denver Broncos (due to the high altitude) and the Miami Dolphins (due to the heat and high humidity) enjoy considerable home field advantages over visiting opponents. Figure 5.8 provides a simplified illustration of what a SWOT analysis would look like. Typically, there are more than just three items under each of the quadrants.

Risk Analysis

Risk analysis was covered in depth in Chapter 2, so there is no need to rehash it in detail in this section. However, we will briefly discuss the topic of risk in the context of the holistic Systems Approach model illustrated earlier in Figure 5.6. You may recall the simple formula outlined in Chapter 2 for determining risk (RISK = Likelihood × Consequence). You may also recall that the likelihood factor is a function of threat and vulnerability. Threat and vulnerability relate to

	Advantageous	Disadvantageous
Internal	Strengths 1. _____ 2. _____ 3. _____	Weaknesses 1. _____ 2. _____ 3. _____
External	Opportunities 1. _____ 2. _____ 3. _____	Threats 1. _____ 2. _____ 3. _____

Figure 5.8 SWOT Analysis Table

SWOT Analysis   Risk Analysis

$$\frac{\text{Threats and}}{\text{opportunities}} = \text{Threat}$$

$$\frac{\text{Weaknesses and}}{\text{strengths}} = \text{Vulnerability}$$

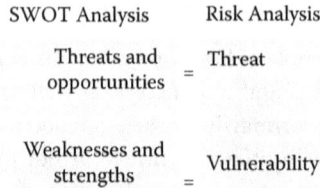

Figure 5.9 Side-by-Side Comparison of SWOT and Risk Analyses

SWOT analysis as outlined in Figure 5.9. In other words, both of these types of analyses can, and should be used in unison.

Cost–Benefit Analysis

Cost–benefit analysis can be summed up with the simple question: "is it worth the trouble?" Better stated: "is the expected benefit worth the cost to attain it?" Cost–benefit analysis is something that companies and organizations do all the time. Good guys do it, and bad guys do it. According to the 911 Commission Report, al Qaeda invested between $400,000 and $500,000 to plan, train for, and execute the September 11 terrorist attacks.[9] From al Qaeda's perspective, the return that they got on their investment was well worth the cost. Consider the impact of the live broadcasts that captured the image of the second Twin Tower being struck by the second airplane. Television cameras from all the major networks: ABC, CBS, CNN, Fox, NBC, and more broadcast the images of September 11 live, and then repeatedly afterward, untold millions of times, via television and the Internet. Compare the cost and benefit ratio that al Qaeda was able to get from the September 11 attacks to the cost–benefit ratio that advertisers are willing to pay for a 30-second commercial during a Super Bowl. A typical 30 second commercial during the Super Bowl costs $3,500,000.[10] That translates to $3.5 million to reach anywhere from 111 to 114 million view-ers for 30-seconds, or roughly 31 cents per viewer. In comparison, al Qaeda "paid" only $400,000–$500,000 for the broadcast of imagery that has been viewed repeatedly throughout the globe. From the standpoint of cost–benefit analysis, it is safe to say that al Qaeda got their money's worth. This was an example of an optimal outcome resulting from a low cost–high benefit invest-ment. This optimal outcome, or *optimal return on investment* is illustrated by the lower right quadrant of Figure 5.10. Another way of saying it is to call that outcome an *optimal value*. The concept of "value" is a function of cost and ben-efit (i.e., Value = Cost × Benefit).

In Figure 5.10, the least desired outcome is the high cost–low benefit return on investment, as illustrated in the top left quadrant titled *poor value*. This quadrant is indicative of wasteful spending as is often seen in some of the out-landish expenditures of the federal government. For example, according to the Washington Examiner, the investigations of 14 inspectors general conducting

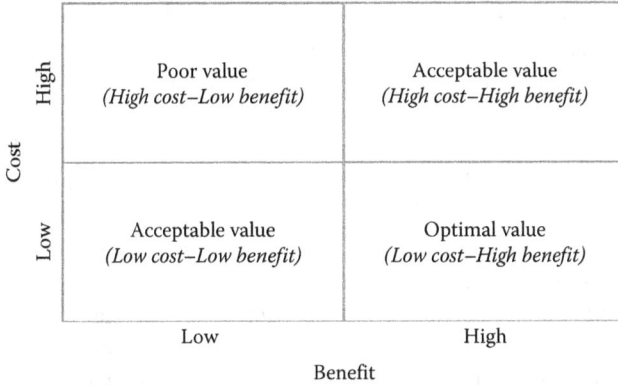

Figure 5.10 Cost–Benefit Matrix

independent audits of various federal agencies found the federal government wasted a total of $43 billion in 2014.[11] We have all heard of wasteful government spending such as $400 screwdrivers and all-expense paid Las Vegas seminars for General Services Administration (GSA) and Internal Revenue Service (IRS) federal employees. Senator Tom Coburn published the last of the annual "Wastebook" in 2014, which highlighted a number of wasteful government programs such as the $50,000 spent to study the effect of sea monkeys swimming on changes in the flow of oceans.[12]

The other two quadrants on the cost-benefit matrix are the "acceptable" outcomes of low cost-low benefit in the lower left quadrant and high cost-high benefit outcome in the upper right quadrant. In simple terms, these two quadrants illustrate the commonly held belief, "you get what you pay for." As long as there is a positive linear relationship between cost and benefit, then most people are willing to accept the outcome to their investment. This linear relationship is illustrated in Figure 5.11.

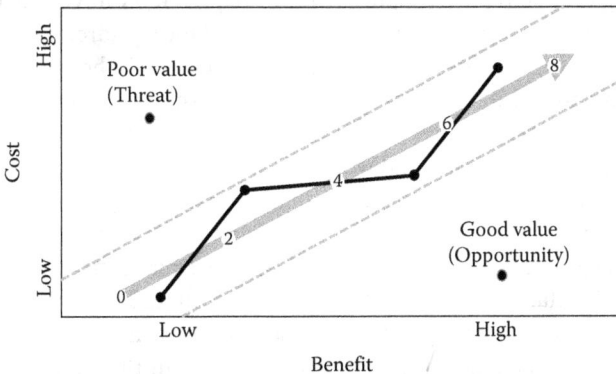

Figure 5.11 Linear Cost–Benefit Relationship

Most people are willing to pay the cost as long as the outcome is commensurate with the investment. The moment that the outcomes start to deviate from the *center line of expectations* (the area between the dotted lines), then a reassessment needs to be done in order to determine whether the right course of action has been taken. In Figure 5.11, the four data points within the dotted lines deviate slightly above and below the center line of expectations. In this figure, two of the data points are slightly higher than expected, and two are slightly lower than expected, but all four fall within an *acceptable area of tolerance.* In other words, these four outcome points were not exactly what was expected, but they were close enough. Close enough to reasonably conclude that the current strategy is working as expected, therefore, the policy makers should stay the course. Also note that there are two data points outside the acceptable area of tolerance. These two data points are outliers. The one on the top left is indicative of a poor value, due to its high cost and low benefit. Going back to the SWOT analysis terminology, another way to describe this poor value data point is that it poses a *threat.* The other outlier data point that is located at the bottom right of the chart indicates a good value, due to its low cost and high benefit. Using SWOT analysis terminology, this data point can be considered to present an unanticipated *opportunity.*

The term "unintended consequences" was coined by Merton[13] in his work, *The Unanticipated Consequences of Purposive Social Action.* In a purposive social action, or an economic one as well, the strategist or investor perceives a positive end result (i.e., a benefit) when a certain investment is made, or a cost is paid. As long as the end result is commensurate with the cost, then all is well. However, if the end result turns out negatively in relation to the costs expended, then that result is considered to be a poor value, and a threat to the growth or existence of the organization. Because it was not intended or expected, that data point on the top left quadrant of Figure 5.10 can also be regarded as an *unintended consequence.* Likewise, the data point on the lower right quadrant that is labeled as "Good Value (Opportunity)" can also be regarded as an *unintended benefit.*

Referring back to the B-17 vignette from Chapter 4, try to visualize the solid diagonal line in Figure 5.10 as the plotted course of the squadron's bombing mission. Any bombs that strike along that center line would be considered to be successful because they had the intended effect. Any bomb strikes within the accepted margin of error (anything between the two parallel dotted lines) would be considered "close enough" and worth the cost. Any bombs that strike outside the two dotted lines would be either an unintended consequence (top left quadrant), or an unexpected benefit (lower right quadrant). An example of an unintended consequence would be a "friendly fire" type situation in which bombs are dropped accidentally on Allied soldiers on the ground. Friendly fire situations in war are so common that planners should expect them to occur. Unintended consequences can be (and should be) accounted for in the plans. The opposite of an unintended consequence would be an unexpected benefit such as a target of opportunity presenting itself, either on the bombing run, or on the trip back while returning to base. A good plan takes into account the possibility of unintended opportunities, and takes advantage of them.

In the realm of critical incident management, unintended consequences and unanticipated benefits occur all the time. The best plans are those that have built-in tolerances to deal with the bad things that happen unexpectedly. In other words, a sound strategy that critical incident managers should strive for is the building of resiliency for the personnel involved in the incident, their equipment, and for the plan itself. The best plans are those that can withstand unexpected threats. Likewise, the best plans are those that can take advantage of unexpected opportunities that present themselves. The best plans have high degrees of tolerance for the unexpected—both threats and opportunities.

Types of Strategies

Nature provides an excellent classroom from which we can learn about strategies that can be applied to war, business, sports, or personal improvement. They can also be applied to the homeland security and critical incident management fields. Animals and plants use a myriad of survival strategies that are often mimicked in the things we do on a daily basis. Indeed, mimicry is one of those survival strategies that we will examine in this section. The ability to learn from others and to mimic their behavior is not unique to the human species, but it is safe to say that humans have used this survival strategy to an extent not seen in any other species on the planet. Vignette 5.2 provides a brief example of how some critical incident planners learned what to do, and what not to do by studying the actions of others.

VIGNETTE 5.2   Lessons Learned from the Seattle WTO Conference, 1999

Planning for the security of the 2003 Free Trade Area of the Americas (FTAA) Conference in Miami, Florida, started more than a year earlier. The law enforcement and emergency management agencies in South Florida and Miami-Dade County in particular are accustomed to these large-scale special events in their jurisdictions. Since 1968, the area has hosted a Republican National Convention; 10 Super Bowls; two Major League Baseball World Series; a Papal visit in 1987; the Summit of the Americas in 1995; and a Presidential Debate in 2004. Moreover, the area had experienced the "McDuffie Riots" in Liberty City in 1980, as well as the "Luis Alvarez" and "Lozano" riots of 1982 and 1989, respectively. There was also the "Elian Gonzalez" civil disturbances in 2000. As a result of all these large-scale events and civil disturbance incidents, Miami-Dade Police Department (MDPD) commanders and policy makers learned a great deal from their past mistakes and became known as innovators of the Mobile Field Force concept, which has been adopted by most police departments throughout the United States. Because of its warm weather and geographic proximity to South America and the Caribbean, Miami had become a place where political and economic conventions and large gatherings of people had become commonplace. As such, it had become a sort of testing area and "proving ground" for new crowd control tactics. Miami had become the place where other police departments would come to observe and learn. But in 1999, the way that police departments plan for large crowds and civil disturbances would radically change.

In 1999, the World Trade Organization held its ministerial conference in Seattle, Washington. This event proved to be a paradigm shift in the way that police departments have had to plan for large-scale special events where large crowds were expected. The WTO Conference in Seattle marked the first time in the United States that a sizeable and well-organized group of protestors had planned and executed a coordinated attack to disrupt an international economic conference in order to bring attention to their political causes. These were not the spontaneous race riots of the 1960s and 1980s. These were professional and well-trained anarchists and other radical left-leaning antiglobalization groups using "direct action" and "Black Bloc" tactics to bring attention to their political causes. In the words of one of the protestors: "There were a lot of us. We blended easily with the local population of youth and other people who were happy to join us at the barricades. And we weren't going to give up no matter how much tear gas was fired at us. We were determined."[14]

The commanders and officers of the Seattle Police Department (SPD) acted admirably and even heroically to meet this new and unexpected challenge. Nevertheless, there is no disputing that the police department and local politicians were caught flat-footed. According to the after-action report completed by the agency,[15] the commanders were surprised by "the high degree of coordinated action orchestrated using walkie talkies and cell phones; the critical mass achieved with the rapid marshaling of forces from all directions nearly simultaneously on the morning of November 30; the conscious use of hit and run tactics and flanking movements through the day and night to follow; and the effective use of peaceful demonstrators to mask and shield law violators."[16]

According to the SPD after-action report, the Seattle WTO riots resulted in 92 injuries as reported by local hospitals, as well as 56 police officers reporting being injured. Local businesses sustained $3 million in property damage, and it was estimated that retailers sustained as much as $17 million in lost sales during the 5 days of the WTO Conference. SPD's after-action report was unique in its frankness and self-criticism. The report cited many lessons learned, but the one that caught the attention of the MDPD planners the most was "The dynamic and rapidly changing character of modern protest activity sometimes resulted in law enforcement being one step behind those committed to unlawful behavior."[17]

Clearly, this was a new beast. No longer could MDPD rely on the old Mobile Field Force tactics that it had developed in the early 1980s. MDPD commanders were determined not to let what happened in Seattle repeat itself for the Free Trade Area of the Americas (FTAA) Conference in Miami. To win in this new paradigm, MDPD planners knew that they had to get ahead of the protestors at every turn. This meant that they needed to be proactive rather than reactive in both their Mobile Field Force tactics and in their overall strategy. They could no longer afford to stand around in static crowd control lines and wait to be attacked from all sides by a well trained and goal-directed cadre of "professional" protestors. In response to the anarchist/antiglobalization protestors expected for the FTAA, MDPD changed its strategic concept to reflect the following organizing principles:

- Emphasis on offense rather than reliance on defense alone
- Inside and outside deployment (i.e., do not put all your forces behind a fence)
- Emphasis on unit mobility rather than the static, linear tactics of the past
- Intelligence driven (know your opponent's every move ahead of time)
- Proactive enforcement (i.e., strike early and strike hard—don't wait until things get out of hand)
- Matching up with the adversary: "The right tool for the right job" (There were many different types of protestors and protest behaviors, therefore different types of units were created to match up against each type)
- Emphasis on strict unit discipline and clearly stated *rules of engagement*

The consensus of the main MDPD planners was that they wanted to get ahead of the protestors and not let what happened in Seattle happen in Miami. They were determined to have more than sufficient forces on hand, and to deploy those forces at the optimal times and places in order to ensure superiority over the hard-core Black Bloc trained protestors. The term "Black Bloc" refers to the tactics used by certain violent protest groups, including anarchist organizations. Being at the right place and at the right time with superior numbers of well-disciplined Mobile Field Force officers would give the impression that the police were everywhere, and thus would act as a deterrence against the planned "direct action" tactics employed by the most violent of protestors. In order to do so, the police needed to have accurate and timely intelligence of the protestors' movements and intentions. That was the single-most important aspect of their strategy going into the FTAA. The second-most important tactic employed by the MDPD was the use of bicycle Mobile Field Force platoons, which acted as light cavalry to quickly maneuver and outflank the marauding groups of protestors.

The third tactic envisioned by the MDPD planners was to deploy six large fire suppression pump trucks and repurpose them to be used as water cannons to disperse protestors. This was the most controversial of all the proposed tactics, and would have been unheard of just a few months prior to the FTAA. However, the MDPD commanders were able to persuade the upper command staff of the department, as well as county policy makers as to the importance of having these water cannons on hand. As it turned out, they were never used to disperse any crowds during the one-week event, but many of the line officers attributed their success to the visual deterrent that these six large water cannons had on the protestors. Their mere presence seemed to deter the more violent protestors from attacking the American Airlines Arena and the adjacent roadway connecting mainland Downtown Miami with Dodge Island, where the Port of Miami was located.

A fourth tactic employed by MDPD was the formation of light, medium, and heavy CUT teams, used to safely and expeditiously separate the "direct action" protestors who were known to chain themselves to fences, or to one another with handcuffs, locks, chains, and PVC pipes. In order to properly outfit these CUT teams, the MDPD spent over $76,000 worth of bolt cutters, sledge hammers, electric saws, generators, and many other tools used to separate any protestors who decided to chain themselves together in order to disrupt the conference. The personnel assigned to these CUT teams received extensive training over a three month period preceding the FTAA event. In the end, despite the expenditures for equipment and training, the CUT teams were never needed. Much of this had to do with the Coast Guard's intercept of the Greenpeace ship *Esperanza*, 1 week before the conference started. The Coast Guard boarded the ship and seized several large crates of chains, hooks, carabineers, and pipes that were intended for use by the Black Bloc protestors.

In the end, all the planning and preparation that the MDPD commanders did prior to the FTAA Conference paid off. It is estimated that 10,000 people from all over the United States and other countries came to the South Florida area to protest. Unlike the WTO in Seattle only 4 years earlier, the FTAA was considered by many to be a successful event. According to the Fort Lauderdale *Sun Sentinel*, a total of $23.9 million was spent on security. There were a total of 234 persons arrested, and the monetary amount associated with property damage was described as "negligible."[18] These numbers reflect a very significant improvement over the problems experienced in Seattle and in other cities that hosted similar economic and political forums such as the 2000 IMF (International Monetary Fund) Conference in Prague, Czech Republic, in which an estimated 11,000 protestors caused over $5 million in property damage, and 123 police officers were reported injured. Another similar event was the 2001 Summit of the Americas/FTAA Conference in Quebec City, which resulted in $10,000 in property damage and 101 officers being injured.[19]

In contrast to these previous events, the police response to the FTAA event was considered to be yet another paradigm shift in which law enforcement agencies adapted from the lessons learned in Seattle and were able to preempt and assertively challenge the violent Black Bloc protestors. Indeed, the "Miami Model" emerged as a new and proactive way of dealing with the new breed of protestors.[20]

Emboldened by their previous successes in Seattle, Prague, Quebec City, and Cancun, many of the hard-core Black Bloc and anarchist protestors came to Miami in 2003 with similar intentions. It is estimated that 150–400 Black Bloc protestors were mixed among the 10,000 nonviolent protestors at the FTAA. The following excerpt was taken from an article titled *The FTAA: Blood in the Streets in the Town of Miami November 2003,* which was one of the articles compiled in the Black Bloc Papers, a 397-page anthology.

The main body of the Bloc itself was small, perhaps numbering 75. However, the Bloc marched in tandem with the Anarchist People of Color Bloc, and other allied groupings bringing its combined strength to maybe 150. This grouping set out from the Miami Convergence Center as an independent feeder march. Their goal was to link up with the large protest contingent. However, from the start the march faced extreme police harassment. This contingent would be bloodied by the cops many times that morning. The simple task of marching the 30 or so blocks to combine with the other demonstrations was effectively curtailed by the well-organized, and violent, tactics of the police department. It would not be until many hours later, well into the afternoon, that the Black Bloc would be able to link up with the primary demonstration. As the main march proceeded, the police, armed to the teeth, quickly moved to blockade the movement of the demonstrators. The protesters found themselves flanked and effectively cut off from all obvious means of escape. Soon, the police moved in. For hours cops, in full riot gear, corralled, pushed, and clubbed protesters from one city block to the next. Anarchists and others sporadically fought back with bottles and fists, but were unable to reverse the tide—their efforts proved ineffective. By 11:00 AM the demonstrators found themselves in front of the ATT amphitheater; surrounded, and unable to move. The nonunion organized actions of protesters in Miami displayed nothing short of a naive and mass failure. Ever since September 11th, we have seen the direct action element of the anticapitalist movement fail to regain the effectiveness and sophistication that we witnessed in Seattle, A16, and in Quebec. Their tactics have been sloppy and ineffectual. Their overall numbers have been way down too. The Black Bloc, for its part, has also failed to recognize the need for tighter organization, as well as better, more realistic plans.[21]

The admission by many in the Black Bloc community affirmed that the Miami-Dade and City of Miami Police Departments had come up with a new and effective strategy to deal with the new age "professional" protestors. The so-called "Miami Model" was seen as an effective countermeasure to the new tactics, first seen in Seattle. But the assertive and proactive strategies used by MDPD and MPD were criticized by some as being over armed, and overly aggressive. That point of view is shared by some, but clearly, the grateful citizens and Downtown business owners would not agree. The Miami Model will serve as the best practice to follow ... at least for now ... until another paradigm shift occurs.

Vignette 5.2 shows how both the police and the Black Bloc protestors learned from past incidents and adapted their strategies and tactics in order to gain a competitive advantage over each other. Whether it is in realm of business, or in sports, or in public safety, or in the clash of human civilizations, the struggle to attain a competitive advantage over one's adversaries seems to be eternal. The Miami-Dade Police vignette provides an excellent laboratory for learning. In 1980, the MDPD and the City of Miami Police Department were faced with 3 days of rioting in Liberty City, Overtown, Brownsville, and Coconut Grove neighborhoods of Miami-Dade County. These riots came as a result of the police killing a black man named Arthur McDuffie. The "McDuffie Riots" were particularly destructive, and resulted in 18 deaths and over 180 serious injuries. The damage caused by the rioting was estimated at $100 million and was thought to have caused the permanent loss of over 3000 jobs in the black communities of Miami.[22]

After the McDuffie Riots, the City of Miami Police Department (MPD) and Miami-Dade Police Department (known as the Dade County Public Safety Department at the time) were criticized for not being prepared and for not taking a more assertive stance to stop the violence. The truth is that both police departments were stretched beyond their capabilities. Morale was at its lowest, and many police and fire-rescue commanders were hesitant in taking assertive action to stop the destruction of property. Some individual officers and firemen acted heroically to save innocent persons who unknowingly wandered into the neighborhoods, but for the most part, the first day of rioting saw the police setting perimeters around the affected areas and letting the place burn down. The outcome of the McDuffie Riots was unacceptable to county and city officials. A review of the incident revealed many deficiencies in the number of officers, their training, their weapons, and their tactics. Shortly after the McDuffie Riots, both police departments increased their recruitment and hiring efforts in order to beef up the understaffed agencies. The other silver lining that came out of the McDuffie Riots was the invention of the *mobile field force* concept.

The Mobile Field Force (MFF) idea came about as a result of the lessons learned from the McDuffie Riots. The concept included new tactics such as high-profile rescues, officer down rescues, better coordinated perimeter control, and "stomp and grind" crowd control tactics that borrowed heavily from the linear warfare tactics employed by the Roman legions during the time of Julius Cesar. Indeed, the MFF tactics innovated jointly by MDPD and MPD cannot be considered to be new ideas *per se*. These new tactics were nothing more than the application of an old idea to a new context. As you will read in Chapter 7, innovation is often driven by necessity, and is usually a reapplication of an old idea in a new way. That is exactly what happened in Miami in the early 1980s.

The Mobile Field Force concept was put to the test in 1982, when another police shooting of a young black man led to an outbreak of lawlessness in the same neighborhoods. That civil disturbance was later referred to as the "Luis Alvarez/Overtown" riots. It happened again in 1989 with another police shooting of a black man. That disturbance was later called the "Lozano" riots, after the name of the officer involved in the shooting. In both incidents, the Mobile Field Forces of the two police departments moved quickly and decisively to quell the civil disturbances. Property damage and injuries were minimal as a result. Due to the proven success of the Miami/Miami-Dade Mobile Field Force model, law enforcement agencies from around the nation adopted the tactics as their own. Up until 1999, the Miami/Miami-Dade Mobile Field Force model was the standard for all police departments. Then came the "Battle in Seattle" and everything changed again.

As we learned from Vignette 5.2, the difficulties encountered by the Seattle Police Department during the 1999 WTO Conference, paired with the expected civil disturbances from the new breed of protestors coming to the South Florida area, prompted a new generation of MDPD commanders to once again innovate their crowd control tactics. But it wasn't just the tactics that were changed. The new Miami Model born from the FTAA in 2003 was also a change of strategy. As listed in the vignette, there were several key components of the strategy, but if we were to reduce it to just a few words, we would call that strategy *early intervention*.

Early Intervention Strategies

In their book titled *Catastrophe Preparation and Prevention for Law Enforcement Professionals,* Baldwin, Irons, and Palin identify three intervention strategies: protection, deterrence, and preemption.[23] The strategy of *protection* is described as "to make people and places less vulnerable through vaccinations, shielding, environmental and architectural design, surveillance, and other technological means."[24] Erecting a fence or wall around a critical infrastructure asset is an example of a protection-based strategy. Other examples of protection strategy include the use of buffer zones, limiting points of entry into a critical infrastructure, and restricting air space. Other protective strategies include the use of flak jackets, helmets, ballistic shields, goggles, and personal protective gear. Examples of protection strategy in the animal and plant kingdoms include the shock delivered by electric eels, the hard shell of mollusks, and the needles of a cactus.

The second early intervention strategy outlined by Baldwin et al. is *deterrence.* They define deterrence as "to influence the thinking of those who threaten the community. For example, deterrence in one area may shift terrorist attention to 'softer' targets. This is called 'displacement.'"[25] Deterrence is a prevention strategy that requires the conscious awareness of the adversary. Examples of deterrence strategies include "Beware of Dog" signs on fences, the bright colors of a poison caterpillar, and a blowfish that triples in size when threatened by a predator.

The difference between protection and deterrence is that the latter depends on the perception and subsequent reaction of the adversary. Take for example the fence with a *Beware of the Dog* sign. The fence itself offers some limited protection, while the Beware of the Dog sign provides a warning that can act as a deterrence. For a deterrence strategy to be effective, the adversary has to be convinced that it is either not worth the effort to attack, or there is a fear of retaliation. In the realm of homeland security and critical incident management, deterrence strategy only works to prevent man-made intentional threats. Deterrence does not work against natural phenomena because we cannot dissuade hurricanes, floods, and tornadoes from coming our way. We can protect against these natural disasters, but we cannot deter them. That is perhaps the easiest way to remember the difference between the two strategies. In law enforcement, an example of a deterrence strategy is high visibility patrol. Generally speaking, deterrence strategy is limited in its effectiveness because it relies only on the perceptions formed by the adversary. If and when the adversary realizes that the initial perception is not truly indicative of reality, then the deterrence value is no longer viable. For example, the purse snatcher simply waits a few minutes for the uniformed patrol car to drive by before committing the robbery. For deterrence strategy to be effective, it needs to be backed up with real retaliatory intent. An example of a very effective deterrence strategy was the *mutually assured destruction* (MAD) strategy used to keep the balance of power between the Soviet Union and the United States during the Cold War. Of course, we know that that strategy was constantly challenged by both sides with proxy wars on the fringes, such as the Korean and Vietnam wars, as well as Soviet inspired Cuban adventurism in Angola, Ethiopia, and Somalia in the 1970s and 1980s.

The third early intervention strategy is *preemption*. Baldwin et al. describe preemption strategy as "to take action during the earliest stages of a threatening event to detect and stop it."[26] Preemption is a strategy used to prevent man-made intentional acts such as terrorism, but it can also apply to man-made accidental incidents, or even natural threats. For example, it was reported in the news that actress Angelina Jolie had voluntarily undergone double mastectomy surgery, and later had her ovaries and fallopian tubes removed as a preemptive measure to prevent cancer. Miss Jolie made that difficult decision based on the revelation that she carries a gene that gives her an 87% chance of developing breast cancer and a 50% chance of developing ovarian cancer.[27]

An example of preemption in warfare is delivering a first strike in order to severely injure the adversary. Examples of preemptive attacks include Imperial Japan's attack on Pearl Harbor, Israel's attack on nuclear facilities in Iraq and Syria, and America's invasion of Iraq to prevent the proliferation of weapons of mass destruction. Preemptive strategy is risky because it opens the possibility and likelihood of a retaliatory attack by the enemy. It also exposes the attacker to criticism that they were unnecessarily the aggressor. That type of criticism is difficult to counter because no one will even know what would have happened if the preemptive attack had not been done. An example of preemptive strategy in firefighting is the practice of conducting controlled burns in forests to eliminate the fuel that builds up over many years of dry leaves and tree branches falling to the ground. The idea is to burn the excess fuel in a controlled manner before it is set off accidentally by a lightning strike, or by a careless camper. Again, this is not without risks, as some controlled fires have gotten out of control.[28]

Early intervention strategies in the critical incident management field, by definition, mostly occur in the *preparedness phase*—the phase that we do the things that we do *before* an incident occurs. However, early intervention can and does occur in the *response phase* of an incident. Early intervention in the response phase is mostly a matter of tactical or operational concern, but it can also be the strategy of a police department as it pertains to response. As we read in Vignette 5.2, the "Miami Model" proved to be a successful strategy for the containment of violence during the 2003 FTAA Conference. That model used elements of all three of the prevention strategies identified by Baldwin et al.—protection, deterrence, and preemption.[29] Protection came in the form of perimeter fencing, buffer zones, checkpoints, and personal protective equipment for the front line Mobile Field Force personnel. Deterrence was used to a lesser extent, but we can consider the prominent display of six large fire pump trucks that were converted for use as water cannons as having a possible deterrent effect during the week of street protests. An example of the preemption strategy was when the participating law enforcement agencies collaborated and shared information that led to the arrest of troublemakers and the impounding of materials, such as in the case of the Coast Guard's intercept of the Greenpeace ship *Esperanza* one week before the event started. In the Miami Model, the strategy of early intervention was the key organizing principle that dictated the preparations before the event and the tactical responses during the event.

The success of the Miami Model, and the early intervention strategy that guided it, was determinant to a great extent by the ability of the commanders and policy makers to predict future occurrences with a high degree of certainty. That capability can be attributed to several important preexisting networks that the Miami and Miami-Dade Police Departments belonged to. One of those was the collaborative network under the umbrella of the Florida Department of Law Enforcement's (FDLE) Southeast Regional Domestic Security Task Force (RDSTF).[30] The RDSTF was comprised of several hundred upper and mid-management personnel from fire rescue, law enforcement, emergency management, and critical infrastructure agencies in the four-county region (Miami-Dade, Broward, Palm Beach, and Monroe counties). The RDSTF is a network where critical incident management practitioners of various disciplines meet to discuss the best practices and lessons learned from each other's successes and failures. The RDSTF is a perfect example of a collaborative network that existed prior to the FTAA Conference in Miami, and which had a great deal to do with the success of the early intervention strategy employed by MDPD and the Miami Police.

The second important collaborative network that the Miami and Miami-Dade Police departments belong to is the South Florida Joint Terrorism Task Force (JTTF).[31] The JTTF concept began in New York City in 1980, but expanded considerably after the September 11 terrorist attacks. Compared to the RDSTF, the South Florida JTTF is a much smaller group of investigators from various local police departments, working under the auspices of the FBI. This is mostly an investigative and intelligence sharing network that works in partnership with the Miami Fusion Center, under the auspices of FDLE.[32] The intelligence provided by the JTTF and the Fusion Center to the FTAA Conference security planners months prior to the event, as well as the "real-time" intelligence from undercover teams imbedded into the protest organizations, proved to be an invaluable asset that allowed the commanders to stay a step ahead of the protestors at every turn. Without the RDSTF, JTTF, and Fusion Center, the planners and commanders in charge of security for the FTAA Conference would not have been able to use the early intervention strategy that worked so well.

Since no one knows for sure what will happen in the future, the best we can do to predict the likely course of future events is to look at past incidents—especially those that we deem as being likely to recur. For the early intervention strategy to work, policy makers must recognize and acknowledge other similar incidents such as was the case in the Miami Model, with the earlier WTO Seattle riots in 1999, and in Quebec City in 2001. If we do not recognize our vulnerabilities and the likelihood of similar incidents happening in our areas, then we will not be able to take advantage of the early intervention strategy, and will be more likely to be surprised when a negative critical incident occurs. The purpose of early intervention strategy is to minimize, or eliminate surprises. In other words, to minimize uncertainty. Next, we will examine a case where early intervention strategy was not used.

VIGNETTE 5.3   Review of the Baltimore FOP After-Action Report

In all my years in law enforcement, I have reviewed the after-action reports of many police departments, as well as state and federal agencies, and congressional. Up until this year, I had never reviewed—or even heard of—an after-action report authored by a police union. Such was the case with the after-action report published by the Baltimore City Fraternal Order of Police (FOP), Lodge #3 on July 8, 2015, in regard to the riots in that city resulting from the in-custody death of a young black man. According to reports in the *Baltimore Sun*, more than 150 police officers were injured by bricks, rocks, and other objects on just one day of the weeklong riots in April of that year.[33] The findings reported in the after-action report were startling in themselves, but perhaps more telling was that the report even existed. That a police union would author and release an after-action report such as this is highly unusual, and in itself is a troubling indicator of severe institutional problems in the Baltimore Police Department and in city government.

The Baltimore City FOP provided a detailed and well-researched 32-page report with the accounts of many of the officers on the front lines for the entire week of the unrest. The report identified 24 key issues. These issues have been directly quoted from the report and condensed below:[34]

Issue 1: Orders were given not to engage protestors

Issue 2: All arrests had to be approved by civilians who work in the Baltimore Police Department's Legal Section

Issue 3: Commissioner Batts seeks to divide the Baltimore Police Department (BPD) rather than unite it. Specifically, Mayor Rawlings-Blake and Commissioner Batts have pointed fingers and shifted blame in regard to what went wrong during the riots. When questions arose surrounding the management of the Baltimore Police Department, Rawlings-Blake and Batts issued scathing public attacks on the rank and file

Issue 4: The National Guard was not called in until April 27, 2015

Issue 5: Officers were told not to wear protective gear during the riots

Issue 6: Officers did not have adequate equipment during initial deployment

Issue 7: Equipment provided to officers was widely ill fitted, mismatched, expired, intended for training purposes, and/or otherwise faulty

Issue 8: Officers did not receive adequate training on how to use equipment provided

Issue 9: Officers do not have utility uniform pants and shirts, made of fire retardant material, for riot or civil unrest situations

Issue 10: Officers had little to no training in riot/civil unrest situations

Issue 11: Officers who receive advanced training do so as individuals rather than squads

Issue 12: The Baltimore Police Department's Education and Training Division lacks adequate personnel and resources to properly train the Department

Issue 13: The riots revealed many intelligence gaps

Issue 14: Officers were ordered to advance and then retreat repeatedly "Officers seemed uncertain of the reason behind this tactic. Many felt it was the result of ineffective command decisions and/or conflicting orders from Police Headquarters"

Issue 15: Officers were not given a chance to rest or come off the line as the situation began to slow

Issue 16: On Monday April 27, 2015, at 11:25 AM, the Office of the Police Commissioner, Media Relations Section, committed a serious error. The Baltimore Police Media Relations Section sent the media an unconfirmed report that there was a "credible threat to law enforcement." The credible threat was, in fact, an unconfirmed rumor. Circulating this rumor undermined the credibility of law enforcement and unnecessarily inflamed tensions

Issue 17: Some officers did not know to whom to report during the riots

Issue 18: In many instances, officers were not provided a safe route of travel and/or staging area

Issue 19: Instructions to officers were unclear, indecisive and/or conflicting throughout the riots

Issue 20: A plan for injured officers was not effectively communicated

Issue 21: Many officers were deployed for 18 or more hours at a time with inadequate food, water or relief. Surveys and focus groups reported squads were left on the line for upwards of 24 hours straight without relief. The majority of the officers reported relying on businesses, bystanders and other jurisdictions for food and water while on duty

Issue 22: Squads were split up during riots. This type of deployment left officers working with others with whom they had no experience, making them less effective than they would have been if deployed with their existing squads and shifts

Issue 23: The Incident Action Plan (IAP) was not communicated to officers

Issue 24: Little action has been taken by the Baltimore Police Department since the riots to ensure the health and welfare of officers

In review, some of these issues are similar to those identified by other police departments in their after-action reports. It is not unusual for departments to report not having adequate, or ill-fitted, mismatched, or expired equipment as was reported in the Fraternal Order of Police (FOP) report. This seems to be a recurring problem for many police departments that are faced with civil unrest of this magnitude for the first time. Another common finding in many after-action reports is that officers did not receive adequate training on how to use equipment provided, or in riot control tactics.

What is not usual was the extent of political meddling and inept leadership at the highest levels of the police department and the City of Baltimore government. No better example of this was evident in words of Mayor Rawlings-Blake herself, who made the following comment during a televised press conference held during the riots, "We also gave those who wished to destroy, space to do that as well." That quotation was highlighted in "all caps" on the front page of the FOP report, and pretty much summarizes why this civil disturbance got so out of control.

Below are three direct quotes lifted from the FOP after-action report:[35]

April 25, 2015 a planned peaceful protest march in downtown Baltimore escalated into unchecked rioting and violence. Orioles' baseball fans, pedestrians and motorists in the area of Camden Yards were attacked. According to information garnered from focus groups, surveys, e-mails and conversations with the After Action Review Committee, officers followed direct orders from command staff not to intervene or engage the rioters.[36]

The predominant characterizations of Baltimore Police Department leadership during the riots by officers surveyed were that they seemed unprepared, politically motivated, uncaring, and confused.[37]

Orders not to engage any protestor, not to wear protective equipment so as not to look intimidating, and orders not to arrest without permission from the legal advisors made officers question the motives of Baltimore Police Department command.[38]

Underlying the now infamous public statement by Mayor Rawlings-Blake seems to be the belief by her and others of like mind that the best approach to these violent civil disturbances is to not inflame the situation by sending police to restore order in an assertive way. It is as if Mayor Rawlings-Blake and others blame the police for the riots. They seem to believe that a passive approach is the answer. They seem to be ignorant of history, or they purposely ignore the failures of the passive approach as evidenced in the 1980 McDuffie Riots in Miami, or in the Los Angeles Rodney King Riots of 1992, or the Seattle WTO riots in 1999. Unfortunately, Mayor Rawlings-Blake is not alone in her belief. It appears that Police Commissioner Anthony W. Batts, the head of the Baltimore Police Department, shares her outlook. Below is another quote from the FOP after-action report.

> Commissioner Batts and command staff members addressed officers during a roll call on April 25, 2015 at Police Headquarters. Of those officers who were present, and with whom the After Action Review Committee spoke, each reported being given direct orders from Commissioner Batts and command staff members not to engage any protestors. Officers were ordered to allow the protestors room to destroy and allow the destruction of property so that the rioters would appear to be the aggressors. According to officers' accounts, they were told "the Baltimore Police Department would not respond until they [the protestors] burned, looted, and destroyed the city so that it would show that the rioters were forcing our hand." The officers were told their primary job was to deescalate any situation with no response rather than to escalate with action. This was confirmed by officers from other jurisdictions who attended that roll call.[39]

The Baltimore riots are an example of poor strategy based on a lack of understanding of human behavior and crowd dynamics. It is a strategy that is based on the naïve belief that passivity on the part of the authorities will deescalate violence. It is a strategy that defies common sense, as well as historical evidence from past civil disturbances. In crowd dynamics, human beings will do things that they would not do under normal circumstances. The sense of anonymity that a large crowd affords the individual is one contributory factor. Another contributory factor is the "herd mentality" whereby individuals sense that their behavior is the right thing to do because everyone else is doing it. Lastly, and most importantly, if the authorities are perceived as being weak, or indecisive, then the crowd will become contemptuous and will challenge their authority. This half-hearted response by police commanders to the civil unrest is what exacerbated the problem. Given their lack of will to fight, they would have been better off not responding at all. Of all the strategies to choose from, the Baltimore Police commanders chose the worst one of all—to respond to the scene and do nothing. Not only does that place the officers unnecessarily in harm's way, it also emboldens the violent crowd to do even more violent actions.

The Baltimore case stands out as the poster child on how *not* to handle domestic civil disturbances. Every police commander in the United States should read this report and learn from it. Not only was it an example of poor judgment in the use of the wrong strategy, more importantly, it was a failure of leadership on the part of the mayor and the commissioner. Putting the officers in harm's way without proper equipment, and tying their hands behind their backs is unconscionable. Purposely allowing the city to be looted and burn down is a total abdication of a public official's duty to serve the public. Sadly, the story doesn't end with the FOP report. Baltimore is a city in a lot of trouble, and they seem to be alienating the very people who they need the most. Below is a direct quote from the FOP report.

> The morale of the men and women of the Baltimore Police Department has suffered greatly. In addition to physical injury, officers feel a lack of support from the Department and report feeling "humiliated" and "dejected" as a result of what occurred and what they experienced during the riots. A significant percentage reported that they are considering resigning or retiring within the next one to two years.[40]

One has to wonder, who are they going to call the next time that the police are needed to quell a riot?

Eloy Nuñez

The review of the Baltimore after-action report in Vignette 5.3 focuses mostly on the passivity exhibited by the Baltimore Police commanders amid a violent and worsening critical incident. Clearly, the strategy of early intervention was not the one favored by city officials and the top brass in the Baltimore Police Department. Most would agree that the strategy of allowing the rioters to have their way and not allow the police to intervene was counterproductive, to say the least. It is important to pause here and consider that the strategy of early intervention need not be a punitive one. In the Baltimore case in particular, top police commanders failed to seize the moment and intervene early to nip the civil unrest before it got completely out of control. But early intervention is not just about a quick and decisive response as the unrest unfolds at the onset. True early intervention should have been practiced days, weeks, and even months before the occurrence. In the ideal situation, a police department would take actions way ahead of time to "weatherproof" their agencies against the sort of violence seen in Baltimore. The problems experienced by the Baltimore Police Department during this 1-week incident are as much a symptom as they are a cause of the problem. Oftentimes, the problems experienced in Baltimore, or in Ferguson, Missouri, are symptomatic of some underlying and unresolved issues that have been neglected by public officials. The next vignette focuses on the efforts of one police commander to establish lines of communications with adversarial stakeholders early on, in order to avoid conflicts further down the road. In other words, this commander saw the importance of early intervention at the strategic level, months before the scheduled date of a special event in his city. This account is about how a commander weatherproofed his police department against an expected onslaught of violent Black Bloc protestors who intended to disrupt the 2012 Republican National Convention in Tampa, Florida.

VIGNETTE 5.4   Assistant Chief John Bennett Plans for the Republican National Convention

I first met Chief John Bennett while I was organizing a panel discussion at Saint Leo University to review the Republican National Convention (RNC) that had been held in Tampa in 2012. I was in the process of assembling a panel of subject-matter experts to conduct an after-action discussion, and I reached out to some of my contacts to find out who the main planner for the security of the RNC event was. From my past experience in planning for Super Bowls and other large-scale events, I knew that it takes the collective effort of hundreds of individuals to get the job done. But I also knew that behind those hundreds of planners, there is usually a core of one or two people who determine the strategic direction of the plan. For the RNC at Tampa, everyone I talked to directed me to contact Assistant Chief Bennett of the Tampa Police Department.

A couple of months before the panel was to convene at the university, I called Chief Bennett on the phone and spoke with him for the first time. I told him my idea of assembling a panel of six subject-matter experts on special event planning to review the RNC, and I asked him if he would come to campus to participate in the discussion. Chief Bennett readily agreed, and I offered him a small honorarium stipend for his time and effort. Chief Bennett told me that receiving payment from the university would not be necessary. He told me that he was a Saint Leo University graduate, and that he would be honored to do it for free. That was my first impression of Chief Bennett, and I immediately sensed that this was a man of duty and devotion— a true public servant. As a side note—a couple of months later, I was able to get the university to process a $500 stipend which was mailed to the Chief, and which he promptly donated the entire amount to a homeless shelter. That should tell you something about his leadership and ethics.

In any regard, we had the panel discussion in October of that same year in front of a number of criminal justice students in the audience. For an hour and a half, we covered several topics, and answered questions from the audience, but of course, an hour and a half is not nearly enough time to cover everything associated with something of the scope of the RNC. What struck me the most from the discussion was learning about the extent that Chief Bennett went to in order to personally reach out to the leaders of certain protest groups before the RNC got started. I have always been a proponent of making early contact with the leaders of various stakeholder groups well ahead of the event. I have learned over the years from my own event planning experience that talking face-to-face with these stakeholder groups and discussing each other's expectations has been a key factor for minimizing surprises and potential points of conflict between the police and certain protest groups. But Chief Bennett has taken this practice to a higher level than I have ever seen. The extent to which Chief Bennett went to reach out to protest groups such as the Occupy Wall Street movement was considered as one of the primary factors that the one-week RNC event concluded with minimal disruptions.

Some people attribute the lack of violent and disruptive protests to the near miss of Hurricane Isaac, which seemed to keep the number of out-of-town protestors to a minimum. One after-action report estimates that there were 30,000 attendees invited at the convention, but only 500 protestors showed up. Undoubtedly, the low number of protestors had a lot to do with the success of the event. Typically, the violent Black Bloc and anarchist-type protestors like to meld into larger crowds of protestors in order to protect themselves with sheer numbers. By comparison, it was estimated that there were up to 40,000 protestors in the 1999 WTO Seattle riots, and as many as 10,000 protestors for the 2003 FTAA civil disturbances in Miami. The large numbers evidenced in Seattle and Miami were enough to provide cover to the Black Bloc protestors to try their violent disruptive tactics, but for the RNC in Tampa, those numbers were simply not there. Nevertheless, this should not detract from the success achieved under the command of Chief Jane Castor and her Assistant Chief John Bennett. For the Tampa RNC, only two event-related arrests were made by police during the week of the event. Contrast that with the more than 800 arrests made at the 2008 Republican National Convention in Minneapolis just 4 years earlier.[41] Much of that had to do with the strategy of early intervention and full engagement used by the Tampa Police Department.

Most would agree that planning and training, which began 2 years before the convention, had a lot to do with the success of the Tampa PD. There were over 3500 law enforcement personnel from 60 agencies, plus National Guard on standby. According to one news story: "a combination of smaller crowds, peaceful protesters and the large law enforcement presence made the convention run smoothly. By the final day, officers were passing out food and water to peaceful protesters."[42]

That the police were perceived as being friendly is a nice by-product, but friendliness was not the intent of Chief Bennett's strategy. The underlying intent of the strategy was to minimize uncertainty, and to avoid surprises whenever possible. By engaging the leaders of the protest groups early on, the police were able to establish a line of communication whereby the expectations of all the parties involved can be made clear. Chief Bennett could hear firsthand what the protestors were thinking, and what their expectations were. At the time, Bennett made clear what the rules were, and what was expected from the protestors. Whenever the parties had a mutual interest, they would build on that shared interest. Whenever the parties disagreed on an issue, they would come to an agreement that was satisfactory to all. The dialogue was respectful and purposeful. It was not intended to be friendly chit-chat. That's an important distinction because some police commanders misunderstand the purpose of this full engagement technique. Some police commanders mistakenly believe that they need to become friends with their adversaries. In doing so, they make a cardinal error that will likely lead to unintended consequences later. These are not people that you want to have over for dinner. I didn't ask Chief Bennett this question, but I think he would tell you that becoming friends with protestors is not a good idea. Engaging them is strictly a business transaction … and very good business indeed.

Eloy Nuñez

The vignette about Assistant Chief John Bennett shows how a leader with a well thought-out strategy can have a positive impact on the outcome of a potentially disruptive situation. Chief Bennett's decision to become fully engaged with his adversaries was an inherently risky approach. It is not unlike the counterinsurgency doctrine conceived by Army General David Petreaus and Marine Corps General James Amos in their 2006 publication, which served as a strategic and tactical guide for field commanders during the "surge" in the Iraq War.[43] This surge of Coalition Forces manpower in 2007, and its underlying counterinsurgency strategy is credited with the successful pacification of a rampant insurgency. Unfortunately, all these gains were ultimately for naught, as the policy decision by a new president and administration to withdraw all forces from Iraq led to the return of the insurgency, and ultimately to the establishment of the Islamic State. Some would argue that President Obama's policy decision to withdraw all American troops from Iraq is what led to the prominence of the Islamic State. Others would argue that the United States should not have gone to war in the first place. We are not going to get into a "chicken-and-egg" argument in this book. However, regardless of one's opinion on the Iraq War, it is safe to say that most experts and politicians would agree that the 2006 counterinsurgency doctrine was a very successful strategy.

Chief Bennett's strategy of getting up close and engaging his potential opponents was done for a purpose. That purpose was not to make friends with the adversary. The purpose was to gain a better understanding of the adversary, minimize uncertainty, and mitigate risk ahead of time. In the end, if no one is injured, and no property is destroyed, then everyone wins. There are parallels between modern day domestic policing and military counterinsurgency. This is not to suggest that the missions of the two are the same. They are not. However, the underlying principles in both arenas are very similar. Both require the police officer, or the soldier to get up close to the population. Both require the police officer, or the soldier to engage the potential adversary. The risk is high for both, and both require "patience, presence, and courage."

VIGNETTE 5.5   Patience, Presence, and Courage

For the first two months of 2006, the Marine platoon of the 22d Marine Expeditionary Unit had walked the streets in Iraq on foot without serious incident. Their patrols had moved fearlessly around lines of cars and through packed markets. For the most part, their house calls began with knocks, not kicks. It was their aim to win the respect of the city's Sunni Arab population.

Suddenly things changed. An armored HMMWV (High Mobility Multipurpose Wheeled Vehicle—"Humvee") on night patrol hit an improvised explosive device. The bomb destroyed the vehicle. Five Marines were wounded and two died shortly thereafter. A third Marine, a popular noncommissioned officer, later died of his wounds as well.

The platoon was stunned. Some of the more veteran noncommissioned officers shrugged it off, but the younger Marines were keyed up and wanted to make the elusive enemy pay a price. A squad leader stood up in the squad bay and asserted that there would be a pile of dead Arabs on the street when the platoon went out the next day.

Just then, the company commander walked in. He was widely respected and generally short on words. He quickly sensed the unit's mood and recognized the potential danger in their dark attitude. Speaking directly to his Marines, the commander urged them to remember why they were there. He reminded them that a very small percentage of the populace was out to create problems. It was that minority that benefited from creating chaos. The enemy would love to see an overreaction to the attack, and they would benefit from any actions that detracted from the Marines' honor or purpose. The commander urged his Marines not to get caught up in the anger of the moment and do something they all would regret for a long time. Rather, they needed to focus on what the force was trying to accomplish and keep their minds on the mission. They had taken some hits and lost some good men, the commander said, but escalating the violence would not help them win. It would fall for the insurgents' strategy instead of sticking to the Marines' game plan of winning the respect of the populace. The commander knew his Marines and understood the operational environment. He assessed the situation and acted aggressively to counter a dangerous situation that threatened mission accomplishment. By his actions, the commander demonstrated patience, presence, and courage.[44]

The story in Vignette 5.5 was quoted directly from the 2006 Counterinsurgency Manual.[45] It provides an excellent example of a forward-looking leader who takes into account the "big picture" and does not allow himself, or his troops to let their emotions get the best of them, and thus avoid becoming embroiled in a bad situation. The preface of the Manual states the importance of forward-looking leadership quite well: "Conducting a successful counterinsurgency campaign requires a flexible, adaptive force led by agile, well-informed, culturally astute leaders."[46] The same holds true for police and emergency management leaders. We are not suggesting that domestic issues such as the spate of highly publicized police shootings in predominantly black neighborhoods are equivalent to insurgencies in Iraq and Afghanistan. However, there are some aspects that are common to both situations, and from which lessons can be learned. Being well informed, culturally aware, and forward-looking leaders who take into account the "big picture" is exactly what effective strategic planning is all about. Let's now examine the "Black Lives Matter" movement, and how it relates to strategic planning for police agencies throughout the nation.

VIGNETTE 5.6   "Hands Up Don't Shoot" Was Built on a Lie

The late evening of August 9, 2014, I couldn't sleep. I was due to substitute-anchor MSNBC's "UP with Steve Kornacki" and should have been asleep. But after looking at my Twitter feed and reading the rage under #Ferguson, I felt compelled to type a reaction to the killing of Michael Brown by police officer Darren Wilson. Tying the shooting to the inane whine of certain politicians about a "war on whites," I decried the next morning the death of yet another unarmed black man at the hands of a white police officer.[47]

These were the words of Jonathan Capehart, a black man and respected opinion writer and member of the *Washington Post* editorial board, on a 2-minute, 10-second video that was broadcast on several national media outlets.

Capehart went on: "In those early hours and early days, there was more unknown than known. But this month, the Justice Department released two must-read investigations connected to the killing of Brown that filled in blanks, corrected the record and brought sunlight to dark places by revealing ugly practices that institutionalized racism and hardship. They have also forced me to deal with two uncomfortable truths: Brown never surrendered with his hands up, and Wilson was justified in shooting Brown."[48]

We now know that Officer Darren Wilson, formerly of the Ferguson Police Department, was justified in the shooting death of Michael Brown. We know that because on November 24, 2014, a St. Louis County grand jury released its report that absolved Officer Wilson of any wrongdoing. The grand jury's report also found that some of the witnesses deliberately lied in their testimony. The claim that Michael Brown held his hands up to surrender prior to getting shot by Officer Wilson was totally discredited by the physical evidence and the testimony of other witnesses.[49]

The U.S. Department of Justice conducted an independent investigation of the Ferguson shooting and concluded the same.[50] "Hands up, don't shoot," never happened. Nevertheless, no one denies that the shooting and the civil disturbances that followed from August 9–25, 2014, opened the door for a closer scrutiny of the pre-existing police–community relations in Ferguson, Missouri. Not only did the incident bring the Department of Justice to the mix, but it also caught the attention of many media outlets.

In March of 2015, the online publication *The Atlantic* published a scathing article with the title of "Ferguson's Conspiracy Against Black Citizens: How the city's leadership harassed and brutalized their way to multiple civil-rights violations."[51] The article cites a number of anecdotal accounts of abuse of power by the Ferguson Police predating the Brown shooting, and concludes that the civil unrest that followed the shooting was the moment that the problem reached a boiling point, which brought a long festering problem into the national consciousness.

The Atlantic article concludes: "Little wonder that black people in Ferguson took to the streets after the killing of Michael Brown. Sooner or later, some event was bound to push them over the edge into protest, and even if Officer Wilson acted totally unobjectionally in that encounter, it wouldn't change the fact that the general lack of confidence expressed in municipal and police leadership was well founded."[52]

The notion that the problems in Ferguson were much deeper than the Brown shooting incident brought to the general public's attention was validated by the findings of the Department of Justice report, which identified six themes that "permeated all aspects of the police response" as it pertained to the pre-existing relationship between the Ferguson Police Department and the community it serves. Listed below are three of the six themes, as they relate to the topic of strategic planning and early intervention strategy.[53]

Failure to understand endemic problems in the community. There was insufficient understanding of community concerns, and relationships between law enforcement and some community segments were lacking.[54]

A reactive rather than proactive strategy. The police response to the mass demonstrations was generally reactive and did not appear to establish a strategic approach to effectively mitigate the complexity of issues and respond more effectively to the mass gatherings.[55]

Use of ineffective and inappropriate strategies and tactics. There were instances where specific actions were taken that infringed upon constitutionally protected activities and were not aligned with current national best practices. These strategies and tactics had the unintended consequence of escalating rather than diminishing tensions.[56]

As is often the case with investigations such as the Justice Department's after-action assessment of the 2014 demonstrations in Ferguson, Missouri, the findings of the investigators go way beyond the scope of the original investigation of the shooting and the civil disturbances that followed. As investigators investigate, they tend to dig deeper to look for the root causes that led to the problem. Invariably, these investigations tend to uncover "other findings" that reveal all kinds of systemic problems within an organization. Like others before it, this investigation revealed a number of institutional weaknesses that sooner or later would have been exposed. This time, a completely justified shooting of a black man by a white police officer, who by all accounts was doing his job correctly, opened a figurative "can of worms" that led to the revealing of the endemic problems of the Ferguson Police Department.

At a broader, national scale, another "can of worms" was opened. The original incident provided the imagery and symbolism which gave a boost to what became the "Black Lives Matter" movement. That the incident itself was based on false testimony, and that the subsequent highly politicized urban myth that resulted from the shooting was false, was totally irrelevant once the "other findings" were revealed by the investigation.

The police–community problems revealed by the Justice Department's investigation of the Ferguson Police Department are not endemic to Ferguson alone. I will conclude this vignette with Jonathan Capehart's comment: "Yet this does not diminish the importance of the real issues unearthed in Ferguson by Brown's death. Nor does it discredit what has become the larger 'Black Lives Matter.' In fact, the false Ferguson narrative stuck because of concern over a distressing pattern of other police killings of unarmed African American men and boys around the time of Brown's death. Eric Garner was killed on a Staten Island street on July 17. John Crawford III was killed in a Wal-Mart in Beavercreek, Ohio, on August 5, four days before Brown. Levar Jones survived being shot by a South Carolina state trooper on September 4. Tamir Rice, 12 years old, was killed in a Cleveland park on November 23, the day before the Ferguson grand jury opted not to indict Wilson. Sadly, the list has grown longer."[57]

Vignette 5.6 was not meant to be critical of the Ferguson Police Department. Any police department in the country that is scrutinized to the extent that the Ferguson PD was, will undoubtedly reveal some flaws. We also understand that police throughout the nation are put in untenable situations. By nature of their work, police officers are thrust into the frontlines and are expected to solve a multitude of social problems that are endemic to our society. The authors contend that those who criticize the police, would be hard-pressed in coming up with better solutions to the problems. It seems like our society expects our frontline police officers to be superhuman. Police officers are held to account like no other profession. Yet, it is also clear that police departments (not just the Ferguson PD), can stand to learn lessons from this incident, and others like it.

Strategic Planning: Before, During, and After

In Chapter 1, we identified the three phases of a critical incident, or a disaster as being: *before, during,* and *after.* This categorization was used to simplify FEMA's four-phase model that includes: *preparedness, response, recovery,* and *mitigation.* We argued that mitigation was not a phase, but was a desired outcome of the three other phases. Arguably, risk mitigation occurs before, during, and after all incidents. For that reason, the phase that FEMA categorizes as mitigation was embedded as an overarching outcome of our simpler three-phase model.

Generally, we think of strategic planning as something that we do in the preparedness (the before) stage. That is because strategic planning generally involves considerable analysis of a broad range of factors, and does not lend itself to the spontaneous improvisation that often occurs during the response phase of a critical incident. Nevertheless, the *implementation* of strategy usually occurs during the response phase. Indeed, the response phase is where an organization's strategic vision is put to the test. Strategy provides a roadmap for an organization's general direction, but it is not meant to tie the hands of operational-level managers in a way that impedes their actions toward a successful resolution of the incident. Well-designed strategic plans must contain sufficient "wiggle room" to allow on-scene commanders to make mid-course adjustments when deemed necessary. Indeed, the acceptance of adaptability and improvisation are part of a sound strategic plan. Good strategy should work in the favor of the on-scene commander to help him or her minimize, or mitigate risk. Strategy should never be so restrictive that it prevents the on-scene commanders from making adjustments as the incident evolves and circumstances change.

The *before, during,* and *after* model provides us with a "snapshot in time" that we can use to better analyze situations. It is similar to a "freeze frame" during a slow motion instant replay of a controversial call at a sporting event. The referees will look at the replay to determine if a player was out of bounds, or if the shot clock had expired, or whether the player's knee hit the ground before he fumbled the football. Often, these slow motion and freeze frame replays reveal things that were not apparent to the eye of the referees when viewed in "real time." Our model serves the same purpose. It is a way of slowing things down and freezing them in time so that we can slowly and deliberately deconstruct and analyze the issues and the causal factors. By examining the lessons learned from our own mistakes, and the mistakes of others during critical incidents, we can take actions to avoid those same mistakes in the future. The lessons learned from incidents *after* they occur, are then analyzed and the best practices are determined. Then steps are taken to implement these best practices before similar incidents occur again. This cycle of learning, and adaption, occurs on a continuous stream, before, during, and after incidents. As policy makers and planners, we understand that what has occurred in the past, is likely to occur again in the future. It is our job to continuously adapt our strategies to new realities. It is likely that by the time that you are reading this sentence, other incidents similar to the Ferguson and Baltimore civil disturbances will have occurred again. Hopefully, those managers and policy makers have learned the right lessons, and have made the right adjustments to their strategy.

References

1. Dictionary.com, n.d. System. Online at http://dictionary.reference.com/browse/system (accessed December 17, 2015).
2. Central Intelligence Agency, n.d. The intelligence cycle. Online at https://www.cia.gov/kids-page/6-12th-grade/who-we-are-what-we-do/the-intelligence-cycle.html (accessed December 17, 2015).
3. U.S. Department of Homeland Security Funding Opportunity Announcement, FY 2014. Homeland Security grant program. Online at http://www.fema.gov/media-library-data/1395161200285-5b07ed0456056217175fbdee28d2b06e/FY_2014_HSGP_FOA_Final.pdf (accessed July 30, 2008).
4. R. Edward Freeman and Reed, D. L., 1983. Stockholders and stakeholders: A new perspective on corporate governance. *California Management Review*, 25(3), 88–107.
5. D. Okes and Westcott, R. T., 2002. *The Certified Quality Manager Handbook* (2nd ed.), p. 63. Milwaukee: American Society for Quality.
6. Ibid.
7. Wikipedia. 2015. List of current National Football League staffs. Online at https://en.wikipedia.org/wiki/List_of_current_National_Football_League_staffs (accessed December 17, 2015).
8. Rolltide.com. 2015. Football Roster. Online at http://www.rolltide.com/sports/m-footbl/mtt/alab-m-footbl-mtt.html (accessed December 17, 2015).
9. National Commission on Terrorist Attacks upon the United States, 2004. *The 9/11 Commission Report*. Online at http://www.9-11commission.gov/ (accessed September 10, 2015).
10. J. Damiano, 2012. How much does a Super Bowl commercial really cost? *Newsday*, January 26. Online at http://www.newsday.com/entertainment/pet-rock-1.811972/how-much-does-a-super-bowl-commercial-really-cost-1.3481154.
11. E. Barton, 2014. Here's how inspectors found $43b Washington could save. *Washington Examiner*, December 29. Online at http://www.washingtonexaminer.com/heres-how-inspectors-found-43b-washington-could-save/article/2557914 (accessed on December 17, 2015).
12. S. Dinan, 2014. Tom Coburn highlights ridiculous government spending in final Wastebook. *The Washington Times*, October 22. Online at http://www.washingtontimes.com/news/2014/oct/22/tom-coburn-highlights-ridiculous-government-spendi/?page=all (accessed on December 17, 2015).
13. R. K. Merton, 1936. The unanticipated consequences of purposive social action. *American Sociological Review*, 1(6), 894–904. Online at http://www.compilerpress.atfreeweb.com/Anno%20Merton%20Unintended.htm.
14. Miami-Dade Police Department. 2003. Open Source memorandum.
15. Seattle Police Department. 2000. The Seattle Police Department After Action Report: World Trade Organization Ministerial Conference Seattle, Washington, November 29–December 3, 1999.
16. Ibid., p. 5
17. Ibid., p. 54
18. D. Marrero. 2004. Trade Meeting Security Costly. Sun Sentinel. (February 24). Online at http://articles.sun-sentinel.com/2004-02-24/news/0402230370_1_florida-ftaa-protesters-police-officials (accessed December 17, 2015).
19. Miami-Dade Police Department. 2003. Internal memorandum.

20. M. R. Chamberlain. n.d. Direct Action Protest Management. Florida Department of Law Enforcement. Online at https://www.fdle.state.fl.us/Content/getdoc/1bbf 4127-0f3d-4044-97b2-e11e9715a04e/Chamberlain-mark-paper-pdf.aspx (accessed December 17, 2015).

21. C. Munson. 2010. The Black Bloc Papers: An Anthology of Primary Texts from the North American Anarchist Black Bloc 1999–2001 The Battle of Seattle (N30) Through Quebec City (A20).

22. A. Driscoll, 2005. The McDuffie Riots 25 years later. *The Miami Herald.* Online at http://www.floridacdc.org/articles/050515-1.html (accessed July 30, 2008).

23. C. Baldwin, Irons, L., and Palin, P. J., 2008. *Catastrophe Preparation and Prevention for Law Enforcement Professionals.* New York, NY: McGraw-Hill.

24. Ibid., p. 114

25. Ibid., p. 118

26. Ibid., p. 118

27. Health. 2015. What you should know about Angelina Jolie's cancer-preventing surgery. Online at http://news.health.com/2015/03/24/angelina-jolie-cancer-preventing-surgery/ (accessed on December 17, 2015).

28. G. McLaren and Comstock, N. 2015. *Controlled Burn Crosses Fire Lines in Yuba County,* June 18. Fox 40. Online at http://fox40.com/2015/06/18/controlled-burn-gets-out-of-control-in-yuba-county/ (accessed on December 17, 2015).

29. C. Baldwin, Irons, L., and Palin, P. J., 2008. *Catastrophe Preparation and Prevention for Law Enforcement Professionals.* New York, NY: McGraw-Hill.

30. Southeast Florida RDSTF. Online at http://www.fdle.state.fl.us/Content/Domestic-Security/Menu/Domestic-Security-Organization.aspx (accessed on December 17, 2015).

31. Federal Bureau of Investigation, n.d. Protecting America from terrorist attack our joint terrorism task forces. Online at https://www.fbi.gov/about-us/investigate/terrorism/terrorism_jttfs (accessed on December 17, 2015).

32. Southeast Florida RDSTF. Online at http://www.fdle.state.fl.us/Content/Domestic-Security/Menu/Domestic-Security-Organization.aspx (accessed on December 17, 2015).

33. J. Fenton and Rector, K. 2015. Police union blasts commanders in 'after action review' of riot. *The Baltimore Sun.* Online at http://www.baltimoresun.com/news/maryland/freddie-gray/bs-md-ci-fop-report-20150708-story.html (accessed December 17, 2015).

34. Baltimore City Fraternal Order of Police Lodge #3. n.d. After Action Review. Online at http://www.fop3.org/wp-content/uploads/2015/07/AAR-Final.pdf (accessed December 17, 2015).

35. Ibid.

36. Ibid., p. 4

37. Ibid., p. 10

38. Ibid., p. 10

39. Ibid., p. 7

40. Ibid., p. 4

41. L. Chapa. 2012. Police planning credited with avoiding problems at Republican National Convention. *Media Law Resources.* (September 4). Online at http://www.rcfp.org/browse-media-law-resources/news/police-planning-credited-avoiding-problems-republican-national-conve (accessed December 17, 2015).

42. Ibid.

43. The U.S. Army/Marine Corps, 2007. *Counterinsurgency Field Manual* (U.S. Army field manual no. 3-24:Marine Corps warfighting publication no. 3-33.5). Chicago: University of Chicago Press.

44. Ibid., p. 7-4
45. Ibid.
46. Ibid., p. vii
47. J. Capehhart. 2015. Hands up, don't shoot was built on a lie, *The Washington Post*. Online at https://www.washingtonpost.com/blogs/post-partisan/wp/2015/03/16/lesson-learned-from-the-shooting-of-michael-brown/ (accessed October 31, 2015).
48. Ibid., p. 2
49. United States Department of Justice. 2015. After-Action Assessment of the Police Response to the August 2014 Demonstrations in Ferguson, Missouri, Institute for Intergovernmental Research. Online at http://ric-zai-inc.com/ric.php?page=detail&id=COPS-P317 (accessed October 31, 2015).
50. Ibid.
51. C. Friedersdorf. 2015. Ferguson's Conspiracy against black citizens: How the city's leadership harassed and brutalized their way to multiple civil-rights violations. *The Atlantic* (March 5). Online at http://www.theatlantic.com/national/archive/2015/03/ferguson-as-a-criminal-conspiracy-against-its-black-residents-michael-brown-department-of-justice-report/386887/ (accessed on December 17, 2015).
52. Ibid.
53. U.S. Department of Justice. 2015. After-Action Assessment of the Police Response to the August 2014 Demonstrations in Ferguson, Missouri.
54. Ibid.
55. Ibid.
56. Ibid.
57. J. Capehhart. 2015. Hands up, don't shoot was built on a lie, *The Washington Post*. Online at https://www.washingtonpost.com/blogs/post-partisan/wp/2015/03/16/lesson-learned-from-the-shooting-of-michael-brown/ (accessed October 31, 2015).

6
Organizing and Planning Training Exercises

The Link between Planning and Training

As has been pointed out throughout this book, critical incident management is a complex endeavor. Invariably, critical incidents and large-scale special events involve a variety of players and stakeholders from a number of organizations and jurisdictions. As a result, there are many moving parts at many different levels. For these reasons, at times, critical incidents can be overwhelming to even the most seasoned practitioners.

Oftentimes, public safety professionals operate in a high-risk, high-liability environment wherein decisions made and actions taken (or not taken) can have far-reaching consequences. Therefore, those organizations that take proactive steps to manage the inevitable complexity and uncertainty associated with these high-profile events will be in a much better position to achieve successful outcomes (see Figure 6.1).

How do public safety organizations best manage complexity and uncertainty? As discussed in Chapter 2, risk analysis is an important consideration in critical incident management. Identifying potential threats, determining vulnerability, assessing potential impact, and taking steps to mitigate risks are key components of this process. Additionally, as stated previously by the authors, risk mitigation actions often occur before, during, and after the incident. In essence, risk analysis and mitigation is at the core of what incident commanders do at various levels (operational, tactical, and strategic). However, once potential threats are identified, risks are analyzed, and plans are formulated, proactive preparedness actions are essential. Unfortunately, far too often, this is where many organizations fall short.

The Importance of Training and Exercising

Over the years, there have been a number of critical incidents that have demonstrated the negative consequences of being unprepared for the inevitable crisis that organizations and communities are likely to encounter at one point or another. In some cases, organizations have expended a considerable amount of time and effort in the planning process, but have failed to follow through on communicating, training, and testing the plan.

Unmanageable		Critical Incident Management		Manageable
Chaos, Uncertainty, Complexity	➡	Communication, Coordination, Collaboration, Command	➡	Order, Predictability, Simplicity

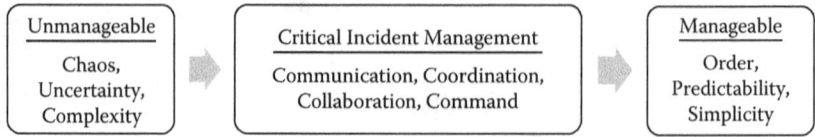

Figure 6.1 Managing Complexity and Uncertainty (Developed by Eloy Nuñez and Ernest G. Vendrell.)

VIGNETTE 6.1   The Planning Officer—The Importance of Follow Through

Lieutenant John Wheeler hung up the telephone and leaned back in his chair. As his agency's designated planning officer, he was deeply troubled by his conversation with Chief Cynthia Bronson regarding events that had negatively impacted his agency and the community. Three consecutive days of mostly peaceful demonstrations near the convention center had led to two back-to-back days of the worst civil unrest that the city had experienced in more than two decades. As the number of demonstrations grew larger, fueled by outside agitators, the crowds became increasingly aggressive and began hurling rocks and bottles at the uniformed officers that were lined up opposite them. The scene quickly became chaotic, with multiple flash points occurring in the downtown area. Before long, numerous demonstrators, police officers, as well as innocent bystanders were injured, some quite seriously. In addition, a multitude of businesses had been looted and set ablaze. Of course, all of this was captured by various media outlets, and became lead-off news across the country. The convention was due to last another 2 days, and the chief had to request the assistance of additional county and state resources, most of which had not yet arrived.

It was clear to Wheeler that his agency had been caught off guard, and the consequences had been quite severe. "How could this have happened?" he muttered to himself. Glancing at the three binders on his shelf, he thought to himself, my team and I developed a detailed emergency response plan for the department, which was presented to the command staff more than 18 months ago. Where did we go wrong? Why wasn't the plan put into effect?

The story that unfolded in Vignette 6.1 illustrates the consequences that can occur when agencies commit personnel and resources to develop an Emergency Operations Plan, but fail to follow through with communicating the plan throughout the organization, followed by training and testing the plan's various components. As past critical incidents serve to reinforce, realistic training, testing, and exercising with applicable stakeholders is what serves to validate the Emergency Operations Plan. Moreover, when emergency planning is done in isolation within organizations, planning documents have a tendency to end up on a shelf collecting dust, instead of being living documents that are reviewed and revised on a regular basis. Of course, when a critical incident does occur, the limitations of such a plan will be painfully obvious to all. For example, the Los Angeles Riots of 1992 are considered one of the worst cases of civil unrest in the United States, and it exposed a number of shortcomings in the LAPD's (Los Angeles Police Department) Emergency Operations Plan. As reported by the *New York Times* in the aftermath of the 1992 Los Angeles Riots, a 5-month study by a panel headed by William H. Webster, a former FBI director, and Hubert Williams, president of the Police Foundation, found "… that what the chief [Daryl Gates] called a riot plan was nothing more than a general training guide. …" Moreover, the *New York Times* further quoted one person familiar with the report, who spoke on the condition of anonymity, "It was just something sitting on a shelf … they really didn't have a plan …"[1]

The Key Components of an Effective Emergency Operations Plan

After potential threats have been identified, risks have been analyzed, and the initial planning process has been completed (operational, tactical, and strategic), being prepared for critical incidents involves a number of key components. These include training, testing, exercising, evaluating, and revising the Emergency Operations Plan (see Figure 6.2).

These components represent the cornerstones of any Emergency Operations Plan. They are the essential ingredients for validating the Emergency Operations Plan, ensuring that the plan will work as designed. FEMA's Emergency Management Institute Web site carries the byline of "Train–Exercise–Educate,"

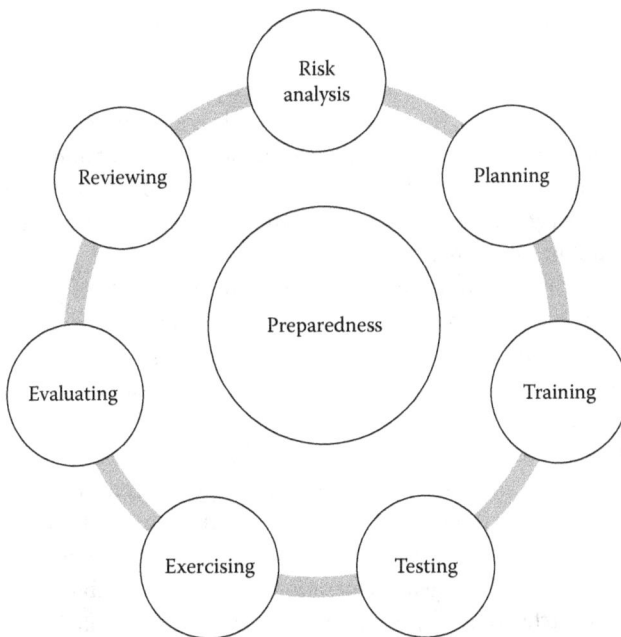

Figure 6.2 Preparedness Links (Developed by Eloy Nuñez and Ernest G. Vendrell.)

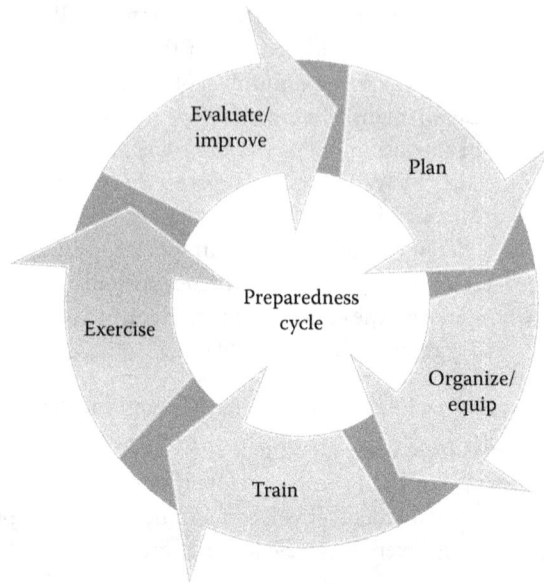

Figure 6.3 FEMA Preparedness Cycle (From FEMA: http://www.fema.gov/exercise#.)

Thereby underscoring the importance of these areas to the public safety community.[2] In particular, with respect to training exercises, FEMA[3] emphasizes that these activities enable organizations to identify both strengths and shortcomings within plans, and existing policies and procedures. They also help to clarify roles and responsibilities, as well as improve communication and coordination among the various stakeholders likely to be involved in a potential critical incident.

As Figure 6.3 illustrates, the preparedness cycle is a circular versus linear process that capitalizes on continuous organizational assessment and improvement. This helps to ensure that organizations are well prepared to respond to a critical incident and manage crisis events. We will discuss various aspects of innovation in greater detail in Chapter 7.

As previously noted, to achieve and maintain high levels of preparedness, it is necessary for planning, reviewing, training, and testing to occur on a regular basis. Nudell and Antokol[4] explain the importance of this concept quite well when they describe these components as an umbrella of preparation against the thunderstorms of a potential crisis. We are certainly reminded on a regular basis that organizations and governments around the world are impacted by a wide range of crisis events. In many of these cases, the impact is quite severe, testing the breadth and depth of emergency preparedness plans. When this occurs, those organizations and governments that have proactively invested in the planning process, as well as trained and tested their Emergency Operations Plan will undoubtedly be in a much better position to effectively respond and minimize the impact on life and property.

Webster and Williams[5] in their report to the Board of Police Commissioners on the Civil Disorder in Los Angeles, titled *City in Crisis*, commented that emergency response training is a critical component of any Emergency Operations Plan. However, the City's preparation for large-scale emergencies focused on earthquake preparedness. According to the report, little attention was given to civil disorder training, even though there was the possibility of civil unrest related to the upcoming trial of the police officers charged in the Rodney King case. It was also concluded that neither the City of Los Angeles nor the LAPD appeared to have conducted any training with adjoining jurisdictions in the event that the City's own resources proved insufficient should there be an emergency. For illustrative purposes, Photo 6.1 depicts a Joint Multi-Agency Training Exercise. Furthermore, the report emphasized that

> No single department or agency has the resources or experience effectively to complete all of the diverse tasks required of an emergency response to a large-scale civil disturbance, all of the City's departments must work together in a coordinated manner. These include not just the obvious examples of the police and fire departments, but all of the departments that make up the City's Emergency Operations Organization. These departments generally have little or no experience in working with other agencies in responding to a large-scale emergency, let alone a civil disturbance.[6]

Webster and Williams[7] further concluded that considering the potential threats to life and property posed by civil disorder, public safety organizations cannot afford to have confusion in their command structures, to include assigned functions and tasks, or fail to have the necessary plans in place to achieve a coordinated response. The panel also emphasized that it was necessary to learn, practice, and perfect responses to civil disorder prior to an actual

Photo 6.1 Joint Multiagency Training Exercise (Courtesy of the Miami-Dade Police Department. Photographer Unknown.)

crisis occurring. Moreover, regardless of the level, training should include three important components: instruction, practice, and testing and evaluation.

The report further provided a number of recommendations relative to training. Among these were the following:[8]

- That the Emergency Operations Board should develop a comprehensive program for emergency preparedness training.
- The program should include all city departments and agencies typically involved in an emergency response, and integrated training be included for all levels within these departments, as well as with mutual aid resources likely to be involved in an emergency response.
- That special attention be given to developing a training program for elected officials, senior managers, and uniformed services commanders. This program would focus on the development of crisis management skills and practical experience.
- That the Chief of Police should be directly involved in the development of citywide plans and training programs related to emergency preparedness. Furthermore, the chief should have overall responsibility for developing a realistic emergency preparedness plan and training program.

Finally, recognizing that many of the recommendations made would result in additional costs to the city, which was operating in a tight fiscal environment, the Webster and Williams[9] report nonetheless emphasized that sufficient funding should be made available to ensure the necessary levels of preparedness. This was certainly an important consideration; one that had wide applicability to other urban law enforcement agencies facing similar challenges at the time.

The civil unrest in Ferguson, Missouri, and Baltimore, Maryland, likewise resulted in local elected officials and police leaders being questioned regarding the ineffective response to events on the ground. In particular, the timing of information being released to the public, various aspects of police tactics and training, as well as the inability to quickly call on sufficient numbers of reinforcements were serious questions that government officials had to contend with on a regular basis. Furthermore, problems related to communications and interagency coordination were among the issues identified as hampering the response by the public safety community.

For example, with respect to the events in Ferguson, one *USA Today* report, entitled "Police Tactics in Ferguson Puzzle Resident, Experts," called into question tactics used by the prosecutor and the police. Noted problem areas included scheduling the announcement of the verdict at night as well as delaying calling in the National Guard, both of which contributed to events spiraling out of control. According to a pastor and protest organizer, "They said they had a plan. They said they were going to protect our businesses and community. ... That plan failed miserably."[10]

The response to natural and technological disasters also pose a number of challenges for public safety organizations as well as government officials at all levels of government. Typically, in times of crisis, leaders have to address a number of critical issues while often operating in an increasingly complex and chaotic environment. Under these uncertain conditions, the protection of life and property is of paramount importance, and those organizations that have been proactive in their planning and preparedness efforts will likely be able respond more effectively and have a smoother transition to the recovery phase. As it has often been said, "you play like you train." Therefore, the interactions and networking that has been established with outside agencies and groups in the front-end can have a very positive impact when communication, coordination, and collaboration is essential during a crisis event. Referring to the need for ongoing preparedness efforts, Smith[11] contends that preparation for the next disaster should occur immediately after the current crisis ends. Furthermore, he notes that those organizations that fail to learn from the mistakes of others, as well as from prior events, are likely to commit the same mistakes in the future.

Both Hurricane Katrina (2005) and Hurricane Sandy (2012) were critical events that impacted many people as well as wide geographic areas. Each one of these hurricane events caused billions of dollars in monetary damage and required a massive governmental response (see Photo 6.2). With respect to Katrina, the failure of the levees caused severe flooding to New Orleans. The federal flood protection system in place proved inadequate, and the resulting flooding submerged entire neighborhoods. FEMA was widely criticized for its response efforts during Katrina. In the aftermath of Katrina, a number of governmental reports revealed that the response was hampered by a lack of leadership, inadequate preparedness,

Photo 6.2 Aftermath of Hurricane Katrina (Photo by Win Henderson/FEMA Photograph—Location: New Orleans, Louisianna. http://www.fema.gov/vi/media-library/assets/images/45252.)

Photo 6.3 Aftermath of Hurricane Sandy (Official White House Photo by Sonya N. Herbert. http://www.whitehouse.gov/issues/hurricane/sandy.)

as well as poor communication and coordination with outside agencies and the general public. In contrast, the governmental response to Hurricane Sandy was better (see Photo 6.3). In particular, FEMA received praise for its role in the Sandy response effort. To many, this was not surprising, since Craig Fugate, the FEMA director since 2009, had focused on building a more effective response organization as well as establishing a culture of individual and community preparedness.[12] In particular, FEMA had come out with the Whole Community Concept in 2011, wherein "… residents, emergency management practitioners, organizational and community leaders, and government officials can collectively understand and assess the needs of their respective communities and determine the best ways to organize and strengthen their assets, capacities, and interests."[13]

In an article to the *Police Chief Magazine,* Fugate would later comment that in preparation for disasters, training exercises that simulate large and small-scale events help to prepare the public safety community and enable participants to better understand resource needs. Mr. Fugate further emphasized the importance of reviewing the Emergency Operations Plan on a regular basis, a critical area that the authors of this book have commented on as well.[14]

As a big proponent of training exercises, Fugate would often have his subordinates undergo surprise drills while director of the Florida Division of Emergency Management. Referred to as "thunderbolt" exercises, these surprise drills helped to prepare his team for a wide range of disaster situations.[15] This type of approach can also serve to develop a team that can readily respond to critical events while adapting to changing conditions. Moreover, team members do not settle into a routine, thereby helping to avoid the problem of complacency.

Faggiano and Gillespie,[16] in their text *Critical Incident Management: A Guide for Law Enforcement Supervisors*, further emphasize that a plan is only as effective as the corresponding training that has taken place to ensure that it can be implemented quickly and effectively. In their view, a book is not a substitute for training. Realistic training and experience is what enables a plan to perform well in times of crisis. Furthermore, training exercises should include the organizations and agencies that are likely to be involved in the response to a critical incident. When this does not occur, it is exceedingly difficult to integrate the strategies and tactics necessary for a coordinated response.

However, the authors contend that none of this can occur without the expressed and visible backing of top leadership within organizations. To this end, the support of top leadership is essential for ensuring that organizations maintain a regular training and exercise schedule that mirrors reality.

Integrating the Emergency Operations Plan

The Importance of Top Leadership

As is often seen, top leadership plays an important role in overall organizational preparedness, thereby setting the tone for the entire organization. Among other things, effective leaders inspire confidence and support among the people that are critical for achieving organizational goals.[17] They are visionary and creative, and use interpersonal influence to have a positive impact on organizational performance. In so doing, ultimately, they help to transform their organizations. Moreover, when a critical incident occurs, decisive action by top leadership can be the steadying force that gets an organization through a difficult period.

There are certainly a variety of ways that top leadership can influence an organization's overall preparedness. For example, Dubrin[18] states that an important aspect of crisis leadership is to prevent a crisis in the first place through proactive planning. As previously mentioned by the authors, the Emergency Operations Plan should not be developed in isolation. Rather, it should be a team approach that includes various organizational units. Doing so ensures that the plan is comprehensive in nature, taking into consideration various organizational viewpoints and requirements, as well as resources and capabilities. For example, referring back to Vignette 6.1, if the Training Bureau had been part of the planning team, the end result might have been quite different. Therefore, top leadership can certainly play a proactive role in the initial stages by putting in place a planning team that includes key organizational units, such as the following:

- Planning
- Specialized services
- Tactical operations
- Personnel management
- Training
- Public information
- Fiscal management

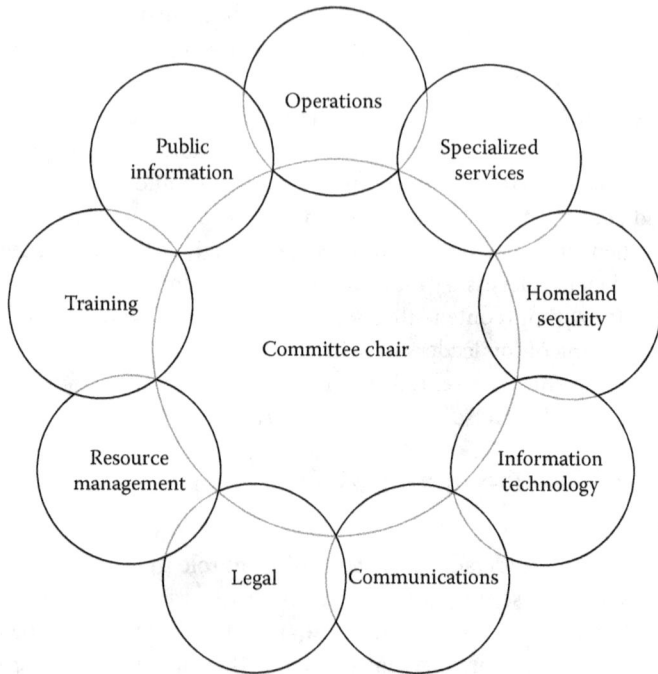

Figure 6.4 Example of Planning Team Organization (Developed by Eloy Nuñez and Ernest G. Vendrell.)

- Communications
- Legal
- Professional compliance
- Homeland security
- Community relations

This list certainly is not all-inclusive. However, it does serve to illustrate the range of organizational entities that have a stake and can play an important role in the planning process.

Regardless of the makeup of the planning team, it is important for top leadership to put someone in charge that will have their full support and authority to carry out the duties and responsibilities associated with the position. Figure 6.4 provides a planning team organization example, illustrating the interaction among various units and functions within the organization.

Communicating the Emergency Operations Plan

Once the initial Emergency Operations Plan has been completed, top leadership can continue to play a key role in communicating the plan throughout the organization. This is important for emphasizing the plan's significance to the organization, as well as highlighting key aspects of the plan and the role that various organizational units and members will be expected to play moving forward.

In addition to helping to align the plan with existing or new policy, it provides top leadership with additional opportunities for endorsing the plan and obtaining buy in from all members of the organization. These are all important considerations, since, as Vignette 6.1 previously pointed out, failure to communicate the plan throughout the organization can lead to disastrous consequences.

Coordination and Collaboration with Various Stakeholders

An examination of past critical incidents reveals that in times of crisis, few, if any, organizations can handle complex and chaotic events alone. Examples here would include the recent incidents of civil unrest that have occurred in various cities across the country, as well as the aftermath of natural disasters such as Hurricane Katrina and Superstorm Sandy. Instead, effective coordination and collaboration among various organizations, agencies, and stakeholders is essential for the successful resolution of these events. Furthermore, the need for high levels of interagency and multi-stakeholder cooperation also becomes quite evident during the planning of large-scale special events. Examples here would include political conventions, Super Bowls, global economic summits, and the Olympics. Oftentimes, the planning for these events takes at least a year. Moreover, the planning that goes into these events typically requires a substantial number of participants from various fields and disciplines. However, although time and resource intensive, they do provide an excellent opportunity for participants to share ideas and learn from each other. They also lay the groundwork for establishing and maintaining networking channels for the future.[19]

Some of the groups and agencies that typically would be involved in planning for or responding to a high-profile critical incident or large-scale special event would include[20]:

- Local police agencies
- State and federal law enforcement organizations
- City or county offices of emergency management
- Local fire and rescue departments
- Emergency medical services
- Local government officials
- Local Emergency Planning Committee
- Electric utilities
- Telephone companies
- Public works departments
- Volunteer agencies
- Essential contractors
- Vendors that supply emergency equipment
- Insurance carriers
- Local businesses
- Trade associations
- National Weather Service

As one can quickly surmise, there are a number of challenges with integrating such a wide array of organizations and stakeholders into the planning process. However, there are a number of clear advantages for doing so. In times of crisis, organizations have a tendency to respond differently based on a number of factors. Some of these variables include variations in tasks and mission, level of preparedness, not to mention various political considerations. Consequently, collaborating with outside agencies, as well as various stakeholders, well in advance will help to avoid confusion and potential delays during the response phase of a critical incident. Additionally, it improves communication and coordination during the management phase, and also provides for a smoother transition to the recovery phase.[21] Moreover, how various partners and stakeholders are going to respond should not be a surprise to anyone. Along these lines, key players should have a good understanding of each other's capabilities and resources in times of crisis.[22] Doing so helps to avoid confusion and delays when events become increasingly complex and uncertain.

Although planning and training with various partners and stakeholders is certainly an important consideration that should not be overlooked, these activities will not be effective if they are not taken seriously. For example, in 2004, FEMA led a simulation exercise called "Hurricane Pam." This fictional hurricane simulated a Category 3 storm striking New Orleans, flooding the city. The Pam simulation identified a large gap in disaster planning.[23] More than one million residents were forced to evacuate, and Pam destroyed 500,000–600,000 buildings. During the Pam simulation, emergency officials from parish, state, federal, and volunteer organizations participated in the five-day training exercise, and numerous deficiencies were noted. Therefore, Hurricane Pam called for a plan of action to prepare for a powerful storm, such as Hurricane Katrina.[24] Instead, a U.S. Senate Committee on Homeland Security and Governmental Affairs Report[25] entitled, *Preparing for a Catastrophe: The Hurricane Pam Exercise*, found that

> As a dry run for the real thing, Pam should have been a wake-up call that could not be ignored. Instead, it seems that a more appropriate name for Pam would have been Cassandra, the mythical prophet who warned of disasters but whom no one really believed. In many ways, the hypothetical problems identified in Pam predict with eerie accuracy the all-too-real problems of Katrina—overcrowded shelters undersupplied with food, water, and other essentials; blocked highways with thousands of people trapped in flooded areas; hospitals swamped with victims and running out of fuel for their emergency generators. The list goes on and on.[26]

Organizing Training Activities

Viewed from this perspective, it becomes increasingly clear that realistic training with applicable stakeholders is critical, as is follow through on noted weaknesses and deficiencies. These important activities help to confirm a number of key areas:

- That the Emergency Operations Plan can be executed properly
- That all participants understand their assigned roles and responsibilities
- That critical resources and capabilities have been identified and are readily available

In particular, testing the plan prior to an actual emergency helps to identify potential problems as well as inherent weaknesses. These areas must be corrected in order to ensure that the Emergency Operations Plan will function as expected.[27]

Typically, the first step in the training process is for the organization to appoint a staff member with the responsibility of developing an overall training plan. This would include the requisite goals and objectives for each component of the plan. Additionally, at this stage, a number of important questions should be asked[28]:

- Who will be trained?
- Who will perform the training?
- Are the training goals and objectives aligned with the Emergency Operations Plan?
- What will the training activities consist of?
- What materials and equipment are necessary to perform the training?
- When will the training take place? Day, night, or both?
- Where will the training take place? Are multiple venues required?
- What is the duration of the initial training?
- How will special circumstances be handled?
- How will the training be evaluated? By whom? Is evaluator training necessary?
- How will the various training activities be recorded and documented?
- How will training costs be budgeted? Will there be any shared expenses? Grant funding opportunities?
- How, where, and by whom will the training debriefing be conducted?
- How will the training outcomes be communicated?

These questions can help organizations to further organize the required training into various categories, as follows:

Training Needs   Identifying the scope of the problem is an important first step. As you can imagine, it is difficult to solve a problem if it has not been properly defined and diagnosed. In particular, organizations need to determine the scope of the present need, problem, deficiency, or area in need of improvement, and whether the issue(s) are internal or external, or perhaps both. Additionally, at this stage, the organizations must determine whether they have the internal resources to lead the training effort. If not, then partnerships are a great way of maximizing capabilities and resources in this important arena.

Training Goals and Objectives   Once the training needs have been clearly identified, there are a number of training variables that need to be considered. First, training goals and objectives are essential, since they tend to drive various activities and efforts moving forward. The goals and objectives need to be specific and consistent with existing law, accreditation standards, and department standard operating procedures (SOPs). Specific goals and objectives will also help to determine the duration of the training as well as the training venue(s) that will be required. In turn, this will assist in calculating anticipated training costs and expenditures.

Training Strategy   After the training needs have been clearly identified and training goals and objectives have been determined, there are a number of training strategies that need to be considered. First, getting budget approval is critical. As it is often said, funding tends to drive everything. Consequently, once the budget is approved, organizations can begin the process of dedicating training personnel to the training effort, finalizing training activities, as well as selecting and training evaluators.

Training Outcomes   Training outcomes can certainly have an important impact on an organization's overall preparedness. As previously discussed in this chapter, it is training, testing, and exercising with various partners and applicable stakeholders that serves to validate an organization's Emergency Operations Plan. Therefore, the performance of personnel, evaluator observations and critiques, exercise debriefings, and after-action reports are important components of the outcomes associated with the training effort.

Organizational Improvement   An important aspect of any training initiative is to communicate outcomes and lessons learned, and to forward any recommendations for improvement to the planning team. In particular, lessons learned need to be applied to appropriate levels within the organization, and, where applicable, necessary changes need to be made to standard operating procedures. This helps to ensure that outcomes and lessons learned are aligned with the organization's policies and procedures. Additionally, an added benefit of conducting training with partners and stakeholders is that they lead to enhanced networking capabilities. In turn, this can serve as a catalyst for future training.

Figure 6.5 provides a visual graphic of the various stages in the training process, from initial training needs assessment to organizational improvement. As indicated in the training outcomes phase, critiques and evaluations are important components, and they should be conducted after each training activity. In particular, exercise debriefings are critical for discussing positive outcomes as well as areas in need of improvement. More importantly, they help to assess how well the Emergency Operations Plan works (see Photo 6.4).

These training activities also serve to reinforce that, whenever possible, organizations should involve outside agencies in the training and evaluation process.

Training Needs	Training Variables	Training Strategy	Training Outcomes	Organizational Improvement
• What is the scope of the problem or area in need of improvement? • Is it an internal or external problem? Both? • Does the organization have the internal resources to lead the training effort, or are partnerships necessary?	• Training goals and objectives • Anticipated training costs and expenditures • Duration of training • Training venue	• Training budget approval • Selection of training activities • Selection of training personnel • Selection and training of evaluators	• Personnel performance • Evaluator observations and critiques • Exercise debriefing • After-action report	• Communicate outcomes and lessons learned • Apply lessons learned to appropriate levels within the organization • Capitalize on enhanced internal/external networking • Use outcomes as a catalyst for future training

Figure 6.5 Various Stages in the Training Process (Developed by Eloy Nuñez and Ernest G. Vendrell.)

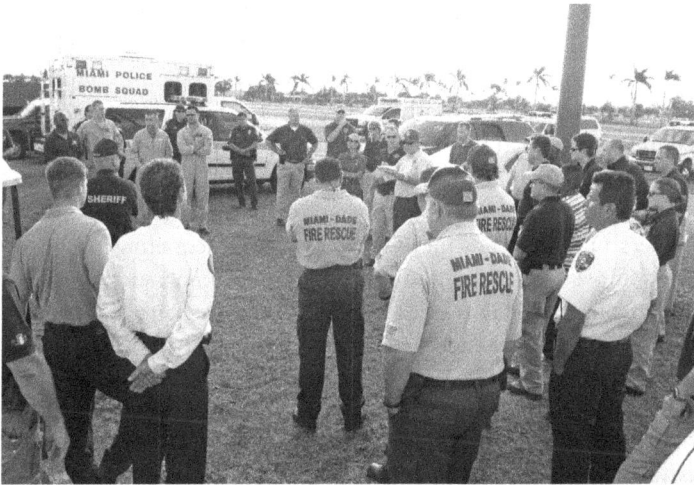

Photo 6.4 Photo of Exercise Debriefing (Courtesy of the Miami-Dade Police Department. Photographer Unknown.)

In addition to helping to promote coordination and cooperation, doing so helps to avoid conflict when a critical incident does occur. Unfortunately, far too often, these areas are not emphasized. When this occurs, organizations miss out on the opportunity for organizational improvement; presumably, this was the purpose of engaging in training activities in the first place. Closely related to this, Chapter 7 will discuss the importance of establishing a culture of innovation and learning within organizations.

VIGNETTE 6.2 The Training Commander—The Journey

Captain Javier Gonzalez approached the podium and prepared to address the men and women assembled in the auditorium of the recently completed state-of-the-art training facility. It spanned more than 20 acres, housing impressive classrooms and outside training areas. "Wow," he thought to himself.

"We certainly have come a long way." Just a few years ago, the bureau was training officers and conducting exercises in makeshift facilities across the county, and the training budget was tight, to say the least. Finally, the county invested heavily in the much-needed training facility, which would serve as a training venue for the rapidly growing sheriff's office. The expansive training complex would allow the department to conduct joint training exercises with nearby agencies and adjoining jurisdictions.

As part of the planning team for the development of the facility, Gonzalez knew all too well the past training problems, and the years of negative consequences that this created. In particular, the lack of realistic training, and inconsistent evaluation of performance, resulted in a myriad of problems when it came to high-profile critical incidents and special events. Additionally, failure to train with the agencies and groups that need to work together in times of crisis led to problems with communications and coordination, and a general lack of trust among key players from the emergency response community.

Today's event marked the culmination of a number of milestones. Since the opening of the facility, Gonzalez used the department's newly revised Emergency Operations Plan to schedule a series of tabletop exercises, and these were followed up with a number of drills and exercises with various stakeholders. On the agenda for today was the final debriefing for the recently completed full-scale exercise. By all accounts it had been a success, identifying positive outcomes, as well as areas in need of improvement. Judging from the excitement among the attendees, he felt confident that considerable progress would continue to be made. However, he did not want this to be viewed as a final destination, but rather as a journey that they were all embarking on.

Vignette 6.2 helps to illustrate the potential outcomes of organizations coming together and collaborating on joint planning and training initiatives. Based on a true story, it is important to note that this type of cooperation and collaboration does not happen by accident. Typically, it involves persistence and perseverance on the part of key players to get people working together, putting aside any past differences, while recognizing the benefits of mutual organizational and community preparedness.

It should be noted that in the actual event, one point of disagreement did surface. In particular, several agencies complained that they had not been included in the after-action team activities that followed the debriefing and wanted to be part of the process. To many in the Training Bureau, this was a sign that the department was moving in the right direction.

Types of Training

There are various types of training options available to organizations seeking to enhance their emergency preparedness capabilities. For example, FEMA's Emergency Management Guide for Business and Industry lists six types of training activities that could be considered[29]:

Orientation and Education Sessions   These are designed to provide information, answer questions, as well as identify needs and concerns. These informal and low-stress sessions, help to familiarize participants with roles and responsibilities, as well as expectations and procedures. They are particularly useful when implementing new plans or adding new staff.

Tabletop Exercise   This is a cost-effective and efficient way for members of the emergency planning team, and key management personnel, to meet in a conference room setting to discuss roles and responsibilities. This also helps to identify areas of concern before engaging in more demanding training activities. Tabletop exercises are also a great way of practicing team building and problem solving (see Photo 6.5).

Walk-Through Drill   The emergency planning team and response personnel actually perform assigned emergency response functions. By design, this involves more personnel, and is more thorough than a tabletop exercise.

Evacuation Drill   This is designed to have participants walk the evacuation route to a designated area where procedures for accounting for all personnel are tested. Participants make note of potential hazards along the way, and the Emergency Operations Plan is revised based on these observations.

Functional Drill   This drill, realistically simulates an event in a controlled environment. Tests specific functions (e.g., emergency notifications, communications procedures and equipment, medical response, etc.), although not necessarily at the same time. The drill is evaluated by the participants, and problem areas are identified. Typically, these drills are detailed and generate a higher level of stress among participants (see Photo 6.6).

Photo 6.5 Tabletop Exercise (Courtesy of the Miami-Dade Police Department. Photographer Unknown.)

Photo 6.6 Functional Training Exercise (Courtesy of the Miami-Dade Police Department. Photographer Unknown.)

Full-Scale Exercise   An emergency event is simulated as close to reality as possible. Personnel, equipment, and resources are deployed to specific locations in real time. This training exercise involves all levels of the organization, as well as outside agencies and groups likely to be involved in the response. Due to the nature of these exercises, they are typically quite detailed, are more expensive, and can generate high levels of stress among participants (see Photo 6.7).

Photo 6.7 Full-Scale Exercise (Courtesy of the Miami-Dade Police Department. Photographer Unknown.)

Critical Incident Management Board   One of the most successful and creative ways of teaching critical incident management to the emergency response community is via a "model city" simulation board. As Photo 6.8 serves to illustrate a "model city" simulator can be designed to represent a small community with various components: a residential area, a business district, an industrial park, and so forth. Therefore, the "model city" simulator provides a realistic environment, which gives participants the feeling of actually having managed a critical incident. In particular, students are able to practice decision-making and leadership skills in a realistic setting where there are no repercussions for making a mistake. Furthermore, participants can immediately see the results of actions taken or not taken.[30]

The primary goal of the "model city" simulator training program is to provide students with a "game plan" for handling critical incidents. This can make the difference in operational personnel taking control of an incident or allowing events to spiral out of control. Therefore, the primary focus of the training is on managing the first 30 minutes of a critical incident. Participants employ a series of critical tasks or decisions as follows:

- Establish communications
- Identify the "hot zone"
- Establish an inner perimeter
- Establish an outer perimeter
- Establish a command post
- Select a staging area
- Identify and request additional resources[31]

It should be noted that the critical incident management simulation board can also be expanded to additional levels and functions within an organization

Photo 6.8 Critical Incident Management Board (Courtesy of John McNall, BOWMAC Educational Services, Inc. http://www.bowmac.com/wp-content/uploads/2013/11/Simulator2.jpg.)

besides first-line supervisors. This could include mid-management personnel, command staff, and so forth.

The Homeland Security Exercise and Evaluation Program (HSEEP) provides guiding principles for conducting exercises.[32] These principles can be applied to the management and execution of exercises to examine capabilities and validate existing plans. As HSEEP points out, "A well-designed exercise provides a low-risk environment to test capabilities, familiarize personnel with roles and responsibilities, and foster meaningful interaction and communication across organizations"[33] (see Figure 6.6).

HSEEP[34] also makes available various templates and guides that can assist organizations in designing, conducting, and evaluating training exercises. These helpful tools can prove invaluable in assessing capabilities and making improvements to their existing Emergency Operations Plans. As HSEEP points out, "Through exercise evaluation, organizations assess the capabilities needed to accomplish a mission, function, or objective."[35]

As previously discussed, the Emergency Operations Plan should be considered a living document that requires regular attention. It is valuable only when all members of the organization understand its various components, and can readily assume their designated roles when a critical incident occurs. This requires that adequate time and effort be expended on training, testing, and exercising the plan. Additionally, it requires the support of the training commander and other top leadership, particularly when others question realistic training tactics and strategies.

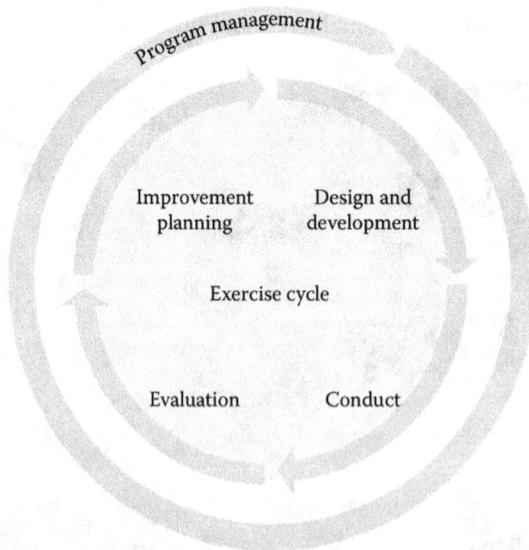

Figure 6.6 The Homeland Security Exercise and Evaluation Program Exercise Cycle (From: http://www.fema.gov/media-library-data/20130726-1914-25045-8890/hseep_apr13_.pdf.)

VIGNETTE 6.3   The Value of Realistic Training

The Monday morning staff meeting with the training division commander had started with business as usual. In attendance were the three section lieutenants and the half-dozen or so training supervisors responsible for managing the department's various in-service programs as well as the increasing number of specialized training courses and programs. However, on the agenda today was the rise in training-related injuries. In particular, despite an enviable safety record over the years, there had been a noticeable increase in injuries during the recently completed annual Mobile Field Force training. Although not debilitating, several of the injuries had been serious enough to require medical attention at local hospitals. The commander was concerned about this trend, and wanted steps taken to ensure that potential risks were being minimized.

The commander now turned to Lieutenant Lisa McCarthy, the training division's representative to the Department's Mobile Field Force Training Committee, and Sergeant Steve Goldbloom, the supervisor in charge of the training activities taking place in the department's recently completed Survival City. "Where are we on this since our last meeting? I have to meet with the director later this afternoon. He has been receiving various inquiries from the County's Risk Management Division, and their representatives will also be in attendance at this meeting. What steps are being taken to ensure that we stay on top of this? Are there any revisions necessary to existing training protocols or departmental SOP's?"

Lieutenant McCarthy was first to address the commander's concerns. "Commander, as you know, this year we incorporated a number of very realistic, and fast-paced, training exercises into our Mobile Field Force training. We added the use of role players into the various scenarios, using both sworn and non-sworn personnel to assume various roles. In an effort to simulate reality as closely as possible, some of the scenarios are pretty intense. They range from controlling chaotic anarchist groups, to diffusing violent crowd confrontations with police during incidents of civil unrest. However, every possible precaution is taken to ensure the safety of all participants, to include the addition of safety officers to quickly identify potentially unsafe situations. Although the risks are higher, it has resulted in higher levels of learning and critical analysis of problems. We believe that this will have a positive impact on performance, both now and in the future."

Sergeant Goldbloom added, "The Survival City scenarios have likewise allowed us to take it to another level in terms of matching reality. We are now able to introduce various high-risk scenarios in a state-of-the-art facility. Those undergoing the training are presented with a number of problems, and we are using trained evaluators as well as role players to bring the scenarios to life. As Lieutenant McCarthy mentioned, the risks are higher, but the goal from the onset was to approximate real-world conditions. The participant evaluations have also been very positive. I also believe that this will pay huge dividends for us in the future."

"Very well," the Commander said. "I would like the two of you to accompany me to this meeting. These programs have been a part of our overall strategic initiatives—all designed to ensure that we will perform more effectively as a Department. We need to make sure that we get this message across."

As Vignette 6.3 serves to illustrate, although there are a number of important, and necessary, benefits associated with public safety organizations engaging in realistic training, there are a number of inherent risks as well. These risks can certainly be minimized by proactive planning and supervision. However, it is unrealistic to think that training for high-risk events that closely simulate reality will eliminate all risks. This is one reason why many public safety organizations use a progression of training with respect to emergency preparedness, ranging from panel discussions to full-scale exercises, each building on the other.

Figure 6.7 depicts the learning value, as well as risks, associated with the various types of training. On one end of the spectrum, orientation and education sessions are considered low-risk, low-stress training. These sessions are also considered more abstract in nature. In contrast, as you begin moving to the other end of the spectrum, full-scale exercises are designed to simulate reality as closely as possible. The risks associated with this type of training are greater, but they offer more concrete learning experiences. Consequently, they are deemed very valuable in enhancing overall preparedness.

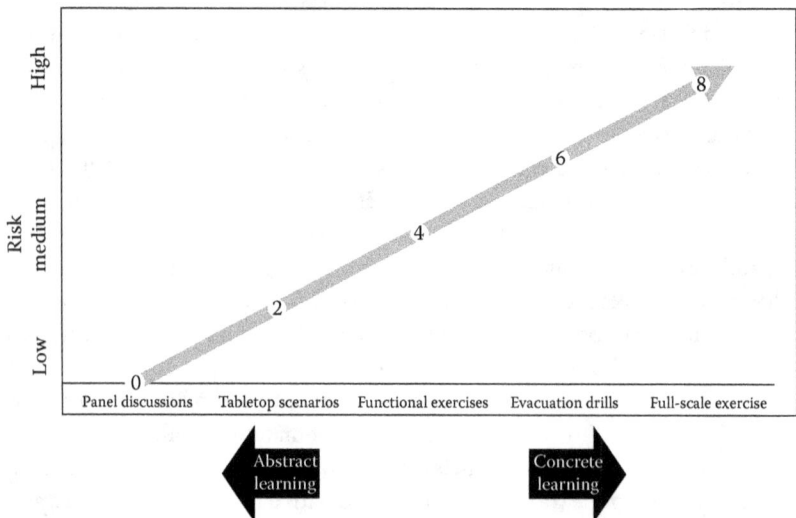

Figure 6.7 Learning Value and Risk Associated with Training Types (Developed by Eloy Nuñez and Ernest G. Vendrell.)

VIGNETTE 6.4 United Airlines Flight 232

On July 19, 1989, United Airlines Flight 232 was flying from Denver to Chicago when the tail engine exploded, resulting in the loss of all flight controls. It was estimated that the odds of this type of failure occurring were one in a billion, and that the odds for surviving were even more remote.[36] However, the pilots did a remarkable job of flying the crippled aircraft. The Captain, Al Haynes, and the flight crew struggled to fly the DC-10 without flight controls. They were assisted by a DC-10 instructor, Al Fitch, who just happened to be seated in the first cabin, flying back to Chicago after teaching a course in Denver. The captain assigned Fitch to coordinate the throttles on the two remaining engines, thus helping to crudely steer the aircraft. Unfortunately, there was no backup plan for total hydraulic failure on a DC-10, resulting in a worst-case scenario for the pilots and flight crew.[37] However, due to the poor condition of the aircraft, the captain knew that time was of the essence, and he decided that the airport in Sioux City, Iowa, was the closest and best airport to attempt a landing. He knew that a landing would be very difficult. A DC-10 is a heavy jumbo jet, and total hydraulics failure meant that there were no brakes. The plan was to set the plane on the runway as early as possible. In this way, the drag would help to slow the plane down. As they approached the runway, the plane sunk too fast and, ultimately, the right wing dipped and scraped the runway. The plane cartwheeled out of control. Fuel spilled, and the plane exploded and broke into pieces.[38] It was a horrendous crash, and eyewitnesses who observed the impact, and resulting fireball, doubted that there would be survivors.

However, out of the smoke and chaos, emergency responders began spotting people, some of whom were walking on their own. Gary Brown, the emergency management coordinator for Woodbury County, had participated in a regional plane crash drill several years prior. He was at the scene and had observed the DC-10 crash on the runway. At first, he was puzzled by seeing people walking towards him, but quickly realized that there were, in fact, survivors.[39]

Of the 296 people on board the flight, 184 survived the crash. Many have praised the skill of the flight crew, as well as the quick and coordinated response of the emergency response community, for so many lives being saved.[40] In particular, Larson et al.[41] have identified a number of reasons for the successful response:

- *The Emergency Response Level Had Been Upgraded*: Realizing the gravity of the situation, ground control decided to issue a higher level alert before the plane actually crashed in Sioux City. This proactive action provided response agencies with additional time to prepare. It also allowed for mutual aid agreements to be put into effect. By the time Flight 232 crash landed, the emergency response community was at the scene ready to take action.

- *Efficient Triage and Ambulance Transportation*: A triage center set up before the crash occurred. In addition, roadblocks were established along the route from the airport to the hospital. Since traffic was eliminated, this enabled ambulances to travel much faster to the hospital and back to the crash site.
- *A Well-Rehearsed and Integrated Emergency Response Plan*: Sioux City had a comprehensive plan that was exercised on a regular basis, and treated as a living document. Two years prior to the crash, a decision was made to better integrate the emergency response plan, taking into consideration the various response agencies. The new plan was exercised annually. Different exercise scenarios were used each year, and this helped to identify weaknesses, enhance coordination, and establish trust among the emergency response community. Coincidently, the 1987 training exercise was based on the crash of a large jumbo jet, which led to the expansion of the mutual aid agreements in place.
- *Effective Use of Medical Teams*: When the crash occurred, hospitals were in the process of changing shifts. Therefore, both the day and evening shift medical personnel were on hand. As a result, teams consisting of one doctor and one nurse were assigned specific patients that they were responsible for until such time as their condition was stable. Additionally, there was a specific group of surgeons and nurses for patients requiring immediate surgery.
- *Mutual Aid Agreements*: The existing mutual aid agreement between Sioux City and adjoining jurisdictions was a contributing factor to the overall success of the emergency response. In particular, an agreement was in place wherein a significant emergency would enable the dispatching of resources from nearby cities. Consequently, prior to the crash, resources were already in position near the runway.
- *Pre-Positioning of Ambulances*: The City had previously determined that positioning ambulances at various points along the highway would minimize travel time should an aircraft crash short of the runway. When Flight 232 crash landed, this resulted in less travel time to the crash site. This proactive measure came about as a direct result of a training exercise.[42]

The events described in Vignette 6.4 highlight the resourcefulness and skill of a flight crew, and the proactive emergency preparedness efforts of various agencies and organizations within a community. Clearly, it was a testament to the cockpit crew that they were even able to make it to the Sioux City Airport. Likewise, the proactive actions undertaken by response agencies, both in terms of advanced preparedness for a potential aviation disaster as well as in preparing for the arrival of United Flight 232, helped to minimize the aftermath, thereby saving lives.

Professional Development

Maintaining high levels of preparedness does not occur by accident. It takes a commitment on the part of organizations to develop their personnel, both individually and collectively, and to always be willing to take it to the next level in terms of preparedness. As past events serve to reinforce, the return on investment (ROI) is well worth the costs associated with maintaining a high level of preparedness.

VIGNETTE 6.5 The Benefits of Professional Development

Sergeant Mark Tolland arrived at the training complex and parked his take-home vehicle near the front door of the main building. He always enjoyed coming to work, but was especially excited today, and it showed as he exited his vehicle and entered the reception area. As usual, he was greeted warmly by the receptionist of many years, Tasha, who barely managed to say as he rushed by "the lieutenant is waiting for you, Mark. He wants to see you right away. What's going on anyway?" But, Mark whizzed past her, blurting out, "It's a good day—Tasha! I'll explain everything later."

Mark walked past the two conference rooms, followed by the administrative office, and then entered the back part of the building where the offices for the various training officers and supervisors were located. There he found Lieutenant Eric Velez, who was on the phone talking with the major from media relations about an upcoming training program. Velez waved him in, and motioned for him to take a seat. However, Mark had a lot of nervous energy, and it was obvious that he was having a difficult time waiting for his turn to speak with the lieutenant.

Lieutenant Velez had been with the department for more than 30 years, and had spent considerable time in uniformed operations, special investigations, as well as organized crime. He was a seasoned veteran who knew the ropes, and was highly regarded by all. Although, at times, he was a stickler for far too many administrative details, the troops knew that he had their best interests at heart, and everyone wanted to work for him.

Finally, Velez hung up the phone, and turned to Mark. "What's going on?" he asked. Mark quickly rattled off, "Lieutenant, remember the police exchange fellowship that I had applied for six months ago? The one for which you wrote me a letter of recommendation? The one that only two officers from the United States are selected for each year? I got it! I leave for Europe in April, and I will remain there for at least two months. As you know, that will provide me with many opportunities to visit with various police organizations, and learn about their policing strategies and training practices. The Fellowship Exchange Commission will provide me with a modest stipend, as long as the department will take care of my airfare and continue to pay my salary while I am away. That sounds like a pretty good deal. I just need to get the final department approval, so I can notify the Fellowship Exchange that I have accepted the award."

Lieutenant Velez was visibly proud of Mark, called everyone over to his office, and publicly congratulated Mark on his accomplishment. Once everyone had left his office, he told Mark, "O.K., I will speak with the major later this afternoon, and will do everything possible to expedite this for you. There is a director's meeting tomorrow, and all of the command staff will be in attendance. That might be a great opportunity for the major to speak with the director, announce the news, and obtain the necessary approval. I will let you know as soon as I hear anything."

Mark left Lieutenant Velez's office feeling pretty confident, and worked on getting all of the necessary paperwork ready to forward to the Fellowship Exchange Commission, pending the director's approval. He felt honored to have been awarded such a prestigious award, and promised himself that he would capitalize on every opportunity presented to him while he was away in Europe.

Late in the afternoon on the following day, Mark's cell phone rang, and he noticed that it was Lieutenant Velez. He cheerfully answered, "Hey LT," but he immediately sensed that the Lieutenant was troubled. "Mark, we have a problem. The major fully supports your award, and he spoke with the director. However, it does not look good at this point. As you know, there is a budget crunch right now, and there is some hesitation about letting you go overseas for two months on full salary, while having to fund the additional expenses associated with this award."

Mark was very disappointed, and Lieutenant Velez allowed him a couple of minutes to vent his frustration. "But, Lieutenant, you know full well the impact of the various critical incidents and special events that the Department has experienced in recent years. And, in the past year alone, the department has repeatedly said that we need to visit with other agencies, review after-action reports of major events, and identify best practices that could potentially be incorporate here. The goal has been to be the best, and be able to anticipate problems as opposed to merely reacting to them. This award does just that. I will have the opportunity to visit with police professionals from highly developed law enforcement organizations. It will benefit not only me, but the Department as a whole. If I am not allowed to go, another agency will gladly send one of their officers. It doesn't make sense?"

Lieutenant Velez then chimed in, "Listen, Mark, the major agrees with everything you just said. He wants you to prepare a presentation that highlights the benefit to both you and the Department. I would suggest that you prepare the presentation as if you were going to deliver it to the entire command staff. Work on it all day tomorrow, and meet me in my office at the end of the day, so we can go over what you have."

Vignette 6.5 exemplifies one type of professional development opportunity that requires a substantial investment on the part of public safety organizations. Examples of professional development activities that might require the support of the organization could include an overseas academic scholarship or fellowship, attending extended police management courses, such as the FBI National Academy (FBINA) or the Southern Police Institute (SPI), attending the National Fire Academy (NFA) Managing Officer Program, or participating in an externship. Although the costs associated with these types of professional development activities, as well as the time that personnel will be away from the agency, might be questioned initially, the benefits to both participants and the organization far outweigh any potential negatives.

Over the years, FEMA has done a good job of providing training support to the emergency response community through the various courses and programs offered through the Emergency Management Institute (EMI). A listing of these courses and programs can be accessed at https://www.training.fema. org. In particular, EMI provides a wide array of residential courses at its campus in Emmitsburg, Maryland, as well as an expansive list of independent study courses, many of which are offered via an interactive Web-based format. Additionally, EMI offers a number of emergency management programs designed to further develop practitioners, as follows:

- Master Exercise Practitioner Program (MEPP)
- Master Trainer Program (MTP)
- Professional Development Series (PDS)
- Advanced Professional Development Series (APS)

Since 1994, EMI has also been providing support to colleges and universities which offer, or seek to develop, degree programs and courses related to emergency management and homeland security through its Higher Education Program. In so doing, FEMA promotes college-level emergency management education for current and future leaders in this important arena. Furthermore, each year, EMI hosts the Higher Education Symposium at EMI, bringing together academics and program directors from across the country and beyond, in an effort to further assist in the development of emergency management higher education programs.

Although not inclusive, it should be noted that free training is typically available through state and local offices of emergency management, Local Emergency Planning Committees (LEPCs), as well as various volunteer organizations and private organizations that play a role, or have an interest in, emergency management or disaster relief. All of these training opportunities can serve to further develop the emergency response community to operate in an increasingly complex and uncertain environment.

Clearly, personnel operating in this important arena need to take advantage of every professional opportunity available to them. Moreover, organizations must continually scan their internal and external environments in order to identify and incorporate best practices. Doing so will help to anticipate problems, instead of merely reacting to them. Along these lines, Chapter 7 will focus on establishing a culture of innovation and learning.

References

1. Panel said to fault Los Angeles Riot Response, 1992. *New York Times*, October 18. Online at http://www.nytimes.com/1992/10/18/us/panel-said-to-fault-los-angeles-riot-response.html (accessed September 27, 2015).
2. Federal Emergency Management Agency, 2015. Emergency Management Institute. Online at http://training.fema.gov/emi.aspx (accessed October 27, 2015).
3. Federal Emergency Management Agency, 2015. The preparedness cycle. Online at http://www.fema.gov/exercise# (accessed September 27, 2015).
4. M. Nudell and Antokol, N., 1988. *The Handbook for Effective Emergency and Crisis Management.* Lexington, MA: Lexington Books.
5. W. H. Webster and Williams, H., 1992. The city in crisis. Office of the Special Advisor to the Board of Police Commissioners. Online at http://www.policefoundation.org/content/city-crisis (accessed September 28, 2015).
6. Ibid., p. 101
7. Ibid.
8. Ibid.
9. Ibid.
10. R. Jervis, 2014. Police tactics in Ferguson puzzle residents, experts. *USA Today*, November 26. Online at http://www.usatoday.com/story/news/nation/2014/11/25/ferguson-riots-police-response/70102410/ (accessed September 28, 2015).
11. J. Smith, 2014. *Crisis Management in Law Enforcement.* Durham, NC: Carolina Academic Press.
12. G. Haddow, Bullock, J., and Coppola, D. P., 2014. *Introduction to Emergency Management.* Waltham, MA: Butterworth Heinemann.
13. Federal Emergency Management Agency, 2011. A Whole Community Approach to Emergency Management: Principles, Themes, and Pathways for Action, FDOC 104-008-1. Online at http://www.fema.gov/media-library-data/20130726-1813-25045-0649/whole_community_dec2011__2_pdf (accessed September 28, 2015).
14. W. C. Fugate, 2013. Law enforcement's role in responding to disasters. *From the Administrator, The Police Chief* 80, 100–101. Online at http://www.nbcnews.com/news/other/old-fema-gone-craig-fugates-cleaned-fema-f4B11229783 (accessed September 28, 2015).
15. E. Chuck, 2013. 'The Old FEMA is Gone': Craig Fugate's Cleaned up FEMA. *NBC NEWS*, September 23. Online at http://www.nbcnews.com/news/other/old-fema-gone-craig-fugates-cleaned-fema-f4B11229783 (accessed September 28, 2015).
16. V. Faggiano and Gillespie, T., 2004. *Critical Incident Management: An On-scene Guide for Law Enforcement Supervisors.* Tulsa, OK: K&M Publishers.
17. A. J. DuBrin, 2010. *Leadership: Research Findings, Practice, and Skills* (6th ed.). Mason, OH: Cengage Learning.
18. Ibid.
19. E. L. Nuñez, Vendrell, E. G., and Watson, S. A., 2015. Managing critical incidents and large-scale special events. In S. J. Davies, C. A. Hertig, and B. P. Gilbride, eds. *Security Supervision and Management: Theory and Practice of Asset Protection* (4th ed.). Burlington, MA: Butterworth Heinemann, 371–394.
20. Federal Emergency Management Agency, 2006. *Emergency Management Guide for Business and Industry.* Washington, DC: U.S. Government Printing Office.
21. E. L. Nuñez, Vendrell, E. G., and Watson, S. A., 2015. Managing critical incidents and large-scale special events. In S. J. Davies, C. A. Hertig, and B. P. Gilbride, eds. *Security Supervision and Management: Theory and Practice of Asset Protection* (4th ed.). Burlington, MA: Butterworth Heinemann, 371–394.

22. J. Walters and Kettl, D. F., 2006. The Katrina breakdown. In R. J. Daniels, D. F. Kettl, and H. Kunreuther, eds. *On Risk and Disaster: Lessons from Hurricane Katrina.* Philadelphia, PA: University of Pennsylvania Press, 255–261.
23. Ibid.
24. R. Longley, n.d. FEMA's "Pam" simulation foretold Katrina disaster. Online at http://usgovinfo.about.com/od/defenseandsecurity/a/femapam.htm (accessed September 28, 2015).
25. Committee on Homeland Security and Governmental Affairs, U.S. Senate, 2006. *Hearings on Preparing for a Catastrophe: The Hurricane Pam Exercise, 109th Cong. 403,* January 24. U.S. Government Printing Office. Online at http://www.gpo. gov/fdsys/pkg/CHRG-109shrg26749/html/CHRG-109shrg26749.htm (accessed September 28, 2015).
26. Ibid., para 7
27. E. L. Nuñez, Vendrell, E. G., and Watson, S. A., 2015. Managing critical incidents and large-scale special events. In S. J. Davies, C. A. Hertig, and B. P. Gilbride, eds. *Security Supervision and Management: Theory and Practice of Asset Protection* (4th ed.). Burlington, MA: Butterworth Heinemann, 371–394.
28. Ibid.
29. Federal Emergency Management Agency, 2004. *Emergency Management Guide;* ASIS International, *Business Continuity Guideline: A Practical Approach for Emergency Preparedness, Crisis Management, and Disaster Recovery.* Alexandria, VA: ASIS International.
30. V. Faggiano, McNall, J., and Gillespie, T., 2011. *Critical Incident Management: A Complete Response Guide.* Boca Raton, FL: CRC Press.
31. Faggiano et al., 1992. *Critical Incident Management;* BowMac Education Services, Inc.; *Critical Incident Management Instructor Notebook.* Rochester, New York: Author. BowMac Education.
32. Department of Homeland Security, 2013. *Homeland Security and Evaluation Program* (HSEEP). Online at https://hseep.preptoolkit.org/docs/HSEEP_Revision_Apr13_Final.pdf (accessed September 28, 2015).
33. Ibid., p. 4
34. Department of Homeland Security, 2013. *HSEEP Police and Guidance Home.* Online at https://hseep.preptoolkit.org/ (accessed September 28, 2015).
35. Ibid., para 5
36. D. P. Finney, 2014. Disaster, Miracle of United 232 Crash Recalled. *The Des Moines Register,* July 13. Online at http://usatoday.com/story/news/nation/2014/07/13/disaster-miracle-recalled-25-years-after-iowa-plane-crash/12574285/
37. Ibid.
38. Ibid.
39. M. Tauscheck, 2014. 25 Years After Major Airline Crash, Survivors Returning to Iowa. Online at http://www.kcci.com/news/25-years-after-major-airline-crash-survivors-returning-to-iowa/26979896
40. D. P. Finney, 2014. Disaster, Miracle of United 232 Crash Recalled.
41. R. C. Larson, Metzger, M. D., and Cahn, M. F. 2006. Responding to emergencies: Lessons learned and the need for analysis. *Interfaces,* 36(6), November–December 2006, pp. 486–501, ISBN 0092-2102. Online at http://pubsonline.informs.org/doi/abs/10-1287/inte.1060.0250
42. Ibid.

7

Learning and Innovation

Creating New Ways for Using Old Ideas

This chapter is devoted entirely to the innovation process. The theme of this chapter is that the core principles of organizational management do not change. What does change is the manner in which those core principles are applied to real-life situations. We often hear the expression, "let's not reinvent the wheel" used in the context of redoing something that someone has already done successfully. From this perspective, it seems like a waste of time and resources to do something that others have already done. However, in this book, we are going to look at "reinventing the wheel" in a different way. In particular, we are going to take the ideas that others before us have created, and we will then determine how we can best apply these to the challenges that we now face.

In previous chapters, we discussed several examples of old ideas being used in new ways. We read about the creation of modern day crowd control tactics in the form of Mobile Field Forces, and how these new tactics borrow heavily from the Roman legions and Greek phalanxes of the past. The innovation of bicycle field forces is nothing more than a reimplementation of light cavalry forces used to outflank and encircle the opponent. Furthermore, the writings of Sun Tzu, Clausewitz, and Machiavelli can be applied as modern day strategies for war, for sports, and for nearly all types of businesses. It is not surprising that the writings of these theorists are still in heavy demand. The core concepts of strategy and tactics are timeless. The only thing that changes is the application of these concepts to the current situation. In essence, the process of innovation is all about "reinventing the wheel."

VIGNETTE 7.1   Black Sunday

Growing up in Miami in the 1960s and 1970s, it was not unusual to see the Goodyear blimp in the skies above the Little Havana neighborhood. At the time, the blimp was based out of nearby Watson Island, and it seemed like it would make an appearance over the Orange Bowl for every Miami Dolphins and University of Miami Hurricanes game. I remember my father telling me stories about the day he rode on the blimp to take aerial photos for the company that he worked for at the time. The Goodyear blimp was a fixture in the skies over Miami, but no matter how many times I saw it, I would always get excited, especially when I was able to get close to it and see its enormous size.

As a young kid, I was a big Dolphins and Hurricanes fan. I remember going to the Orange Bowl many times to watch University of Miami (UM) games with great players such as Ted Hendricks, the "Mad Stork." I remember paying $10 for season tickets and sitting in a special section in the west end zone for Huddle Club kids in the early, pre-Shula Dolphin games. The new Dolphins team that played its inaugural season in 1966 had a hard time filling the seats of the stadium, and would practically give away tickets to youngsters. Looking back, that was a smart marketing strategy because not only did they fill some seats, they also got kids to become Dolphins fans for life. Of course, in 1970, when the great Don Shula took over as head coach, and the team became instant winners, the Huddle Club was disbanded and ticket prices increased as more fans started attending games. Luckily for me, my older brother purchased season tickets in the upper deck of the north stands, and invited me to every Dolphins home game.

The 1975 season was not a memorable one for the Dolphins. After winning two Super Bowl championships in a row, and going undefeated in the 1972 season, the team lost three of its best players to a new upstart league. The 1975 team was a pretty good one, but they were clearly in decline, and that year, they failed to make the playoffs for the first time in the Shula era, even though they finished with ten wins and tied for first place in their division. They were beaten out by their archrivals at the time—the Baltimore Colts. It was at a home game against the Colts that year which I remember the most. It was not the game itself—which the Dolphins lost. What I remember the most of that day was the filming of the movie *Black Sunday*. I never got to see the movie at the theater, but I got to see the filming of it live at the Orange Bowl. In the movie plot, a terrorist group hijacked the blimp and used it to crash into the stadium during the 1976 Super Bowl between the Pittsburgh Steelers and the Dallas Cowboys. Indeed, part of the filming of the movie took place during the actual Super Bowl that year, but what most people don't know is that many of the scenes where the blimp comes close to crashing into the south-side upper deck of the stadium were shot during the Colts game earlier that year. I wasn't at the Super Bowl, but I do remember watching during the Colts game as the blimp would approach from the south and dip its nose downward, as if it was getting ready to dive into the middle of the stadium. From what I recall, the blimp made at least three runs for the filming—each time getting closer and closer to the stadium. It was an impressive sight, to say the least. There certainly would have been panic in the stands had it not been that several announcements were broadcast over the stadium's public address system letting people know that a movie was being shot and that a blimp would be getting close to the stadium.

Later, the game ended … the Dolphins lost in a non-memorable performance … but the memory of the blimp approaching the Orange Bowl would be ingrained in my mind for a long time. Little did I realize as an 18 year old at the time, that one day I would be tasked with conducting a vulnerability assessment for a Super Bowl, and that that image of the blimp crashing into a stadium would shape my thoughts and recommendations. As the commander of the Emergency Operations Unit at Miami-Dade Police, I was tasked with assembling a team of bomb squad and critical incident management unit personnel to conduct a vulnerability assessment of Dolphin Stadium in preparation for the 1999 Super Bowl. I would later repeat that assignment for the 2007 Super Bowl. The difference between those two events could not be any more distinct. In 1999, my bomb squad team was brought into the planning only a couple of months before the game. Typically, the planning for a special event the size and scope of a Super Bowl will take as much as 2 years. Security plans are well in place at least a year in advance. Two months out from the event, most of the planning activity has to do with the positioning of equipment, training for specialized units, and for last minute meetings and tabletop exercises to rehearse prior to the event. Since I was not part of the core planning committee for the 1999 Super Bowl, I am not sure why NFL Security and my own police department had waited so long to ask us to conduct a vulnerability assessment. Nevertheless, we undertook the assignment with a sense of urgency, and got it done in less than a week.

It was not the first time that I had conducted a vulnerability assessment, but it was by far the most complex and labor-intensive assessment that I had been involved in to date. In 1999, the security plan for the Super Bowl did not have a buffer zone around the stadium grounds. The area immediately surrounding the stadium was open to anyone who wished to be there. To gain entry into the stadium itself required a ticket, but there was nothing to prevent pedestrians or vehicles to walk or drive right up to the stadium structure. There were no searches of bags at the ticket gates, no magnetometers, no fencing, no concrete barriers, and no clearly designated exclusionary zones. The result was that there were as many people outside the stadium as there were inside the stadium during the game. Many people just showed up for the tailgate party outside the stadium, with no intention of actually going inside to watch the game. In 1999, the Super Bowl event was more like a mega party than the heavily secured event that it is now.

As we conducted our vulnerability assessment, we made special note of the air handler system which could conceivably spread an intentionally released chemical agent throughout the stadium. We also noted the unimpeded passage into the stadium through the east end zone, in which a terrorist's vehicle could be driven right onto the field from the east parking lot, without any barriers to stop it, or even slow it down. We noted the on-scene hazards such as the bags of fertilizer stored at the ground level. All these items were noted and recorded on our report to our command staff, but the one thing that bothered me the most was that the air traffic around the stadium would not be restricted on game day. Those images of the Goodyear blimp crashing into the Orange Bowl were still very vivid in my memory.

When I presented a report of our vulnerability assessment findings, I got a positive reception from my command staff. They were equally concerned about the many issues that we had noted on the report. Among my recommendations were to implement a buffer zone around the stadium, with a clearly defined perimeter and a fence to keep unauthorized persons out. I also recommended restricted access into the stadium secure zone, with magnetometer searches of all persons entering with tickets for the event. I recommended a single point of entry for all delivery vehicles, team buses, and for officials with the proper credentials. Lastly, I recommended flight restrictions around the stadium grounds to prevent an aircraft from crashing (intentionally or accidentally) into the stadium.

While my commanders took my concerns seriously, I was told that it was too late to make many substantive changes at that point. Never mind that the Oklahoma City bombing in 1995, and the Khobar Towers bombing in Saudi Arabia the following year had brought the threat of large vehicle bombings to the attention of the American public. Never mind that an FBI wanted poster of Osama bin Laden had been pinned to the bulletin board at our bomb squad offices immediately after the 1998 twin bombings of U.S. embassies in Nairobi, Kenya, and in Dar es Salaam, Tanzania. Despite all these occurrences, NFL Security, which is almost exclusively comprised of retired U.S. Secret Service agents, had convinced the Miami-Dade top planners that the recommendations that I had made were too costly and too late to implement. There would be no buffer zone, or limited access to deliveries, or flight restrictions. The best they could do for me was to increase the number of security personnel at the ground level to guard against any intruders gaining access to the stored fertilizers, and to give me an additional squad of officers to patrol the outside of the stadium, with the sole mission of keeping vehicles from parking next to the stadium structure, and to prevent a vehicle from barreling through the east end zone gate onto the field. I was assigned to be the supervisor of that squad during the event. That was the extent of my involvement in the 1999 Super Bowl.

The 2007 Super Bowl was an entirely different matter. This time, I was brought in early into the planning process, and I was one of the core planners. Early on, I realized how much things had changed post-September 11. The site plan presented by NFL Security and their contractors included a clearly defined buffer zone with fencing and concrete barriers, restricted entry for all vehicles, magnetometer searches for persons with tickets, and restricted air space around the stadium. More importantly, the *attitude* of the top NFL Security personnel had changed significantly. This time around, they were much more receptive to suggestions from others. When I pointed out that the Vehicle and Cargo Inspection System (VACIS) que line used to screen incoming delivery vehicles was too close to the stadium grounds, and that it lacked a sacrificial zone to render safe vehicle bombs, the NFL readily agreed to move the VACIS que line to where I suggested, south of the stadium, where there was sufficient space to screen the vehicles and render them safe if necessary. This time around, the relationship between NFL Security, the U.S. Secret Service, the FBI, the ATF, and Miami-Dade Police was much better than in 1999. It seems that it took the tragedy of September 11 to finally get us to work toward a common cause.

On the day of Super Bowl XLI, I sat in my seat at the Command Post perched high above the 50 yard line of Dolphin Stadium. I looked at the sky and noted that not a single aircraft was there. At that moment, I couldn't help but remember that Sunday afternoon in 1975, when I first saw the Goodyear blimp come so perilously close to the upper deck stands at the Orange Bowl. Prior to September 11, who would have ever thought of crashing an aircraft into a building in order to bring attention to a political cause? Apparently, someone did. Someone with an imagination had written a book with the same idea, and a movie shortly followed. Unfortunately, terrorists watch movies too. Once again, life imitates art.

Eloy Nuñez

As Vignette 7.1 serves to illustrate, past experience had a direct impact on the approach taken on two similar events, separated in time by almost a decade, as well as the events surrounding 9/11. For the 1999 Super Bowl, due to a variety of factors, including the late involvement of the bomb squad conducting the vulnerability assessment, many of the security recommendations that were submitted for consideration were not accepted by policy makers and event planners. By contrast, for the 2007 Super Bowl, the core planning team was brought in much earlier in the process, the relationship among the various participants was much better, and NFL Security was much more receptive to security recommendations. A clearer perspective of threats, vulnerability, and potential impact had occurred, and there was a sense of urgency to get things right in the post 9/11 world.

Innovate or Die

Peter Drucker, who is considered to be one of the foremost authorities on the subject of innovation (*Innovation and Entrepreneurship: Practice and Principles,* 1985) wrote an article about the city of London's financial services industry titled *Innovate or Die,*[1] in which he discusses the necessity for financial institutions to innovate and adapt to the changing environment, or risk becoming extinct. In Drucker's world, innovation has to do with the survival of companies. In the realm of critical incident management, the statement *"innovate or die,"* can be taken quite literally. Today, we live in an increasingly complex and dangerous global arena. We face a multitude of threats from a variety of foes, many of which have openly expressed their desire to do us harm by any means possible. Our enemies organize themselves in agile and decentralized organic structures, and many have proven successful at incorporating innovative strategies into their strategic and operational planning efforts. In many respects, they use sound business practices to gain a competitive advantage. They are adept at conducting their own risk assessments and assessing cost–benefit analysis, and they rely on imagery and symbolism to spread their message to a wide audience, using the Internet and social media to further their cause.

For example, as previously discussed, the 9/11 Commission Report estimated that al Qaeda spent between $400,000 and $500,000 to plan, train for, and execute the 9/11 attacks.[2] Viewed from al Qaeda's perspective, they received a substantial return on their initial investment. The devastating images from the attacks on the Twin Towers and the Pentagon, as well as the crash of United Airlines Flight 93 in western Pennsylvania (it is believed that this plane was headed for the U.S. Capitol Building before the passengers fought back), were broadcast repeatedly throughout the world to a horrified viewing public. In particular, the Twin Towers symbolized American economic power, the Pentagon represented American military power throughout the world, while Washington, DC, embodied the center of American government. As the 9/11 Commission Report stated:

> America stood out as an object for admiration, envy, and blame. This created a kind of cultural asymmetry. To us, Afghanistan seemed very far away. To members of al Qaeda, America seemed very close. In a sense, they were more globalized than we were.[3]

It is important to note here that the World Trade Center had been previously attacked. On February 26, 1993, Middle Eastern terrorists detonated a truck bomb in the parking garage beneath the World Trade Center. The explosion caused a massive crater, killing six and injuring more than 1000.[4] The mastermind behind the attack, Ramzi Yousef, had wanted the explosion to topple one tower, with the resulting debris helping to knock down the second tower. Although this did not occur, the 1993 attack on the World Trade Center served as a dress rehearsal for the 9/11 attack.[5] It is notable that when Ramzi Yousef was captured and brought back to the United States, upon viewing the Twin Towers from the air, an FBI agent made a point of commenting to him that they still stood. However, Yousef coldly commented that this would not have been the case had they simply had more help.[6] In many respects, this serves to highlight the mentality of Middle Eastern terrorists and their future plans for America.

There were a number of terrorist plots uncovered in the intervening years between the 1993 attack on the Twin Towers and the 9/11 attacks. For example, in June of 1993, Sheik Omar Abdel Rahman, a prominent member of the Egyptian Islamic Group and extremist Sunni Muslim cleric with ties to al Qaeda, was arrested for complicity in the 1993 World Trade Center bombing, as well as conspiring to bomb a number of important landmarks in New York City.[7] Furthermore, before Yousef was caught and brought back to the United States, he was planning an operation from the Philippines that would have brought down a dozen American jetliners over the Pacific Ocean during a two-day period, resulting in thousands of deaths. Additionally, Khalid Sheik Mohammed, Yousef's uncle who had ties to al Qaeda and was instrumental in the planning of the 1993 World Trade Center attack, as well as a planned attack on the Los Angeles Airport in 2000 (which was prevented), was later found to be the mastermind behind the 9/11 attacks.[8]

These examples serve to highlight the extent to which terrorist organizations will adapt and innovate over time, probing for weaknesses and taking advantage of opportunities. Like many successful organizations in the West, they are continually scanning their internal and external environments, and learn from their mistakes, making corrections and adjustments along the way. They assess strengths, weaknesses, opportunities, and threats (SWOT analysis), just like we do. They consider the costs and the benefits, just like we do. They use the information gathered to formulate long-term strategies and develop operational plans, just like we do. As you can see from the pattern of attacks in the previous examples, the terrorists began focusing on airplanes and the air transportation system, and they eventually carried out a second successful attack against the World Trade Center; one which brought the Twin Towers down.

Terror as a Business

Let's set aside for now our revulsion to the tactics of killing innocent people and our value judgments concerning the underlying religious/political ideology. Let's examine this as a *rational* business decision on the part of the terrorists. But first, it needs to be said that the term "rational" does not suggest sensible or smart, or moral or ethical. As used here, the word "rational" only means that a logical and methodical approach to reasoning was used by the terrorists. It does not suggest that their thought processes were well intended, well thought out, or very smart. We make a mistake when we deem terrorist organizations such as al Qaeda as being irrational. Al Qaeda is many things, including evil, dogmatic, stupid, and so forth but irrational they are not. Just because we do not agree or understand their ideology does not mean that their thought processes are irrational. Failure to understand the rationality of their thinking is a huge wasted opportunity for us in the counterterrorism business.

To continue our examination of al Qaeda's effectiveness as an organization, we will go by the premise that terrorism is a rational business decision. First, let's look at the *inputs*—in other words, how much capital was invested into this "business" venture? We already know from the 9/11 Commission Report that the cost to fund the 19 hijackers for the attack was estimated to be between $400,000 and $500,000. This estimated figure accounts for the cost of the airplane tickets, food, lodging, entertainment, box cutters, and flight lessons for four of the 19 hijackers (we later learned about the "20th hijacker" Zacarias Moussaoui).

Now let's examine the *outputs* resulting from the September 11 attacks. In other words, how much *return on investment* did al Qaeda get out of their half-million dollar expenditure? To answer this question, we need to consider that the desired return on investment by al Qaeda involves political *outcomes*. However, determining political outcomes is a tricky proposition because it usually requires a much broader and time extended perspective that we simply do not have yet. Maybe 25 or 50 years from now, we will be better able to answer whether al Qaeda achieved its intended return on investment from the September 11 attacks. Instead of examining the long-range political *outcomes*, we will look at specific short-term *outputs* to try to get an idea of how much al Qaeda got back from their $500,000 investment. To do so, we will have to look at both the *intrinsic* values and *symbolic* values that we assign to things that we hold in high regard. Let's start with intrinsic values because they are a lot easier to determine than symbolic values.

For now, let's just look at some of the intrinsic values of things that were damaged or destroyed in the attack. The intrinsic value of things is relatively easy to determine. For example, the cost of the four airplanes destroyed is valued at $385 million. The cost to replace the World Trade Center buildings is estimated to range from $3 billion to $4.5 billion. Damage to the Pentagon building is estimated at $1 billion. Other property and infrastructure damage is estimated to be anywhere from $10 billion to $13 billion. The amount of damaged or unrecoverable property was $21.8 billion.[9]

These output figures reflect only the *replacement value* of property that was damaged or destroyed. Not counted were cleanup costs, the loss of business as the result of the disruption, the loss of tax revenue, the loss of air traffic revenue, and most importantly, the loss of almost 3000 innocent people. What price tag can be placed on each of those lives? Some would say, "you cannot put a price on a person's life," but that is not true. Insurance companies do it all the time. What is the cost of a person's life? Actuaries working for insurance companies would tell you, "it depends." As a quantitative measure, some people's lives are worth more than others. But for the sake of discussion, let's consider what the insurance companies have determined that the average first responder's life is worth. *New York Magazine* reports that the average benefit already received by each widow of a New York City police officer or firefighter was $1 million.[10] So, how much did al Qaeda get in return for its investment? When taking into account the broader losses to the overall economy directly or indirectly attributed to the September 11 attacks, the figure reaches a remarkable $2 trillion level.[11] Not a bad return for al Qaeda's $500,000 investment.

If a $2 trillion loss of intrinsic value was not enough, consider the more difficult-to-discern effect on *symbolic* value sustained as the result of the September 11 attacks. Symbolic value is much more difficult to calculate, but let's compare the effect that the visual impact of the September 11 attacks had worldwide with another event that is viewed worldwide every year—the Super Bowl. It is estimated that 111.3 million viewers watched Super Bowl XLVI on television. These viewers included our soldiers, airmen, and sailors stationed on bases and assigned to fleets overseas. The football game was just part of the draw. The *Nielsen* data indicate that the halftime show with Madonna as the headliner was actually viewed by more people than the game itself. That halftime show drew a record-setting 114 million viewers.[12]

Clearly, it is not just football fans who watch this iconic moment of American life. In fact, the viewership data indicates that many of the viewers tuned in for the commercials alone. A typical 30-second commercial during the Super Bowl costs the advertiser $3,500,000.[13] This amounts to $3.5 million to reach anywhere from 111 to 114 million viewers for 30 seconds, or roughly 31 cents per viewer. While $3.5 million may seem like a lot for a 30-second commercial, it must be worth it to the companies doing the advertising. Otherwise they would not be doing it.

So, who got the better return on investment—al Qaeda, or the companies paying for Super Bowl commercials? Stop and consider how many times you have seen the images of the second hijacked plane hitting the World Trade Center tower ... either on television, magazines, newspapers, or documentary films. Like most of Americans, you probably have seen those images hundreds, if not thousands of times—from many different angles. It would be next to impossible to determine how many people worldwide have seen the image of the second plane (United Flight 175) crashing into the south World Trade Center tower. In the United States alone, it is estimated that all Americans combined watch 250 billion hours of television per year. About 53.8% of that viewing is attributed to stories about crime, disaster and war,[14] so it is a good bet that a lot of those hours were devoted to the September 11 attacks ... especially the images of the plane hitting the second tower.

Even more difficult is to try to put a number that accurately reflects the emotional reaction of these millions of viewers watching billions of hours of TV coverage. While intrinsic value is relatively easy to determine, symbolic value is much harder. The intrinsic value of gold, or paper currency, or real estate tends to stay relatively stable over time, with some minor fluctuations depending on market forces. Intrinsic value of things is determined by the invisible hand of market forces, or the calculations made by actuaries based on the law of large numbers. In other words, the intrinsic value of an item is not absolute or sacrosanct. It is based on what the aggregate population says it is.

Symbolic value is more difficult to determine because things have different meanings for each of us. There are no market forces or laws of large numbers to put a number on the symbolic value of things. Symbolic values vary between cultures, political and religious ideologies, and individuals. What is symbolically significant to one person may not be symbolically significant to someone else. Nevertheless, most of us will agree that certain symbols and iconography carry considerable weight when it comes to symbolic value. For example, the American flag has a very high symbolic value to most Americans. Likewise, certain places, events, music, and objects have great symbolic value. Baseball, the World Trade Center, the Super Bowl, the *Star Spangled Banner*, Mount Rushmore, and the American flag, just to name a few.

It is clear the World Trade Center towers had a high symbolic value. It is not just Americans who believe that. Clearly, al Qaeda believed it as well. Ramzi Yousef and others stated as much when the first attempt to bring down the

Photo 7.1 World Trade Center on Fire (Photo by Michael Foran. https://commons.wikimedia.org/wiki/File:WTC_smoking_on_9-11.jpeg.)

buildings in 1993 failed. But why would al Qaeda target the two towers in New York City, and ostensibly, direct two of the hijacked planes to Washington, DC? (see Photo 7.1). If you were one of the core al Qaeda planners, why would you not disperse the attack by sending one of the planes to high symbolic value targets in Los Angeles, and another to Chicago, and make it seem like the entire nation was under attack? You have probably already figured it out, but we will stop here and let you ponder this question for a bit. At the end of this chapter, we will revisit this question, and offer our hypothesis.

The Learning Organization

Peter Senge is a professor at the Massachusetts Institute of Technology who has had a significant impact on the way organizations conduct business. His 1990 book, *The Fifth Discipline*, focused on the concept of the *Learning Organization*. Senge described a *Learning Organization* as:

> Organizations where people continually expand their capacity to create the results they truly desire, where new and expansive patterns of thinking are nurtured, where collective aspiration is set free, and where people are continually learning to see the whole together.[15]

The basis for Senge's concept is that in times of rapid change, organizations must have the capacity to be flexible and adaptive to succeed. They do this by taking advantage of the dedication and commitment of organizational members to learn at all levels.[16]

The above definition of a learning organization may very well describe the type of organization that many of us would like to work for. However, in many respects, it also describes a number of terrorist organizations today. For example, over the years, al Qaeda has been described as flexible, adaptable, resilient, nimble, invisible, malleable, fluid, dynamic, and difficult to penetrate.[17]

Al Qaeda as a Learning Organization

After the U.S. invasions of Afghanistan and Iraq, al Qaeda transformed from a predominantly centralized hierarchical organization into a decentralized and geographically dispersed network of loosely related cells.[18] However, al Qaeda's strength is also its weakness in that its decentralized structure is conducive for innovation, but it also exposes it to risk. Calvert Jones of the University of Cambridge stated, "dispersed al Qaeda fragments, operating more independently and looking outwardly for assistance and support, may be more vulnerable to infiltration as a result."[19] Ultimately, this proved true, and Osama bin Laden was eventually located and killed in Pakistan by U.S. Navy Seals.

Nonetheless, we continue to feel the impact of the 9/11 attacks to this day, and al Qaeda has served as a source of inspiration for a number of terrorist organizations. A number of these terrorist organizations have proven quite adept at using the World Wide Web to further their cause. In particular, terrorist organizations have been effective in using the Internet and social media to recruit potential members, acquiring funding, as well as planning and executing operations. In an article appearing in *The Police Chief* magazine entitled *Social Media and the Homegrown Terrorist Threat*, Kunkle reported that terrorists "… are recruiting, inspiring, and guiding global strategies not just by Internet operations but through an organized, steady infusion of propaganda videos and call-to-action messages circulated via social media platforms, such as blogs, Facebook, YouTube, and Twitter …"[20] According to Kunkle, social media is contributing to the dissemination of bomb-building capabilities around the world, to include the United States. For example, Kunkle discussed how al Qaeda used its media branch, the Global Islamic Media Front, to make available an English version of a bomb making manual, written by a well-known Egyptian bomb maker, over the Internet using various social media sites. The manual went viral. Therefore, social media served as a platform for potentially teaching homegrown terrorists the skills necessary for making bombs and carrying out attacks. Furthermore, in the same article, Kunkle provided an example of the importance of social media to political unrest in Egypt. Activists would use Facebook to schedule demonstrations, and then use Twitter to coordinate their protest activities. YouTube would then be used to provide a visual presentation to the viewing public across the globe.

To add to this growing threat, in an audio recording made public in September of 2015, al Qaeda leader Ayman al-Zawahiri, called for lone wolf attacks in the United States. The al Qaeda leader also pleaded for greater unity among jihadists across the globe.[21] Earlier, in August 2015, a group by the name of the Islamic State (ISIS) Hacking Division made public the personal information of hundreds of military and government personnel via Twitter.[22] The group urged "lone wolves" to use this information to kill people on the list.[23] Already, a number of lone wolf attacks, such as the 2009 Fort Hood shooting, the Boston Marathon Bombing in 2013, and the Charlie Hebdo attack in Paris in 2015, have resulted in much concern, both in the United States and across the globe. Viewed from this perspective, the threats are real, and the stakes remain quite high for Western governments, including the United States.

The question then becomes, "how can we win a protracted war against radical Islam?" The opponent is nimble, well organized, politically and technologically savvy, and understands how to manipulate public opinion with imagery and symbolism. Furthermore, the opponent is willing to take a long-view approach to achieving their aims, and believes that they cannot lose because God is on their side. Perhaps we can revisit Peter Drucker's notion, *"innovate or die"* for answers.

Innovation and Homeland Security

Peter Drucker is considered by many to be the founder of modern management.[24] Drucker asserts that innovation results from thoughtful analysis and systematic review. The process involves hard work and a systematic approach. Moreover, these concepts can be taught and learned.[25]

Drucker asserts that although innovations can indeed spring from a flash of genius, most innovations, particularly those which prove successful, occur from a determined search for innovation opportunities. Therefore, it is a purposeful activity that should be managed accordingly.[26]

According to Drucker, innovation begins with an analysis of opportunities that should be conducted on a recurring basis. He identified seven sources of opportunity that can drive innovation[27]:

- Unexpected successes and failure
- Incongruities between "what is" and what "ought to be"
- Process needs
- Unanticipated changes in the "market" (Strategic environment)
- Demographic changes
- Changes in meaning and perception
- New knowledge becomes available

Drucker further asserts that innovation which is both purposeful and systematic starts with the analysis of new opportunities. In particular, because innovation is a conceptual and perceptual process, organizations must seek out potential opportunities. In essence, they must "... go out and look, ask, and listen ..."[28]

VIGNETTE 7.2   Model City Simulator

I joined what is known today as the Miami-Dade Police Department in 1975. At the time, the department was known as the Dade County Public Safety Department. South Florida had certainly undergone considerable changes prior to that time. However, a barrage of social, political, and economic changes were forthcoming as well, since Miami-Dade County continued to grow at an accelerated pace. Unfortunately, by the early 1990s, South Florida had already experienced three major riots, as well as a bloody drug war, which included the "Cocaine Cowboys" shooting at one another on the streets of this growing metropolitan area. Having worked in Vice, Intelligence, and Narcotics (VIN) units, as well as the Organized Crime Bureau, during this time frame, I can remember just how crazy the drug scene was in Miami-Dade County during the 1970s and 1980s.

By 1992, I was working at the Miami-Dade Police Department Training Bureau. The department had developed a national reputation for its emphasis on training and professional development, and the Training Bureau was delivering a wide array of training courses and programs to not only its in-service personnel, but to a growing number of officers from outside agencies as well. Fortunately, as a department, we had gotten into the habit of continually scanning our internal and external environments in an effort to identify innovative policing strategies and best practices. This proactive strategy served us well for many years to come, helping us to anticipate problems or trends, as opposed to merely reacting to them.

The year 1992 was quite eventful for a number of reasons. In particular, in April, Los Angeles erupted into one of the worst cases of civil unrest ever experienced in the United States, resulting in considerable death and destruction. Former *ABC News* anchorman Ted Koppel did a television special, "Anatomy of a Riot," which examined the *Los Angeles Riots* (sometimes referred to as the *Rodney King Riots*) from a variety of perspectives. It is still so relevant that I continue to use this resource in various courses and programs.

Realizing that the policing environment was becoming increasingly complex, the Training Bureau started looking for innovative strategies for managing the initial stages of critical incidents, and began searching for best practices across the country. After reviewing a number of options, the Training Bureau focused on a company, BowMac, which had developed an innovative "Model City" Simulator for public safety personnel. As mentioned in Chapter 6, a "model city" simulator can be designed to represent a small community with various components: a residential area, a business district, an industrial park, and so on. Therefore, the "model city" simulator provides a realistic environment, which gives participants the feeling of actually having managed a critical incident.[29] The primary goal is to provide students with a "game plan" for handling critical incidents. This can make the difference in operational personnel taking control of an incident or allowing events to spiral out of control,[30] as had occurred in prior incidents, such as the 1980 McDuffie Riots in Miami-Dade County as well as the 1992 Los Angeles Riots.

Before long, a Model City Simulator was built on behalf of the department, and a number of sergeants and lieutenants completed the facilitator training, including myself. As we were getting ready to start offering the program to the department's first-line supervisors, Hurricane Andrew struck in August of 1992. This devastating category 5 hurricane left an unbelievable path of destruction in the southern part of Miami-Dade County. In particular, the cities of Homestead and Florida City were the hardest hit, as was the Cutler Ridge area of the county. Of course, this meant that many officers were reassigned to assist with the response and recovery efforts. For example, I was assigned to the Culter Ridge Command Post, and worked there through December.

By early 1993, most of the personnel who had received facilitator training were back at the Training Bureau, and we began offering Critical Incident Management (CIM) training using the "Model City" simulator to first-line supervisors. In addition to the intensive hands-on training, each 24-hour course included a block of instruction on dealing with Hazardous Materials, which was taught by Hazmat Technicians from the Miami-Dade Fire Rescue Department. Getting the fire department involved was one of the best decisions we ever made. After a period of time, fire and police personnel got to know each other, readily recognized each other at the scene of critical incidents, and established an ongoing level of trust and rapport that was beyond measure.

In fact, the CIM training was so well received, that it was expanded to mid-management personnel, and then again to the command staff. Before long, field training officers (FTOs) also began attending the training program. Finally, we received approval to begin offering the program in an abbreviated format (8 hours) to all police recruits. Once this took place, a good portion of our sworn personnel, from police recruits to command staff had been exposed to the training in one format or another.

Perhaps no other program proved more successful over the long term than the CIM Training Program using the "Model City" simulator. In essence, it helped to change the culture of the department with respect to how emergencies and disasters are viewed and dealt with, and it all started with a concerted search for an innovative best practice based on an identified need.

Ernest G. Vendrell

Look, ask, and listen! If only it would be that simple. Only a few days after the 2015 San Bernardino terrorist attack, we found out that one of the terrorists (the female, Tashfeen Malik) had posted multiple messages on Facebook about her radical Islamic views. If anyone in the federal government had paid any attention to this publicly available information, it is quite possible that the subject could have been stopped from entering the United States in the first place, and thus, the attack would have been prevented. Unfortunately, and inexplicably, the U.S. Department of Homeland Security (DHS) had explicitly prohibited immigration officials from looking at social media as a means to vet foreign citizens applying for U.S. visas.[31] Instead of taking advantage of an open source of information to keep our nation safe, the DHS decided to erect yet another bureaucratic barrier that further endangers our citizens.

In the article, *Fostering a Culture of Innovation,* Thornberry examined the post 9/11 reforms, such as the creation of the Department of Homeland Security, to meet the threats posed by modern terrorist organizations, such as al Qaeda. With respect to the reforms, Thornberry contends that:

> Transformation is about creating an adaptive national security apparatus that can deal with changing circumstances and emerging threats. Organizational changes—like the creation of the new Department of Homeland Security— will help, but the real challenge is to capture hearts and minds.[32]

So, out of the ashes of the September 11 attacks, what did our Congress and executive branch do to defend against attacks from this nibble adversary? We responded by clumping a number of unrelated government agencies, and creating a very large and ponderous bureaucracy—the U.S. Department of Homeland Security. The DHS is a 29-element hierarchy that clumps together under one Department umbrella, such unrelated government agencies as the Coast Guard, U.S. Secret Service, and FEMA.

As we can see in Figure 7.1, the DHS appears to be a highly mechanistic hierarchical organizational structure. BusinessDictionary.com defines mechanistic organizations as: "Hierarchical, bureaucratic, organizational-structure characterized by (1) centralization of authority, (2) formalization of procedures and practices, and (3) specialization of functions. Mechanistic organization are comparatively simpler and easy to organize, but find it difficult to cope with rapid change."[33] The only part of this definition that does not pertain to the DHS is the "simpler and easy to organize" due to its sheer size. Hierarchies are designed for efficiency and unity of command, not for innovation. In fact, the many levels of reporting in a hierarchical organization make it difficult to get creative ideas implemented as innovations.

By contrast, al Qaeda and the Islamic State are considered to be organic organizations. Organic organizations are defined as:

> Organizational structure characterized by (1) Flatness: communications and interactions are horizontal, (2) Low specialization: knowledge resides wherever it is most useful, and (3) Decentralization: great deal of formal and informal participation in decision making. Organic organizations are comparatively more complex and harder to form, but are highly adaptable, flexible, and more suitable where external environment is rapidly changing and is unpredictable. Also called open organizations.[34]

There certainly are a number of examples of proactive organizations from the public and private sectors that nurture a culture of innovation, and much can

U.S. Department of Homeland Security

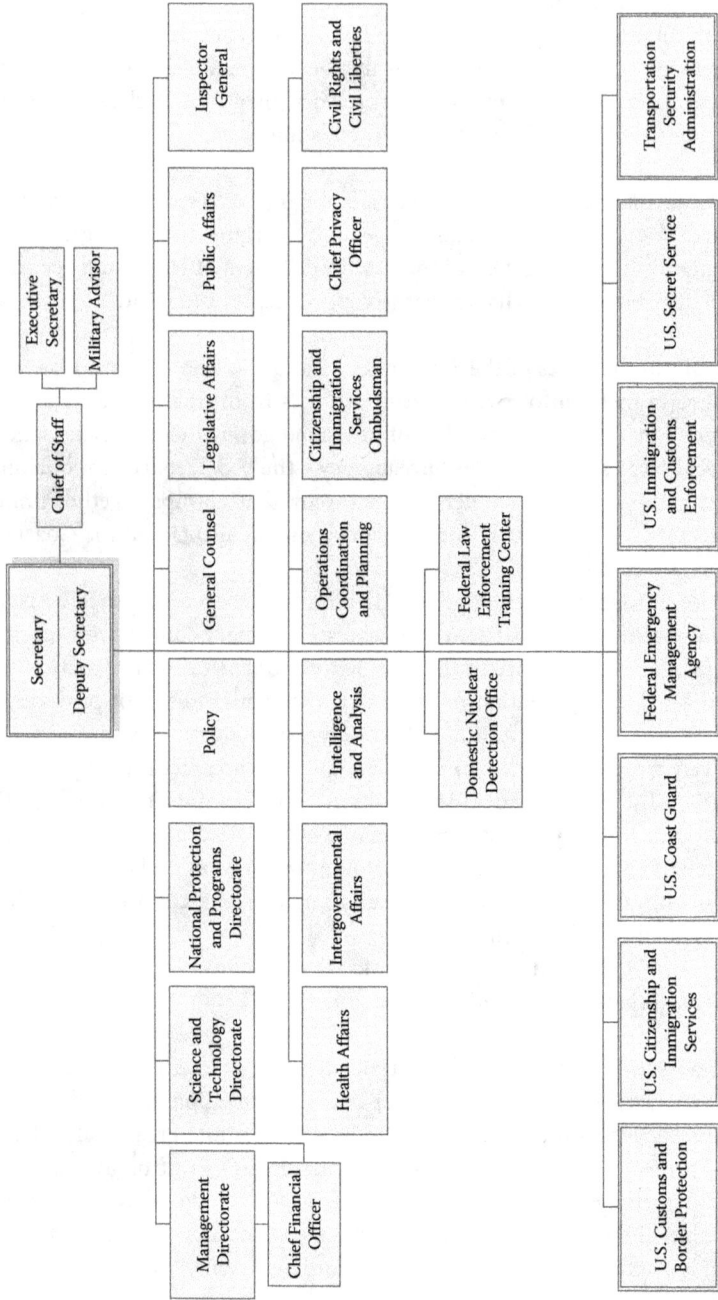

Figure 7.1 DHS Organizational Chart

be learned from them. These *learning organizations*[35] see their members as part of a team, and make them feel that their contributions are important. They also are quick to recognize, and capitalize, on potential opportunities. Some of the high-tech companies such as *Google* and *Apple* come to mind when we think of *"organic"* learning organizations.

Improvisation versus Innovation

It is important to make a distinction between the concepts of improvisation and innovation. These are two similar constructs, but they are not the same. Improvisation is like jazz music, and innovation is like classical music. They are both adaptive and beautiful, but they differ in significant ways. Improvisation can be described as an unplanned and spontaneous adaptation. Innovations are also adaptations, but as Drucker stated, innovations come from thoughtful analysis and systematic review. It is true, however, that spontaneous improvisations can sometimes turn into long-term innovations. For example, the Miami-Dade Bomb Squad developed several improvised solutions to help the Special Response Teams (SRTs—also commonly known as "SWAT") during hostage situations. While on the scene of one hostage call, the SRT team was having a difficult time breaking the glass window, and then pulling aside the curtains, in order to put a long extended pole camera to see inside the second floor apartment where the subject had barricaded himself with his hostage. The SRT commander asked the bomb squad if they could rig some tools together to solve the problem. The bomb squad immediately got to work and put together two long poles with some duct tape holding together a wood splint to stabilize the connection. At the end of one of the poles, they rigged what looked like a small rake contraption that they manufactured on the scene. The SRT entry team then used the rigged contraption and the end of two long poles to break the second floor window all the way from the ground floor, which was the only safe approach that they had for this particular situation. The rake at the end of the pole was used to pull the curtains so that the long extended pole cam could be introduced into the room. By doing so, the SRT team was able to see inside the apartment and to know exactly where the hostage and the hostage taker were located. As it turned out, the situation was resolved without incident and there were no injuries to anyone. After the incident was resolved, the bomb squad officers returned to their office and went to work on their milling machines and lathes at their machine shop and produced a medieval-looking contraption that was something like an extended pike tool with rake teeth. The punch at the end was used to break the glass window, and the rake teeth was used to pull back the curtains. What began as an impromptu short-term solution for unanticipated problems at a hostage call turned into a long-term innovation that was later adapted for several applications, including mounting the rake device to a tactical robot. Photo 7.2 shows the result of the innovation that came about from the initial improvisation. That simple pike and rake tool was used successfully in many more hostage and barricaded calls thereafter. Photo 7.3 shows the tactical teams practicing with the new tool during

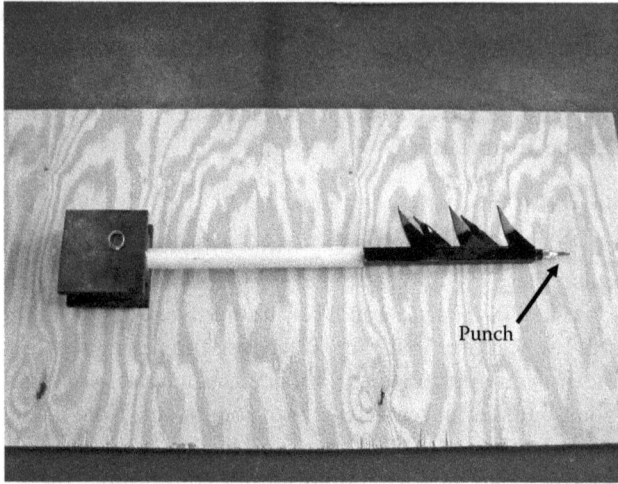

Photo 7.2 Pike and Rake Tool (Courtesy of the Miami-Dade Police Department. Photographer Unknown.)

training. The actual machine shop used by the Bomb Squad is depicted by Photo 7.4. It should be noted that the bomb squad did not invent the pike. Nor did they invent the rake. All they did was put all the features from ideas that had been thought of thousands of years ago and reapplied them to a new set of challenges. That is what innovation is all about.

While improvisation is a good thing, it can also be indicative of deficiencies in an organization. When organizations seem to be in a perpetual state of

Photo 7.3 Example of How an Improvisation Turned into Innovation (Courtesy of the Miami-Dade Police Department. Photographer Unknown.)

Photo 7.4 Bomb Squad Machine Shop (Courtesy of the Miami-Dade Police Department. Photographer Unknown.)

improvization, that suggests that the organization may not be learning from its mistakes and successes, and thus has to constantly be relearning and "flying by the seat of its pants." An *auto-adaptive organization* is not the same thing as a *learning organization*. Louise Comfort from the University of Pittsburgh describes the auto-adaptive organization as being a system that is continuously learning and adapting to its threat environment.[36] The auto-adaptive organization is continuously shifting its resources to meet new challenges. The auto-adaptive organization differs from the learning organization in that its adaptations are considered as "ad hoc" improvisations rather than long-term innovations. The differences between the improvisational auto-adaptive organization and the innovative learning organization are illustrated in Figure 7.2.

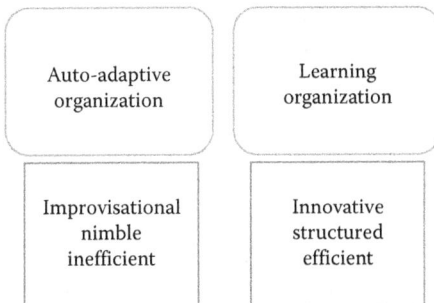

Figure 7.2 Differences between the Auto-Adaptive Organization and the Learning Organization

Soldiers, Artists, Writers, and Magicians

All warfare is based on deception.

Sun Tzu

Earlier in this chapter we asked the question: Why would al Qaeda target the twin WTC towers in New York City, instead of attacking other highly symbolic value targets in large cities across America such as Los Angeles, and Chicago? The key to answering that question is to ask yourself, how often have you seen a video of the plane crashing into the Pentagon? How often have you seen a video of the first plane crashing into the WTC tower? The answer is most probably, "never, or not very often." The images of both of these crashes were captured on very short videos. The only video of the Pentagon crash came from a security camera set at half-second intervals. This video captured fleeting images of American Flight 77 right before it struck the building and then the ensuing fireball.[37]

A slightly better video captured the image of American Airlines Flight 11 crashing into the north World Trade Center tower. That video was taken by fire-fighters from the New York City Fire Department, who just happened to be conducting a training exercise in the vicinity that day. That video clearly shows the first plane crashing into the tower, but it is not as well known as the many videos of United Flight 175 crashing into the south Tower.

Of course, there are no known videos of United Flight 93, which crashed into a field in Pennsylvania. The only artifacts remaining from that flight came in the form of audio recordings from the plane's black boxes and witnesses' accounts of the now famous phone conversations from the heroic Todd Beamer and other passengers.[38] From that, we got the now famous battle cry "let's roll" that was used to unite and motivate the American public shortly after the attacks.

Heroic battle cries aside, the images that we remember the most from the September 11 attacks were those of United Flight 175 crashing into the south World Trade Center tower. The reason that there were so many videos capturing that crash is that all the major television networks rushed their crews to the area and set up their cameras to report on the first crash. Had it not been for the coverage of the first crash, the images of the second crash would not have been captured by so many cameras, and from so many different angles.

How much "bang for the buck" did al Qaeda get for its investment in 2001? There is no way to know for sure what al Qaeda leadership had in mind when they targeted the two WTC towers with two different planes, but they seem to have a fairly good understanding of the art of propaganda in general, and the ways of the American media in particular. Al Qaeda planners had to know that the first crash would guarantee live coverage of the second crash. With the cameras already in place, and crews reporting live, the stage was set for a perfect and spectacular propaganda "commercial." This one–two punch makes perfect sense to the media savvy terrorist group.

If our premise is correct, then we have to wonder what other highly symbolic places or events would offer al Qaeda or Islamic State leaders a tempting target that will provide as much "bang for the buck" as September 11 did. What places or events have cameras and crews already in place to capture the images of a catastrophic in-progress attack? Clearly, having cameras already in place and shooting live images makes for an optimal force multiplier for the terrorist's asymmetrical warfare strategy. The media savvy terrorists know that television coverage of a mass casualty incident is most effective when it is captured "live" as it unfolds in real time. Images captured after the fact are OK, but have nowhere near the effect that a live, in-progress image has.

Imagine what it would be like if a massive terrorist attack of the magnitude of a September 11 attack occurred during the live broadcast of a Republican or Democratic National Convention, or worse yet, during a Super Bowl broadcast. Imagine a plane crashing into the stands, or a runaway truck bomb barreling into the halftime show entertainers as they muster outside prior to the show, precisely at a time that television viewership is at its high watermark. NBC deployed a total of 57 cameras to provide coverage of Super Bowl XLVI (including pregame, and postgame coverage). Add to that another 75 security cameras installed in or around Lucas Oil Stadium for the Super Bowl and we can see how the media savvy al Qaeda would perceive such large-scale special events to be so desirable.[39]

The live images of such an attack would be captured by many cameras, from many angles. Not only would the events be streaming live from the stadium, but the videotaped images would be replayed over, and over, and over by television networks worldwide. The psychological effects of such an attack would be unimaginable. With cameras and crews already in place, all the terrorists would have to contribute to the effort is the "big bang" itself. Most of the manpower costs for this investment would be provided by the terrorists' opponent ... the American television media. As far as asymmetrical warfare, it doesn't get much better than this type of cost–benefit ratio. It would be the terrorists' equivalent of winning a $337 million Powerball lottery on a purchase of a $1 ticket ... only more. A successful attack during the halftime show of a Super Bowl is the "Holy Grail" of terrorist targets.

With such a tempting target as the Super Bowl, the question remains, why haven't the terrorists already targeted a Super Bowl event? The answer to this question is not because they haven't considered it. Clearly, al Qaeda and ISIS have demonstrated a good knowledge of American customs and iconography. Indeed, several of al Qaeda's top leadership have been American born individuals. The best known being Anwar al-Awlaki and al Qaeda magazine editor Samir Khan, both killed by a CIA drone strike in Yemen in 2011.[40]

Another was the American born media specialist for al Qaeda, Adam Yahiye Gadahn (AKA *Azzan the American*). Gadahn is an example of how media savvy the terrorist organizations have become. He has appeared in several al Qaeda propaganda videos, both as a recruiting tool, and as a way to poke the U.S. government in the eye. Clearly, al Qaeda knows the American psyche, and they know the things that we value the most. They know that a terrorist strike during a Super Bowl broadcast would be devastating.

The reason that al Qaeda has not struck during a Super Bowl is simply because they have not been able to. Clearly, the War on Terror has significantly disrupted their operations and their ability to coordinate and to fund attacks. The killing of Osama bin Laden may have been the most newsworthy counterstrike against the al Qaeda network, but the most significant counterstrikes on the top operational leadership of the organization shortly after the War on Terror began in 2001 did not end the war. Right now, al Qaeda is an organization that is in disarray. That's not to say that it won't reconstitute itself. But at this moment, al Qaeda has been weakened considerably. It hasn't hit the Super Bowl because it has not been able to. Clearly, the Islamic State has become the predominant radical Islamist organization in the world right now. Indeed, the two organizations seem to be competing with each other, trying to see who can kill the most innocent people, and who can do the most horrific acts of barbarism.

It is not just the lack of capability that has hampered the terrorists. Another important factor that has kept Super Bowls from being hit is the increased level of security post-September 11. There is no comparison between the security of Super Bowls held before the September 11 attacks and those held after the attacks. Many of the recommendations that were made by law enforcement planners (and ignored by policy makers) in 1999, became standard procedures for the 2007 Super Bowl. These recommendations included flight restrictions, buffer zones, closed circuit video surveillance, magnetometers, mass casualty treatment areas, and mass evacuation and decontamination corridors, among others. Not that we should stop being wary of a terrorist attack against a Super Bowl. But clearly, the likelihood of such an attack is much less than it was prior to 2001. In the standard risk formula: RISK = Likelihood × Consequence, the consequence factor of a Super Bowl attack remains extraordinarily high. However, the likelihood part of the equation has dropped considerably. That is because the two factors that comprise likelihood, threat and vulnerability, have both shifted to our advantage. The threat of a terrorist strike has decreased due to their lack of operational efficacy. Likewise, the vulnerability of the Super Bowl venue has also decreased significantly due to better security. The remaining al Qaeda and ISIS leadership know this. Therefore, in order to remain relevant, they need to figure out other targets that are not as difficult to strike, but yet offer a high return on their investment—a "big bang for their buck" so to speak.

Given their weakened operational state, al Qaeda and ISIS have been forced to reconsider the large-scale catastrophic attack, and has had to shift toward "soft targets" which offer less return on their investment, but are more doable. Crowded shopping malls with little security offer an easy and tempting target with a relatively high consequence factor. Among all the soft targets in the homeland, the one that causes the most concern for police officers, firefighters, and parents alike, is a Beslan-like coordinated military assault by a group of terrorists on a middle school somewhere in the heartland of the United States.[41] We have seen how much media attention attacks by lone gunmen at schools and universities have garnered over the past few years. The Columbine incident, the Virginia Tech shootings, and more recently the Sandy Hook Elementary School shooting in Newtown, Connecticut, demonstrate how vulnerable we are to such incidents. A Beslan-style attack on a school full of children is a different animal altogether. Such an attack would involve a protracted siege that would play out over days, and perhaps weeks. Multiple attackers and the taking of young children as hostages would provide the terrorists a stage where they can play to the extended live media coverage that is sure to ensue.

Osama bin Laden is dead. But this war is far from over. No one knows for sure where and when al Qaeda or ISIS will strike next. Even when they do nothing, they affect our lives. Late in 2015, a threatening email was received by the New York City and Los Angeles school systems. New York ignored the email, citing it as being non-credible. However, the superintendent in Los Angeles made the decision to order that all 900 schools close. This mass closure affected over 640,000 students, their parents, and teachers.[42] The superintendent's erroneous and poorly thought-out decision avoided the catastrophic error, but caused a major nuisance error. He played it safe, and by doing so, he almost guaranteed that more hoax emails will be sent to the school district. The chances are that the next time he will not order another school closure. Clearly, the superintendent of the Los Angeles school district did not fully think this through. He has not prepared himself mentally for the Long War. The email threats will happen many more times, and sooner or later, one of them will come to fruition. It will happen on the day that the superintendent decides to not close the schools.

We are in the midst of a multigenerational clash of civilizations between the West and radical Islamic fascism. This is the *"Long War,"* or the *Global War on Terror*.[43] It will take soldiers, Marines, airmen, and sailors to fight overseas. It will take police and firefighters to defend the homeland. It will take magicians and illusionists to make it seem that we are few when we are many, and many when we are few. Magicians and illusionists played a vital role in beating Nazi Germany and Imperial Japan in World War II. It will take the artists, musicians, and videographers to capture the images and put those images together into a story. It will take writers to document the facts, and to write the story so no one will ever forget.

References

1. P. Drucker, 1999. Innovate or die. *Economist*, 352(8138), 25–28. Retrieved from Academic Search Premier database (accessed August 7, 2008).
2. National Commission on Terrorist Attacks Upon the United States, 2004. *The 9/11 Commission Report*. Online at http://www.9-11commission.gov/ (accessed August 27, 2015).
3. National Commission on Terrorist Attacks Upon the United States, 2004, p. 340.
4. Ibid.
5. FBI, 2008. FBI 100. First strike: Global terror in America. Online at https://www.fbi.gov/news/stories/2008/February/tradebom_022608

6. R. Wright, 1996. First of 2 trials to open for key N.Y. blast figure. *Los Angeles Times*, May 12. Online at http://articles.latimes.com/1996-05-12/news/mn-3425_1_world-trade-center-attack (accessed on December 18, 2015).

7. J. White, 2009. *Terrorism and Homeland Security* (6th ed.). Belmont, CA: Wadsworth Cengage Learning.

8. Ibid.

9. IAGS.org, 2003. How much did the September 11 terrorist attack cost America? Institute for the Analysis of Global Security. Online at http://www.iags.org/costof911.html (accessed December 17, 2015).

10. NYMag.com, 2012. 9/11 by the numbers: Death, destruction, charity, salvation, war, money, real estate, spouses, babies, and other September 11 statistics. *New York Magazine*. Online at http://nymag.com/news/articles/wtc/1year/numbers.htm (accessed December 17, 2015).

11. IAGS.org, 2003. How much did the September 11 terrorist attack cost America? Institute for the Analysis of Global Security. Online at http://www.iags.org/costof911.html (accessed December 17, 2015).

12. A. Riccobono, 2012. How many people watched the Super Bowl? *International Business Times*. Online at http://www.ibtimes.com/articles/293912/20120206/super-bowl-rating-giants-patriots.htm (accessed December 17, 2015).

13. J. Damiano. 2012. How much does a Super Bowl commercial really cost? *Newsday*. Online at http://www.newsday.com/entertainment/pet-rock-1.811972/how-much-does-a-super-bowl-commercial-really-cost-1.3481154.

14. N. Herr, 2007. *Television Statistics. The Sourcebook for Teaching Science.* Online at http://www.csun.edu/science/health/docs/tv&health.html

15. M. K. Smith, 2001. Peter Senge and the learning organization. Online at http://www.infed.org/thinkers/senge.htm (accessed August 7, 2008).

16. Ibid., para. 7

17. C. Jones, 2006. Al-Qaeda's innovative improvisers: learning in a diffuse transnational network. *Cambridge Review of International Affairs*, 19(4). Online at http://www.gvpt.umd.edu/sites/gvpt.umd.edu/files/pubs/Jones_AQInnovativeImprovisers.pdf (accessed on December 16, 2015).

18. Ibid.

19. Ibid., p. 566

20. J. Kunkle, 2012. Social media and the home-grown terrorist threat. *The Police Chief*, 79(June), 22–28.

21. T. Jocelyn, 2015. Al Qaeda leader calls for lone-wolf attacks in the U.S., Unity among terrorists. Online at http://www.defenddemocracy.org/media-hit/thomas-joscelyn-al-qaeda-leader-calls-for-lone-wolf-attacks-in-us-unity-among-terrorists/

22. O. Pawlyk, 2015. ISIS hacking group tweets support for 'lone wolf' attacks on military personnel. Online at http://www.militarytimes.com/story/military/pentagon/2015/08/12/isis-hacking-group-tweets-support-lone-wolf-attacks-military-personnel/31550919/

23. Ibid.

24. S. Denning, 2014. The best of Peter Drucker. Online at http://www.forbes.com/sites/stevedenning/2014/07/29/the-best-of-peter-drucker (accessed December 17, 2015).

25. R. Leubke, 2010. Peter Drucker on innovation. Online at http://www.innovationexcellence.com/blog/2010/07/30/peter-drucker-on-innovation/ (accessed December 17, 2015).

26. P. Drucker, 1985. *Innovation and Entrepreneurship.* New York, NY: HarperCollins Publishers.

27. P. Drucker, 2002. The discipline of innovation (re-print of 1985 article). *Harvard Business Review*, 80(8), 95–103. Online at Business Source Complete database (accessed August 7, 2008).

28. Ibid., p. 13

29. V. Faggiano, McNall, J., and Gillespie, T., 2011. *Critical Incident Management: A Complete Response Guide*. Boca Raton, FL: CRC Press.

30. Faggiano et al., 1992. *Critical Incident Management*; BowMac Education Services, Inc. *Critical Incident Management Instructor Notebook*. Rochester, NY: Author. BowMac Education.

31. B. Ross, Schwartz, R., Meek, J. G., and Margolin, J., 2015. Secret U.S. policy blocks agents from looking at social media of visa applicants, former official says, December 14. *ABC News*. Online at http://abcnews.go.com/US/secret-us-policy-blocks-agents-social-media-visa/story?id=35749325 (accessed December 15, 2015).

32. C. Thornberry, 2003. Fostering a culture of innovation. U.S. Naval Institute Proceedings. p. 1.

33. Mechanistic organization. BusinessDictionary.com. WebFinance, Inc. Online at http://www.businessdictionary.com/definition/mechanistic-organization.html (accessed December 16, 2015).

34. Organic organization. BusinessDictionary.com. WebFinance, Inc. Online at http://www.businessdictionary.com/definition/organic-organization.html (accessed December 16, 2015).

35. M. K. Smith, 2001. Peter Senge and the learning organization. Online at http://www.infed.org/thinkers/senge.htm (accessed August 7, 2008).

36. L. Comfort, 2002. Managing intergovernmental response to terrorism and other extreme events. *Publius: The Journal of Federalism*, 32(4), 29–49.

37. *Fox News*, 2006. Pentagon releases video of plane hitting building on 9/11. FoxNews.com, May 16. Online at http://www.foxnews.com/story/0,2933,195702,00.html

38. J. McKinnon, 2001. The phone line from Flight 93 was still open when a GTE operator heard Todd Beamer say: Are you guys ready? Let's roll. *Post-Gazette*, September 16. Online at http://old.post-gazette.com/headlines/20010916phonecallnat3p3.asp

39. C. White, 2012. Super Bowl 2012 by the numbers. *Mashable Entertainment*, February 4. Online at http://mashable.com/2012/02/04/super-bowl-2012-by-the-numbers/

40. J. Griffin and Fishel J., 2011. Two U.S.-born terrorists killed in CIA-led drone strike. Fox News.com, September 30. Online at http://www.foxnews.com/politics/2011/09/30/us-born-terror-boss-anwar-al-awlaki-killed/#ixzz1s2jPebNZ

41. J. Giduck, 2005. *Terror at Beslan: A Russian Tragedy with Lessons for America's Schools*. Golden, CO: Archangel Group.

42. H. Branson-Potts, Ceasar S., and Blume H., 2015. L.A. schools to reopen Wednesday; threat against schools was "not credible," officials say. *Los Angeles Times*, December 15. Online at http://www.latimes.com/local/lanow/la-me-ln-all-lausd-schools-closed-threat-20151215-story.html (accessed December 16, 2015).

43. *The Long War Journal*. Online at http://www.longwarjournal.org/about (accessed December 16, 2015).

8
Planning for Large-Scale Special Events—Putting It All Together

The overarching theme of this book has been that planning for large-scale special events is the best possible context to examine all aspects of critical incident management. Whether you will ever be part of the planning of such an event is not as important as what lessons can be learned by using these complex and all-encompassing events as the backdrop for our examination. A large-scale special event such as a Super Bowl, or a presidential election brings all elements associated with homeland security and emergency management together to one table. There is no better context to examine the *before, during,* and *after* of a critical incident, or the *tactical, operational,* and *strategic* spheres of command than a preplanned event, in which all these factors come into play. A secondary reason for using the large-scale special event as a backdrop is that the lessons from it can be applied to the planning of much smaller events. For example, the writers of this book have applied the principles of large-scale event planning to the planning of smaller events such as United Way and Rotary Club fundraisers. You probably won't ever need to define a total flight restriction zone for your church's Thanksgiving Day turkey giveaway event, but the concepts related to crowd control and the need for clearly marked zones will be useful, even for such a small and informal event.

Yet another benefit of large-scale special events is that they act as *focusing events* whereby people from many different organizations and diverse disciplines converge at the same place and time to solve a common problem. When that happens, magic occurs. Ideas are exchanged. Technologies from one discipline are integrated to solve problems in another discipline, and as a result, new innovations are born. The synergy that occurs at these focusing events reminds us of the old *Reese's Peanut Butter Cup* television commercials where a young man is walking down a busy city sidewalk, obliviously listening to music on a headset and happily chewing on a chocolate bar. The young man is not paying attention and accidentally bumps into a young woman walking in the opposite direction. The young woman is eating peanut butter out of a jar. As they collide into each other, the young man's chocolate bar ends up in the young woman's peanut butter jar. The young lady says, "Hey, you put chocolate in my peanut butter!" The young man says, "You put peanut butter on my chocolate!" Then they both take a bite out of the new chocolate-peanut butter concoction and they simultaneously say, "Delicious!" The couple then walks away together eating their new invention. We know how well Reese's Peanut Butter Cups turned out … although we cannot be certain about the ensuing relationship of the young man and young lady. The point is that when people from different organizations and disciplines get together at the same time and place, and for a common goal, incredible things happen. Many organizations try to mimic the effects of a focusing event by artificially creating *innovation incubators*[1] at their place of business. The purpose of these innovation incubators is to put people together at the same place and time, and with common interests, and then provide tools to help them communicate and exchange ideas. Focusing events create the same conditions as innovation incubators, but even more so, since the event is "real" and there is a sense of urgency to collaborate and innovate so that the end result is a positive one.

A 31 Point Checklist for Planning Large-Scale Special Events

In Chapter 3, we identified nine steps for planning a simple special event at the operational level. These steps are listed below as a brief review.

Step 1: Conduct a Threat Assessment
Step 2: Meet with Event Organizers and Stakeholders
Step 3: Conduct a Site Survey (Vulnerability Assessment)
Step 4: Develop a Site Plan
Step 5: Develop a Crowd Control Plan
Step 6: Determine Necessary Resources
Step 7: Develop an Organizational Chart
Step 8: Assign Specific Personnel
Step 9: Conduct Training and Rehearsals

These are nine simple steps that a planner at the operational level can take for planning a special event. However, as we mentioned in the earlier chapters, we have devised a comprehensive 31-point checklist of things to do for planning a large-scale special event that takes into account the tactical, operational, and strategic spheres of command. This checklist incorporates the nine steps mentioned earlier, and adds several more aspects that should be considered when planning large-scale events. In this section, we will discuss each of these 31 items. It is important to note that these items are not listed in any sequential order; however, it is wise to start with the first two items on the list. This list is available as Appendix I at the end of the book.

Identify the Stakeholders

At the core of planning for events, or incidents that may happen during those events is the knowledge of who is who, and in what way they relate to you and to each other. There are many types of stakeholders—some friendly, some adversarial, and some that could go either way, depending on the situation. Stakeholders may be external to your organization, or internal. Some stakeholders may have a direct claim or may be impacted by the event (claimants), while others seek to influence the outcome of the event (influencers).[2] Because there are so many moving parts to the universe of stakeholders, it is a good idea to find a way to identify and categorize them. One way is to make a list of all the stakeholders involved in the event. The list can be subdivided into smaller lists that categorize the type of stakeholder and what they bring to the table.

Another useful tool for planners to get a full understanding of the stakeholder system is to devise a stakeholder map. Stakeholder maps are simple diagrams that illustrate the relationships of all the stakeholders involved in the event, and how they interrelate to the central unit of analysis (your organization). There is no one single way of drawing these maps. The important thing is that the illustration makes sense to you. As we mentioned in Chapter 5, the point of the stakeholder map is to oversimplify the stakeholder system so that the planners can get a grasp of it in a holistic sense. Once that is accomplished, other illustrations and lists can be added to it in order to include more detail and substance. These maps and lists can be used by the planner of the special events so that everyone can be on the same conceptual page. They can also be used by planners for making PowerPoint presentations to some of the external stakeholders, so that they too can be aware of the stakeholder system as a whole. For the special event planner, the purpose of using stakeholder maps is the same as the purpose of the critical incident manager—to make simplicity out of complexity, order out of chaos, and predictability out of uncertainty.

Meet with Event Organizers and Stakeholders

Early on in the process of special event planning, it is vital that the planners meet with the outside organizers of the event who are likely to be the main claimant stakeholders. The chances are that the main external organization that is planning the event will reach out to you first, since they need the police and fire department more than you need them. For example, for the planning of a Super Bowl, representatives from the NFL (National Football League) Security will contact the sheriff or chief of police of the local agency as early as 2 years prior to the event. Even before that, the NFL will contact local policy makers, such as county managers or city mayors to form discussion groups and "host committees" to ensure cooperation between the NFL and the local government agencies at the earliest stages of planning. Cities such as Miami, Tampa, New Orleans, Los Angeles/Pasadena, and Phoenix/Glendale, which have hosted multiple Super Bowls over the years, tend to be more prepared with the existing shells of host committees already in place. Other venues such as Indianapolis or Jacksonville have had to start their host committees from scratch since they have hosted the event only once.

The initial meeting between the police and fire department representatives and the representatives of the main claimant stakeholder (the organization planning the event) is vital to the success of the event because this is where the main players meet face-to-face and become familiar with each other, and where they exchange contact information for follow-up meetings. The initial meeting is where each side should state their expectations, so that all parties are aware of where everyone else stands. If there are conflicting expectations, this is where they should be ironed out.

After the initial meeting with the core planners of the main agencies and organizations, there will be many more meetings, where subgroups or subcommittees will get together to work on solutions to discipline-specific problem areas. The next step will require decisions on which stakeholders to meet, and which ones not to meet with. It is not a bad idea to meet with leaders of certain influencer organizations in order to hash out each other's expectations ahead of time. The stakeholder map and accompanying stakeholder analysis can be very helpful for deciding on who to meet with and who not to meet with prior to the event. Not every group will want to meet with you, nor should you want to meet with them. As a general rule of thumb, it is a good idea to meet with the leaders of violent adversarial groups that may have common interests with the local authorities. For example, there are organizations that seek to gain publicity and attention by protesting during the event, but they also want to avoid violent confrontations with the police. We recommend that you meet with those leaders ahead of time to make each other's expectations known. The more rules that are established ahead of time, the less uncertainty there will be during chaotic times. Organizations that on the surface may seem to be adversarial oftentimes become best friends with the police during chaotic times. An example of this occurred during the Free Trade Area of the Americas (FTAA) Conference in Miami, in 2003, when leaders of the Teamsters and AFL-CIO labor unions formed an impromptu symbiotic relationship with the leaders of the Miami-Dade Police Mobile Field Forces (MFF) on the worst day of that civil disturbance. Due to an unexpected last minute change on the fourth day of the event, the main staging area for the labor unions somehow ended up behind the MFF lines. The recreational vehicle (RV) trailers that served as command posts and food and water dispensing centers for the Teamsters and AFL-CIO protestors now found themselves on the wrong side of the police lines. As it turned out, the leaders of those two unions inside the trailers were very grateful to be on the "safe" side of the protests, as things on the other side of the frontline got out of control. Out of the estimated 10,000 protestors at the FTAA, it was estimated that 400–500 of them were violent "Black Bloc" types, who were intent on causing harm and destruction to the city. The vast majority of protestors were peaceful. The Teamsters and AFL-CIO unions were among the peaceful majority, and their leaders showed their appreciation by providing some of the police MFF commanders with beverages and use of their restroom facilities. This unintended and unexpected symbiotic relationship between the police field forces and some of the protest groups is an example of how the police can establish temporary partnerships with organizations that may be perceived at first as being adversarial, but which turn out to have common interests. If those common interests can be established ahead of time, before the event or incident, then so much the better.

Identify All Related Critical Infrastructure Assets

Now we turn our attention from people to infrastructures. Obviously, for a preplanned event, the infrastructure at the core of the planning is the event venue itself. However, for many large-scale special events, the area of operation "footprint" can be very large and dispersed over a wide geographic area. Most people think of a Super Bowl as being a one day event at a specific stadium location. The fact is that the actual event takes an entire week and involves multiple venue sites, where parties, festivals, exhibitions, and other gatherings take place. Each of these locations must be considered as a critical infrastructure asset that must be protected.

In addition to infrastructure assets within the identified area of operation footprint, there are other critical infrastructure assets that must be accounted for. These assets are deemed critical infrastructure because they provide functional services to people in and outside the area of operation (such as utility companies, airports, seaports, hospitals, jails, courts, fire, and police stations). These critical infrastructure assets must also be protected for the good of the general public, as well as the protection of the people within the area of operation. Just like we did a stakeholder map to gain a better understanding of who the players of an event are, it is also a good idea to compile a listing of all critical infrastructure assets that affect, or are affected by, the activities during the special event. This listing will often coincide with the stakeholders identified in the stakeholder map. The difference is that this list of critical infrastructure assets focuses more on the *what* and *where*, rather than on the *who* question. The compilation of this list is the first step of a five-step risk analysis process that follows this section. That process is summarized as:

1. Identify critical infrastructure assets
2. Conduct consequence assessments on those assets
3. Conduct threat assessments
4. Conduct vulnerability assessments
5. Conduct an overall risk analysis

Conduct a Consequence Assessment of All Identified Critical Infrastructure Assets

By definition, *consequences* are things that happen after. However, for the purpose of conducting risk analyses, we start by looking at the possible outcomes of an event or incident, and then work our way backward. We start with the end because it is the desired outcome that steers our strategies and tactics. Without a vision of the desired outcome, we have no basis on which to plan for the future. Determining the consequence scores of critical infrastructure assets provides planners of special events a starting point for conducting the overall analysis of risk, and for the later determination of where and when to best direct manpower and equipment resources to get the job done. Ultimately, this helps us to manage resources so that our most valuable assets are protected.

No one can predict the future with 100% certainty, but we can get reasonably close by conceptualizing what would occur if we lost an infrastructure asset that we depend on a great deal. For example, what would happen if we were to lose, or have a temporary disruption of our electric supply, or water supply? One good way of determining the value of an asset is to consider what it is worth to us if it is gone, or temporarily disrupted. In Chapter 2, we discussed how determining the value of an asset takes into consideration its *intrinsic value*, as well as its *symbolic value*. We also mentioned that intrinsic and symbolic values can be quantified, and that they are both determined by the subjective assessments of human beings. We tend to think of intrinsic value as being more quantifiable, and thus more "objective" than symbolic value, but that is simply not true. The only thing that makes intrinsic value more tangible is that we tend to ascribe a monetary cost to it, and thus make it easier to for us to grasp conceptually. In the end, the values that we ascribe to an asset, whether intrinsic or symbolic, are determined individually, or collectively by people who make subjective assessments, based on their own value systems. Intrinsic value is usually determined by large numbers of people through the *invisible hand* of the free market, whereas symbolic value is determined by small numbers of people making "rational" value assessments. The best we can do to avoid making arbitrary decisions as to the relative value of an asset is to approach it in a systematic manner. The more formal and systematic the consequence assessment procedure is, the more likely that people will accept it.

Conduct a Threat Assessment

The next step in a risk analysis is to try to predict the *likelihood* of something bad happening. For something bad to happen, there has to be two basic elements: the thing that is harmed, and the thing that causes harm. In the law enforcement realm, the armed robber is the threat, and the victim is the element that is harmed. In the realm of firefighting, the fire is the threat, and the building and any people inside are the elements that are harmed. In the realm of emergency management, a hurricane may be the threat, and an entire coastal community may be the element that is harmed. Because these two elements (threat and vulnerability) go hand-in-hand, it is difficult to separate them when conducting a risk analysis. Indeed, there is no good reason to separate them because the determination of one is often a function of the other. Without a victim, there is no crime. Without a bad guy, there is no crime. When those two meet, then there is a high likelihood that a crime will occur. Indeed, the element of *consequence* also factors in to the determination of the *likelihood* of risk. The only reason that we separate these elements here is so that we can eat this elephant, one small bite at a time.

As discussed earlier in Chapter 2, threats can be natural, man-made intentional, or man-made accidental. There are experts in different disciplines that are better suited for assessing these different types of threats. That is why we should rely on subject-matter experts from different disciplines to help us determine the threat factor. Nobody is better suited to assess the threat of an impending hurricane than a meteorologist working for the National Hurricane Center. Likewise, nobody is better suited to conduct an on-site assessment of hazards than a Hazmat technician. For the best assessments of man-made intentional threats, look to the Joint Terrorism Task Forces (JTTFs) and regional fusion centers to provide the best possible information on terrorists and violent protest groups that may be actively targeting your special event.

Conduct a Site Survey/Vulnerability Assessment

Site surveys and vulnerability assessments go hand-in-hand, but they are not quite the same thing. Site surveys are usually conducted by a small team several days, or even a few hours before an event. The purpose of the site survey is to look around for glaring vulnerabilities, or on-site hazards which can be corrected or mitigated ahead of time. Site surveys are more limited in scope, and tend to be more informal in their approach. A typical site survey involves one, or a couple of planners, carrying clipboards and jotting down notes on vulnerabilities and hazards as they encounter them.

Vulnerability assessments basically do the same task as site surveys, but they are more formal in approach, and tend to be larger in scope, with more experts involved at a broader and deeper level. Whereas site surveys rely mostly on qualitative notations, vulnerability assessments usually use industry-specific quantitative tools, with a formal scoring system in which the scores are later tabulated and combined as part of a broader assessment of the overall vulnerability/threat of all the identified critical infrastructure assets associated with the special event.

Site surveys and vulnerability assessments are an important part of the overall risk analysis process. They also help to determine the placement of resources to fill coverage gaps and vulnerabilities in order to address potential problems before they occur. As mentioned in Chapter 2, *red teams*, by mimicking enemy attacks provide the most aggressive and realistic assessments of vulnerability; however, because of the surprise factor and realism, they are a risky proposition.

Conduct an Overall Risk Analysis

As mentioned previously in Chapter 2, the fifth and final step of the risk analysis involves the calculation and final determination of the overall risk by using a formula that combines causal factors (threat and vulnerability) with effect factors (i.e., consequences). The numerical scores (if using a quantitative approach) or the written observations (if using a qualitative approach) for the consequence, threat, and vulnerability assessments are combined to determine an overall risk score.

Incorporate Best Practices and Lessons Learned

Much of what we do as critical incident managers to minimize risk is done way ahead of time with due diligence and preparation. Many agencies do a lot of work to prepare lengthy and detailed after-action reports following major incidents and events. Unfortunately, it has been a long standing practice that once those after-action reports are completed, they are filed away and are never read by anyone. Oftentimes, critical incident managers are going from one incident to another, and rarely have the time to stop and read their own agency's after-action reports, much less, those of other agencies. That is unfortunate because many of the lessons learned from previous incidents and events are lost, and have to be relearned by the new incident commanders. Whenever possible, we recommend that special event planners take the time to examine the after-action reports from their own agency, as well as from other agencies that have held similar events in the past. These reports are readily available upon request, and can often be download from the Internet.

Whenever possible, we also recommend that critical incident managers and special event planners personally visit venues that are holding similar events so that they can get an up-close view of what their special event may look like. When they go to the special events of other agencies, they can observe and learn the best practices to emulate, and also to learn the lessons from the mistakes that others have made. For a typical Super Bowl planning regimen, the top commanders of the jurisdictions selected for the event, will personally travel and observe Super Bowl preparations 2 years, and then 1 year ahead of their own event to observe and learn. Another example of how law enforcement and firefighting agencies cooperate in this manner was evidenced by the preparations for the 2003 FTAA in Miami, where one of the writers of this book was sent along with three other lieutenants to Cancun, Mexico, to observe the World Trade Organization (WTO) riots earlier that same year. Many of the lessons learned by the Miami-Dade Police contingent at Cancun of the things to do, and not do, were incorporated into the strategy and tactics used during the FTAA Conference. Likewise, a contingent from Savanah, Georgia, came to Miami that same year to observe the preparations for the FTAA Conference. Savanah and Sea Island Georgia were scheduled to host the G-8 Conference a year later, and the commanders and planners for that event learned from the commanders and planners of the FTAA event.

Develop a Site Plan

The purpose of the site plan is to clearly define the area of operation (also called a "footprint") for the event. Developing a site plan is one of the first things that is done at the operational level of planning. This step is different than the initial "site survey" step, which is done earlier to assess the vulnerabilities of an existing site *before* actions are taken to address those vulnerabilities. A site plan includes all measures taken to address the vulnerabilities exposed by the site survey/vulnerability assessment. That is not to say that a second and subsequent site surveys cannot be done after the site plan is created in order to test for other vulnerabilities that were not apparent the first time around. In fact, vulnerability assessments should not just be a step in the early planning process. The assessment of vulnerability should continue throughout the event, and into the response (i.e., "during") phase of the event or incident because many gaps in the security are likely to be exposed during the actual event.

A site plan usually starts with a map or satellite photograph (such as Google Maps or Google Earth) of the area affected by the event. We recommend that *Microsoft Word* or *PowerPoint* be used to overlay polygon shapes over the map or satellite photograph to clearly delineate the area of operation, restricted areas, buffer zones, command posts, staging areas, and other important features. Other more advanced computer software are available for this task, but the use of *Microsoft* products is simple and available to most at an affordable price. It doesn't take a lot of computer savviness to figure out how to overlay a rectangle marked with yellow dotted lines over a satellite photograph background.

Designate Command Post Locations

Depending on the size and scope of the special event, there may be more than one command post. For most special events, one Incident Command Post (ICP) will suffice, and that ICP will usually be located somewhere within, or close to the area of operation as delineated in the site plan. However, for very large events such as a Super Bowl, there will be multiple command posts to serve in the various levels of command (strategic, operational, and tactical), and also to provide redundancy in the event of a catastrophic incident. For the 2007 Super Bowl, we had a strategic command post, located at the Broward County Emergency Operations Center (EOC). Co-located at this strategic command post was a multiagency Bomb Management Center which served as a Unified Command structure for any CBRNE or terrorist-related incidents occurring in Miami-Dade, or Broward counties during the entire week preceding the day of the football game. The strategic command post at the EOC also served as a redundant command center in the event that the stadium operational command was destroyed or became incapacitated.

The second command post for Super Bowl XLI was a Unified Command (UC) at the operational level. This command post was located in a specially constructed perch at the upper level of the stadium, looking over the 50 yard line. From this high vantage point, the Unified Command post, in which the major law enforcement and fire-rescue agencies were located, was where all major operational decisions would be made.

In addition to the above-mentioned command posts, there was also the command post that the Miami-Dade Police and fire-rescue agencies use on a day-to-day basis for regular football and baseball game operations. From this command post, the officers and firefighters working regular security details were dispatched.

The next level of command post was at the tactical level. There were several Tactical Operations Command (TOC) posts prepositioned at various places in and around the stadium grounds in the event of an incident. One tactical command was positioned at a forward base of operations on a strip of land directly north of the stadium. Another tactical command was staged a mile away at a nearby high school. These tactical command (TOCs) were positioned at different locations to provide redundancy in the event of a totally incapacitating incident. In order to maintain lines of communication between all these levels of command posts, there were individuals assigned as liaisons from each Command Post (CP) to all the other CPs.

Obviously, this level of redundancy is not for every special event. In fact, we discourage having so many points of command because it could get confusing, and there could be conflicts between the different commands. The scope and level of complexity of the Super Bowl event dictated the need for this many levels of command. More often than not, all you will ever need is one incident command post, and an *ad hoc* TOC if a tactical incident occurs during the event. Otherwise, keep the command structure as simple as possible and the location of the CP at a safe distance from the event (not too close, but not too far).

Identify Redundant Staging Areas

Part of the site plan would be a defined location for a staging area. The more complex the event, the more types of staging locations there will be, and the more need for redundancy. The purpose of a staging area is to provide a place where units gather before responding to an incident. Staging areas are not the same thing as command posts, although in some events and incidents, the command post may be colocated with the staging area. This happens from time to time, but we recommend against it because staging areas are busy places, with a lot of commotion. The heavy commotion and noise can be distracting to the commanders working the event or incident.

As a general rule of thumb, staging areas need to be located close, but not too close to the area of operations. The choice of location must take into consideration obstructions such as train tracks and heavy traffic that may slow down response of the units responding from the staging area in the case of an emergency. In some cases, the staging area may be located inside the area of operations. Such was the case in Super Bowl XLI, in which several JHRT (Joint Hazard Response Teams) were prepositioned inside the stadium for rapid response.

Ideally, staging areas should provide some degree of comfort and security to the personnel being staged. It is not unusual for personnel to be placed on standby status at these staging locations for up to 8–12 hours, so it is important that they are provided with the basic needs such as restroom facilities, shelter, and food and water. Ideally, staging areas are placed at discrete locations that provide some limited cover and concealment to the personnel and their vehicles. Large staging areas should have a staging area manager to keep things organized, and confusion to a minimum. Additionally, there should always be some units assigned to security details to maintain the integrity of the staging area perimeter. Nobody wants an adversary sneaking up on them while they are waiting and relaxing at a staging location.

For Super Bowl XLI, in addition to the interior stadium staging areas, we had several redundant staging locations. We already mentioned the forward base of operations (FOB) on the strip of land by the canal, north of the stadium. Staged at that location were several elements of Miami-Dade and Miami Bomb Squads, Miami-Dade Fire Rescue, FBI and ATF bomb techs, and the Florida National Guard 44th Civil Support Team. Another redundant staging area was located at a high school approximately 1 mile east of the stadium. The same elements as in the FOB were also staged at the high school. A *helispot* for the landing of police and fire-rescue helicopters was also designated in a field at this location. Another operational-level staging area was located at an elementary school a couple of miles west of the stadium. This is the staging area where the Mobile Field Forces were located, and where all regular uniformed officers working stadium security reported to. A shuttle service was established at this location to bring in "new crew" officers, and take back "old crew" officers as their shift began or ended.

Incorporate a Plan to Control Ingress and Egress

Two weeks prior to the Super Bowl game, and one week prior to other event-related activities (such as the NFL Experience exhibit and fair), all access to the stadium grounds is restricted. All football games have a great deal of traffic activity involving the delivery of food and beverages and supplies. The Super Bowl takes the regular delivery of goods into the stadium and multiplies it by 10. In addition to the regular deliveries of goods, the entire field is re-sodded a couple of weeks before the game, which involves the delivery of giant rolls of sod and fertilizer on trucks, along with forklifts and other machinery to lay the sod. The halftime shows are very elaborate, and require the construction of stages on wheels and other related items. We already mentioned how a temporary structure was built on the highest part of the upper deck for one of the command posts. With all these deliveries of sod and construction materials, and food and beverage items, it would be very easy for a terrorist group to smuggle weapons and other destructive devices into the stadium and then hide them until they were ready for use during an assault. For that reason, the NFL Security and the Miami-Dade Police Department jointly devised a plan to have all entry into the secured area of operation footprint controlled at a couple of locations. There were limited entry points designated for first responders. Another controlled entry point was designated for the team buses, the media buses and personnel, the halftime show performers, and stadium staff. All trucks making deliveries of goods had to go through a multi-station que in a specifically designated "sacrificial" area south of the stadium footprint. All delivery vehicles were checked at the various stations by explosive detection canines, then by the VACIS x-ray machine and other visual checks, as well as brief interviews of the drivers to ensure that they had the proper identification and delivery documents. The que was considered a sacrificial area because that would be the place where any vehicle bomb that was found would have had to be rendered safe. This sacrificial place was at a relatively safe distance from the stadium and from the main gathering of fans attending the game.

Controlling ingress and egress to the secured area within the designated area of operations can be done several ways. The simplest way is to have unrestricted access. That means that anybody can go anywhere. Unrestricted access works well for open festivals that do not charge an admission fee. This type of access requires the least amount of manpower and least amount of perimeter control. There is no need for fencing or barricades since foot and vehicular traffic is allowed anywhere. Of course, an event with totally unrestricted access is very rare. There usually exists at least some level of restriction. The restriction could be as simple as foot traffic only, or vehicles only.

The second level of restricted access calls for some people and vehicles to be allowed to enter the restricted area. Restricted access will require some sort of fencing or barricades along the perimeter of the defined restricted area. Entry for patrons is usually granted by the purchase of a ticket and/or a parking pass for their vehicles. Restricted access to ticketed events requires a lot of manpower resources to manage. Entry points need to be minimized to only a few gates to better control the flow of foot traffic into the event grounds. Depending on the level of security for the event, there may be various levels of intrusive or non-intrusive body searches at these entry gates. For the Super Bowl, there were many people selling and buying counterfeit tickets to the game. Provisions had to be made to single out those people to ensure that they did not gain access into the stadium.

The third level of restricted access involves the use of credentials to gain entry into the secure area. These credentials are provided to all persons working the event. These include first responders, the team coaches and players, the cheerleaders, the media, stadium security staff, food and beverage vendors, media staff, the halftime show performers, and many other essential personnel. Depending on the scope of the event, credentials may be something as simple and inexpensive as a wristband, or as elaborate and expensive as biometric identification.

The difference between the 1999 Super Bowl and the 2007 Super Bowl was striking. In 1999, there was no designated buffer zone around the stadium perimeter. The lack of a buffer zone allowed crowds and vehicles to come up to the fence line of Dolphin Stadium, only a few feet away from the stadium superstructure. In fact, there were no barriers at the time to stop or impede any vehicle from driving straight into the ground-level tunnel and onto the field of play. It would have been very easy for a terrorist to drive a large vehicle bomb straight onto the field and detonate it during the crowded halftime show back then. When this writer brought this vulnerability to the attention of the NFL Security, it was met with the attitude of, "well it's too late now to make any changes." Apparently, neither the 1996 Khobar Towers bombing[3] nor the bombing of the Murrah Building in Oklahoma City in 1995[4] had made much of an impression on those responsible for the site plan of the 1999 Super Bowl. Of course, the attitudes of security policy makers changed considerably after the September 11 attacks, and all the risk mitigation suggestions that we made (and that were ignored) for the 1999 Super Bowl were now the new normal.

Develop an Emergency Evacuation Plan

The "new normal" security paradigm that came about as a result of the September 11 attacks was not just about how to get the right people into the secured area (while keeping the undesired ones out). The new paradigm also had to do with how best to get people out in an emergency. As first stated in Chapter 2, in situations where people are in imminent danger, critical incident managers are faced with the fundamental decision as to whether to order an evacuation or a shelter-in-place. Some situations call for a partial evacuation of certain areas and a lock-down (i.e., "shelter in place") of others during the same incident. But regardless of whether an evacuation, or a shelter in place is deemed most appropriate for a particular set of circumstances, a good evacuation plan clearly defines where the evacuees should go, and who will be assigned to ensure that they get there. A good evacuation plan must be flexible enough to allow decision makers to change the direction of the evacuation routes in order to steer the evacuees away from the threat, rather than directing them to go toward the threat. As such, for preplanned events, there should be different contingencies for evacuation routes and for mustering locations where the evacuees gather.

Develop an Emergency Decontamination Plan

As we evacuate people out of a hot zone, we need to be mindful that those coming out may be contaminated with the chemical, biological, or radiological element that they were exposed to. In order to save peoples' lives, we should not put other peoples' lives in danger. In essence, decontamination of evacuees and returning first responders must be done in a way that minimizes the spread of the threat. For this reason, we must develop an emergency decontamination plan that is consistent with, and takes into account the evacuation plan. A good plan should take into account the three levels of decontamination: mass decon, technical decon, and tactical decon.

Develop a Mass Casualty Plan

Closely related to the evacuation and decontamination plan should be the mass casualty plan. It is very possible that all three of these aspects may intersect during a critical incident. In a mass casualty incident, there will likely be some sort of evacuation, and quite possibly, some degree of decontamination of the victims. Mass casualty plans must first deal with the dead, the injured, the ambulatory, and the nonambulatory. Mass casualty plans must have a triage protocol wherein first responders determine who among the dead and injured should be treated first, and who should not be treated at all. This is usually done with the color-coded tags or ribbons affixed to the victims. The START (Simple Triage and Rapid Treatment) method uses four colors (red, yellow, green, and black) to designate the treatment priorities in a mass casualty situation. The color red indicates that there is an emergent urgency due to an immediate threat to life or limb. The color yellow is used to designate an urgent situation involving "significant injury or illness, but can tolerate a delay in care." The color green is used to designate a nonurgent situation whereby the victim can safely wait for treatment. The color black is used to designate victims that are either deceased, or are expected to die shortly. For victims designated with black tags, there will be no treatment, except for: "expectant patients after initial 'Reds' are cleared, if resources exist and it does not delay care for Yellows."[5]

The mass casualty plans must also take into consideration the likelihood of an overwhelming surge of patients into area hospitals. Mass casualties will likely place extraordinary stress on hospital trauma centers and emergency rooms. Redundant layers of hospital care must be planned for at the regional level, as an overload on normal capacity is to be expected. Because a mass casualty incident is likely to overwhelm the normal manpower resources during a regular scheduled event, it can be expected that resources outside the defined area of operation will be needed. Thus, mass casualty plans must involve both the operational sphere and the strategic sphere of command.

Develop a Crowd Control Plan

Crowd control plans have to do with large numbers of people in small confined areas. Crowd control plans are related to the ingress and egress plans of the people who are supposed to be at the event, but also have to account for people who are not supposed to be there. Many special events attract television coverage. Whenever there is television coverage, there exists the possibility that people who are unaffiliated with the event will attempt to "crash" it, or do something to bring attention to themselves outside the confines of the event. When an event occurs on private property, the owners of the property and the law enforcement personnel working as security can eject trespassers and give them a warning not to come back. If the individuals ignore the trespass warning, then they can be arrested by the authorities.

The issue changes when large crowds of people show up to protest on public lands. Individuals have a constitutional right to protest when the land they're protesting on is not privately owned. That does not mean that the protestors can do whatever they want. The Constitution protects free speech and expression, but it does not give anyone the license to break the law. The purpose of the crowd control plan is to provide a way that balances the constitutional rights of individuals with the safety of all concerned. One way that event planners can reduce uncertainty and gain a better control of the situation when protestors are expected to show up at an event is to predesignate a "First Amendment zone" for protestors to converge at. First Amendment zones are typically designated by law enforcement planners, but often involve input from influencer stakeholders who desire a safe location at which protestors can gather and peacefully demonstrate somewhere near, but not inside the secured area of the planned event. Negotiations between law enforcement planners and the leaders of protest groups can often be cooperative in that both sides have a mutual interest for allowing the protestors to express their concerns while maintaining a peaceful and safe protest environment. However, at times, the negotiations for the placement of the First Amendment zone in relation to the event footprint can become contentious, as the protest groups typically ask for unrestricted access to the event, or at least be allowed to get as close as possible. When there have been disagreements between the police planners and the leaders of protest groups, the courts have had to intervene and dictate where the First Amendment zone should be placed.

In order to avoid a court mandated order that places the First Amendment zone at a location that may be less than ideal for law enforcement purposes, it is a good idea to do it in a reasonable manner in the first place, so that the influencer stakeholder groups can agree with it, and not take it to court for litigation. Once the courts get involved in the decision making, it is less than likely that the best location for First Amendment zone will be chosen.

There are several "rules of thumb" that can prove helpful for planners to select the best possible location for First Amendments zones. First, is what we like to refer to as the *"Goldilocks principle"*—not too close, and not too far—just right. The protestors typically want to get as close to, if not inside, the actual event so that they can be seen and heard. Their objective is to get attention from the invitees who are authorized to be inside the event, and to get the attention of the television cameras. If in their opinion, the First Amendment zone is set up too far from the event footprint, then they will more likely contest the placement with an unwanted court litigation. On the other hand, the police planners want to have the protestors at a safe distance from the secured area of the event. The attendees at the event, and all those claimant stakeholders who will be inside the secured area will want to know that their safety has been ensured. To achieve a balance that takes into account these divergent interests, it is a good practice to have the First Amendment zone set up at a distance and location that is within the *line of sight* to where the event is being held. The principle is simple—if they can see it, they will feel as if they are part of it. People tend to rely on symbolic representations to help them define where something is located. Often, a symbolic representation of the event venue is already in place, and can be used by planners as a focal point to determine a good line-of-sight location for the First Amendment zone. Usually, the higher and more prominent the symbol is, the further it can be seen from, and thus, the further the unimpeded line of sight can extend. For example, the U.S. Capitol building on one end, and the Lincoln Memorial on the other end of the National Mall provides a very long line-of-sight distance (approximately half a mile) where protestors can turn their attention from one end to the other. In a crowded urban landscape with many tall buildings obstructing the line of sight, the distance between the event footprint and the First Amendment zone may have to be much shorter. If a symbol of the event location does not already exist, it may be in the best interests of both the police planners and the protest group leaders to make one. Fence lines that are used to secure the restricted areas often become symbolic of the event itself. Claimant stakeholders inside the fence line want to feel safe. Influencer stakeholders outside the fence line want to use the imagery of the fence as a symbol of how they are being kept out of whatever is going on inside. That way, the protestors can portray the image that is consistent with their storyline of the elite insiders erecting barriers to keep out the "common" people. Because fences serve both a tangible protective purpose, and an intangible symbolic purpose as well, it may be a good idea for event planners to set up concentric rings of fencing around the event footprint so that the inner fence serves as a final protective ring, while the outer fence serves more as a symbol where protestors can demonstrate at a safe distance. This is especially a good idea because at some events, such as the 2003 WTO in Cancun, the outer fence line was torn down by the protestors, not once, but twice.

The second important principle to use for determining the best placement of a First Amendment zone is what we call the *"Field of Dreams"* principle. The famous line from that movie was, "if you build it, they will come." We use this principle as a way of determining the location of the First Amendment zone, as well as how best to configure it. The best First Amendment zones are those that provide all the creature comforts to the protestors. The idea is to configure the area so that it has sufficient shade (on a hot sunny day), and restroom facilities (usually porta toilets), and a place that provides drinking water to the protestors. Usually, a grass surface is better than a hard asphalt of concrete surface because both the protestors and the police may have to stand for prolonged periods. It stands to reason that the more comfortable the zone is configured, the more likely the protest groups will come to gather at. Conversely, planners can use discomfort to dissuade protestors from gathering at locations that are not in the best interest of the police and internal stakeholders. For example, in the late 1980s, this writer was part of a Mobile Field Force that responded to a protest organized by Haitian organizations to demonstrate their grievances against the detention of Haitian immigrants at the Krome Detention facility on the outskirts of the Everglades. This remote site had a very long lone access roadway, which the protestors decided to use to get as close as possible to the outer fence line of the facility. The Mobile Field Force was deployed inside the fence line, while the protestors (about 50 of them) gathered outside the fence. While the Mobile Field Force officers were rotated every half hour, one squad at a time on the front line, while the other seven squads were kept well hydrated and under the shade of a large "chickee" shelter, the 50 protestors stood under the broiling hot sun of a typical South Florida summer day. To make things worse, there were no shade trees for the protestors to stand under, and the heat reflecting from the asphalt roadway put the ambient temperature in the 100° Fahrenheit range. Needless to say, that demonstration did not last very long. The main lesson when it comes to the control of large crowds is that much can be done ahead of time to persuade—and on the other side of the coin—to dissuade people from gathering at places and times that are in the best interests of the event planners and the claimant stakeholders.

Develop a Mass Arrest Plan

Like the mass casualty plan required the cooperation of area hospitals, the mass arrest plan requires a partnership with local jails and detention facilities. By definition, the occurrence of a mass arrest will likely overwhelm the regular booking procedures at local jails. Mass arrests will also affect the arraignments and bond hearings at the county courts. For that reason, the court system—most likely represented by the chief administrative judge, and the court liaison officers and deputies from the county where the event will take place—will also be stakeholders and partners for the planning of the event. Procedures need to be in place to handle a large number of arrests. Those procedures should include mobile or temporary prisoner processing facilities to expedite the booking procedures while safeguarding the safety of the prisoners and their personal property. The procedures should also take into account sufficient means to transport the prisoners and their personal property to the regular jail facilities. Often, these procedures involve quick booking and release of the nonviolent misdemeanor

offenders, while the violent felons are held in custody through the regular detention procedures. Likewise, the administrative judge of the county court can
devise procedures for expedited arraignments and bond hearings.

The other important component of mass arrest plans are the Mobile Field
Forces (MFFs), which are the units most likely to actually place the arrestees in
custody. A typical Mobile Field Force is comprised of 64 personnel, although in
some cases it may be smaller, and in other cases, there can be as many as 84 for
an enhanced MFF. Examples of a typical MFF lineup, and an enhanced MFF
lineup that were used by the Miami-Dade Police for the 2003 FTAA Conference,
are provided in the Appendix of Resources immediately following this chapter
(Appendices II and III).

The larger enhanced field forces were used in anticipation of mass arrests.
Because the effectiveness of the field force concept depends on disciplined and
coordinated line movements, the integrity of the front line needs to be maintained at all times. If that line integrity breaks down during a chaotic situation,
then the opponents can exploit gaps in the line, and the effectiveness of the MFF
will be compromised. In order to maintain the necessary line discipline, field
forces make arrests in a very deliberate and methodical manner. Only one of
the seven eight-person squads in a regular field force is dedicated to making the
actual arrests. Typically, squads 10, 20, 30, 40, and 50 form the front line. Squad 70
provides rear guard security. That leaves Squad 60 as the designated arrest team.
Only eight personnel out of the 64 are dedicated for the sole purpose of arresting
subjects. Depending on whether the subjects are violent, nonviolent compliant,
or nonviolent and noncompliant, it could take anywhere from 1 minute to several
minutes for an eight-person arrest team squad to project themselves beyond the
front line to arrest one or two subjects at a time. The subjects have to be handcuffed (usually with plastic flex cuffs) and then patted down to ensure that they
have no weapons. If the subject has any personal belongings, those need to be
picked up, searched, and brought back behind the line, along with the arrestee.
The task of arresting subjects is a strenuous ordeal that takes considerable time
to do correctly, and places a great deal of stress on the arrest team officers. Under
these circumstances, a typical 64 person MFF can make up to 20 arrests per hour
if the subjects are nonviolent compliant, and usually no more than six arrests
per hour for noncompliant subjects. The 84 person enhanced MFF, with an extra
eight-person arrest team, may be able to double that rate. Nevertheless, arresting
people at a mass level is a very labor-intensive task. For that reason, most MFF
commanders opt to arrest two or three of the biggest troublemakers and follow
that up with chemical agents to disperse the remaining crowd. In a situation such
as the FTAA Conference, where multiple field forces from a number of partner
agencies are making mass arrests, the prisoner processing aspect can get backed
up considerably. That is why the coordination between the MFF arrest teams and
the corrections officers doing the "booking" procedures at the mobile prisoner
processing facilities is so important. The longer the MFF arrest teams are tied up
in dropping the prisoners off at the prisoner processing facility and transferring

custody to the corrections officers, the less effective the MFF will be. Those field forces need to get back into the "game" as soon as practicable. Without a doubt, the arrest of mass numbers of violators is a very labor-intensive task, and one that is fraught with legal liability, as it is difficult to keep track of all the prisoners' personal belongings, which are sometimes left behind in the confusion.

Develop a Flight Control Plan

A flight control plan involves more than the concentric circles of a TFR (temporary flight restriction) on a map around the event's area of operation. Unlike the very visible fence lines on the perimeter of the event footprint, the concentric circles that delineate the boundaries of the TFR cannot be seen. For that reason, we need to have in place a procedure that lets pilots know that they are approaching a restricted "no fly" zone. TFR no fly zones associated with the security of a special event are usually configured in two concentric circles—the inner ring at 10 miles from the center of the area of operation and the outer ring at 30 miles from the center. All aircraft entering the outer ring, including those arriving or departing local airports, must maintain two-way radio contact with the local Air Traffic Control and must be able to continually "squawk" an assigned discreet beacon code that identifies the aircraft as being authorized to be in the restricted air space. Aircraft that wander into the 30 mile restricted airspace without the correct beacon code will be hailed via two-radio and intercepted by U.S. Air Force aircraft. If unable to establish radio contact with the pilot of the aircraft, the Air Force plane will get close enough to make visual contact and signal him to turn around. If the wayward aircraft ignores the radio and visual signals to turn around, the Air Force pilot will be authorized to shoot down the violator. According to U.S. Code Title 49, the FAA has the authority to apply restrictions within airspace under its jurisdiction. That authority includes the imposing of civil penalties and criminal charges for violators, and also allows for the use of deadly force to prevent the violating aircraft from continuing toward the restricted area of operation, as stated in Section C of the code: "The United States Government may use deadly force against the airborne aircraft, if it is determined that the aircraft poses an imminent security threat."[6] The decision to shoot down the trespassing aircraft is usually made once it enters the 10 mile inner ring. This may be done either by an Air Force jet or by U.S. Customs and Border Protection helicopters within the 10 mile ring. The decision to shoot down an aircraft that violated the TFR is not made lightly. In highly populated urban areas where the event is likely to take place, the crashing aircraft is likely to hit innocent people on the ground. The trade-off that decision makers have to make is to consider that it is "less bad" to have a few casualties off site as a result of the crash than it would be to have mass casualties if the aircraft continued on course and deliberately crashed into a crowded stadium or other large-scale event.

There are three ways that the pilots of aircraft flying in the proximity of the event's area of operation are given. We already mentioned the radio warnings that an approaching aircraft is given, as well as the visual signals to turn around.

The other warning is done *before* the aircraft even takes off from its point of departure. The crew of commercial airline flights that are scheduled to take off, land, or come in proximity of the event's TFR area can be informed ahead of time via informational bulletins and announcements. Likewise, noncommercial pilots intending to fly in the proximity of the TFR no fly zone can receive these same warnings prior to departing from general aviation airports in the region. In order to convey this pre-takeoff informational warning, it is imperative that the event planners reach out to the FAA (Federal Aviation Administration) early on in the planning process. It is the FAA that issues *Notices To Airmen* (NOTAM) to disseminate the information about TFR no fly zones.[7] The authorities at regional general aviation airports should also be included as stakeholders in the early planning process because much of the control of non-authorized civilian aircraft can be done before the aircraft leaves the ground. For the 2007 Super Bowl, we had teams of investigators assigned on the ground at four regional general aviation airports to ensure that any suspicious behavior was addressed early on, before a would-be terrorist took off.

The 10 and 30 mile radius of the TFRs may sound like they would provide sufficient time to react to an incoming terrorist attack by air, but when taking into consideration the speed of the aircraft, it really does not allow for much reaction time. For example, the top speed for a Cessna Skyhawk general aviation aircraft is 124 ktas (knots true air speed).[8] This translates to 143 mph (miles per hour), which means that the aircraft can cover a distance of 2.38 miles per minute. A Boeing 737 commercial airliner's top speed is 974 kph (kilometers per hour).[9] This aircraft can cover 10 miles in 1 minute. A 737 can enter the 30 mile ring and be on target within 3 minutes. That leaves very little time for contemplation of options. For that reason, it is vital to the security of the event that open lines of communication are established early between the event planners, the U.S. Air Force, the FAA, U.S. Customs and Border Protection, and the local authorities. There should be a TFR committee established with representatives from all these agencies on board. Coordination between these agencies is crucial in order to avoid allowing a catastrophic error (terrorist aircraft crashes into a crowded venue), or even a nuisance error (in this case, the "nuisance" would be quite severe in that innocent civilians on the ground could be killed).

Incorporate the Three Phases of Critical Incident
Management (Before, During, and After)

We will not spend a lot of time on this task, other than to say that all plans should have a before, during, and after component. In essence, the planning of a special event requires three sub-plans—one for each of the phases. Oftentimes, many of the same personnel who served on planning committees may transition into operational units or teams during the response phase as well. For example, in preparation for the 2007 Super Bowl, all matters related to CBRNE response were planned by the EOD/Canine Workgroup that was comprised of Miami-Dade Police, Miami-Dade Fire Rescue; Miami Police; FBI; ATF; Florida National Guard's 44th Civil Support Team; U.S. Postal Service; Broward County Sheriff's Office; Palm Beach County

Sheriff's Office; U.S. Customs and Border Patrol; and U.S. Department of Energy; among others. Some of the personnel assigned to that workgroup transitioned into roles in the JHRTs (Joint Hazard Response Teams) and the K-9 sweep teams for the event itself. The post-event demobilization required less personnel because there were no notable adverse incidents during the event. However, if there had been a CBRNE attack, the post-incident recovery effort would have been substantial, thus requiring many of the same personnel to continue working.

It has been our experience that agencies tend to do a good job in planning the *before* and *during*, but not so good in planning for the *after* of special events. There seems to be a human tendency to relax after an event is done, and if nothing went wrong, to go on vacation right afterward. That is understandable because the planning for such complex events can take as long as a year, and in some cases 2 years. At the end, the core planners are exhausted and in need of some relaxation. However, just because the event is over and nothing bad happened does not mean that the commanders and planners can relax too much. Bad things can still happen after the event is over. For example, there tends to be a large infusion of equipment and supplies at a great cost for these events. For the 2003 FTAA, the Miami-Dade Police Department spent over $900,000 for munitions, weapons, tools, protective clothing, and other supplies. Some of those expenditures were for perishable items or for supplies with short shelf lives. For those things, it is a good idea to have a plan to dispose of the supplies that were not used by giving them away to charitable organizations (such as homeless veterans groups) or to use for training purposes. For example, bottled water can spoil after a while if not kept in an air-conditioned warehouse. Other equipment, such as bolt cutters, sledge hammers, power drills and saws (for the CUT teams) can vanish at the end of an event. Great care should be taken to properly account for these expensive tools. After the FTAA, we assigned the bomb squad to conduct a full inventory of all the CUT team tools, which totaled in excess of $76,000. After the inventory was conducted, these tools were kept in safe storage in a utility closet at the bomb squad office.

Develop an Organizational Chart

Having a clearly delineated organizational chart of the command structure for the event early in the planning process is integral for the plan's success. Organization charts are important because they reduce uncertainty as to who reports to whom. Every person who works the event needs to know what their position is in the organization, relative to everyone else. A well-designed organizational chart is as important as a stakeholder map, or a site plan. All these provide a spatial orientation as to where an individual component stands in relation to all the other components. The reason that new organizational charts need to be made for new events is that the regular organizational structures of the agencies involved are not going to work for these special events. Each event requires a different organizational configuration in order to deal with the particular challenges of that event.

There are generally two basic types of organizational charts—*hierarchical configuration* and *spoke and wheel configuration*. The Incident Command System is an example of a hierarchical configuration. Almost every organization in the world—whether private or publically owned, nonprofit or for-profit, military or civilian—are organized in some sort of hierarchical configuration. The reason that hierarchies are almost universal is that they work really well. Figure 8.1 is an example of a hierarchical organizational chart configuration for the various planning committees used by Miami-Dade Police as the lead agency for the planning of the 2007 Super Bowl. This organizational chart depicts the many committees, subcommittees, and interdisciplinary workgroups involved in the *before* phase leading up to the event. This was not the configuration of command *during* the actual event.

Figure 8.2 illustrates a *spoke and wheel* configuration for one of the committees from Figure 8.1. In this case, the Canine/EOD (bombs) Workgroup is used as an example. The spoke and wheel configuration is best used when the planners seek to deemphasize authority-based linear relationships and emphasize coequal partnerships in workgroups instead. In reality, the spoke and wheel configuration used to illustrate committee structures is nothing more than a snapshot of the same thing, but from a different angle. Think of it as a hierarchy being the side view of an organizational structure, while the spoke and wheel configuration is the same thing, but from a top view. In essence, they portray the same linear relationships, but one emphasizes top-down hierarchy, which is best depicted from the side view; while the other emphasizes coequal partnerships, which is best depicted from the top view. Regardless of whether you use the preferred hierarchical configuration or the spoke and wheel configuration, this is something that should be done early in the planning process. The sooner that every participant knows their position relative to others, the smoother the planning process will go. We recommend *Microsoft PowerPoint* for the creation of these organizational charts. PowerPoint provides some very easy to use *SmartArt* graphics for this purpose.

Develop Interdisciplinary and Multiagency Specialized Mixed Teams

In Chapters 3 and 4, we discussed the purpose of having multiagency mixed teams. The fundamental purpose of these teams is to address the multiple threats posed by an all-hazards CBRNE environment. These mixed teams are intended to be problem solvers at the most basic and up-close level of critical incident management. They have to be interdisciplinary because nobody is an expert at everything. They need to be multiagency because no single agency has the manpower, expertise, or equipment to solve every problem. The members of these mixed teams need to work together and practice together in order to get to know each other's capabilities. In essence, these teams form a Unified Command at the most basic level of response. A blank roster of the multiagency mixed team assignments that was used for the 2007 Super Bowl can be found in Appendix IV.

Develop an All-Hazards Render Safe Plan

There are two fundamental ways to render safe a suspected explosive device. One way is to pick up the device (preferably with a robot), and to place it inside

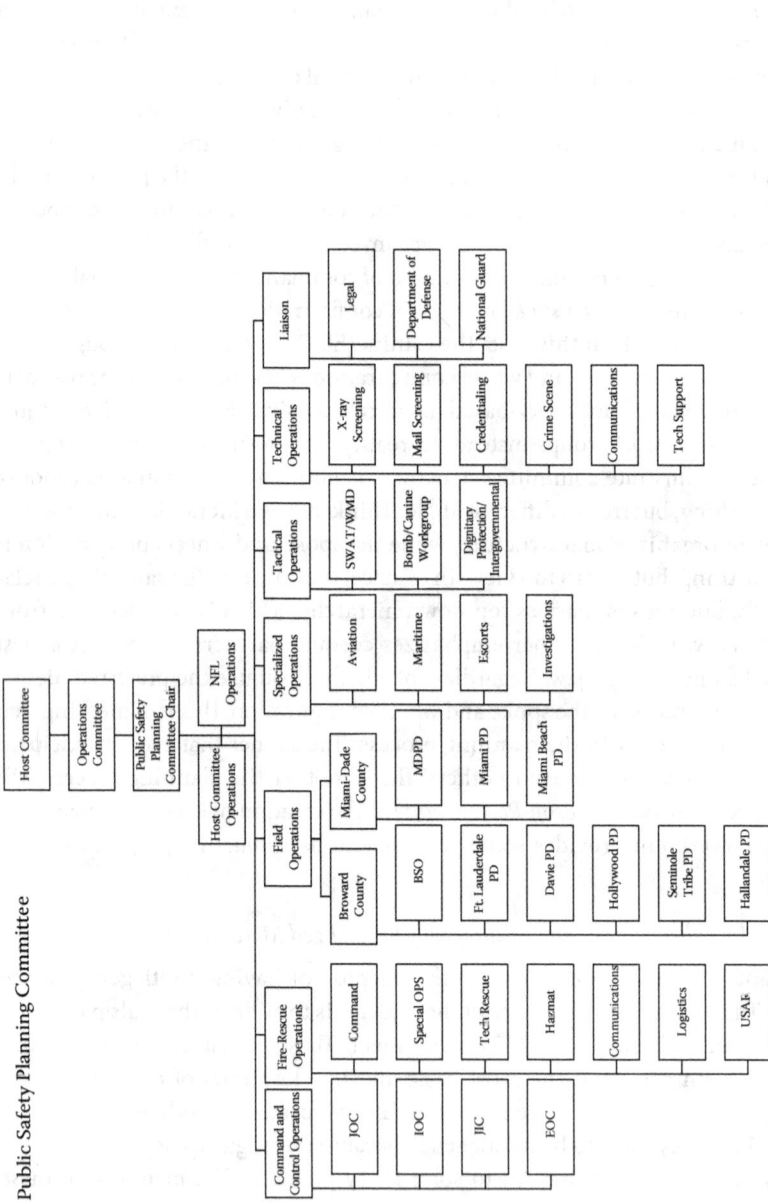

Figure 8.1 Example of a Hierarchical Organizational Chart 2007 Super Bowl Public Safety Planning Committee (Courtesy of the Miami-Dade Police Department.)

Canine/EOD Workgroup

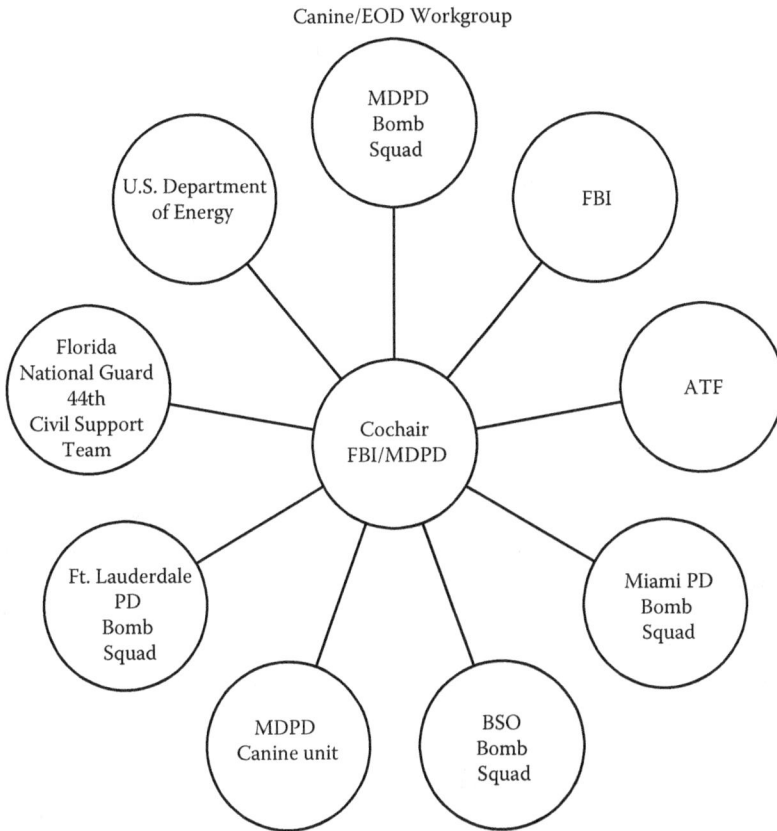

Figure 8.2 Example of a Spoke and Wheel Organizational Chart (From the 2007 Canine/EOD Workgroup.)

a containment vessel, and then transport the device to a location where it can be disposed of in a safe manner. Oftentimes, the preferred way to neutralize an explosive device is to render it safe while "in-place" so that the suspected device is not moved, therefore minimizing the risk that it will accidentally detonate and cause harm to the bomb technicians, or to anyone else in proximity of the explosion. There are advantages and disadvantages to both approaches. The preferred render safe in-place approach is done in two general methods. The first is to "counter-charge" the suspected device by exploding it in a controlled manner. A more precise method is to separate the components of the device so that it will not detonate as designed. There exists a variety of PAN (percussion actuated non-electric) and water-based disruptors that are aimed and shot at the suspected device after x-rays have identified the precise location of the vital components. The disadvantage of the preferred render safe in-place method is twofold. First, the loud bang of a countercharge, or even a PAN disruptor could cause panic in a large crowd situation such as a concert or sports event. Second, a controlled detonation or a precise disruption may cause greater harm if the device is combined with either a chemical or radiological component. The controlled explosion may actually help to disperse the chemical or radiological component and make things worse, rather than better. Given that most large-scale special events have a lot of people at them, and given that evacuations of large numbers of people can be difficult and problematic, the better approach may be to use the robots and the total containment vessels to move the suspected devices away from the event crowds and to a remote location where the devices can be disposed of safely. In the end, however, the decision on what approach to take—whether to render safe in-place, or to move and dispose the device—has to be made by the bomb technicians and bomb squad commanders who are most affected by the outcome of the decision.

An all-hazards render safe plan has to take into account all these factors and needs to have equipment in place should any CBRNE incident occur. Because the large crowds and crowd dynamics makes the move and dispose method a more likely option, there needs to be several containment vessels prepositioned at various locations to allow for quick response to the incident. More importantly, protocols need to be in place ahead of time to ensure that communication between the hazardous devices teams and the Incident Command Post is maintained. There may be a need for a partial or total evacuation of the premises, and thus public announcement scripts should already be in place, should such an eventuality occur. As discussed earlier, evacuations require not just an order to get out. The best evacuations are those that instruct the evacuees to take a particular path while they are leaving the premises in order to steer them away from the known threats. In the end, decisions regarding evacuations and render safe procedures will require the decision makers to understand the consequences of the threat, and to make trade-offs that may turn out to be the "least worst" decision possible.

Develop Contingency Tactical Response Plans

This plan has to do with being able to react accordingly to an active shooter, suicide bomber, hostage taking, or barricaded subject incident. The main components of this plan will be the SWAT teams and the bomb squads. Also involved in a support capacity would be K-9 teams and the aviation units. The key to any tactical response plan lies with the establishment of a viable *overwatch*. An overwatch refers to the ability to establish advantageous positions (usually up high) from where the location and movement of the "bad guys" can be observed and reported back to the tactical commander at the Tactical Operations Command (TOC). The ability to know the adversary's position and their movements, and being able to react quickly to any changes, is paramount for a successful SWAT response. The role of overwatch is usually that of the SWAT counter sniper. The counter sniper has the capability and the legal authority under certain situations to use his/her weapon to use deadly force to protect him/herself and others. But more important than the long range shooting aspect of the counter sniper is the ability to provide real-time intelligence to the TOC commander about the movements of the subjects. In active shooter and hostage/barricaded subject incidents, one of the first responsibilities of a tactical team is to establish a secure inner perimeter around the hot zone where the shooters are. The second important task is to set up an overwatch with the counter snipers in place. The advantage of a preplanned event is that the counter-sniper positions can be set up ahead of time. For example, at Super Bowls, several counter-sniper teams are set up in various high locations throughout the stadium. These counter snipers are typically dressed in regular police uniform, and their weapons hidden from view, as to not attract attention from the fans at the game. In addition to their overwatch responsibility inside the stadium, the counter snipers also maintain an overwatch outside to ensure that no vehicles crash through the fence or the serpentine barriers at the cargo delivery checkpoints.

A good tactical plan also pre-positions SWAT entry teams, both inside and outside the area of operation, in order to give them sufficient response flexibility. This part of the plan intersects with the plan for selecting staging areas. Because police helicopters may need to lift the SWAT, bomb squad, and K-9 teams from one place to another in a hurry, details such as the weights and volume displacement of the personnel and their equipment need to be known ahead of time and calculated so that the helicopters are not overburdened with too much weight. For example, the body weights of every tactical team officer, including their weapons and gear, was recorded, as was the weight of the police dogs and bomb squad robots. Had an urgent need to move tactical teams from one location to another by helicopter arisen, it would not have been necessary to waste time trying to figure out if the helicopter had been dangerously overloaded. Trying to calculate total weights during the stress of the moment of an active shooter or hostage situation would not have been a good thing. The more planning is done ahead of time, the less uncertainty there will be during the actual incident.

Identify and Procure the Necessary Specialized Equipment for Each Mission

We mentioned earlier how the Miami-Dade Police Department spent over $900,000 for new weapons, munitions, equipment, and protective gear in preparation for the FTAA Conference. Part of the reason why so much money was spent was that many new tactics and munitions were being put into effect in order to adapt to the new tactics of the Black Bloc antiglobalization protestors. Miami-Dade policy makers realized that the Mobile Field Force needed to become more mobile and better equipped. Every one of the 1094 MDPD personnel assigned to Mobile Field Force was issued ballistic helmets, riot vests, and fire retardant uniforms and underwear to protect them from the projectiles and incendiary devices being used by the protestors against the police in previous violent protests. Bicycles were used for the first time for riot control by the bicycle field forces. Those required special equipment as well, including *Camelbak* hydration packs. The bottom line is that new tactics required the purchase of new equipment at high cost to the County. That the County administrators and policy makers agreed to spend so much money in such a short period of time on equipment for the police department was in itself an incredible story. Perhaps it had something to do with the genuine concern for the safety of the officers. But it could also have been attributed to smart policy. While $900,000 for equipment alone may sound like a lot of money, the workmen's comp claims from injured officers could have exceeded that amount many times over. The policy makers in the County were wise to spend the money. Besides, many of these items could be carried over and used for future events.

Develop a Communications Plan

A communications plan starts with a listing of all radio frequencies that will be used during the event. That is done to help manage the communications of the many agencies and organizations that may be involved in the event. There is another reason for having a comprehensive list of the authorized radio frequencies. We know that cell phone transmissions are used by terrorists to remotely actuate improvized explosive devices (IED). Because of this, some of the larger bomb squads around the nation have electronic countermeasure (ECM) equipment that is capable of jamming all wireless signals within a limited radius in order to negate the possibility of a remote actuation of an IED while it is being rendered safe by the bomb techs. In order for ECM to work as intended, it is important to preprogram all the essential radio frequencies (primarily police and fire) so that they do not get knocked out when all the other ambient frequencies are jammed. For a large-scale special event such as a Super Bowl, there are untold numbers of wireless transmissions in the stadium during a game. The game officials use wireless transmissions to communicate with each other, and the lead referee uses wireless to communicate the outcome of penalties over the public address system. The coaches on the field for both teams communicate with the coaches up high in the press box to relay vulnerabilities in their opponents' defenses and to plot strategy. The director of the television broadcast relies on wireless communication to coordinate with the camera crews and broadcasters. Each security guard has a radio, as do the maintenance workers. Every taxi, bus, or limousine driver outside the stadium has either a radio, or a cell phone. Obviously, all police and fire rescue, and emergency medical staff are also equipped with radios. Not to mention, all the fans in the stands, each one likely with their own personal cell phones. A bomb squad equipped with an ECM would be able to knock out all the unessential radio signals and leave the essential ones unmolested.

Develop a Surveillance and Intelligence Gathering/Dissemination Plan

Arguably, the single most important aspect for a successful special event is the ability to collect and disseminate intelligence regarding potential threats. Critical incident managers and policy makers rely heavily on the intelligence that is provided to them by Joint Terrorism Task Forces (JTTF) and/or from fusion centers. The ability to prevent, and in some cases, preempt a threat before it occurs is crucial. One of the most basic ways of gathering information about potential threats is to simply monitor the websites and blogs of the organizations that are most likely to pose a threat. The overwhelming majority of valuable information comes from these *open sources* that are available to anyone who has the time to look for them. For example, there were reports that the U.S. Department of Homeland Security (DHS) explicitly prohibited immigration officials from looking at social media to vet foreign citizens applying for U.S. visas. This policy came to light after the investigation of the 2015 San Bernardino terrorist attack revealed that one of the terrorists had posted multiple messages on Facebook about her radical Islamic views. The information that would have prevented the attack—indeed, would have precluded Tashfeen Malik's entry into the United States—was available for all to see, but the DHS purposely turned a blind eye to it.[10]

The collection of information from open sources is a low risk, but a labor-intensive endeavor that reveals a great deal of valuable intelligence. However, this method should not be relied upon exclusively because it does not reveal what is not open to the public. To get to the innermost secret discussions of terrorist and other criminal groups, it becomes necessary to take more intensive action for gathering intelligence. These methods include wire taps, and either active, or passive surveillance. By far, the riskiest, time consuming, and most costly method for gathering information is to embed undercover agents or confidential informants deep into the terrorist organizations and criminal groups. Obviously, it is very difficult to infiltrate many of these criminal organizations because entry into their inner circles is done by invitation only, and requires months, if not years to gain sufficient confidence of their leaders. Instead of embedding undercover officers, it is easier to recruit confidential informants who already have ties to the criminal organization. However, what is gained in ease of access is lost in the lack of veracity of some informants.

Before and during the FTAA Conference, the gathering of information regarding violent protest groups was gained by a combination of the techniques mentioned above. Undercover officers were infiltrated into the criminal organizations well ahead of the event. The information provided by those undercover officers was invaluable. In addition, the multiagency intelligence task force also embedded undercover officers among the 10,000 protestors during the actual event. These undercover officers provided very useful "real time" information that kept the police one step ahead of the protestors the entire week of the event. Being able to anticipate the opponent's every move is a huge advantage and acts as a force multiplier because the police can move its limited resources to the right place, at the right time, thus giving the appearance that there were many more police than there actually were.

The other component of a successful intelligence campaign is provided by the use surveillance cameras and software technology that can recognize facial features and other biometric data. Another very useful technology that was used in the 2007 Super Bowl involved a system that recognized and alerted security personnel whenever a package was left unattended. This computer system was programmed to identify and visually isolate anything in its field of view that was motionless for more than 10 seconds (or whatever time span that was programmed), thus alerting the security personnel watching the TV monitors of a possible parcel bomb being placed among a large crowd. There are many surveillance and information gathering systems available to event planners. The best way is to integrate multiple approaches to create an "umbrella" of coverage, whereby a number of threats can be monitored and dealt with ahead of time. A coordinated surveillance and intelligence gathering/dissemination plan is integral for the successful resolution of the event.

Develop a Unified Information Dissemination Protocol

The previous section dealt with information coming in. This section has to do with the control of information going out. One of the most counterproductive things that can occur during a critical incident is the dissemination of inaccurate, or premature information to the public. The repercussions resulting from an unauthorized, or careless release of information can have significant effects on the outcome of the incident, and may also affect the criminal prosecution of defendants further down the road. The careless release of information can be done by any one agency, but is even more likely to occur when many agencies work the same incident or event. If there is no coordinated information dissemination protocol, then there is a greater likelihood for unintended consequences to occur. For this reason, it is important to abide by the simple principle of "speaking with one voice." The Incident Command System places the public information officer (PIO) high on the hierarchy, and reporting directly to the incident commander. That is how important the function of information dissemination is deemed to be. In events and incidents where a Unified Command of multiple agencies has been established, the function of the PIO becomes that of a unifier of information dissemination. For large events, the Unified Command of the PIO function is usually located at a predetermined Joint Information Center (JIC), where all press releases and television interviews are given. The coordination of information release also involves social media posts and tweets.

In order to ensure the "one voice" doctrine, it is imperative that all personnel from all agencies involved are briefed ahead of time of the restrictions regarding the release of information by individual employees during the event or incident. It is also important to let the employees know that the prohibition extends to personal email usage and social media posts. The employees need to be made aware that they face disciplinary actions against them if they violate these rules. This is not a First Amendment issue. As a term of employment, all law enforcement and government agencies have the legal right to limit the release of certain information by its employees if that information is job related and has expressly been prohibited from being released. A good information dissemination protocol should address all these concerns ahead of time.

Develop Response Protocols for Nonevent-Related Incidents Outside the Area of Operations

There is a world outside the area of operations. That is something that some event planners tend to forget or ignore. It is understandable that after spending an entire year planning for an event, planners would get so focused on what they are responsible for that they would ignore the broader interests of the community they serve. The old saying, "no man is an island" comes to mind here. In this case, *no plan* is an island. Being that large-scale special events draw assistance from neighboring localities, it stands to reason that during these events, resources can be stretched thin. State and federal agencies fill many gaps, but ultimately, it is likely that any large-scale special event is likely to draw resources away from the day-to-day operations of the community that the event is located in. As such, the planners need to include contingencies for response to nonevent-related incidents outside the area of operations. Since there will likely be mutual aid agreements that bring in resources from neighboring jurisdictions, we need to consider what would be the best way to use these resources. Is it better to have the "out of town-ers" respond to emergencies outside the event area of operation, or is it better to have the "out of towners" handle event-related responsibilities, while the regular units respond to emergencies outside the area of operation? Usually, it is better for the local authorities to handle the regular calls for service in their own juris-diction. That is because the local authorities are more familiar with the geogra-phy and characteristics of the area, and thus are presumed to be more prepared to handle calls for service more efficiently and more effectively. One alternative is to employ a hybrid solution, whereby the personnel from the visiting agencies are paired off with the personnel of the host agency. That approach was used in South Florida during the recovery phase in the aftermath of Hurricane Andrew in 1992. Officers from other agencies were paired off as two-man units with the Miami-Dade officers. Not only did this provide an added officer safety issue dur-ing the long 12-hour shifts (over a prolonged recovery period), but it also reduced the need for having extra "interoperable" radios since the visiting personnel were matched up with the personnel from the local agency.

Develop a Budget

A budget is nothing more than a guess about what the future will be. It is sup-posed to be an "educated guess," but it is a guess nonetheless. The formulation of a regular operating budget relies on the projection of needs, based on the previ-ous years' expenditures. Typically, budget makers take an average of the previous 3 or 5 years, and use that to estimate what the upcoming year's expenditures will be. Oftentimes, a 3%–5% increase is built in to account for inflation or growth. This practice works generally well for most organizations. The only downside is that it often creates a "spend it, or lose it" mentality among budget makers. That means that agencies often purchase items that they do not need. Often, the unneeded items are hoarded and placed into storage, where they are either pilfered by employees or the shelf life of the product expires, and the items are wasted. This is a problem endemic to many bureaucratic government agencies, and is really not an issue as it pertains to the budgeting for special events, except that the typical mentality used by budget makers will not work as well when it comes to the formulation of a budget for a preplanned event.

Budgeting for a preplanned event differs from regular budgeting in that there may not be a 3 or 5 year period preceding it to compare and average. In other words, it is more difficult to project costs when there is no previous point of reference. Even if the event is a recurring one, the differences from one year to another can be significant. For example, Miami-Dade has hosted ten Super Bowls.[11] However, the set of circumstances from the events in 1968, 1969, 1971, 1976, 1979, 1989, 1995, 1999, were completely different from the set of circumstances faced by the planners of the event in 2007 and 2010. The planners of the events in the new millennium could not, and should not rely on the record of expenditures from the previous four decades. Everything changes after the September 11, 2001, terrorist attacks.

The planners of new events, having no point of reference, have to make their best guesses based on other similar events in other places. That is one way of approaching it. Or they can base their projections on other similar past events within their own jurisdictions. One thing that we recommend that they do is to not exaggerate the threat in order to get more money for their budget. The best approach is to give an honest appraisal of the threat, and to request only as much money as is required to get the job done. The old story of "the boy who cried wolf" comes to mind here. If a special event planner exaggerates the threat in order to get more money budgeted than is necessary, then the next time it comes to ask for money for another event, it will be more difficult to convince policy makers. One simple piece of advice that we offer is: never do anything that will compromise your credibility. Once you lose that, you never get it back. Be genuine and forthright. Never ask for more than you need. Never hoard. Always share with other agencies when you have a surplus. Always be a responsible steward of the taxpayers' money.

Develop a Training and Rehearsal Schedule

There is an old axiom that states: "train as you fight … fight as you train." That saying could not be any more accurate. In 2003, the training regimen for the Miami-Dade Police Mobile Field Forces leading up to the FTAA Conference was so realistic and so rigorous that by the time that the field forces faced off against 10,000 protestors, they were ready to deal with just about anything. The front lines maintained their discipline throughout the weeklong event. They held up against all the taunting behavior that some of the more provocative protestors used to test the police. That is because they had been subjected to the same, if not worse, taunting during the training that preceded the event.

Training was provided for the general Mobile Field Force officers as well as the commanders, and special training for certain specialized positions such as grenadiers, CUT team members, and water cannon operators. Appendix V provides an overview of all the training conducted prior to the FTAA Conference by the MDPD. Appendix VI shows the training regimen in preparation for the 2007 Super Bowl. The two events were different in nature, and the differences in the training regimens reflected that.

Develop a Timeline

Very early in the planning process, it is imperative that a timeline be implemented to keep the project on time and going in the desired direction. Large-scale special events have a lot of moving parts, and keeping track of things can be daunting at times. Whereas the stakeholder map provides a context of who is who, and the organizational chart provides a map of the command structure for the event, timelines provide an equally important point of reference for the temporal factor. One of the first things that needs to be done is to list all the things that need to be done prior to the event. Significant milestones such as meetings, training, rehearsals, and other important dates need to be identified and then ordered in a sequence that makes sense. Start with the date of the event at one end, and the current date on the other, and then fill in all the significant milestones in the middle. Do not forget to include the post-event demobilization milestone at the end of the timeline.

There are some project management software programs on the market, but we recommend that you keep it simple. Any *Microsoft* product, such as *Word*, *Excel,* or *PowerPoint,* can be used to create a timeline. Figure 8.3 is an example of a planning timeline for the 2004 Presidential Debates in Coral Gables, Florida. This simple timeline was done with Microsoft PowerPoint. Another example of a timeline is provided in Appendix VII, which shows an example of a simple training timeline using *Microsoft Word* tables.

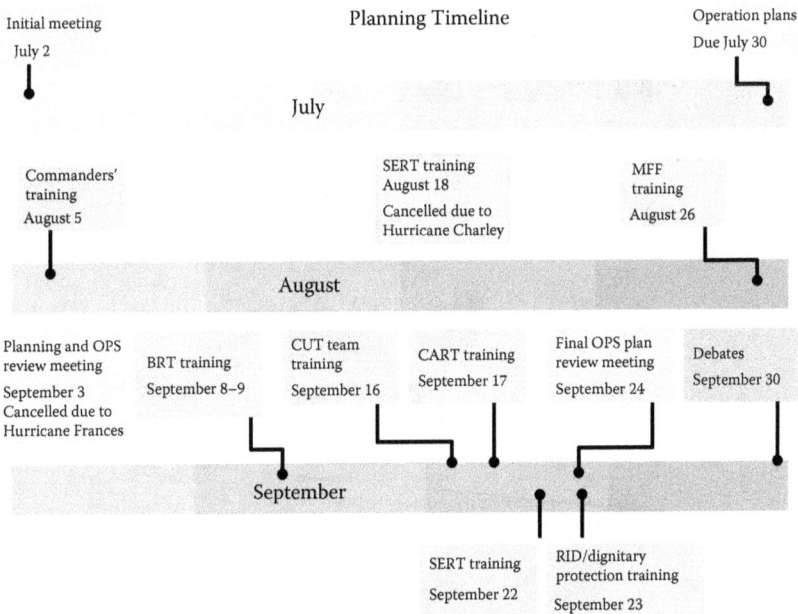

Figure 8.3 Example of a Planning Timeline

Applying the Lessons of Special Event Planning to Scale

In this chapter, we focused on the planning of a large-scale special event because that is the context that allows us to cover all aspects of special event planning. We realize that most readers of this book will never be part of something as large and complex as a Super Bowl, or an FTAA Conference. Nevertheless, many of the principles learned from this book can be applied to events and incidents at a much smaller scale. Moreover, these events and incidents do not have to be related to law enforcement or emergency management. Indeed, the writers have applied many of the best practices outlined in this book to projects in other fields. One example is illustrated in Figure 8.4, which shows how a simple stakeholder map and flowchart were combined to organize the flow of money and supplies from the United States to an impoverished hospital in Bulgaria, as part of a Rotary Club international project. The flowchart shows how an initial $500 contribution and an idea from a former Peace Corps worker evolved into the raising of $40,000 to pay for the shipping container which delivered $400,000 worth of medical supplies from California, to the hospital in Bulgaria. The flow map/flowchart shows how one Rotary Club was able to partner with other Rotary Clubs, and with multiple international agencies such as Project Cure, the International Red Cross, and Peace Corps to get this mission accomplished. This was a monumental and complex task for a small Rotary Club in Florida to accomplish. But with the help of a simplified flowchart to get everyone to understand the process, we were able to parlay $500 into $400,000 of much-needed medical supplies in less than one year's time.

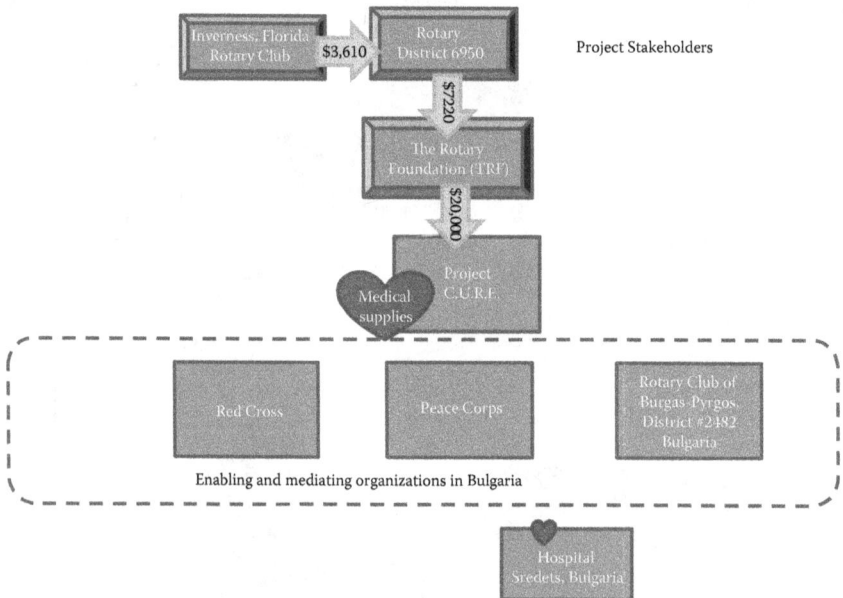

Figure 8.4 Flowchart of a Rotary Project

The Rotary Club example reminds us that the lessons of critical incident management can be applied to just about everything. In the end, making sense of our world is about learning how to simplify the complex, bring order to chaos, and predictability to uncertainty.

References

1. J. Borden. Innovation Incubator. Saint Leo University. Online at http://innovation. saintleo.edu/ (accessed December 4, 2015).
2. J. Kaler, 2002. Morality and strategy in stakeholder identification. *Journal of Business Ethics*, 39(1/2), 91–99. Online at ProQuest database (accessed November 27, 2002).
3. W. S. Cohen, 1997. Report: Personal accountability for force protection at Khobar towers. *Secretary of Defense*, July 31. Online at http://www.dod.gov/pubs/khobar/ report.html (accessed December 11, 2015).
4. The Oklahoma Department of Civil Emergency Management After Action Report Alfred P. Murrah Federal Building Bombing 19 April 1995 in Oklahoma City, Oklahoma. Online at https://www.ok.gov/OEM/documents/Bombing%20After%20 Action%20Report.pdf (accessed December 11, 2015).
5. Florida Department of Health, n.d. Hospital medical surge planning for mass casualty incidents. Online at: http://www.floridahealth.gov/programs-and-services/emergency-preparedness-and-response/healthcare-system-preparedness/_documents/ hosp-ms-planning-for-mci.pdf (accessed December 11, 2015).
6. Federal Aviation Administration, 2015. *Super Bowl XLIX Flight Advisory*, January 2. Online at https://www.faasafety.gov/files/notices/2015/Jan/150102_Advisory_Super_ Bowl_XLIX.pdf (accessed December 14, 2015).
7. Federal Aviation Administration, n.d. *FAI FSS—NOTAM Overview*. Online at http://www.faa.gov/about/office_org/headquarters_offices/ato/service_units/systemops/fs/alaskan/alaska/fai/notam/ntm_overview/ (accessed December 14, 2015).
8. Cessna. Cessna Skyhawk, n.d. Online at http://cessna.txtav.com/single-engine/skyhawk (accessed December 14, 2015).
9. Top Speed.com. n.d. *Boeing 737-700 Plane Review*. Online at www.topspeed.com/.../ boeing/1998-2010-boeing-737-700-ar85339.html (accessed December 14, 2015).
10. B. Ross, Schwartz, R., Meek, J. G., and Margolin, J. 2015. Secret U.S. policy blocks agents from looking at social media of visa applicants, former official says, December 14. *ABC News*. Online at http://abcnews.go.com/US/secret-us-policy-blocks-agents-social-media-visa/story?id=35749325 (accessed December 15, 2015).
11. M. Avila, 2010. Which city has hosted the Super Bowl the most times? *Live Science*, May 25. Online at http://www.livescience.com/32607-which-city-has-hosted-the-super-bowl-the-most-times.html (accessed December 15, 2015).

Glossary

3-Phase Model of Critical Incident Management: This model corresponds with FEMA's phases of preparedness, response, and recovery, but it shows mitigation, not as a temporal phase, but rather as something that is done before, during, and after a critical incident.

9/11 Commission: The National Commission on Terrorist Attacks Upon the United States.

9/11 Commission Report: Chartered by Congress in 2002 to investigate the circumstances of the September 11, 2001 terrorist attacks on the United States. The report was released to the public on July 22, 2004.

ACLU: American Civil Liberties Union

Adam Yahiye Gadahan: Also known as Azzan the American. An American-born media specialist for al Qaeda.

All-Hazards Approach: Considers a variety of hazards and threats to determine risk and vulnerability.

All-Hazards Render Safe Plan: There are two fundamental ways to render safe a suspected explosive device. One way is to pick up the device (preferably with a robot), and to place it inside a containment vessel, and then transport the device to a location where it can be disposed of in a safe manner. Oftentimes, the preferred way to neutralize an explosive device is to render it safe while "in-place" so that the suspected device is not moved, therefore minimizing the risk that it will accidentally detonate and cause harm to the bomb technicians, or to anyone else in proximity of the explosion. However, the decision on what approach to take has to be made by the bomb technicians and bomb squad commanders.

Anwar al-Awlaki: American-born individual that became part of al Qaeda's top leadership. He was killed by a CIA drone strike in 2011.

APS: Advanced Professional Development Series. This program is offered through FEMA's Emergency Management Institute (EMI).

Area of Operation: Clearly defining the area of operation is an important step with respect to event planning since it serves as a focal point for the planning and organization of the entire event. The area of operation may contain fenced-in security exclusionary zones, or it could simply be open to the public with no barriers at all, depending on the type of event.

ATF: U.S. Bureau of Alcohol, Tobacco, and Firearms

Auto-Adaptive Organizations: Louise Comfort from the University of Pittsburgh describes the auto-adaptive organization as being a system that is continuously learning and adapting to its threat environment. The auto-adaptive organization is continuously shifting its resources to meet new challenges. The auto-adaptive organization differs from the learning organization in that its adaptations are considered as "ad hoc" improvisations rather than long-term innovations.

Ayman al-Zawahiri: In an audio recording made public in September of 2015, this al Qaeda leader called for lone wolf attacks in the United States. He also pleaded for greater unity among jihadists across the globe.

Beslan Massacre: A 2004 attack on a school in Beslan, Russia by Chechen terrorists who took a large number of hostages, mostly children. The siege lasted three days, and ended with the death of more than 300 hostages.

BIG Suits: Biological Isolation Garments (BIG suits) similar to today's personal protective equipment garb, but unlike modern PPE, the BIG suits were designed to keep any biological hazards in, rather than out. Used by the Apollo 11 astronauts upon returning from the first landing on the moon in 1969.

"Black Bloc" Protesters: Refers to the tactics used by certain violent protest groups, including anarchist organizations.

Black Lives Matter: A movement that advocates against violence towards black people.

Black Sunday: A 1977 film about a Palestinian terrorist group attempting to blow up the Goodyear Blimp over the Miami Orange Bowl during the Super Bowl.

CBRNE: Refers to chemical, biological, radiological, nuclear, and explosive attacks.

Chicane (or Serpentine): An effective practice used to address the threat of an explosive-laden vehicle approaching at a high rate of speed. The serpentine configuration with three concrete or water-filled barricades force all incoming vehicles to slow down as they drive around the curves.

CIA: U.S. Central Intelligence Agency

City in Crisis: A report by William Webster and Hubert Williams to the Board of County Commissioners on the Civil Disorder that occurred in Los Angeles, California, in 1992.

Cold Zone: The area outside the outer perimeter is referred to as the *cold zone.*

Command and Control: The words *command* and *control* are similar, but they are not the same. *Control* is temporary and task specific. By contrast, *command* is a broader term, and is usually related to rank and authority (although not always). An example here would be the incident commander ceding temporary control of a "hot zone" to a tactical commander with specialized knowledge, expertise, and equipment.

Communications Plan: A communications plan starts with a listing of all radio frequencies that will be used during the event. That is done to help manage the communications of the many agencies and organizations that may be involved in the event. In addition, we know that cell phone transmissions are used by terrorists to remotely actuate Improvised Explosive

Devices (IED). We also know that cell phone transmissions are used by terrorists to remotely actuate improvised explosive devices (IED). Because of this, some of the larger bomb squads around the nation have Electronic Countermeasure (ECM).

Conceptual Perimeter: Yet another type of "perimeter" that we do not give much thought to is the conceptual perimeter that strives to control information from being released prematurely, and thereby increasing the risk to first responders and other citizens in the area. For example, news media helicopters now have very powerful telescopic cameras that are gyroscope steadied, and can shoot a live feed of ongoing tactical situations.

CONR: Continental U.S. NORAD Region

Contingency Planning: The practice of planning for possible unanticipated incidents that are likely to arise during an event.

COOP: Continuity of Operations Plan

Cornerstones of Critical Incident Management: All structures have a foundation upon which they are built. The same can be said for critical incident management. These "cornerstones" are communication, collaboration, coordination, and command.

Cost–Benefit Analysis: When the perceived benefits outweigh the estimated costs, then the decision should be to implement the mitigation action. Conversely, if the estimated costs outweigh the perceived benefits, then the decision should be to not implement the mitigation action. Although the concept is relatively simple, the estimates on both sides of the cost–benefit calculation are not.

Craig Fugate: Director of the Federal Emergency Management Agency.

Critical Incident Management: Complex events, such as incidents of widespread civil unrest, or venues drawing national or global attention, which present a variety of problems for organizations and communities if not managed correctly.

Crowd Control Plan: The purpose of the crowd control plan is to provide a way that balances the constitutional rights of individuals with the safety of all concerned. One way that event planners can reduce uncertainty and gain a better control of the situation when protestors are expected to show up at an event is to predesignate a "First Amendment Zone" for protestors to converge at.

CST: National Guard Civil Support Team

CUT Teams: Specially trained and equipped teams that use power saws to safely defeat obstructions, such as the "Sleeping Dragon" technique, employed by protesters.

Decon Corridor: The designated pathway that technicians use to enter and exit the hot zone. This corridor is located in the warm zone, and acts as a vestibule to contain the spread of the hazard from the hot zone to the cold zone.

Denial: Defined by FEMA as "… the process of minimizing or delaying the degree of site or building infrastructure damage or loss of life or protecting assets by designing or using infrastructure or equipment designed to withstand blast and chemical, biological, or radiological effects …"*

Detection: Defined by FEMA as "… the process of using intelligence sharing and security services response to monitor and identify the threat before it penetrates the site perimeter or building access points …"†

Deterrence: Defined by FEMA as "… the process of making the target inaccessible or difficult to defeat with the weapon or tactic selected …"‡ Is dependent on the adversary being convinced that the attack is not worth the cost. Deterrence as a prevention strategy only works in situations involving human-based threats.

Deterrence Strategy: Deterrence is a prevention strategy that requires the conscious awareness of the adversary. Examples of deterrence strategies include "Beware of Dog" signs on fences, the bright colors of a poison caterpillar, and a blowfish that triples in size when threatened by a predator.

Devaluation: While deterrence seeks to psychologically discourage the adversary by making the consequences of their actions too costly, devaluation strategy seeks to devalue the perceived benefits of the actions.

DHS: U.S. Department of Homeland Security

DOE: U.S. Department of Energy

ECM: Electronic Counter Measures

Elian Gonzalez Civil Disturbance: Elian Gonzalez's immigration and custody status was at the center of controversy. The Attorney General at the time, Janet Reno, ordered the return of the boy to his father in Cuba. However, the Miami relatives of Elian refused to comply.

Emergency Decontamination Plan: As we evacuate people out of a hot zone, we need to be mindful that those coming out may be contaminated with the chemical, biological, or radiological element that they were exposed to. A good plan should take into account the three levels of decontamination: mass decon, technical decon, and tactical decon.

Emergency Evacuation Plan: A good evacuation plan must be flexible enough to allow decision makers to change the direction of the evacuation routes in order to steer the evacuees away from the threat rather than directing them to go toward the threat. As such, for preplanned events, there should be different contingencies for evacuation routes and for mustering locations where the evacuees gather.

EMI: The Federal Emergency Management Agency's Emergency Management Institute

---

* FEMA (January, 2005). [SHORT CITE, p. 5-5]
† Ibid.
‡ Ibid.

Engineered Enticement Approach: A variation of the free access category whereby the event planners modify the site layout in ways that entice people to converge in a desired area while dissuading them from converging in an undesired area. First Amendment zones are an example of an engineered enticement approach.

EOD: Explosive Ordinance Disposal

EOP: Emergency Operations Plan

Evacuation Drill: Designed to have participants walk the evacuation route to a designated area where procedures for accounting for all personnel are tested. Participants make note of potential hazards along the way, and the Emergency Operations Plan is revised based on these observations.

Event: Something that is anticipated and planned for ahead of time.

FAA: Federal Aviation Administration

FBI: Federal Bureau of Investigation

FBINA: Federal Bureau of Investigation's National Academy

FDLE: Florida Department of Law Enforcement

FEMA: Federal Emergency Management Agency

Field of Fire (sacrificial area): The location that the site planners have designated as the best (least harm) location for the truck bomb to detonate in the event that a terrorist decides to prematurely detonate explosives.

FIRESCOPE: Firefighting Resources of California Organized for Potential Emergencies

First Amendment Zone: Event planners have the authority to restrict access to certain areas in order to ensure the public's safety. However, at no time do the planners have the authority to restrict free speech. Unfortunately, "First Amendment zone" has been accepted widely as the term to describe the patch of land that is designated for protestors to muster at, but it does not truly describe what that patch of land is for. A better term for that piece of land would be "designated protest area."

Flight Control Plan: Temporary flight restrictions (TFR) no fly zones associated with the security of a special event are usually configured in two concentric circles—the inner ring at 10 miles from the center of the area of operation and the outer ring at 30 miles from the center. There should be a TFR committee established with representatives from all these agencies on board. Coordination between these agencies is crucial in order to avoid allowing a catastrophic error (terrorist aircraft crashes into a crowded venue) or even a nuisance error (in this case, the "nuisance" would be quite severe in that innocent civilians on the ground could be killed).

FOB: Forward Operating Base

Free Access: Control of crowds of people starts with the determination of who is allowed access to the site, and who is not. Free access means that anyone can move freely within the site.

French Barricades: These barricades serve as a buffer zone that separate opposing groups.

FTAA Conference: Free Trade Area of the Americas. The 2003 conference was held in Miami, Florida.

FTO: Field Training Officer

Full-Scale Exercise: An emergency event is simulated as close to reality as possible. This training exercise involves all levels of the organization, as well as outside agencies and groups likely to be involved in the response. Due to the nature of these exercises, they are typically quite detailed, are more expensive, and can generate high levels of stress among participants.

Functional Drill: Realistically simulates an event in a controlled environment. Tests specific functions (e.g., emergency notifications, communications procedures and equipment, medical response, etc.), although not necessarily at the same time. Typically, these drills are detailed and generate a higher level of stress among participants.

GIS: Geographic Information System

Green Groups: Segment of protesters which are neither violent nor do they use the passive resistance techniques that the Yellow Groups use. They may be vocal and loud, but they are peaceful and compliant with the law, and they disperse when given lawful dispersal orders by the police. The color green used to identify these peaceful protesters has nothing to do with the common use of the word "green" to describe environmental issues.

HAAT: Hazardous Agent Assessment Teams. Used during the 2003 Free Trade of the Americas Conference and the 2004 Presidential Debates at the University of Miami. Both HAAT and HDAT were later merged into a single element that was comprised of experts from various disciples, and which reported their findings and recommendations through a unified chain of command.

"Hands-Up, Don't Shoot": The claim that Michael Brown raised his hands up to surrender before being shot by Ferguson, Missouri, police officer Darren Wilson.

Hazard: Usually associated with natural or man-made non-intentional threats. Typically, it is passive and pre-existing.

Hazardous Devices Team: Comprised of bomb technicians from the Miami-Dade Police Department (MDPD); the Federal Bureau of Investigation (FBI); the U.S. Bureau of Alcohol, Tobacco, and Firearms (ATF); as well as bomb technicians from other agency bomb squads during the 2007 Super Bowl in Miami, Florida.

Hazmat: Hazardous materials

HDAT: Hazardous Devices Assessment Teams. Used during the 2003 Free Trade of the Americas Conference and the 2004 Presidential Debates at the University of Miami. Both HAAT and HDAT were later merged into a single element that was comprised of experts from various disciples, and which reported their findings and recommendations through a unified chain of command.

Holistic Approach to Systems Analysis: Starts with a stakeholder analysis and is followed by a SWOT analysis. The SWOT analysis is then followed by a risk analysis and then a cost–benefit analysis.

Hot Washes: On-scene debriefings that are conducted as soon as possible after an incident or training session.

"Hot Zone" or "Kill Zone": Area considered to be hazardous or dangerous. The term *hot zone* is used primarily by firefighters, whereas police officers typically refer to it as the *kill zone*. For the purposes of this book, we refer to the area within the inner perimeter as the *hot zone,* since that is the term most used by emergency managers and the National Incident Management System.

HSEEP: Homeland Security Exercise and Evaluation Program. Provides guiding principles for conducting exercises. HSEEP also makes available various templates and guides that can assist organizations in designing, conducting, and evaluating training exercises.

Hurricane Pam Exercise: An exercise led by FEMA in 2004 that simulated a Category 3 storm striking New Orleans and flooding the city. The Hurricane Pam simulation identified a large gap in disaster planning.

ICAO: The International Civil Aviation Administration

ICP: Incident Command Post. The broader mission of the critical incident must be the realm of the overall Incident Commander, and that mission must be centered at the ICP.

IED: Improvised Explosive Devices

Incident: Something that occurs unexpectedly.

Incident Command System (ICS): ICS organizational structure and related processes have brought much-needed uniformity to critical incident management. It uses a standardized and fully modular organizational structure, which uses only the elements that are necessary to solve the problem at hand. ICS is typically structured around five functional areas: command, operations, planning, logistics, and administration/finance.

Inner Perimeter: Its purpose is to contain the threat so it does not escape.

Institutional Learning: The passing on of lessons learned and best practices within organizations.

Intrinsic Value: The intrinsic value of an item, or an asset, can be calculated by how much it originally cost to construct it, or how much it would cost to replace it.

ISIS: Islamic State in Iraq and Syria

JHRT or JHAT: Multiagency, interdisciplinary Joint Hazardous Assessment Response Teams employed during the 2007 Super Bowl to respond to any suspected CBRNE type of call to assess the threat and report back to the Bomb Management Center at the Incident Command Post. The concept of the JHRT mixed teams is to have the combined expertise of multiple disciplines to assess an unknown threat.

JIC: Joint Information Center whereby representatives of the PIOs of all the major participating agencies will meet in order to plan out and release information to the public in unison, and with "one voice."

JTTF: Joint Terrorism Task Force. Began in New York City in 1980, but expanded considerably after the September 11 terrorist attacks. It is of a group of investigators from various local police departments working under the auspices of the FBI. It is mostly an investigative and intelligence sharing network that works in partnership with the Miami Fusion Center under the auspices of FDLE.

John Bennett: Assistant Chief of the Tampa Police Department. Played a key role in the planning for the 2012 Republican National Convention in Tampa, Florida.

Khalid Sheik Mohammed: Ramzi Yousef's uncle who had ties to al Qaeda and was instrumental in the planning of the 1993 World Trade Center attack.

Learning Organizations: Peter Senge in his 1990 book, *The Fifth Discipline*, focused on the concept of the *Learning Organization*. The basis for Senge's concept is that in times of rapid change, organizations must have the capacity to be flexible and adaptive to succeed.

LEPC: Local Emergency Planning Committee

LETPP: Law Enforcement Terrorism Prevention Program

Level A PPE: Requires positive air pressure, totally encapsulated chemical protective suit with a self-contained breathing apparatus (SCBA). Level A protection is used by trained personnel to enter the hot zones of some CBRNE hazards. Because of the cumbersome properties of the Level A suit and butyl gloves, it is not practical for SWAT usage, although many SWAT teams have trained with Level A PPE.

Level B PPE: Is described by OSHA as, "the highest level of respiratory protection is necessary but a lesser level of skin protection is needed." Level B protection is also based on self-contained breathing apparatus (SCBA), but is much less cumbersome than the totally encapsulated positive air pressure Level A suit. Unlike Level A, the Level B suit does have practical application by SWAT and bomb squad officers.

Level C PPE: Differs from Levels A and B in that it does not rely on self-contained breathing apparatus (SCBA). For Level C to be appropriate, the oxygen level in the immediate atmosphere must be sufficient to sustain the user's respiration.

Level D PPE: Is defined by OSHA as simply a work uniform offering only minimal protection.

Lone Wolf Terrorists: Individual(s) who act alone, but are inspired by radical Islam.

Los Angeles Riots: Took place following the Rodney King trial. Considered one of the worst cases of civil unrest in the United States, and it exposed a number of shortcomings in the Los Angeles Police Department's Emergency Operations Plan.

Lozano Riots: Came about as a result of the police shooting of a black man in 1989.

LRL: Lunar Receiving Laboratory. An 83,000 square foot facility that was designed to house the Apollo 11 astronauts and all support staff that had come into contact with them, including crew surgeons, recovery engineers, medical laboratory technicians, cooks, and stewards. The LRL also kept the Command Module capsule and even the helicopter used to transport the crew and capsule to the aircraft carrier U.S.S. Hornet.

Luis Alvarez/Overtown Riots: Came about as a result of the police shooting of a young black man in 1982.

MAD: Mutually Assured Destruction policy strategy used to keep the balance of power between the Soviet Union and the United States during the Cold War.

Man-Made Accidental Disasters: Also referred to as technical disasters. Usually involves some sort of negligence or error.

Man-Made Intentional Disasters: Occurrences such as active shooter incidents, suicide bombings, small unit coordinated military or terrorist attack, etc.

Mass Arrest Plan: The mass arrest plan requires a partnership with local jails and detention facilities. A mass arrest situation will likely overwhelm the regular booking procedures at local jails. Procedures need to be in place to handle a large number of arrests. Those procedures should include mobile or temporary prisoner processing facilities to expedite the booking procedures while safeguarding the safety of the prisoners and their personal property.

Mass Casualty Plan: Mass casualty plans must first deal with the dead, the injured, the ambulatory, and the nonambulatory. Mass casualty plans must have a triage protocol wherein first responders determine who among the dead and injured should be treated first, and who should not be treated at all. This is usually done with the color-coded tags or ribbons affixed to the victims. The mass casualty plans must also take into consideration the likelihood of an overwhelming surge of patients into area hospitals.

Mass Decon: Used to decontaminate large numbers of people who are evacuating or fleeing from a CBRNE incident in a place with large concentrations of people, such as a crowded subway station or a preplanned event like a Super Bowl.

McDuffie Riots: Came about as a result of the 1980 police killing a black man named Arthur McDuffie in Miami-Dade County.

MEPP: Master Exercise Practitioner Program. This program is offered through FEMA's Emergency Management Institute (EMI).

Meta System: Refers to a larger system of systems.

Meth Lab: A clandestine drug laboratory that produces methamphetamine (meth).

MDPD: Miami-Dade Police Department (previously known as the Dade County Public Safety Department).

MFF: Mobile Field Force

Miami Model: A successful police strategy for the containment of violence during the 2003 FTAA Conference in Miami. In the Miami Model, the strategy of early intervention was the key organizing principle that dictated the preparations before the event and the tactical responses during the event.

Mitigation: Efforts to reduce losses to life and property.

Mixed Teams: Can consist of personnel from one agency or multiple agencies. Also see "Strike Teams."

Mobile Field Force: A specially trained Mobile Field Force (MFF) is used to deal with riots and civil disturbances. The Mobile Field Force idea came about as a result of the lessons learned from the 1980 McDuffie Riots. A typical MFF consists of 64 personnel.

Model City Simulator: Provides a realistic environment, which gives participants the feeling of actually having managed a critical incident. In particular, students are able to practice decision making and leadership skills in a realistic setting where there are no repercussions for making a mistake. Participants can immediately see the results of actions taken or not taken.

MOU: Memorandum of Understanding

MPD: City of Miami Police Department

MQF: Mobile Quarantine Facility

MTP: Master Trainer Program. This program is offered through FEMA's Emergency Management Institute (EMI).

NASA: National Aeronautics and Space Administration

National Incident Management System (ICS): A standardized approach to incident management. Initially developed by DHS in 2004.

Natural Disasters: Naturally occurring events such as earthquakes, tornadoes, hurricanes, etc.

NEADS: NORAD's Northeast Air Defense Sector

New Mexico Tech, Energetic Materials Research and Testing Center: Under the auspices of the Department of Homeland Security, this center provides bombing related training to first responders.

NFA: National Fire Academy

NFL: National Football League

NFPA: National Fire Protection Administration

NFPA Decontamination Classification: The National Fire Protection Administration classifies six levels of decontamination as follows: A—light hazards; B—medium hazards; C—extreme hazards; D—dry contamination for water-reactive substances; E—for etiologic agents and certain dry pesticides; and R—radiological materials.

NHC: National Hurricane Center

Nine Steps of Operational Pre-Event Planning for Special Events: Conduct a threat assessment; meet with event organizers and stakeholders; conduct a site survey (vulnerability assessment); develop a site plan; develop a crowd control plan; determine necessary resources; develop an organizational chart; assign specific personnel; conduct training and rehearsals.

NMCC: The Pentagon's National Military Command Center

NOAA: National Oceanographic and Atmospheric Administration

Norden Bombsight: Instrument used by bombardiers during World War II to deliver bombs to their intended targets.

NOTAM: Notices to Airmen

NSA: National Security Agency

NSSE: National Special Security Event, as designated by the Department of Homeland Security.

NTAS: National Terrorism Advisory System

Occupy Wall Street Movement: Started from a blog post in July of 2011 and quickly spread throughout the United States and throughout the world. Protesters camped out on streets and parks in many cities. When the police were called to remove the protesters, the protesters used techniques of noncompliance.

Organic Organizations: View their members as part of a team and value their contributions. High-tech companies such as *Google* and *Apple* come to mind when we think of *"organic"* learning organizations.

Orientation and Education Sessions: Designed to provide information, answer questions, as well as identify needs and concerns. They are particularly useful when implementing new plans or adding new staff.

Osama bin Laden: Leader of al Qaeda that was killed by Navy Seals in 2011.

OSHA: Occupational Safety & Health Administration, under the U.S. Department of Labor.

Outer Perimeter: Its purpose is to keep undesired elements from coming in and making the situation worse.

Overall Risk Analysis: Involves the calculation and final determination of the overall risk by using a formula that combines causal factors (threat and vulnerability) with effect factors (i.e., consequences). The numerical scores (if using a quantitative approach) or the written observations (if using a qualitative approach) for the consequence, threat, and vulnerability assessments are combined to determine an overall risk score.

PDS: Professional Development Series. This program is offered through FEMA's Emergency Management Institute (EMI).

Peter Drucker: Considered one of the foremost authorities on the subject of innovation. Drucker believes that innovation begins with an analysis of opportunities that should be conducted on a regular basis.

Peter Senge: Professor at MIT who has had a significant impact on the way organizations conduct business. His 1990 book, *The Fifth Discipline*, focused on the concept of the *Learning Organization*. The basis for Senge's concept is that in times of rapid change, organizations must have the capacity to be flexible and adaptive to succeed.

PIO: Public Information Officer (Media Relations)

POB: Police Operations Bureau, Miami-Dade Police Department

POMTOC: Port of Miami Terminal Operating Company

PPE: Personal Protection Equipment. PPE can include ballistic resistant vests for regular patrol officers, bomb suits for bomb technicians, and heavy ballistic vests and ballistic helmets for SWAT personnel in the police realm. In the fire department, PPE can include fire resistant wear, helmets, gloves, and self-contained breathing apparatus (SCBA), among other things.

PPO: Probationary Police Officer

Preemption Strategy: Preemption is a strategy used to prevent man-made intentional acts such as terrorism, but it can also apply to man-made accidental incidents or even natural threats. An example of preemptive strategy in firefighting is the practice of conducting controlled burns in forests to eliminate the fuel that builds up over many years of dry leaves and tree branches falling to the ground.

Probability: Is a function of two factors (threat and vulnerability). Regardless of whether the threat is natural, man-made accidental, or man-made intentional, the prediction of probability is based on the interplay between the threat and the vulnerability of a structure or a function.

Protection Strategy: Erecting a fence or wall around a critical infrastructure asset is an example of a protection-based strategy. Other examples of protection strategy include the use of buffer zones, limiting points of entry into a critical infrastructure, and restricting air space. Other protective strategies include the use of flak jackets, helmets, ballistic shields, goggles, and personal protective gear.

Ramzi Yousef: Considered the mastermind behind the 1993 World Trade Center attack.

RAP Team: Department of Energy's Radiological Assistance Program

RDSTF: The Florida Department of Law Enforcement's Southeast Regional Domestic Security Task Force. The RDSTF is a network where critical incident management practitioners of various disciplines meet to discuss the best practices and lessons learned from each other's successes and failures.

Red Groups: Segment of protesters that come to events with the specific intent of destroying property and causing injury to others. They can be easily identified because they often wear masks, body padding, and other protective equipment in anticipation of a clash with police. Sometimes Red Groups will mix into larger groups for their own protection, and also as a force maximizer by appearing to be larger than they really are.

Red Teams: Comprised of individuals who take on a simulated adversarial role to infiltrate otherwise well-defended assets. Red team probes can also be conducted through computer-generated simulations. The advantage of using red team probes is that they tend to reveal vulnerabilities that may not otherwise be apparent.

Restricted Access: There are two basic types of restricted access: ticketed access and credentialed access. Ticketed access simply means that a person has to provide a ticket to gain entry into the event site. The advantage of ticketed access is that it funnels the flow of incoming attendees to a limited number of entry points that can be used to screen the persons and their belongings. Credentialed access control has all the benefits associated with ticketed access control, but has the added advantage of allowing the event coordinators to limit entry to specific persons whose identities are known ahead of time.

Risk Analysis: The act of weighing the factors (probability and consequence) that determine risk. Threat + Vulnerability × Consequence. Formal threat and vulnerability are usually conducted at the tactical and operational levels of command. Formal consequence assessment tends to be done at the strategic level.

Risk Mitigation: Steps taken to reduce the likelihood of something adverse occurring. Occurs in all three phases of an incident: Before, during, and after. FEMA classifies its mitigation strategies into three broad categories: regulatory measures, repair and strengthening of existing structures, and protective and control measures. With regard to man-made intentional incidents, FEMA identifies the following risk mitigation measures: deterrence, detection, denial, and devaluation.

Risk Reduction: Reducing the likelihood of something bad happening *before* it happens, or reducing the consequences of something bad happening *after* it happens.

Ruckus Society: This group claims to work with 43 partner organizations such as Greenpeace, Earth First, and the War Resisters League. In addition to the training camps where protestors are taught the techniques of passive resistance, the organization also publishes a number of informational manuals, including a 14-page Scouting Manual for Activists, which is available for download on their website.

Samir Khan: American-born individual and *al Qaeda Magazine* editor. Was killed by a CIA drone strike in 2011.

SCBA: Self-Contained Breathing Apparatus

SERT: Special Events Response Teams were developed by the Miami-Dade Police Department in anticipation of political demonstrations by opposing groups for the 1994 Summit of the Americas. They were designed as an intermediate step between regular patrol and a full-blown mobile field force deployment.

Sheik Omar Abdel Rahman: A prominent member of the Egyptian Islamic Group and extremist Sunni Muslim cleric with ties to al Qaeda, who was arrested for complicity in the 1993 World Trade Center bombing, as well as conspiring to bomb a number of important landmarks in New York City.

SHSP: State Homeland Security Program

Site Plan: Developing a site plan is one of the first things that is done at the operational level of planning. This step is different than the initial "site survey" step, which is done earlier to assess the vulnerabilities of an existing site *before* actions are taken to address those vulnerabilities. A site plan includes all measures taken to address the vulnerabilities exposed by the site survey/vulnerability assessment.

Situation-Driven Tactical Approach: The practice of the police using a specific approach to react to the specific tactics used by protesters. The situation-driven tactical approach is akin to picking the right tool out of a toolbox to fix a problem. The effective management of protesters requires the right tool and tactics at the right time.

SPB: Special Patrol Bureau, Miami-Dade Police Department.

Sleeping Dragon Technique: Tactic where protesters chain themselves together and cover the chain with PVC pipes to make it more difficult for the police to separate them.

SOPs: Standard Operating Procedures

SPI: Southern Police Institute at the University of Louisville

SRT: Special Response Team

Stages of a Critical Incident Response: Initial onset, first response, the dust settles, incident resolution, and post-incident review.

Staging Area: The purpose of a staging area is to provide a place where units gather before responding to an incident.

Stakeholder Analysis: Consists of listing all organizations or individuals that have an effect, or are affected by, the actions of the organization at the center of the analysis. The organizations and individuals are then examined closer to determine whether they are friendly or adversarial. The analysis of the listed stakeholders would also take into account the common issues of concern, and whether there are possible points of agreement, or possible points that may lead to conflict.

Stop Sticks: Can be remotely deployed to puncture the tires of a vehicle in order to slow its approach.

Strike Teams: Single-purpose specialized teams designed to solve a specific problem. Can consist of personnel from one agency or multiple agencies (Mixed Team). FEMA defines strike teams as "… A set number of resources of the same kind and type with common communications operating under the direct supervision of a Strike Team Leader …"*

Sun Tzu: Ancient Chinese general and military strategist.

---

* Federal Emergency Management Agency, "ICS 100—Lesson 3: ICS Organization: Part II," (n.d.). Online at: http://www.usda.gov/documents/ICS100Lesson03.pdf (accessed September 10, 2015).

Surveillance and Intelligence Gathering/Dissemination Plan: Critical incident managers and policy makers rely heavily on the intelligence that is
provided by Joint Terrorism Task Forces (JTTF) and/or from fusion centers. The ability to prevent, and in some cases, preempt a threat before it
occurs is crucial. One of the most basic ways of gathering information
about potential threats is to simply monitor the websites and blogs of the
organizations that are most likely to pose a threat. The overwhelming
majority of valuable information comes from these *open sources* that are
available to anyone who has the time to look for them.

SWAT: Special Weapons and Tactics Team

SWOT Analysis: Consists of analyzing strengths, weaknesses, opportunities,
and threats.

Symbolic Value: Difficult to determine because things have different meanings
for each of us. There are no market forces or laws of large numbers to put
a number on the symbolic value of things. Nonetheless, most Americans
would argue that baseball, the World Trade Center, the Super Bowl, the
Star Spangled Banner, Mount Rushmore, the American flag, etc., have
great symbolic value.

Systems Approach: Helps us to look at the "big picture" as it relates to the strategic sphere of critical incident management. Provides planners with an
understanding of where their organization stands in relation to other
organizations, both friendly and adversarial.

Tabletop Exercise: A cost-effective and efficient way for members of the emergency
planning team and key management personnel to meet in a conference
room setting to discuss roles and responsibilities. Tabletop exercises are a
great way of practicing team building and problem solving.

Tactical Decon: Is defined as the decontamination equipment that one person
can carry and is used for hasty cleanups of light or medium hazards
when no other option for decontamination exists.

Tactical Team: A group of individuals specifically assembled to perform a specialized task. These individuals are presumed to be specialists at their
specific disciplines. The two key elements that distinguish tactical teams
from hastily assembled teams are specialized training and accessibility
to specialized equipment.

Tashfeen Malik: One of the terrorists in the 2015 San Bernardino attack.

Task Forces: A type of mixed team which is defined by FEMA as "… a combination of single resources assembled for a particular tactical need with
common communications and a leader …"* Task forces are different from
strike teams in that they are comprised of interdisciplinary elements.

TFR: Temporary flight restrictions that are imposed during certain large-scale
special events, such as Super Bowls, or presidential debates. TFRs are
commonly referred to as "no fly zones" and typically are designated in

---

* FEMA, ICS Glossary (May 2008).

concentric circles around stadiums or NSSE event venues at intervals of 10 miles for the inner ring, and 30 miles for the outer ring.

Threat: Broader and more inclusive than the word Hazard. That is because all hazards can be considered threats, but not all threats are hazards.

Threat Assessment: A step in the risk analysis process that tries to predict the *likelihood* of something bad occurring. Considers various threats applicable to a specific location or venue. Important for assessing risk and determining vulnerability.

Thunderbolt Exercises: Surprise drills instituted by Craig Fugate while he was the Director of the Florida Division of Emergency Management. This type of approach can serve to develop a team that can readily respond to critical events while adapting to changing conditions. It also helps team members to not settle into a routine, thereby helping to avoid the problem of complacency.

TOC: Tactical Operations Command. Because situations involving armed subjects can happen anywhere, at any time, the Tactical Operations Command (TOC) is a mobile command post that is usually set up in close proximity to the hot zone, but never inside the hot zone. The TOC is the place where the tactical commander sets up his command post.

Traffic Control Perimeter: This perimeter is sometimes used in large incidents such as manhunts for armed and dangerous escaped prisoners, along with traffic checkpoints at strategic points of ingress and egress. The purpose of this perimeter can be either to keep things in, or keep them out.

TSA: Transportation Safety Administration

Type I, II, and III Bomb Squads: The Department of Homeland Security/FEMA classifies bomb squads throughout the United States as Type I, Type II, or Type III, depending on their capability to perform in various environments, including CBRNE (chemical, biological, radiological, nuclear, and explosive) situations. Type I is the highest level for bomb squads, and consists of a full-time unit that has the ability to manage a complex incident. In contrast, Type III bomb squads have the lowest level of capability. These units have the ability to handle a small incident.

UASI: Urban Area Security Initiative

Unified Information Dissemination Plan: It is important to abide by the simple principle of "speaking with one voice." The Incident Command System places the public information officer (PIO) high on the hierarchy, and reporting directly to the Incident Commander. That is how important the function of information dissemination is deemed to be. For large events, the Unified Command of the PIO function is usually located at a predetermined Joint Information Center (JIC), where all press releases and television interviews are given. The coordination of information release also involves social media posts and tweets.

Unintended Benefits: In contrast to unintended consequences, this is a benefit that was neither planned for nor anticipated.

Unintended Consequences: The term "unintended consequences" was coined by Merton (1936) in his work, *The Unanticipated Consequences of Purposive Social Action.* In a purposive social action, or an economic one, the strategist or investor perceives a positive end result (i.e., a benefit) when a certain investment is made or a cost is paid. As long as the end result is commensurate with the cost, then all is well. However, if the end result turns out negatively, it is considered to be a poor value, and a threat to the growth or existence of the organization.

USAR: Urban Search and Rescue Team

VACIS: Vehicle and Cargo Inspection System in place during the 2007 Super Bowl. VACIS is used to inspect incoming cargo at delivery checkpoints and has the capability to detect anomalies that may indicate the presence of explosive devices in vehicles.

Value: It is a function of cost and benefit (Value = Cost × Benefit).

Vulnerability: Pertains to the state of the asset that is being protected. Vulnerability must be assessed in the context of the threats that are posed to it.

Vulnerability Assessment (site survey): Can be as simple as a quick walk-thru of an event venue by the incident commander and his team prior to the event, or it can be as complex as a comprehensive vulnerability conducted by subject-matter experts. The bigger and more complex the event, the more involved the site survey should be. Reveals possible vulnerabilities of the event venue, and also sets the stage for the development of the site plan.

Walk-Through Drill: The emergency planning team and response personnel actually perform assigned emergency response functions.

Warm Zone: The ground between the inner and outer perimeter is the *warm zone.*

WTC: World Trade Center

WTO: World Trade Organization. In 1999, the WTO Ministerial Conference was held in Seattle, Washington. The WTO in Seattle marked the first time in the United States that a sizeable and well-organized group of protestors had planned and executed a coordinated attack to disrupt an international economic conference in order to bring attention to their political causes.

Yellow Groups: Segment of protesters that use peaceful but noncompliant tactics. Although Yellow Groups do not pose the threat that violent Red Groups do, their noncompliance tactics pose a different set of unique problems for law enforcement.

Appendix I: Steps for Planning a Special Event

	Task	Done	N/A
1	Identify and map out all stakeholders (include partners, adversaries, claimants, and influencers)		
2	Meet with event organizers and stakeholders		
3	Identify all related critical infrastructure assets		
4	Conduct a consequence assessment of all identified critical infrastructure assets		
5	Conduct a threat assessment		
6	Conduct a site survey/vulnerability assessment		
7	Conduct an overall risk analysis based on the findings of the consequence, threat, and vulnerability assessments		
8	Incorporate best practices and lessons learned: Examine the after-action reports from agencies that have held similar events in the past. If possible, personally visit those venues during the events to observe and learn the best practices to emulate, and also to learn the lessons from the mistakes made		
9	Develop a site plan with a clearly defined area of operations, buffer zone, restricted areas, and fencing/barriers (if applicable)		
10	Designate redundant command post locations for all levels of command		
11	Identify redundant staging areas (on-site and off-site)		
12	Incorporate a plan to control ingress and egress from the restricted areas. The plan should include ticketing or credential control measures		
13	Develop an emergency evacuation plan that includes criteria for partial and full evacuations, as well as shelter-in-place		
14	Develop an emergency decontamination plan that includes provisions for mass decon, technical decon, and tactical decon		
15	Develop a mass casualty plan that includes the participation of all regional trauma centers		
16	Develop a crowd control plan that takes into consideration the possibility of adversarial protest groups. Identify "First Amendment zones" for protestors to gather		
17	Develop a mass arrest plan that involves the local jails and court system as factors		

Continued

	Task	Done	N/A
18	Develop a flight control plan that includes enforceable TFRs (temporary flight restrictions) around the venue, as well as "on the ground" preventive measures at nearby airports		
19	Develop a plan that takes into consideration the three phases of critical incident management (before, during, and after)		
20	Develop an organizational chart based on Incident Command System principles. The organizational chart should take into consideration the three levels of command (strategic, operational, and tactical), and include Unified Command structures at all three levels		
21	Develop interdisciplinary and multiagency specialized mixed teams to respond to "all-hazards" incidents		
22	Develop an all-hazards render safe plan that considers in-place disruption/mitigation versus safe removal and transportation off-site		
23	Develop contingency tactical response plans in the event of an active shooter, suicide bomber, hostage taking, or barricaded subject incident		
24	Identify and procure the necessary specialized equipment for each mission		
25	Develop a communications plan that takes into account all radio and wireless frequencies (including TV and commercial radio)		
26	Develop a surveillance and intelligence gathering/dissemination plan (usually involving fusion centers and JTTFs)		
27	Develop a unified information dissemination protocol involving representatives of all the primary agencies and organizations (JIC)		
28	Develop protocols and backup systems for response to nonevent incidents outside the area of operations		
29	Develop a budget of projected costs, including equipment/supply purchases and manpower costs (including regular and overtime hours)		
30	Develop a training and rehearsal schedule for the weeks and months leading up to the event		
31	Develop an overall timeline that identifies key dates/times and significant milestones		

Appendix II: Typical Field Force Lineup

DISTRICT/UNIT	COMMANDER-LIEUTENANT: _____	DATE
_____	Vehicle#_____	/ /

EXECUTIVE-SERGEANT: _____

1ST GRENADIER-OFFICER: _____

2ND GRENADIER-OFFICER: _____

MFF ADVISOR: _____
      Vehicle#_____

#10: SERGEANT _____
      Vehicle# _____
      OFFICER: _____
      OFFICER: _____
      **OFFICER: _____

#11: OFFICER: _____
      Vehicle# _____
      OFFICER: _____
      OFFICER: _____
      OFFICER: _____

#20: SERGEANT _____
      Vehicle# _____
      OFFICER: _____
      OFFICER: _____
      **OFFICER: _____

#21: OFFICER: _____
      Vehicle# _____
      OFFICER: _____
      OFFICER: _____
      OFFICER: _____

#30: SERGEANT _____
      Vehicle# _____
      OFFICER: _____
      OFFICER: _____
      **OFFICER: _____

#31: OFFICER: _____
      Vehicle# _____
      OFFICER: _____
      OFFICER: _____
      OFFICER: _____

#40: SERGEANT _____
      Vehicle# _____
      OFFICER: _____
      OFFICER: _____
      **OFFICER: _____

#41: OFFICER: _____
      Vehicle# _____
      OFFICER: _____
      OFFICER: _____
      OFFICER: _____

#50: SERGEANT _____
        Vehicle# _____
        OFFICER: _____
        OFFICER: _____
        *OFFICER: _____

#51: OFFICER: _____
        Vehicle# _____
        OFFICER: _____
        OFFICER: _____
        ****OFFICER: _____

#60: SERGEANT _____
        Vehicle# _____
        OFFICER: _____
        OFFICER: _____
        *OFFICER: _____

#61: OFFICER: _____
        Vehicle# _____
        OFFICER: _____
        OFFICER: _____
        ****OFFICER: _____

#70: SERGEANT _____
        Vehicle# _____
        OFFICER: _____
        ***OFFICER: _____
        ***OFFICER: _____

#71: OFFICER: _____
        Vehicle# _____
        OFFICER: _____
        ***OFFICER: _____
        ***OFFICER: _____

#39: OFFICER: _____
        OFFICER: _____

Pris Van# _____

#91: OFFICER: _____
        OFFICER: _____

Equip Van# _____

> Grenadiers = *
> Pepperballs = **
> Less Lethal = ***
> Cut Officer = ****
> Note: One additional
> Grenadier will be attached
> to each Arrest Team

Appendix III: Enhanced Mobile Field Force Lineup

DISTRICT/UNIT		DATE / /

COMMANDER-LIEUTENANT:_____

Vehicle#_____

EXECUTIVE-SERGEANT:_____

1ST GRENADIER-OFFICER:_____

2ND GRENADIER-OFFICER:_____

MFF ADVISOR:_____
Vehicle#_____

#10: SERGEANT_____
Vehicle#_____
OFFICER:_____
OFFICER:_____
OFFICER:_____

#11: OFFICER:_____
Vehicle#_____
OFFICER:_____
OFFICER:_____
**OFFICER:_____

#20: SERGEANT_____
Vehicle#_____
OFFICER:_____
OFFICER:_____
OFFICER:_____

#21: OFFICER:_____
Vehicle#_____
OFFICER:_____
OFFICER:_____
**OFFICER:_____

#30: SERGEANT_____
Vehicle#_____
OFFICER:_____
OFFICER:_____
OFFICER:_____

#31: OFFICER:_____
Vehicle#_____
OFFICER:_____
OFFICER:_____
**OFFICER:_____

#40: SERGEANT_____
Vehicle#_____
OFFICER:_____
OFFICER:_____
OFFICER:_____

#41: OFFICER:_____
Vehicle#_____
OFFICER:_____
OFFICER:_____
**OFFICER:_____

#50: SERGEANT_____
Vehicle#_____
OFFICER:_____
OFFICER:_____
OFFICER:_____

#51: OFFICER:_____
Vehicle#_____
OFFICER:_____
OFFICER:_____
***OFFICER:_____

#60:   SERGEANT_____
            Vehicle#_____
            OFFICER:_____
            OFFICER:_____
            OFFICER:_____

#61:   OFFICER:_____
            Vehicle#_____
            OFFICER:_____
            OFFICER:_____
        ***OFFICER:_____

#70:   SERGEANT_____
            Vehicle#_____
            OFFICER:_____
            OFFICER:_____
         **OFFICER:_____

#71:   OFFICER:_____
            Vehicle#_____
            OFFICER:_____
      ****OFFICER:_____
      ****OFFICER:_____

#80:   SERGEANT_____
            Vehicle#_____
            OFFICER:_____
            OFFICER:_____
         **OFFICER:_____

#81:   OFFICER:_____
            Vehicle#_____
            OFFICER:_____
      ****OFFICER:_____
      ****OFFICER:_____

#90:   SERGEANT_____
            Vehicle#_____
            OFFICER:_____
            OFFICER:_____
       ***OFFICER:_____

#91:   OFFICER:_____
            Vehicle#_____
            OFFICER:_____
      ****OFFICER:_____
      ****OFFICER:_____

#39:   OFFICER:_____
            OFFICER:_____

Pris Van#_____

#92:   OFFICER:_____
            OFFICER:_____

Equip Van#_____

#93: ***OFFICER:_____
    ***OFFICER:_____
    ***OFFICER:_____
     **OFFICER:_____

Vehicle#_____

Personnel assigned:

Lieutenants:_____
Sergeants:_____
Officers:_____
TOTAL:_____

Grenadiers = *
Pepperballs = **
Less Lethal = ***
Cut Officer = ****
Note: Vehicle #93 will have additional Launchers in case they must assist the Grenadiers in launching chemical agents.

Appendix IV: Multiagency Team Assignments

Personnel/Agency		Assignment	Location	Hours
Cpt_____	MDPD	BMC	JOC	
Lt._____	MDPD	EOD leader	At large	0700–2400
Lt._____	MDPD	K9 leader	At large	0700–2400
SABT_____	FBI			
SA_____	ATF			
Sgt._____	MDPD	JHRT 1	Dolphin Stadium East	1200–2400
_____	FBI			
_____	FBI Hazmat			
EEO_____	ATF			
_____	44th CST			
Off._____	MDPD	JHRT 2	Dolphin Stadium West and NFL Experience	0900–2100
_____	FBI			
_____	FBI Hazmat			
EEO_____	ATF			
_____	44th CST			
Off._____	MDPD	JHRT 3	Stadium Interior Ground Level	1200–2400
_____	FBI			
_____	FBI Hazmat			
EEO_____	ATF			
_____	44th CST			
Off._____	MDPD	JHRT 4	Stadium Interior 100 Level	1200–2400
_____	FBI			
_____	FBI Hazmat			
EEO_____	ATF			
_____	44th CST			

Continued

Personnel/Agency		Assignment	Location	Hours
Sgt. _____	MDPD	JHRT 5	Stadium Interior	1200–2400
_____	FBI		200–300 Levels	
_____	FBI Hazmat			
EEO _____	ATF			
_____	44th CST			
Off. _____	MDPD	JHRT 6	Stadium Interior	1200–2400
_____	FBI		400 Level	
_____	FBI Hazmat			
CES _____	ATF			
_____	44th CST			
Off. _____	BSO	HDT 1	Stadium Inner	1200–2400
Off. _____	BSO		Perimeter	
Off. _____	PBSO	HDT 2	Stadium Inner	1200–2400
Off. _____	PBSO		Perimeter	
SABT _____	FBI	HDT 3	Outside	0900–2100
SABT _____	FBI		Perimeter West®	
EEO _____	ATF	HDT 4	Outside	1200–2400
EEO _____	ATF		Perimeter East®	
Off. _____	MDPD	HDT 5	Countywide®	0700–1900
SABT _____	FBI			
Off. _____	MDPD	HDT 6	Countywide®	1200–2400
SABT _____	FBI			
EEO _____	ATF	HDT 7	ARTS/VACIS	1500–2400
EEO _____	ATF			
EEO _____	ATF	HDT 8	ARTS/VACIS	0700–1600
EEO _____	ATF			
Off. _____	MDPD (SPB)	K9 1	NFL Experience and Stadium	1200–2400
Off. _____	MDPD (SPB)	K9 2	NFL Experience and Stadium	1200–2400
Off. _____	MDPD (SPB)	K9 3	NFL Experience	0700–1900
Off. _____	MDPD (SPB)	K9 4	NFL Experience	0700–1900

Appendix V: FTAA-Related Training

FTAA-Related Training (Completed)

Type of Training	Number of Sessions	Number of Personnel Trained
Commanders' updates	2	62
TF commanders' round table	1	6
Grenadier/Pepperball operator	17	262
MFF training—16 hours	22	1244
SERT training—24 hours	4	103
Cut team training—24 hours	2	48

FTAA-Related Training (Upcoming)

Type of Training	Number of Sessions	Number of Personnel Trained
MFF training—8 hours	5	320
SERT training—24 hours	2	50
Grenadier/Pepperball operator	3	45
Less-lethal operator	6	120
Crash truck operator—16 hours	2	24
Commanders' course—40 hours	1	62
Leadership course—40 hours	1	62

As of 9/26

Appendix VI: Example of a Training Schedule

Date	Type of Training	Units Involved
March 21, 2006	Responding to and rendering safe suspected IEDs in the stands of Dolphin Stadium (Levels 100 and 400). The capabilities of the following equipment will be tested: • Bomb suits • Hook-and-line kits • Robots	Bomb Squad
April 19, 2006	Familiarization walk-through and site survey	Canine Unit
May 15, 2006	Barricaded subject. Incorporating various areas of the stadium; to include locker rooms, suites, stands, and offices	SRT
June 20, 2006	Response and render safe procedures for vehicle borne improvised explosive devices. The capabilities of the following equipment will be tested: • Bomb suits • Hook-and-line kits • Robots • WMD equipment	Bomb Squad
July 26, 2006	Explosives detection sweeps of designated areas (locker rooms, press box, suites, and tunnel areas)	Canine Unit
August 14, 2006	Active shooter and hostage rescue. Incorporating various areas of the stadium; to include locker rooms, suites, stands, and offices	SRT
September 19, 2006	Familiarization with stadium site to include bomb technicians from FBI, ATF, Miami PD, and Broward SO	Bomb Squad
October 4, 2006	Explosives sweeps and actual explosives detection scenarios	Canine Unit
November 13, 2006	WMD response incorporating SCBAs	SRT
December 6, 2006	Joint explosives detection and removal exercise of primary and secondary devices	Bomb Squad Canine Unit

Continued

Date	Type of Training	Units Involved
January 15, 2007	Final walk-through and joint exercise	Bomb Squad SRT Canine Unit Critical Incident Management Unit (CIMU)

Appendix VII: Example of a Training Timeline (2003 FTAA)

MOBILE FIELD FORCE FTAA PLANNING TIME FRAME 2003

	April				May				June				July				August				September				October				November				December			
	Weeks				Weeks				Weeks				Weeks				Weeks				Weeks				Weeks				Weeks				Weeks			
	1	2	3	4	1	2	3	4	1	2	3	4	1	2	3	4	1	2	3	4	1	2	3	4	1	2	3	4	1	2	3	4	1	2	3	4
MFF Committee Planning (April 01 to June 27)	▬	▬	▬	▬	▬	▬	▬	▬	▬	▬	▬	▬																								
Task Force & MFF Commanders Training (June 30 to July 02)												▬																								
MFF Training (July 07 to Sept. 23)														▬	▬	▬	▬	▬	▬	▬	▬	▬	▬													
Cut Team Training (Aug. 18 to 20 and 27 to 29)																			▫		▫															
Supplemental MFF Training (Oct. 20 to 30)																													▬							
Task Force & MFF Commanders Updates (Oct. 01 and Nov. 05)																									▫					▫						
Chemical Agent Training (April 03 to Sept. 05)	▬	▬	▬	▬	▬	▬	▬	▬	▬	▬	▬	▬	▬	▬	▬	▬	▬	▬	▬	▬	▬															

MOBILE FIELD FORCE FTAA PLANNING TIME FRAME 2003

	April Weeks				May Weeks				June Weeks				July Weeks				August Weeks				September Weeks				October Weeks				November Weeks				December Weeks			
	1	2	3	4	1	2	3	4	1	2	3	4	1	2	3	4	1	2	3	4	1	2	3	4	1	2	3	4	1	2	3	4	1	2	3	4
Water Cannon Familiarization (Oct. 13 to 17)																											▫									
Rental Water Cannon Familiarization (Nov. 03 to 07)																														▫						
Less Than Lethal Training (Sept. 29 to Oct.03)																									▬											
Bicycle Response Team Training (July 07 to 18)														▬																						
SERT Training (July 30 to Aug. 1) (Aug. 13 to 15) (Aug. 27 to 29) (Sept. 24 to 26) (Oct. 1 to 3) (Oct. 22 to 24)													▫		▫		▫				▫		▫			▫										

Index

For Product Safety Concerns and Information please contact our EU
representative GPSR@taylorandfrancis.com
Taylor & Francis Verlag GmbH, Kaufingerstraße 24, 80331 München, Germany

www.ingramcontent.com/pod-product-compliance
Lightning Source LLC
Chambersburg PA
CBHW070556270326
41926CB00013B/2329